The Radical Enlightenment

EARLY MODERN EUROPE TODAY
Series Editor: J. H. Shennan

Popes and Princes J. A. F. Thomson
Radical Religious Movements in Early Modern Europe
M. Mullett

Minerva Duce by Bernard Picart, 1722 *Teylers Museum, Haarlem.*

The Radical Enlightenment

Pantheists, Freemasons and Republicans

MARGARET C. JACOB
The Graduate Center and Baruch College
City University of New York

London
GEORGE ALLEN & UNWIN
Boston   Sydney

First published in 1981

GEORGE ALLEN & UNWIN LTD
40 Museum Street, London WC1A 1LU

© Margaret C. Jacob, 1981

British Library Cataloguing in Publication Data

Jacob, Margaret C
   The radical Enlightenment. – (Early modern
   Europe; 3).
   1. Freemasons – History   2. Europe –
   Civilization – 17th century
   3. Europe – Civilization – 18th century
   I. Title   II. Series
   940.2'5   HS414   80-41893

ISBN 0-04-901029-8

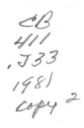
Set in 10 on 11 point Times by Inforum Ltd, Portsmouth
and printed in Great Britain
by Billing and Sons Ltd.,
Guildford, London and Worcester

Contents

Editor's Preface

In introducing a new historical series it is difficult not to begin by offering some justification for its appearance. Yet if we accept that history is ultimately unknowable in the sense that our perception of the past as distinct from the past itself is forever changing, then no apologia is required. That is certainly the premise on which this series is posited. In the last several decades the changes have been particularly rapid, reflecting fundamental shifts in social and political attitudes, and informed by the growth of new related disciplines and by new approaches to the subject itself. The volumes contained within this series will seek to provide the present generation of students and readers with up-to-date history; with judgements and interpretations which will no doubt in turn form part of the synthesis of future scholarly revisions. Some of the books will concentrate on previously neglected or unconsidered material to reach conclusions likely to challenge conventional orthodoxies in more established areas of study; others will re-examine some of these conventional orthodoxies to discover whether, in the light of contemporary scholarly opinion, they retain their validity or require more or less drastic reassessment. Each in its own way, therefore, will seek to define and illumine some of the contours of early modern Europe, a coherent period at once remote from our own world yet crucial to an understanding of it. Each will combine considerable chronological range with thematic precision and each, finally, will be introduced by a significant bibliographical chapter. It is hoped that this last, prominent feature, which will make the series especially distinctive, will be of value not only to readers curious to explore the particular topic further but also to those seeking information on a wide range of themes associated with it.

Acknowledgements

The completion of a book inevitably reminds its author of how deeply indebted she is to a web of personal and professional ties that defy easy description. A long time ago Henry Guerlac suggested that I work on John Toland and, of course, out of those manuscripts came a crucial piece of evidence that led ultimately to the subject of this book. As a teacher and as a friend, he has provided vital support and encouragement. So too did H. G. Koenigsberger, also a former teacher, and of course, Dorothy Koenigsberger, with whom I have shared much merriment and serious scholarship around matters of mutual interest. Ernst Wangermann first introduced me to the Enlightenment and gave me the necessary confidence to pursue topics into the second half of the century. Both Ernst and Maria Wangermann have given loyally of their time and encouragement.

Various libraries, and in particular their excellent librarians, require special acknowledgement. Dr P F J Obbema at the Universiteits-bibliotheek, Leiden, and his staff, in particular C. L. Heesakkers, J. van Groningen and C. Berkvens-Stevelinck, provided vast quantities of xeroxed material promptly and efficiently. Ms Berkvens-Stevelinck and I have oftentimes corresponded, always to my benefit, although we do not agree on all matters concerning Marchand. G. J. Brouwer at the Bibliotheek van de Vereeniging ter Bevordering van de Belangen des Boekhandels in Amsterdam helped me through the catalogues of that splendid library. The librarians at the rare book room of the Spencer Research Library were especially efficient. B. Croiset van Uchelen at the Masonic Library in The Hague gave invaluable assistance with its records and with the early history of Dutch Freemasonry. Some of my most pleasant research hours were spent in that library. As always the staffs of the University Library, Cambridge, and the British Library, London, were extremely gracious and helpful. I wish to thank the Marquis of Cholmondeley for permission to cite material in the Cholmondeley manuscripts in Cambridge. The Widener Library, Harvard University, proved an excellent place to do much of the background reading for the subjects here explored. Financial assistance over the years has come from the National Endowment for the Humanities in the form of a Fellowship for Independent Study and from the Research Foundation of the City University of New York.

The opening chapters were first written at Currier House, Harvard University, where I had an appointment in the History of Science department. My time at Currier House, with its excellent facilities for quiet reflection and writing, is among the most memorable of the past few years. This book owes much to the support given by the house masters, Barbara and Paul Rosenkrantz, as well as to the good conversation and companionship provided by certain of the house's students and tutors. One of the latter, Margaret Hunt, then kindly and expertly read portions of the completed text with an eye to clarity and readability. The facilities provided at Harvard were matched only by those made available at the Institute for Advanced Study, Princeton, where most of this book was actually written during my fellowship year, 1978–9, and where it was expertly typed by Margaret Van Sant. My time there again mixed the personal and professional in especially pleasing ways and I am grateful to Quentin Skinner, Susan James, Karen Blu, Joan Scott and Bill Sewell for good scholarly company and conversation. Joan Scott also made valuable suggestions on the text. I. Leonard Leeb read portions of the text, while Aram Vartanian gave many hours to reading the text and to assisting with Rousset de Missy's impossibly written letters. What errors in transcription remain are all of my own doing.

Over the years a few scholars have assisted either in the search for fellowships or in the securing of research appointments. I am very grateful to Elizabeth Eisenstein, Frances Yates, J. G. A. Pocock, I. B. Cohen, J. H. Elliott and Everett Mendelsohn. At my home institution, Baruch College, then acting vice-president Sidney Lirtzman, unfailingly supported my requests for sabbatical salary and leaves while Stanley Buder, Edward Pessen, and Randolph Trumbach, among other loyal colleagues, always recognised the value of scholarly endeavour. In addition to her professional support Elizabeth Eisenstein also read portions of the text with meticulous care and saved me from many excesses of judgement. As always, the ones that survive, as well as any errors, are all of my own doing. While in disagreement with my methodology, Herbert Rowen gave an invaluable reading to many chapters, and I am very grateful to this hard-working critic. Many scholars provided bibliographical assistance. In that respect I want to thank I. H. van Eeghen, Pat Rogers, Ed Ruhe, Robert Darnton, Frank Kafker, S. J. Larkin, R. Mortier, Henry Snyder, C. M. Bruehl, Louis Trenard, Howard Weinbrot, and various British Masonic historians and antiquarians (despite their occasional and perplexing habit of responding to James Jacob whose name also appeared on the stationery). J. H. Shennan gave his unfailing support to this project from its earliest days, while Martin Staum read selected portions of the text. Once again the Baruch College Scholar Assistance Program made a contribution to the final preparation of the text. And likewise, Margaret Fidanza gave very generously of her time in checking notes and collating lists; vital assistance with research and translation came from Clarissa Campbell Orr. My debt to her is very great.

This book is dedicated to my long-time companion and fellow scholar, James Jacob, who now knows more about the origins of Freemasonry and related topics than he may ever have imagined possible. His abiding interest and patience over the years have sustained me through a variety of endeavours, not least of them scholarly, as well as through seemingly endless travel to various institutions and libraries. Other loyal friends and family, notably my mother, Margaret O'Reilly Candee, and Pat Cunningham, deserve special thanks. For those who have read or helped in other ways yet another project will have to be undertaken some day, for they too deserve a dedicatory acknowledgement.

MCJ
The Institute for Research in History,
New York,
September 1979

Abbreviations

AQC	*Ars Quatuor Coronatorum*
BL	British Library
BN	Bibliothèque Nationale
Chol. MSS	Cholmondeley Manuscripts, University Library, Cambridge
DNB	*Dictionary of National Biography*
MSS ADD.	Additional Manuscripts
ÖN	Österreiche Nationalbibliothek, Vienna
PRO	Public Record Office, London
UL	University Library
ULC	University Library, Cambridge

Items numbered in the Bibliographical Essay are then cited in the body of the text as follows: (1,20) with the second number referring to the page, or occasionally to the volume number and then the page. Items numbered as notes in the text are listed in the conventional manner, at the end of each chapter. Where a source is so basic as to be cited in its entirety, the reader is simply referred back to the Bibliographical Essay, by the number of the item, for example (1).

To Jim

Bibliographical Essay

Books seldom exist outside a scholarly tradition, and this one is no exception. Although differing in fundamental ways from earlier works, this book asks some of the same questions found in Lucien Goldmann, *The Philosophy of the Enlightenment. The Christian Burgess and the Enlightenment,* trans. H. Maas (Cambridge, Mass.: Harvard University Press, 1973)(1). But the new evidence presented here contradicts Goldmann's indictment of the enlightened man as incapable of political action. Similarly, this new evidence takes us far beyond the analysis found in Franco Venturi, *Utopia and Reform in the Enlightenment* (Cambridge: Cambridge University Press, 1971)(2). Nevertheless, Venturi saw Toland's importance for the reforming and utopian impulse in the Enlightenment and for that reason his book is often cited in these pages. All scholars who work on the Enlightenment have benefited from Peter Gay, *The Enlightenment: An Interpretation. The Rise of Modern Paganism* (London: Weidenfeld & Nicolson, 1967)(3). But like so much of Anglo-American scholarship that book does not deal with the social context and political involvements of the major *philosophes*. A general view of their philosophy can be found in the stimulating account by Lester Crocker, *An Age of Crisis* (Baltimore, Md: Johns Hopkins University Press, 1959)(4).

On the clandestine tradition and its vital importance in disseminating materialism and pantheism certain books are absolutely basic: Ira Wade, *The Clandestine Organization and Diffusion of Philosophic Ideas in France from 1700 to 1750* (Princeton, NJ: Princeton University Press, 1938)(5) and Philomneste Junior [Pierre Gustave Brunet], *De tribus impostoribus* (Paris, 1861)(6). Without the labours of those authors it would have been impossible to uncover the origins of the *Traité des trois imposteurs,* one of the most important clandestine manuscripts of the Enlightenment. Of course, it is now known that Freemasons played a significant part in that clandestine traffic (see pp.217–20). Of all the subjects examined in this book, Freemasonry is fraught with the greatest bibliographical difficulties. For that reason I shall return to it again, but at the outset two works should be cited. The standard history of Freemasonry, to be used with extreme caution, remains Dudley Wright, *et al.* (eds), *Gould's History of Freemasonry*

(New York: Scribner, 1936)(7). That no work in English with a scholarly perspective has been written to replace it suggests the paucity of research available on Anglo-American Freemasonry. Such is not the case for Continental countries. One book in particular provides much of the evidence for Rousset de Missy's role in Amsterdam Freemasonry and those primary sources are published in French in a Dutch work by W. Kat, *Een Grootmeestersverkiezing in 1756* (The Hague: Eigen uitgave van de Loge, 1974)(8).

Since the radical Whigs of the 1690s figure so prominently in transmitting a variety of English traditions: pantheism (as Toland called his particular brand of materialism), republicanism, and Freemasonry; and because English science was taken up so avidly by Marchand, s'Gravesande and their circle, the English context and background for the Radical Enlightenment requires explication. Certain books are particularly helpful in orienting the reader to both the English Revolution and English natural philosophy: J. R. Jacob, *Robert Boyle and the English Revolution* (New York: Burt Franklin, 1977)(9); Christopher Hill, *The World Turned Upside Down* (London: Temple Smith, 1972)(10); Margaret C. Jacob, *The Newtonians and the English Revolution* (Ithaca, NY: Cornell University Press, 1976)(11). For the Renaissance background to the conflict between the mechanical philosophy of the moderates and the pantheism of the radicals the basic book remains Frances Yates, *Giordano Bruno and the Hermetic Tradition* (London: Routledge & Kegan Paul, 1964)(12). One of Bruno's most important works has now become accessible to English readers in a useful translation by Arthur D. Imerti (trans. and ed.), *The Expulsion of the Triumphant Beast* (New Brunswick, NJ: Rutgers University Press, 1964)(13). Of course, Frances Yates has also written a controversial book on the seventeenth-century version of the Hermetic tradition entitled *The Rosicrucian Enlightenment* (London: Routledge & Kegan Paul, 1972)(14).

Descartes became a hero to some radicals in the Enlightenment who simply and conveniently ignored his Christian orthodoxy. One recent study makes their adoration more understandable and emphasises the extreme individualism found in Descartes's philosophy: A. J. Krailsheimer, *Studies in Self-Interest. From Descartes to La Bruyère* (Oxford: Oxford University Press, 1962)(15). Of equal importance for the history of materialism and hence for the history of the Radical Enlightenment is the valuable study by Aram Vartanian, *Diderot and Descartes. A Study of Scientific Naturalism in the Enlightenment* (Princeton, NJ: Princeton University Press, 1953)(16). Whether the radical insistence on conflating matter and spirit, a direct by-product of one reading of the new science, should be attributed to Descartes and Hobbes or to Spinoza, in other words to materialism or pantheism, receives a careful analysis in Paul Vernière, *Spinoza et la pensée française avant la revolution*, Vols 1 and 2 (Paris: Presses Universitaires de France, 1954)(17). For a brief history of the word 'pantheism' see Hassan El Nouty, 'Le Panthéisme dans les lettres françaises au XVIII siècle: aperçus sur la fortune du mot et de la notion', *Revue des sciences humaines*, vol. 27 (1960), pp. 435–57(18). In the course of these studies the difference between 'materialism' and 'pantheism' is rendered largely semantic.

Not semantic, however, is the difference between my approach to the radical Whigs and that found in James O'Higgins, SJ, *Anthony Collins. The Man and His Works* (The Hague: Nijhoff, 1970)(19). That account makes little of Collins's connections with the Knights of Jubilation and indeed O'Higgins appears to have been unaware of the existence of that secret club. Likewise, he did not have access to Collins's letters in the Spencer Research Library, University of Kansas.

Just as important for the Radical Enlightenment, if not more important than the natural philosophy of Descartes, stands the philosophy of Spinoza. Not always an accessible philosopher, Spinoza can be approached through the magisterial work of Harry A. Wolfson, *The Philosophy of Spinoza* (Cambridge, Mass.: Harvard University Press, 1958, reprint of 1934 edn)(20). Many books and articles have been written on the dissemination of Spinoza's writings on 'spinozism' as it was called at the time, but one in particular is especially useful in describing the response of orthodox natural philosophers to his pantheism: Georges Friedmann, *Leibniz et Spinoza* (Paris: Gallimard, 1962)(21). For our purposes, Leibniz is a particularly important exponent of the new science because he became increasingly distressed by the machinations of the radicals. The most historically useful exposition of his thought occurs in a perhaps excessively Hegelian work by R. W. Meyer, *Leibnitz and the Seventeenth-Century Revolution*, trans. J. P. Stern, (Cambridge: Bowes, 1952)(22). The scholarly world still awaits a complete edition of Leibniz's writings and letters, but in the meantime for his politics the student should consult Patrick Riley (ed.), *The Political Writings of Leibniz* (Cambridge: Cambridge University Press, 1972)(23).

All the major philosophers of the late seventeenth century got into the fray with the radicals and for help with their special relationship to John Locke readers should consult my work cited above(11). For the present, Locke's relationship to the radical Whigs of the 1690s remains a tortured question which may only be illuminated when the chronologically relevant volumes of his correspondence finally appear. To date, the first four volumes up to 1694 are available in E. S. de Beer (ed.), *The Correspondence of John Locke* (Oxford: Clarendon Press,

1977)(24). Also very useful for Locke's reputation on the Continent is an essay by Rosalie Colie, 'John Locke in the Republic of Letters', in J. S. Bromley and E. H. Kossmann (eds), *Britain and The Netherlands* (London: Chatto & Windus, 1960)(25).

No better example of the complexity of Locke's relationship to the republican faction of his party can be found than in his ambiguous response to John Toland. He, of course, provides in his unpublished manuscripts at the British Library the crucial evidence for the existence of the secret coterie whose history we are attempting here to trace. In the past ten years there has been an explosion of printed material on Toland and his many involvements, intellectual as well as political. Much of this research has come from Italian scholars, and can be most easily surveyed in an extremely useful monograph by Chiara Giuntini, *Pantheismo e ideologia republicana: John Toland (1670–1722)* (Bologna: Il Mulino, 1979)(26). Giancarlo Carabelli has produced an indispensable bibliography, *Tolandiana* (Florence: La Nuova Italia Editrice, 1975, with a supplement, 1978)(27). For a summary of Toland's career in English the reader can consult my book on the Newtonians (11) as well as the new material discussed here (pp. 151–6). Toland's role in the intricacies of party political life in England during the 1690s is surveyed in A. B. Worden (ed.), *Edmund Ludlow. A Voyce from the Watch Tower. Part Five: 1660–62*, Camden Fourth Series, Vol. 21 (London: Royal Historical Society, 1978)(28). Worden does not, unfortunately, deal effectively with Toland's religious beliefs or his philosophy of nature.

In early modern Europe philosophies of nature often served to reinforce other power relationships, for example, between king and people, priest and parishioner, lord and servant. Predictably then, the development of a scientific rendering of the natural order could easily become entwined with religious and political conflict. In seventeenth century Europe that moment when such conflict produced a new social order occurred most dramatically in England during the mid-century revolution. One of the first scholars to document the impact of religious belief on the new science argued that English Puritanism gave a vital impetus to scientific inquiry. Robert K. Merton's arguments, first published in 1938, appear in *Science, Technology and Society in Seventeenth Century England* (New York: Harper & Row, 1970)(29). Since that time, however, historical analysis has gone far beyond Merton and the most recent understanding of the relationship between science and the English Revolution can be found in the following books and essays: J. R. Jacob's work on Boyle, previously cited (9); Charles Webster, *The Great Instauration. Science, Medicine and Reform, 1626–60* (London: Duckworth, 1975)(30); Christopher Hill, *The Intellectual Origins of the English Revolution* (Oxford: Clarendon Press, 1965)

(31); James R. Jacob and Margaret C. Jacob, 'The Anglican origins of modern science', *Isis* vol. 71 (June 1980), pp. 251–67(32).

The relationship between science and the English Revolution must be grasped before the subversive implications of pantheism can be fully comprehended. Science rendered nature knowable, but a pantheistic understanding of nature, once coupled with science, made nature a plausible substitution for God. Of course, to many early modern Europeans, to eliminate God also meant to eliminate kings, bishops and established churches.

As a consequence of their power, the mid-seventeenth century saw few actual theoreticians of republicanism. Yet in the light of subsequent history those few are terribly important, especially for the Radical Enlightenment. For an analysis of one of the most important of these theoreticians, James Harrington, the student should consult J. G. A. Pocock (ed. and intro.), *The Political Works of James Harrington* (Cambridge: Cambridge University Press, 1977)(33). Also important for interpreting Harrington's often difficult prose is C. B. Macpherson, *The Political Theory of Possessive Individualism: Hobbes to Locke* (Oxford: Oxford University Press, 1962)(34), and George H. Sabine, *A History of Political Theory* (London: Harrap, 1949)(35).

Some defenders of monarchy, on the other hand, were false friends, at least as the clergy saw it. Hobbes was a materialist who also supported monarchy. Given the ideological context of natural philosophy, however, 'Hobbism' became one of the weapons in the radical's arsenal. Hobbes can best be understood by reading him in the original, and the most accessible edition is Thomas Hobbes, *Leviathan*, ed. and intro. by C. B. Macpherson (Harmondsworth: Penguin, 1968)(36).

The Revolution of 1688–9 intervened to reshape the contours of mid-century English political thought and to render the republicans into extreme Whigs, or 'Commonwealthmen' and 'old' Whigs as the language of the time preferred. For that transformation and the critically important 1690s, a variety of books and essays should be consulted: Caroline Robbins, *The Eighteenth Century Commonwealthman* (New York: Atheneum, 1968)(37); J. G. A. Pocock. *The Machiavellian Moment. Florentine Political Thought and the Atlantic Republican Tradition* (Princeton, NJ: Princeton University Press, 1975)(38); Henry Horwitz, *Parliament, Policy and Politics in the Reign of William III* (Manchester: Manchester University Press, 1977)(39); William L. Sachse, *Lord Somers. A Political Portrait* (Manchester: Manchester University Press, 1975)(40); Margaret Jacob, 'Newtonianism and the origins of the Enlightenment: a reassessment', *Eighteenth Century Studies*, vol. 11 (1977), pp. 1–25 (41); J. P. Kenyon, *Revolution Principles. The Politics of Party, 1689–1720* (Cambridge: Cambridge University Press, 1977)(42); Geraint Parry,

John Locke (London, Allen & Unwin, 1978)(43); Gerald Straka, *Anglican Reaction to the Revolution of 1688* (Madison, Wis.: State Historical Society, 1962)(44); and his '1688 as the Year One', in *Studies in Eighteenth-Century Culture,* ed. Louis T. Milc, (Cleveland, Ohio: American Society for Eighteenth Century Studies, 1971)(45); J. H. Plumb, *The Growth of Political Stability in England, 1675–1725* (London: Macmillan, 1967)(46). As a result of the Revolution of 1688–9 a new, more tolerant intellectual era begins in England, and after 1695 and the lapsing of the Licensing Act the publication of anti-clerical and 'deistic' writings began in earnest. It is possible, therefore, to date the beginning of the European Enlightenment, as a coherent intellectual milieu, in England during the 1690s.

The clerical leaders of this new age were the Newtonians and by the reign of Anne (1701–14) the new scientific culture they represented had captured the imagination of the educated classes. Presiding over it, of course, was Newton, the leading scientific figure of the age, but students should not be intimidated. Newton's natural philosophy and his public role can be explored in two fairly accessible collections: A. Rupert Hall and Marie Boas Hall (eds), *Unpublished Scientific Papers of Isaac Newton* (Cambridge: Cambridge University Press, 1962)(47), and H. W. Turnbull (ed.), *The Correspondence of Sir Isaac Newton,* vols 1–7 (Cambridge: Cambridge University Press, 1959–77)(48). For the political and legal context within which the Newtonian vision of order and harmony prevailed see Edward Thompson, *Whigs and Hunters: the Origins of the Black Act* (New York: Pantheon Books, 1976)(49). Also useful in describing the varieties of scientific interpretations given to Newton's speculations (although completely eccentric in its use of the term 'materialism') is Robert Schofield, *Mechanism and Materialism. British Natural Philosophy in An Age of Reason* (Princeton, NJ: Princeton University Press, 1970)(50). For critics of the Newtonian philosophy coming from 'the right', in some cases from the Tory camp, see A. J. Kuhn, 'Hutchinson vs. Newton', *Journal of the History of Ideas,* vol. 22 (1961), pp. 303–22(51).

Newton's science, as interpreted by the first and second generations of his followers, gave small consolation to those seeking a materialistic account of natural phenomena. By the 1740s, however, other evidence seemed to be available from zoological experiments done in The Hague by Abraham Trembley. For that fascinating episode consult Aram Vartanian, 'Trembley's polyp, La Mettrie, and eighteenth century French materialism', *Journal of the History of Ideas,* vol. 11 (1950), pp. 259–86 (52). In general the supporters of Newton's science never abandoned the attack against the materialists begun during the 1690s, and this is nowhere truer than in the case of Voltaire. Amid the vast bibliography on his writings I would single out certain particularly useful books and essays: Ira O. Wade, *Studies on Voltaire* (Princeton, NJ: Princeton University Press, 1947)(53); Martin Staum, 'Newton and Voltaire: constructive sceptics', *Studies on Voltaire and the Eighteenth Century*, vol. 62 (1968), pp. 29–56(54); Dennis J. Fletcher, 'Bolingbroke and the diffusion of Newtonianism in France', *Studies on Voltaire and the Eighteenth Century*, vol. 53 (1967), pp. 29–46(55); P. Valkhoff and J. Fransen, 'Voltaire en Hollande', *Revue de Hollande*, vol. I (1915), pp. 734–54(56); J. Vercruysse, *Voltaire et la Hollande*, *Studies on Voltaire and the Eighteenth Century*, vol. 46 (1966)(57); T. Besterman, 'Voltaire, absolute monarchy, and the enlightened monarch', *Studies on Voltaire and the Eighteenth Century*, vol. 32 (1965)(58); Ira O. Wade, *The Intellectual Development of Voltaire* (Princeton, NJ: Princeton University Press, 1969)(59); and especially useful for this study, André Michel Rousseau, 'L'Angleterre et Voltaire', *Studies on Voltaire and the Eighteenth Century*, vol. 145 (1976)(60). For an overview of Voltaire's beliefs and especially for the religious meaning he attached to Newton's science see René Pomeau, *La religion de Voltaire* (Paris: Librairie Nizet, 1956)(61). Previously, scholars have tackled the question of Voltaire's relationship to Collins and Toland, but without the evidence for the Netherlands that we now possess: nevertheless, see Norman L. Torrey, *Voltaire and the English Deists* (New Haven, Conn.: Yale University Press, 1938)(62).

The camaraderie between the radical Whigs and the Knights of Jubilation, that secret society lead by Marchand, Fritsch and Levier, among others, instantly raises the question of their role in the origins of Freemasonry. Much of what has been written on Freemasonry is worthless and every library is filled with non-scholarly literature on the subject. The items singled out here are not uniformly professional, but in some cases they are all that is available. The best place to begin is with the 1723 Masonic *Constitutions*, partially reprinted here in the appendix, or consult an original copy of James Anderson, *The Constitutions of the Freemasons . . . For the use of the Lodges* (London, 1723)(63). For the mediaeval background to the Masonic guilds, that so-called 'operative' phase of Freemasonry, two studies are scholarly and useful: George Unwin, *The Gilds and Companies of London* (London: Methuen, 1963)(64) and D. Knoop, *The Medieval Mason* (Manchester: Manchester University Press, 1967)(65). For the transition to speculative Freemasonry, a process well underway by the 1690s in London, the now standard account is by A. S. Frere, *The Grand Lodge, 1717–1967* (Oxford: Oxford University Press, printed for the United Grand Lodge of England, 1967)(66). That transition is also documented in D. Knoop, G. P. Jones and D. Hamer, *Early Masonic Pamphlets* (Manchester: Manchester University Press, 1945)(67). One detailed description exists for the transformation of an operative lodge into a 'speculative' one: Harry Carr, *Lodge Mother Kilwinning, No. 0. A Study of the Earliest Minute Books* (London: Quatuor Coronati Lodge no. 2076, 1961)(68).

By far the most important Freemason and its guiding spirit after the formation of the Grand Lodge in 1717 was Jean Theophile Desaguliers (1683–1744). There are a few good places to start, aside from the *Dictionary of National Biography*: Duncan Campbell Lee, *Desaguliers of No. 4 and His Services to Freemasonry* (London, privately printed: 1932)(69); Margaret Rowbottom, 'John Theophilus Desaguliers', *Proceedings of the Huguenot Society*, vol. 21 (1965–70)(70), and for Desaguliers's patron, C. H. Collins Baker and Muriel I. Baker, *The Life and Circumstances of James Brydges. First Duke of Chandos. Patron of the Liberal Arts* (Oxford: Clarendon Press, 1949)(71). A glimpse at Desaguliers as ideologue can be found in J. T. Desaguliers, *The Newtonian System of the World. The Best Model of Government* (Westminster, 1728)(72).

There is not much manuscript evidence that has survived on Desaguliers, but the British Library, Additional manuscripts 32556, ff. 191–3(73) should be used. One excellent source exists for Desaguliers's own lodge at the Horn Tavern: Rev. Arnold W. Oxford, *No. 4. An Introduction to the History of the Royal Somerset House and Inverness Lodge* (London: Quaritch, 1928)(74).

It is very doubtful that the present Grand Lodge in London has any other important manuscripts, beyond the ones it has already published. The catalogues of its contents, both its library and picture gallery, are most interesting: A. Tudor-Craig (ed.), *Catalogue of Portraits and Prints at Freemasons' Hall in the Possession of the United Grand Lodge of England* (London, 1938)(75); A. Tudor-Craig (ed.), *Catalogue of Manuscripts and Library at Freemasons' Hall* (London, 1938)(76). Some years ago Rae Blanchard saw the significance of Picart's edition of an engraving of the early lodges now used to adorn the jacket of this book: Rae Blanchard, 'Was Sir Richard Steele a Freemason?', *Publications of the Modern Language Association*, vol. 63 (1948), pp. 903–17(77). The earliest records for speculative Freemasonry after 1717 have been published in W. J. Songhurst (ed.), *Quatuor Coronatorum Antigrapha. Masonic Reprints of the Quatuor Coronati Lodge, No. 2076*, vol. 10 (London, 1913)(78). Frequent reference will be made to that volume.

For the official establishment of Freemasonry in the Low Countries, one of the first Continental areas where that was done by English Masons (the establishment of French Freemasonry is a much more complex matter), the political context is crucial. There are certain standard places to start: Gilbert W. Daynes, 'The Duke of Lorraine and English Freemasonry in 1731', *Ars Quatuor Coronatorum*, vol. 37

(1924), pp. 107–28(79). Indeed the entire journal, *Ars Quatuor Coronatorum* (hereafter cited as *AQC*), an official Masonic publication, should be consulted for any topic, although the older volumes should be used with caution. Far more reliable, however, are the histories of Dutch and Belgian Freemasonry found in E. A. Boerenbeker, 'The relations between Dutch and English Freemasonry from 1734 to 1771', *AQC*, vol. 83 (1970), pp. 149–92 (80); Hugo de Schampheleire, *De Antwerpse Vrijmetselaars in de 18ᵉ eeuw* (Antwerp: Ontwikkeling, 1969)(81); Bertrand van der Schelden, *La Franc-Maçonnerie Belge* (Louvain: Librairie Universitaire, 1923)(82). Both works date the existence of Freemasonry in Belgium considerably later than the evidence here presented warrants. See also H. de Schampheleire, *Aperçu des principaux travaux récents relatifs à l'histoire de la franc-maçonnerie belge . . . organisé par 'la Lessing-Akademie', (Wolfenbüttel)* (Brussels: Lessing-Akademie, 1976)(83). Peter Geyl has done the basic historical narrative for Anglo-Dutch relations in the 1730s and 1740s: P. Geyl, 'Holland and England during the War of Austrian Succession', *History*, vol. 10 (1925), pp. 47–51(84); and his *Willem IV en Engeland* (The Hague: Nijhoff, 1924)(85). On the Austrian role in Belgian history and on the northern alliance of Austria, England and the Netherlands against France see the Comte Charles de Villermont, *Le Comte de Cobenzl. Ministre plénipotentiaire aux Pays-Bas* (Lille: Deselée, 1926)(86); André Puttemans, *La Censure dans les Pay-Bas autrichiens* (Brussels: Palais des Académies, 1935)(87); and Jeroom Vercruysse, 'Candide journaliste J. H. Maubert de Gouvest, gazetier à Bruxelles, 1758–61', *Cahiers Bruxellois. Revue d'histoire urbaine*, vol. 19 (1974), pp. 46–83 (88); Ghislaine de Boom, 'Les Ministres plénipotentiaires dans les Pays-Bas autrichiens principalement Cobenzl', *Académie Royale de Belgique, Mémoires*, 10th ser., vol. 31 (Brussels, 1932)(89).

Of all the Masonic histories the French has been most systematically and professionally written. A good starting place is the whole of vol. 41, 1969, of *Annales historique de la révolution française*(90). Still useful is the older work by the Masonic writer, Hiram [Emanuel Bon], *Les Ancêtres de la Franc-Maçonnerie en France*, reprinted from *Revue internationale des sociétés secrètes*, 1938(91). The bridging figure between English and French Freemasonry, and one who best illustrates the religious temper of the leadership of the French lodges was the Chevalier Ramsay. All of the following items should be consulted for an outline of his career and beliefs: D. P. Walker, *The Ancient Theology* (London: Duckworth, 1972)(92); C. N. Batham, 'Chevalier A. M. Ramsay; A New Appreciation', *AQC*, vol. 81 (1968), pp. 280–315 (93), with a useful appendix giving Ramsay's 1737 speech(94); G. H. Luquet, *La Franc-maçonnerie et l'état en France au XVIIIᵐᵉ siècle*

(Paris: Editions Vitiano, 1963, pp. 157–8)(95) on Ramsay's political intrigues. The foremost historian of French Freemasonry is now Pierre Chevallier and, although I take exception to his reading of certain important pieces of evidence (pp. 127–30), I still heartily recommend: Pierre Chevallier, *La Première profanation du temple maçonnique ou Louis XV et la fraternité, 1737–1755* (Paris: Librairie Philosophique J. Vrin, 1968)(96); also very useful is his more general account found in *Histoire de la franc-maçonnerie française. La Maçonnerie: école de l'égalité, 1725–1799* (Paris: Fayard, 1974)(97). I think that Robert Shackleton underestimates the importance of Freemasonry for Montesquieu, but his superb biography should always be consulted: *Montesquieu. A Critical Biography* (Oxford: Clarendon Press, 1961)(98).

Readers should never forget the web of intrigue that engulfed British politics and international relations as a result of the Jacobite threat. Not only was French Freemasonry heavily Jacobite, so too it would seem were some of the networks used by Walpole's agents. The best introduction to this world of intrigue occurs in Paul S. Fritz, *The English Ministers and Jacobitism between the Rebellions of 1715 and 1745* (Toronto: University of Toronto Press, 1975)(99) and his 'Anti-Jacobite intelligence, 1715–1745', *Historical Journal*, vol. 16 (1973), p. 276n, and pp. 273–4 on spies in the postal system (100). But no one should miss an account of the career of the Baron von Stosch, art collector, secret agent and Freemason: Lesley Lewis, *Connoisseurs and Secret Agents in Eighteenth Century Rome* (London: Chatto & Windus, 1961)(101). To assist in keeping the cast of characters in these plots in order also consult J. C. Sainty, *Officials of the Secretaries of State, 1660–1782* (London: University of London, Institute of Historical Research, 1973)(102).

But Masonic involvement in political intrigue should not obscure the largely educational mission of the lodges. Some attention is paid to that subject by N. Hans, *New Trends in Education in the Eighteenth Century* (London: Routledge & Kegan Paul, 1951)(103). Fairly good evidence also suggests that the first encyclopaedia of the eighteenth century was compiled by a Freemason, that is, E. Chambers, *Cyclopaedia: Or an Universal Dictionary of Arts and Sciences . . .* (London, 1728; printed for James and John Knapton, John Darby, Daniel Midwinter, Arthur Bettesworth, John Senex, Robert Gosling, John Pemberton, *et al.*)(104). Court Whigs were very commonly active in the new Masonic lodges, but we should not be deluded into thinking that Walpole had captured the intellectuals into his camp. Their antagonism to him is intelligently discussed in Bertrand Goldgar, *Walpole and the Wits. The Relation of Politics to Literature, 1722–1742* (Lincoln Nebr.: University of Nebraska Press, 1976)(105).

Beginning in the 1720s, the British government had managed to undercut both the political effectiveness and publishing freedom of the radicals. Yet signs of radical activity are occasionally visible. England still attracted foreigners of a decidedly subversive temper, and the career of one such unwelcome visitor is poignantly described in Franco Venturi, *Italy and the Enlightenment,* ed. Stuart Woolf (London: Longman, 1972)(106). Yet evidence for the survival after 1720, indeed the flourishing of radicalism under the aegis of Freemasonry, mostly comes from the Netherlands. Predictably the circle whose history is narrated in Chapter 5 began its intellectual life around the preservation of the works of Pierre Bayle. Both French refugees, Marchand and Picart, were significantly involved in the 1720 edition of Bayle's *Dictionnaire*, and for the history of Bayle's reputation in the Enlightenment the reader should begin with Pierre Rétat, *Le Diction-naire de Bayle et la lutte philosophique au XVIIIe siècle* (Paris: Université de Lyon, 1971)(107). The political milieu of the French Huguenot refugees involved in the publishing centres of the Netherlands is also illuminated in Pierre J. W. van Malssen, *Louis XIV d'après les pamphlets répandus en Hollande* (Amsterdam. II. J. Paris, 1936)(108), and William I. Hull, *Benjamin Furly and Quakerism in Rotterdam,* Swarthmore College Monographs on Quaker History (Swarthmore College, 1941)(109); Guy Howard Dodge, *The Political Theory of the Huguenots of the Dispersion* (New York: Columbia University Press, 1947)(110). Two absolutely indispensible guides to journalism in this period, much of it emanating from the Netherlands, should always be consulted: Jean Sgard, *Dictionnaire des journalistes* (Grenoble: Presses Universitaires de Grenoble, 1976)(111); and I. H. van Eeghen, *De Amsterdamse Boekhandel, 1689–1725,* Vols 1–4 (Amsterdam: Scheltema-Holkema, 1962–7)(112). Also useful, although now dated, is E. F. Kossmann, *De Boekhandel te 's-Gravenhage tot eind de 18^e eeuw* (The Hague: Nijhoff, 1937)(113).

The centres of subversive philosophising found in Paris in the early decades of the eighteenth century, and with which radicals in the Netherlands may have had contact, are surveyed in an unfortunately unpublished Cambridge PhD thesis: E. R. Briggs, 'The Political Academies of France in the Early 18th Century, with Special Reference to the Club de l'Entresol, and Its Founder, the Abbé Pierre Joseph Alary', (D. Phil. dissertation, Cambridge University, 1931) (114). The efforts of the French authorities to control the presses in their kingdom is well documented in Joseph Klaits, *Printed Propaganda under Louis XIV. Absolute Monarchy and Public Opinion* (Princeton, NJ: Princeton University Press, 1978)(115). For a brief survey of French freethinking the reader may also consult J. S. Spink, *French Free-Thought from Gassendi to Voltaire* (New York:

Greenwood reprint, 1969)(116), as well as Antoine Adam, *Le mouvement philosophique dans la première moitié du XVIII siècle* (Paris, SEDES, 1967)(117).

The link between publishing in the Netherlands and the dissemination of subversive ideas did not begin in the eighteenth century. The fascinating antecedents can be surveyed in Herman de la Fontaine Verwey, 'The Family of Love', *Quaerendo,* vol. 6, no. 3 (1976), pp. 219–71(118). Cf. P. J. Buijnsters, 'Les Lumières hollandaises', *Studies on Voltaire and the Eighteenth Century,* vol. 87 (1972), pp. 197–215(119); B. Rekers, *Benito Arias Montano (1527–1598)* (London: Warburg Institute, 1972)(120); and L. Voet, *The Golden Compasses* (Amsterdam: Van Gendt, 1969)(121), as well as in Elizabeth Eisenstein, *The Printing Press as an Agent of Change,* Vol. I (Cambridge: Cambridge University Press, 1979)(122). Sixteenth-century political theories of resistance, as revealed in Chapter 7, also contributed to the origins of the Radical Enlightenment, and for those theories the reader should consult Quentin Skinner, *The Foundations of Modern Political Thought* (Cambridge: Cambridge University Press, 1978)(123); Julian Franklin (ed. and trans.), *Constitutionalism and Resistance in the Sixteenth Century. Three Treatises by Hotman, Beza, and Mornay* (New York: Pegasus, 1969)(124); Donald R. Kelley, *François Hotman. A Revolutionary's Ordeal* (Princeton, NJ: Princeton University Press, 1973)(125). See also J. A. van Dorsten, *The Radical Arts. First Decade of an Elizabethan Renaissance* (Oxford: Oxford University Press, 1970)(126). And on the question of Hermetism and its influence on these sixteenth-century revolutionaries, see Jeanne Harrie, 'Duplessis-Mornay, Foix-Candale, and the Hermetic religion of the world', *Renaissance Quarterly,* vol. 31 (1978), pp. 506–8(127). The link between the *Traité* and those theories does not, however, rest on pantheism. Rather those theories were directly compatible with the republican and Commonwealth tradition.

One of the best republican libraries in the Netherlands during the late seventeenth and early eighteenth centuries to which the radicals had access was housed in the home of Benjamin Furly. For a survey of its contents see *Bibliotheca Furliana, sive Catalogus librorum* (Rotterdam: 1714)(128). The British Library copy, 11901.a.11, contains John Furly's manuscript notes on buyers and their purchases. One of the important French refugee converts to Whiggery who also plied his trade as an historian in the Netherlands was Rapin de Thoyras. His manuscript letters to his publisher and Knight of Jubilation, Charles Levier, are in the Marchand collection at the University Library in Leiden. A worthwhile account of his influence during the eighteenth century occurs in H. Trevor Colbourn, *The Lamp of Experience. Whig History and the Intellectual Origins of the American Revolution*

(Chapel Hill, NC: University of North Carolina Press 1965)(129). The inner circle of publishers and journalists who made up the Knights of Jubilation and their attendant literary society has never been previously discussed. Their history had to be pieced together from a variety of sources, most of them primary. Their engraver and iconographer, Bernard Picart, left a large volume of engravings; the finest collections are at the Teylers Museum, Haarlem, the Netherlands, and at the Metropolitan Museum of Art, New York. For a list of his engravings the reader should consult Bernard Picart, *Imposteurs innocentes, ou recueil d'estampes* (Amsterdam, 1734)(130). Marchand now has an excellent biography, although I disagree at various points with the interpretations found in C. M. G. Berkvens-Stevelinck, *Prosper Marchand et l'histoire du livre; quelques aspects de l'érudition bibliographique dans le première moitié du XVIII' siècle, particulièrement en Hollande. Académic Dissertation for the Degree of Doctor of Letters at the University of Amsterdam* (Bruges, 1978)(131). For Marchand's literary circle and their journal see P. Hemprich, *Le Journal littéraire de la Haye, 1713–37* (Berlin: Fritz Herrmann, 1915)(132); as well as M. Bruys, *Mémoires historiques, critiques et littéraires* (Paris, 1751)(133). S'Gravesande, one of the most active members, is discussed in a variety of places: G. Gori, *La fondazione dell'esperienza in s'Gravesande* (Florence: Nuova Italia, 1972)(133); Edward G. Ruestow, *Physics at Seventeenth and Eighteenth Century Leiden* (The Hague: Nijhoff, 1973)(134). Of course, Marchand gave his own account of the literary society in P. Marchand, *Dictionnaire historique, ou mémoires critiques et littéraires* (The Hague, 1759), Vol. 2, pp. 215–16(135).

Once again an unpublished thesis, this one in Paris, proved essential before the life of Saint-Hyacinthe could be reconstructed: E. Carayol, 'Themiseul de Saint-Hyacinthe. Thèse, 3ᵉ cycle, Lettres', 2 vols, University of Paris, IV, 1971, typewritten(136). This, of course, had to be combined with the Marchand manuscripts in the University Library, Leiden, which contain letters from Saint-Hyacinthe to his publisher, Levier. Saint-Hyacinthe's bibliography has been hopelessly confused with that of his friend, Albert-Henri de Sallengre. Carayol(136) goes a long way to sorting out the confusion but readers should be warned that many library catalogues are incorrect.

Justus Van Effen has fared better than his 'frères' in the literary society as far as bibliography is concerned. He is discussed in Harry M. Bracken, *The Early Reception of Berkeley's Immaterialism, 1710–33* (The Hague: Nijhoff, 1959)(137), as well as in W. J. B. Pienaar, *English Influences in Dutch Literature and Justus Van Effen as Intermediary* (Cambridge: Cambridge University Press, 1929)(138).

Two essays describe the intellectual milieu within which the literary society founded by the Knights operated: G. C. Gibbs, 'Some intellectual and political influences of the Huguenot émigrés in the United Provinces, c. 1680–1730', *Bijragen en Mededelingen betreffende de Geschiedenis der Nederlanden,* vol. 90 (1975), pp. 265–87(139); and Rosalie Colie, *Light and Enlightenment. A Study of the Cambridge Platonists and the Dutch Arminians* (Cambridge: Cambridge University Press, 1957)(140). But it should be remembered that while many French Hugenot refugees were either strict Calvinists or liberal Protestants, many of the Knights and their associates took the road to deism or even pantheism. On the links between these freethinking refugees and English political and journalistic circles another unpublished thesis is very useful: J. H. Broome, 'An Agent in Anglo-French Relationship: Pierre des Maizeaux 1673–1745', D. Phil. dissertation (London: University of London, 1949)(141). Some of these international connections are also mentioned in Aubrey Rosenberg, *Tyssot de Patot and His Work, 1655–1738* (The Hague: Nijhoff, 1972)(142).

By far the most elaborate set of detective records ever compiled on an eighteenth-century text must converge around the authorship of the *Traité des trois imposteurs.* A useful modern edition is P. Rétat (ed.), *Traité des trois imposteurs. Manuscript clandestin au début du XVIIIᵉ siècle (ed. 1777)* (Grenoble: Universités de la Région Rhône-Alpes, 1973)(143). This edition includes Rousset de Missy's commentary on the *Traité,* which I commonly refer to as his *Réponse*(143). There is a now dated work in German that surveys the problem: Jacob Presser, *Das Buch 'De tribus impostoribus'* (Amsterdam: H. J. Paris, 1926) (144), but his conclusions do not stand in the light of more recent scholarship. Another, less exact survey occurs in a work by Pierre Gustav Brunet (pseudonym Philomneste Junior) (previously cited as 6). Then in 1964 Don Cameron Allen made an educated guess that Rousset de Missy had actually written the *Traité*; see Don C. Allen, *Doubt's Boundless Sea. Skepticism and Faith in the Renaissance* (Baltimore, Md.: Johns Hopkins Press, 1964)(145). As my analysis shows that was good detective work done without the evidence we now possess.

The literary projects, open and clandestine, that can be traced to the Knights continue to grow, and in that respect a new look should be taken at the career of Jean Frédéric Bernard. His influence on Montesquieu has been shown in G. L. Van Roosbroeck, *Persian Letters before Montesquieu* (New York: Publications of the Institute of French Studies, 1932)(146). Indeed, all of the names on the official membership list of Rousset de Missy's lodge, La Bien Aimée, in Amsterdam ought now to be studied. The list is at the Grand Lodge of the Netherlands, 22 Fluwelenburgwal, The Hague, under the citation 'Annales de Dagran. Persoonsnamen, Correspondentie'. An aged catalogue exists for the contents of that library, the core of which was collected by George Kloss, *Beschrijving der Verzamelingen van het Groot-Oosten der Nederlanden. Handschriften der Klossiansche Bibliotheek* (The Hague, 1888)(147). These records have only recently been made available to scholars largely through a series of extraordinary and even bizarre events. During their occupation the Nazis originally confiscated the records of the Dutch lodges (we sometimes forget that they believed there was a Jewish–Masonic conspiracy). These records were then shipped to Germany and only recovered after the war quite by accident. Gradually, but in disarray, they were returned to The Hague where they have been superbly catalogued and made available to all scholars. Those records should be supplemented, of course, by Rousset's correspondence to Marchand at the University Library in Leiden. The manuscript contents of that library are catalogued in G. Geel, *Catalogus Librorum manuscriptorum qui inde ab anno 1741 bibliothecae Lugduno Batavae accesserunt* (Lugduno Batavae, 1852) (148).

There is some important published and now also accessible pamphlet literature about Freemasonry in Amsterdam: Harry Carr (ed.), *The Early French Exposures* (London: Quatuor Coronati Lodge, no. 2076, 1971)(149).

For the Enlightenment in the Netherlands after 1750 one family predominated, and various works serve as a useful introduction to the Bentincks: Paul-Emile Schazmann, *The Bentincks. The History of a European Family,* trans. Steve Cox (London: Weidenfeld & Nicolson, 1976)(150); Jacques Marx, 'Charles Bonnet contre les Lumières, 1738–1850', vols 1–2, *Studies on Voltaire and the Eighteenth Century,* vol. 157 (1976)(151); M. Paquot, 'Voltaire, Rousseau, et les Bentincks', *Revue de littérature comparée,* vol. 6 (1926), pp. 293–320 (152). Diderot also visited the Bentincks; see H. L. Brugman, 'Diderot, le Voyage de Hollande' in M. Boucher, *et al.* (eds), *Connaissance de l'Étranger. Mélanges offerts à la mémoire de Jean-Marie Carré* (Paris: M. Didier, 1964)(153). For their diplomatic involvements the following collection is essential: Arnoldina Kalshoven, *De Diplomatieke Verhouding tusschen Engeland en de Republiek der Vereenigde Nederlanden, 1747–1756* (The Hague: Nijhoff, 1915)(154).

The full implications of radical philosophising about nature and politics did not become clear until the political turmoil of the 1740s and the French invasion of the Netherlands. In the meantime Rousset and his friends had continued to publish political propaganda or to translate English Whig tracts: for example, Rousset de Missy (trans.), *Le Chevalier de St. George, rehabilité dans sa Qualité de Jacques III* (Whitehall, 1745) [originally by Gilbert Burnet](155); Rousset de Missy, *The History of Cardinal Alberoni* (London, 1719)(156);

Mémoires du Regne de Catherine Imperatrice et Souveraine de toute la Russie (The Hague, 1728)(157); *La Magazin des événemens de tous genres passez, présens et futurs ou L'epilogueur* (Amsterdam, 1741–5) (158), 13 vols in all and a weekly that was resolutely pro-Whig and pro-Protestant. As a result of these activities, among others, Rousset and his friends were questioned by the authorities: see M. M. Kleerkooper and W. P. van Stockum, *De Boekhandel te Amsterdam voornamelijk in de 17ᵉ eeuw*, 4 vols (The Hague: Nijhoff, 1916)(159). But it was not until the War of Austrian Succession that the weaknesses in the Dutch political and military system became fully evident.

For the role of oligarchy in Dutch political life various good secondary works are available: P. Geyl, 'Historical appreciations of the Holland Regent Regime', in A. O. Sarkissian (ed.), *Studies in Diplomatic History and Historiography in Honour of G. P. Gooch* (New York: Barnes & Noble, 1961)(160); and Simon Schama, *Patriots and Liberators. Revolution in the Netherlands, 1780–1813* (New York: Knopf, 1977)(161).

A useful summary of the 1740s is also found in Alice C. Carter, *The Dutch Republic in Europe in the Seven Years War* (London: Macmillan, 1971)(162); and Michel Richard, *Les Orange-Nassau* (Lausanne: Editions Rencontre, 1968), pp. 210–24 for a good description of William IV (163); see also W. C. van Huffel, *Willem Bentinck van Rhoon. Zijn Persoonlijkheid en Leven, 1725–47* (The Hague: Nijhoff, 1923)(164); and Peter Geyl, 'William IV of Orange and his English marriage', *Transactions of the Royal Historical Society*, 4th ser., vol. 8 (1925), pp. 14–37(165). For the Revolution of 1747 the letters of William Bentinck are essential: C. Gerretson and P. Geyl (eds), *Briefwisseling en aanteekeningen van Willem Bentinck, heer van Rhoon (tot aan de dood van Willem IV 22 October 1751)* (Utrecht: Kemink en Zoon, 1934)(166). For a general and sensitive discussion of the revolution see I. Leonard Leeb, *The Ideological Origins of the Batavian Revolution. History and Politics in the Dutch Republic, 1747–1800* (The Hague: Nijhoff, 1973)(167); and for Rousset's role the best source is Nico Johannes Jacques de Voogd, *Die Doelistenbeweging te Amsterdam in 1748* (Utrecht: De Vroede, 1914)(168).

As official historian of the revolution Rousset wrote a very interesting justification: J. Rousset de Missy, *Relation historique de la Grande Révolution arrivée dans la République des Provinces-Uniés, en DCC LXII* (Amsterdam, 1747)(169). After Rousset broke with the Bentincks and was finally arrested and exiled, his important journal, *Mercure historique et politique*, was condemned in 1749. Few books in the Netherlands ever made that category, and for a list see W. P. C. Knuttel, *Verboden Boeken in de Republiek der Vereenigde Nederlanden* (The Hague: Nijhoff, 1914)(170). And for the details of his sudden political demise see T. Bussemaker (ed.), *Archives ou correspondance inédité de la maison d'Orange-Nassau* (Leyden: A. W. Sijthoff, 1908), 4th ser., Vols 1–4 (171). Rousset's political career should also be followed by consulting his manuscript letters in the Haus-Hof-und Staatsarchiv, Vienna, in 'Alphabetischer Index zur Grossen Korrespondenz', G. C. 277, 328, 395 (some letters incorrectly listed under 'Roussel') (172). Throughout, Rousset is listed as the 'agent de S. A. le Duc de Brunswick Wolfenbuttel'.

The implications of the radical underside of the Enlightenment for the history of the High Enlightenment require more attention than I have been able to give in the epilogue. There is new evidence for the career of the Abbé Yvon, Diderot's associate and the writer of certain key essays on materialism for the *Encyclopédie* (1751). For the background to Yvon and the *Encyclopédie* the reader should consult the Comte de Montbas, 'Quelques encyclopédistes oubliés', *Revue des travaux de l'Académie des Sciences Morales et Politiques*, 4th ser. (1952), pp. 32–40; Kathleen S. Wilkins, 'A study of the works of Claude Buffier', *Studies on Voltaire and the Eighteenth Century*, vol. 66 (1969), pp. 102–5 on Yvon's use of Buffier; John Lough, *The 'Encyclopédie' in Eighteenth Century England and Other Studies* (Newcastle-upon-Tyne: Oriel Press, 1970), p. 160; F. Venturi, *Le origini dell' enciclopedia* (Rome: Edizioni U, 1946); D. W. Smith, *Helvétius. A Study in Persecution* (Oxford: Clarendon Press, 1965); J. Lough, 'Luneau de Boisjermain vs. the publishers of the *Encyclopédie*', *Studies on Voltaire and the Eighteenth Century*, vol. 23 (1963), pp. 82–3; and his *The Contributors to the 'Encyclopédie'* (London: Grant & Cutler, 1973). (All these items are cited as 173.) Then there is the extraordinary episode provoked by the Abbé de Prades' materialistic thesis written for the Sorbonne. It caused him and his friend, Yvon, a great deal of trouble, and that whole episode can be reconstructed from a variety of sources: D. W. Smith, *Helvétius*, pp. 144–52(173); a copy of the thesis is in BN MSS Joly de Fleury, 292, f. 354. For a summary see Francisque Bouillier, *Histoire de la philosophie cartésienne* (Paris: Ch. Delagrave et Cie, 1868), Vol. 2, pp. 632–7; R. R. Palmer, *Catholics and Unbelievers in 18th Century France* (Princeton, NJ: Princeton University Press, 1939), pp. 117–31; Voltaire, *Oeuvres complètes* (Paris: Garnier Frères, 1879), Vol. 24, pp. 17–28 (although probably not by Voltaire). (All cited as 174.) The Abbé de Prades' exile is surveyed without the new evidence presented here in Donald Schier, 'The Abbé de Prades in Exile', *Romanic Review*, vol. 55 (1954), pp. 182–90(175).

Now that we know that the Abbé Yvon was a Freemason the whole question of Freemasonry and the *Encyclopédie* has to be reopened. That enormous historiography is admirably surveyed by Robert

Shackleton, 'The *Encyclopédie* and Freemasonry', in W. H. Barber *et al.*, *The Age of the Enlightenment. Studies Presented to Theodore Besterman* (London: Oliver & Boyd, 1967), pp. 223–37(176). Information about one of the publishers of the *Encyclopédie*, Laurent Durand, who figures in this debate, can be found in the Bibliothèque Nationale, Paris, BN MSS français 22107, f. 26; and in 22106; Jacques Proust, *Diderot et l'Encyclopédie* (Paris: Colin, 1962), pp. 75, 94; and Arthur Wilson, *Diderot* (Oxford: Oxford University Press, 1972), pp. 119, 352n. (All cited as 177.) His relationship to Freemasonry is raised in a very important essay by Dorothy Schlegel, 'Freemasonry and the *Encyclopédie* reconsidered', *Studies on Voltaire and the Eighteenth Century*, vol. 90 (1972), pp. 1,433–60(178). Also very useful for the years just prior to the publication of the *Encyclopédie* is a recent essay by Aram Vartanian, 'The politics of *Les Bijoux indiscrets*', in A. Bingham and V. Topazio (eds), *Enlightenment Studies in Honour of Lester G. Crocker* (Oxford: Voltaire Foundation, 1979), pp. 349–76(179). Indeed, it was Lester Crocker who first saw the influence of Toland on Diderot: Lester Crocker, 'John Toland et le matérialisme de Diderot', *Revue d'histoire littéraire de la France*, vol. 52 (1953), pp. 289–95; see also L. Flam, 'De Toland en d'Holbach', *Tijdschrift voor de studie van Verlichting*, vol. 1 (1973), pp. 33–54. (Both items cited as 180.)

Not only can Yvon be tied to the Radical Enlightenment, but so too can the undoubtedly pious, although republican, French Huguenot, the Chevalier de Jaucourt. Various essays and monographs now exist for his life: Madeleine Morris, *Le Chevalier de Jaucourt. Un Ami de la Terre* (Geneva: Droz, 1979); see also John Lough, 'Louis, Chevalier de Jaucourt', in his *The 'Encyclopédie' in Eighteenth Century England* (Newcastle-upon-Tyne: Oriel Press, 1970), pp. 31–42. Jaucourt was also known as 'Neuville' and 'L. de Neufville'; see R. Schwab, 'Un encylopédiste Huguenot – le chevalier de Jaucourt', *Bulletin de la société de l'histoire du Protestantisme français*, vol. 113 (1962), pp. 45–75, and Dennis Fletcher, 'The Chevalier de Jaucourt and the English sources of the Encyclopedic article, *Patriote*', *Diderot Studies*, vol. 16 (1973), p. 25. (All cited as 181.)

Of all the major *philosophes* none was influenced more deeply by the Radical Enlightenment than the Baron d'Holbach. A good survey of current literature on the baron appears in D. Roche, 'Lumières et engagement politique: la coterie d'Holbach dévoilée', *Annales. Economies. Sociétés. Civilisations*, vol. 33 (1978), pp. 720–8(182). The most important recent work on d'Holbach is by A. C. Kors, *D'Holbach's Circle. An Enlightenment in Paris* (Princeton, NJ: Princeton University Press, 1977)(183).

Finally, the reader planning to begin a research topic on intellectual history in the eighteenth century should first consult the annual volumes of *The Eighteenth Century: A Current Bibliography,* ed. Robert R. Allen and published by the American Society for Eighteenth Century Studies. All back issues of *Eighteenth Century Studies* and the *Journal of the History of Ideas* are also worth surveying. There is also one bibliographical technique that is invaluable, that is, reading the footnotes of any author, this one being no exception.

Introduction

In this study of eighteenth-century culture, the student with a basic knowledge of the intellectual contours of the period and of the lives and ideals of the major *philosophes*, as well as the scholar interested in new sources and interpretations for the early decades of the Enlightenment, will meet a cast of interesting, if so-called minor, characters. Most of them were literary journalists or political propagandists, many of them, Freemasons; a significant number were also intellectual and political radicals. Immediately that anachronistic term 'radical' applied to the Enlightenment raises queries. If these be radicals, who are the moderates? The radicals were intellectual dissenters, men, and possibly a very few women, often with a refugee background, who could not share the willingness of the major *philosophes* like Voltaire and d'Alembert, or liberal churchmen like the Newtonians in England, to put their faith in enlightened monarchy. They sought, therefore, through a variety of methods, propaganda as well as intrigue, to establish a republican ideal, if not always a republican reality, worthy of European-wide imitation. Predictably they, like the moderates were the intellectual heirs of the mid-century English Revolution, only unlike the moderates they sided more with the radical sectaries, that is, with the losers rather than the winners of that first major European revolution.

Thus the radicals of the Enlightenment defy one of its stereotypes, that 'the man of the Enlightenment remains incapable of reaching beyond reason and intellect to the essence of life, historic action' (1, 12). On the contrary they were political activists, who, unlike the major *philosophes*, attached themselves to political patrons in England and courts on the Continent not as philosophers but as polemicists, spies and official historians. And Jean Rousset de Missy, one of the central characters in this book, in turn became a revolutionary. These radicals circulated within an international republic of letters, but after the 1720s they are found most strikingly in the Dutch Republic. Their social nexus had been established almost precisely at the turn of the century when the radical Whigs, in their disillusionment with the outcome of the Revolution of 1688–9 at home, and in their desire to strengthen the alliance against France abroad, ventured across the Channel to seek out followers. They found them predictably in the

Netherlands, in the clusters of angry French Protestant refugees recently forced into exile by Louis XIV's repressive policies. This new evidence for the early infiltration of English political culture and in the case of Freemasonry, of English social institutions, into the Low Countries, both north and south, adds further weight to the contention that the beginning of the European Enlightenment can in many instances be traced to post-revolutionary England.[1] The unique characteristic of that post-revolutionary culture was its scientific maturity, and perhaps inevitably that new scientific culture proved a distinct force in shaping the reforming philosophy and programme advocated by Enlightenment radicals.

The culture of Locke and Newton existed within a political context transformed by the first of the modern revolutions. In the last twenty years or so we have learned a great deal more about the English Revolution and we have come to understand more clearly its exact relation to the origins of modern science. This new historiography that illuminates both the English Revolution – understood as a matrix of social and political upheaval beginning in 1640 and culminating at the Revolution of 1688–9 – and the social origins of modern scientific culture, offers important revisions for our understanding of the Enlightenment. It is no longer possible, given what we now know about the social relations of English science, to divorce eighteenth-century culture from its seventeenth-century origins(3). The opening chapters of this book aim to correct that older historiographical tendency. Secondly, the custom in Enlightenment historiography of treating science and natural philosophy, in particular theories about the nature of matter, as simply progressive forces and a-historical ideas, devoid of social content and meaning, requires revision. Because the social meaning of scientific ideas and programmes has not been assessed in relation to the interests of their proponents we have obliterated a fundamental tension now apparent in the earliest manifestations of enlightened culture. The version of Enlightenment culture supported by the Newtonian synthesis, as it was articulated by Newton and his closest followers, asked that educated men and women acknowledge a providentially guided polity where diversity of Christian creeds was to be tolerated, where learning about nature and society was encouraged, but where both were put to serve the interests of court-centred and ministerial government and the concomitant but loosely defined political oligarchy that came to dominate Hanoverian England. In other words, in the first half of the eighteenth century Anglican hegemony and 'court' government, as opposed to legal equality for all religious creeds and the rule of parliamentary or 'country' interests, received vital support from the Newtonian assumption that the deity instilled hierarchy, order and place, that spiritual forces controlled nature just as kings and oligarchs managed their states. In early modern and pre-industrial Europe the assumption was uniformly held that ideas about nature, in particular its physical manifestations and metaphysical properties, bore relation to the way people, educated and uneducated, understood the social and moral order. However, there was a vast difference between the social assumptions held by certain heretics who believed that God or spirit dwelt in nature, that in effect nature contained within it sufficient explanations of its various phenomena, and the assumptions held by essentially orthodox Newtonians, among them even Voltaire, who argued that God controlled nature from outside, as it were by laws and spiritual agencies. The first approach, which I have chosen to call pantheistic because that is the word used by some of its most-aggressive eighteenth-century proponents, tended inevitably in a socially levelling direction because it undermined the theoretical foundations for established churches and their priestly caste.

The radicals of the Enlightenment, from their first stirrings within Whig circles after the Revolution of 1688–9, tended to subscribe to this pantheistic conception of the universe, to a metaphysic that conflated spirit and matter and tended to proclaim nature, and not God, as the sole object of worship and study. They were represented most prominently by John Toland (1670–1722). Indeed it was Toland who invented the English word, 'pantheist' (1705), and it was quickly taken up by his associates in the Netherlands. In contrast to the providentialism and in some cases the deism of the moderate, Newtonian Enlightenment, the radicals postulated pantheism, or if we use the more historiographically commonplace term, materialism, and it horrified the liberal exponents of the new science who invariably brought their influence to bear against it. Eighteenth-century materialism had many origins and faces. One version, heavily indebted to Descartes, emphasised the mechanical and self-moved properties of matter; another, that is here called pantheism, emphasised the vitalistic, spirit-in-matter qualities of nature and tended inevitably to deify the material order. The latter philosophy belonged to the radical coterie whose history we are tracing, but it should be emphasised that they were also comfortable in praising the writings of La Mettrie, a mid-century exponent of a mechanistic version of materialism. All these philosophies of nature, whether the property of materialists or deists or providentialists, drew heavily upon their reading of the methodology and metaphysics of the new science. However, in the case of the radicals they also found support for their pantheism in the naturalistic writings of the late Renaissance. In Chapter 1 I explore their probable use of Bruno, Vanini and Des Périers, and suggest ways in which these naturalistic and vitalistic philosophies, often of ancient lineage, could be made compatible with a scientific culture whose major representatives had in large measure attempted to refute them.

The first occasion in early modern history when philosophies of nature and their prescriptions for the social order took on revolutionary significance occurred in England between 1640 and 1660. For the intellectual history of that period and its relevance to the new science, as discussed in Chapter 2, I have relied heavily on the writings of Christopher Hill, J. R. Jacob, and Charles Webster to set the stage for the emergence of early Enlightenment culture, in both its moderate and radical phases. In the late 1640s the revolutionary implications of pantheism were made all too clear in the preachings and political programme of the radical sectaries, and in a very attenuated sense, they became the ancestors of the various eighteenth-century republicans who form the subject of this book. Likewise the scientific culture first articulated by Robert Boyle and his followers in the Royal Society (1662) was intended in part to combat the philosophical and political radicalism of the late 1640s. It also in turn provided a basis for later polemical assaults aimed against the freethinkers and republicans of the early eighteenth century. The mechanical philosophy of Boyle and his associates directly contributed to the triumph of Newton's science and to the articulation of the liberal Anglicanism to which it was so neatly grafted.

Yet even after we distinguish the Radical Enlightenment from that of the Newtonians, as I have tried to do before plunging into its social network and heretical ideas, we have still not fully grasped its uniqueness. A definition of the *philosophe* of the Enlightenment, whether liberally Christian (although within the mainstream of the French Enlightenment there were few enough of those), deist or atheist, which sees him as a combative thinker who 'refused to abide by Christian doctrines and dogma . . . [who] searched for the truth in the light of reason and experience' and who entertained a strong interest in the new science and its applications (4, xv), although still valid for most Enlightenment thinkers, does not adequately encompass what the new evidence about these early eighteenth-century radical coteries now tells us. Not only did they refuse to accept Christian doctrine, and indeed reject the most basic assumptions of Christian metaphysics, they also formulated an entirely new religion of nature and gave it ritualistic expression within Freemasonry. That startling conclusion, documented in Chapters 5 and 6, forces a reappraisal of the traditional histories of European Freemasonry, not to mention a reworking of its traditional chronology. Generally it has been assumed, largely on the basis of Masonic historiography, that speculative Freemasonry begins in London in 1717 with the establishment of the Grand Lodge.[2] In an official sense that is still true, only the picture, as we shall see, is infinitely more complex than that.

Toland has long been suspected of writing a Masonic ritual (*Pantheisticon*, 1720) intended to praise nature and not God, and one as a result never officially adopted. Aside from that published text, ostensibly written for his 'Socratic Brotherhood', Toland's role in the establishment of European Freemasonry, that vastly popular and uniquely eighteenth-century phenomenon, has never until now been adequately demonstrated. The present volume began to take shape with the discovery of a manuscript in Toland's unpublished papers, here printed for the first time in the appendix, which was the record of one meeting in 1710 of a secret society at work in The Hague.[3]

Surprisingly the meeting record contained not only a date but crucially important names. It was written by Prosper Marchand (1678–1756), a journalist and minor *philosophe*, who, as a young French Protestant refugee, became an admirer of Pierre Bayle (d. 1706) and the editor of the 1720 edition of his immensely popular *Dictionnaire historique*. The meeting record in Toland's manuscripts led to Marchand's vast collection of unpublished manuscripts at the University Library, Leiden, where a larger social world, long hidden, was suddenly revealed. The Marchand manuscripts attest to the Masonic character, although not in every instance to the Masonic membership, of a vast network of publishers and journalists, English Commonwealthmen and French refugees, and one prominent Dutch scientist, Willem Jacob s'Gravesande.

All of these disparate figures were 'brothers', intent upon preserving their 'secret', and loyal to their various grand masters. Most prominent among Marchand's associates and his close friend, was Jean Rousset de Missy (1686–1762), another French Protestant who became one of the leaders of organised Dutch Freemasonry in the period after its official establishment in 1735. From Leiden it was a short journey, both geographically and intellectually, to the library of the Grand Lodge of the Netherlands in The Hague, one of the finest Masonic libraries in Europe, that is also proudly (unlike its London equivalent) open to all scholars. Rousset's role in organised Dutch Freemasonry could then be documented(8), and the historian could inspect a previously clandestine world that stretches at least from 1710 and Toland's private record, into the 1750s, by which time many of these radicals have been seasoned and aged by experience, and in some cases, by disappointment. This secret world, although not some of the pantheistic tracts that can be traced to it, turned out to be far tamer than we might have been led to suspect by the various paranoid accounts of European Freemasonry perpetrated by early nineteenth-century conservative and anti-Masonic historians and propagandists.

Yet, as I shall argue, eighteenth-century Freemasonry, although resolutely Newtonian in its official posture, could and did house a variety of radical thinkers. Their dedication to Masonry, perhaps more than any other single characteristic, distinguished them from the purely intellectual concerns, as previously defined, of the major *philosophes*. Most of the latter never ventured into this daring attempt to found an international movement that had within it the potential of creating a new European religion, resolutely civil to be sure, but no less compelling than its alternatives. In politics, the radicals were republicans and 'politicians', to use their word; in philosophy they were drawn to materialism, or pantheism as they preferred to call it; in religion they came dangerously close, through the agency of Freemasonry, to challenging the established churches, not simply doctrinally or philosophically, but more fundamentally on the level of social existence and ritualistic expression. Most important, the Radical Enlightenment was not simply spawned, as it were, by liberal parents. It existed simultaneously and in harsh dialogue with the more dominant and moderate version of enlightened belief and practice, a dialectic that owes much to its English and revolutionary origins. Before there was a High Enlightenment in Europe, during that violently anti-Christian post-1750 climate that briefly dominated the great salons of Paris and that is best represented in the writings of the Baron d'Holbach and his atheistic friends, there was a Radical Enlightenment. If it had a capital, it was The Hague and there, of course, it was directly in touch with the nerve centre of Enlightenment propaganda, the Dutch publishing houses.

We are on the verge of a major reassessment of the role of the printing press in early modern European culture (122). Rather than being seen as a mere vehicle for the dissemination of new ideas, its practitioners and technology are being advanced as distinct forces for cultural change in themselves. Here that thesis receives re-enforcement and extension into the first decades of the eighteenth century. In this account of radical coteries in the Netherlands, with access to the presses and their own publishing firms, the distinction between *philosophe* and publisher, between the enlightened man and the printed word, is inevitably blurred if not obliterated. Not by any means were all publishers and journalists like the radical ones we shall encounter in these pages; most were business men, pure and simple. But various books and manuscripts that played crucial roles in shifting the eighteenth-century debate about God's role and existence in the direction of materialism and into a frontal assault on the very foundations of Christianity, in particular the infamous *Traité des trois imposteurs*, can now be traced to this major coterie whose existence first emerged from that important manuscript in Toland's possession. Calling themselves, and what I shall argue was their private Masonic lodge, the Knights of Jubilation, Marchand, Levier and their friend, Rousset, put into writing an old accusation, and one that would still be offensive in some quarters today, namely, that Moses, Jesus and Mohammed were mere impostors. Fritsch, the Grand Master of the Knights, among others, circulated manuscript copies of the *Traité*, while various other members produced now very rare published editions.

Inevitably the historian must admit her sympathy for such a cast of fascinating characters. These lesser-known figures are being put forward for inspection partly because their story needed to be written (new evidence entails the writing of new history), and also because perhaps it is time that we shift our vision, if only momentarily, away from the major *philosophes*; not because they have been rendered less important, but solely because we do, or should, know a great deal about them already.

Yet shifts of vision are sometimes controversial. The links asserted here between Whig culture in England, the spread of Freemasonry and the Dutch Revolution of 1747, may cause some unease. That seemingly 'irrational' activities might play a role in the social lives of the lofty guardians of the Whig constitution, from Walpole through to the Bentincks, and in the cultural life of their Austrian allies, not to mention in the creed of their radical critics and agents, may at first blur our image of 'the age of reason'. But that shibboleth, to use a favourite and secret Masonic 'word', may need some de-mystifying even if it has to come somewhat ironically from the world of secrecy and ritual.

It must not be forgotten that here we are looking at Freemasonry in its golden age. That eighteenth-century phenomenon bears little or no relation to some of its twentieth-century varieties. The curiously anachronistic and even sinister role of Freemasonry in the contemporary religious conflicts (not unrelated to the events of 1689) that still plague the last bastion of seventeenth-century religious culture to be found in the British Isles, namely Northern Ireland, should not be associated with the story here related. All that remains there in the linkage between some Masonic lodges and the Orange order seems to be secrecy and an exaggerated cult of a Protestant past. By contrast, the Masonic lodges of the eighteenth century on both sides of the Channel offered men, and most surprisingly some women, of all religions an opportunity to create what must have been an extraordinarily fascinating and tolerant social world, where, if only briefly and of course secretly, 'brothers' from a variety of backgrounds could meet, as the Masonic phrase asserted, 'upon the level'.[4]

Our primary purpose in the chapters that follow is to give the student a new understanding of the radical side of Enlightenment culture, and initially to relate its earliest manifestations to the major revolutions of the seventeenth century, to both the English and Scientific Revolutions. To do so we must enter into a culture that was by the early eighteenth century international, yet at moments, purposely clandestine. Its existence, but not its personnel, have been known for some decades, ever since the pioneering work of Gustave Lanson and Ira Wade.[5] They pointed to the singular importance of clandestine literature in creating the intellectual ferment so central to the early decades of the European Enlightenment. In the period prior to 1750, those clandestine manuscripts, passed from hand to hand, fed the flames of what became after mid-century a massive conflagration intended to destroy the Christian churches and their doctrines, as well as to invalidate the claims made to authority by established élites and absolutist institutions of government. Surveys of clandestine manuscripts have seldom, if ever, been able to locate their actual purveyors. The book trade network engaged in the circulation of these manuscripts still remains largely obscure. Here some new evidence is presented for one such network operating in this crucially important early period, and we now have a sense of how at least this publishing coterie, dedicated to the clandestine, might have trafficked in its forbidden wares (see Chapter 6).

The ideas and beliefs we can now associate with the Radical Enlightenment, of course, made their greatest impact in select Parisian salons operating during the second half of the eighteenth century. In summation we must look briefly at those decades, in particular at two projects, Diderot's *Encyclopédie* (1751) and d'Holbach's *Système de la Nature* (1770), for the relation they bear to this earlier culture. In the first case, the old question of the relationship of Freemasonry to Diderot's project must be reframed, not to assert the Masonic character of that project (for it was in no sense a Masonic 'plot'), but rather to analyse its relation to this earlier Masonic network centred in the publishing world of the Netherlands. Likewise the pantheism of d'Holbach, now acknowledged to be deeply indebted to Toland, merits some final attention. So, too, do the social contacts of that great publisher of the High Enlightenment, Marc-Michel Rey, who profited so handsomely from the publication of those earlier manuscripts, as well as from the services he rendered to Rousseau and d'Holbach, among others.

We are at the source of a long tradition, with a very large cast of characters. Only a few of them have survived the passage of time, at last to reveal themselves and their private world into which, for our own enlightenment, we are obliged to enter.

Notes: Introduction

1 See my 'John Toland and the Newtonian Enlightenment', *Journal of the Warburg and Courtauld Institutes*, vol. 32 (1969), esp. pp. 329–31; cf. J. G. A. Pocock, 'Post-Puritan England and the Problem of the Enlightenment', William Andrews Clark Library Lecture, 24 October, 1975.

2 For example, John Lane, *Masonic Records, 1717–1784: Being Lists of All the Lodges at Home and Abroad* (London, 1895); H. Harry Rylands, *Records of the Lodge Original, No. 1. Now the Lodge of Antiquity, No. 2 of the Free and Accepted Masons of England* (London, privately printed, 1928), 2 vols; Wilfred G. Fisher, 'A Cavalcade of Freemasons', *AQC*, vols. 76–7 (1963–4), pp. 44–58.

3 BL, MSS ADD. 4295, ff. 18–19; see pp. 267–9.

4 Jacob Katz, *Jews and Freemasons in Europe, 1723–1939* (Cambridge, Mass.: Harvard University Press, 1970), pp. 8–16; the pattern does not, by and large, hold for German lodges, pp. 21–2.

5 G. Lanson, 'Questions diverses sur l'histoire d' l'esprit philosophique en France avant 1750', *Revue d'histoire littéraire de la France*, no. 19 (1912), esp. pp. 20–1; also A. A. Barbier, *Dictionnaire des ouvrages anonymes et pseudonymes* (Paris, 1806–9) and his manuscript notations in BN, n.a. fr. 5184, ff. 53–5.

CHAPTER 1

Science and the Philosophical Origins of the Radical Enlightenment

During the seventeenth century Europeans witnessed two great, although profoundly different revolutions. Each in its way shaped the contours of the radical side of the European Enlightenment. The English Revolution of the 1640s and 1650s left a legacy of political thought and experience that nurtured republican thought throughout the eighteenth century. In the early 1700s English republicans transmitted that legacy to small, but important, coteries of converts in the Netherlands and they, in turn, spread republican ideas to French-speaking readers throughout Europe.

Yet the term 'revolution' also correctly describes the central intellectual transformation of the 1600s, the Scientific Revolution. Although begun during the second half of the sixteenth century with the publication of Copernicus's *De revolutionibus orbium coelestium* (Nuremberg, 1543), that intellectual transformation had its greatest impact and reached its culmination during the second half of the seventeenth century, in particular with the publication of Isaac Newton's *Philosophiae naturalis principia mathematica* (1687). The Scientific Revolution of the late sixteenth and seventeenth centuries established the intellectual context for the Radical Enlightenment, and in this chapter we shall explore the background and significance of that revolution.

In early modern Europe ideas about nature and its workings were linked to the way people conceived the human condition, whether moral or political. Before we can deal with the enlightened prescriptions for the human order proclaimed by eighteenth-century radicals we must understand the natural or cosmic picture they extracted from the new body of scientific or natural philosophical learning.

The central achievements of the Scientific Revolution were the development of a new methodology for investigating nature based upon experiment and upon the newly invented mathematical skills, and the articulation of a mechanical understanding of the natural world. Both achievements fired the imagination of the educated élite and by the late seventeenth century presented reformers and critics of the established order in church and state with the philosophical and methodological foundations for an assault upon established authority.

Up until the mid-seventeenth century widely known explanations for natural phenomena had relied upon essentially scholastic and Aristotelian notions of matter in motion. Bodies move in a filled universe because of tendencies inherent in their God-given nature. For example, heavy bodies fall because it is in their nature to do so. Scholastic explanations of natural phenomena, whether the motion of the planets in the heavens or the rising of water in a hollow reed when pressure is applied through suction, falsely supposed, in the words of Robert Boyle, a harsh critic of scholasticism and one of the first mechanical philosophers, 'that there is a kind of *anima mundi* [soul of the world], furnished with various passions, which watchfully provides for the safety of the universe; or that a brute and inanimate creature, as water . . . has a power to move its heavy body upwards . . .'(9, 113).

The new mechanical philosophy banished spiritual agencies, inherent tendencies, and *anima* from the universe. In their place were put explanations based upon those natural properties capable of mathematical calculation. Nature had to be observed and experienced, and wherever possible given mathematical expression. The physical universe became a place with spatial dimensions within which bodies moved at measurable speeds. Bodies moved one another by impulse, that is, by pushing one another and to explanations of the natural world based upon impulse we commonly ascribe the term 'mechanical'.[1]

The mechanisation of the world picture was in fact but one aspect of the Scientific Revolution. For our purposes, however, and for eighteenth-century reformers who were not themselves scientists but who possessed a keen interest in the new science, it was by far the most important aspect of that intellectual revolution. The discovery of a new explanation of man's physical environment inevitably entailed implications for the political, social and religious environment. In the words of Isaac Barrow, a leading mathematician and the tutor of Isaac Newton (1642–1727), the 'world natural' provided a model for the operation of the 'world politick'.

But what lessons were to be derived from this new mechanical model of the natural world? In the older, magical view of nature upon which rested the sciences of astrology and alchemy, the movements of the planets, or earthquakes and natural disorders, were interpreted as portents of future political upheavals or of moral disorders. Theologians argued that these natural disorders were signs of God's displeasure. By the late seventeenth century certain mechanical philosophers such as Newton still allowed for occasional divine intervention in the course of nature and the German philosopher and mathematician, Leibniz, believed cautiously in astrology. But by and large a more sophisticated, analogous relationship between natural and human events had come to prevail. The ordered and regular structure of the universe, its laws, its mechanism, or simply its heliocentricity, provided a foundation for new kinds of religious beliefs, and a very compelling argument for order, stability and progress in human affairs.

The great mechanical philosophers of the seventeenth century, from Descartes through Newton and Leibniz, were profoundly aware of the social and religious implications of the new science. All, with the exception of Hobbes and Spinoza, laboured to use these new explanations of the natural order to emphasise the dependence of the created world on the will and power of the Creator. In short they lent their support to the established Christian churches of their various societies, and often to the maintenance of established monarchical authority. Western science at its very origins was perceived and used to enhance the power of ruling élites and prevailing Christian orthodoxy.

In England during the seventeenth century that search for stability and order on the part of Christian and Protestant *virtuosi* like Boyle entailed the demolition of scholastic, and generally Catholic, versions of scientific explanation. That battle was but one phase of the war against the reinstitution of Catholicism in England, a goal long associated with the Stuarts and nearly attained during the reign of James II (1685–8).[2]

The assault upon scholasticism, which in Protestant countries like England and the Netherlands was replete with political and ideological meaning, was but one of the intellectual battles undertaken by the new mechanical philosophers. They also repudiated those explanations of nature that rested upon magic and animism. On one level we regard this assault upon magic as one of the great steps forward in the articulation of Western rationalism. Yet to leave the matter at that would be to ignore the historical context within which that step occurred.

During the seventeenth century magical explanations of the natural order were intrinsically bound up with popular heresy and social protest coming from the lower orders of society. Given that association, the assault upon magical and animistic explanations of nature undertaken by the major Christian scientists can no longer be seen simply as a step in the struggle between 'rational' versus 'irrational' ways of explaining the natural order. Political and social motives were entwined with that assault, and indeed those motives are most clearly illustrated in the role played by English scientists during the English Revolution. That first revolution in modern Western history led to a breakdown of established authority of such major proportions that lower-class spokesmen were for the first time capable of putting in print coherent statements of their democratic and republican goals. At every turn these Levellers, as well as a variety of other sectaries not directly affiliated with them, described the human condition and the natural world in language best described as pantheistic and materialistic(10).

The pantheistic materialism of seventeenth-century radicals owed its origin to the magical and naturalistic view of the universe which Christian churchmen and theologians had laboured for centuries to defeat. At the heart of this natural philosophy lay the notion that nature is a sufficient explanation or cause for the existence and workings of man and his physical environment. In other words, the separation of God from Creation, creature from creator, of matter from spirit, so basic to Christian orthodoxy and such a powerful justification for social hierarchy and even for absolute monarchy, crumbles in the face of animistic and naturalistic explanations. God does not create *ex nihilo*; nature simply is and all people (and their environment) are part of this greater All. Of course there are mystical tendencies in this pantheism and indeed the practice of magic can be but one of its logical conclusions.

The new science and mechanical philosophy of the seventeenth century repudiated magical explanations that relied upon the random working of spirit or animus in the universe or upon the ability of the *magus* or magician to control nature. As a result by the late seventeenth century radical reformers who repudiated the authority of Christian churches and absolute monarchs were caught in an intellectual quandary of serious proportions. As educated men they embraced the new science and its mechanical explanations; they too repudiated magic. Yet the burden of the new mechanical philosophy had been brought to support established institutions and traditional religious and political authority. More precisely, the version of the mechanical philosophy that most captivated European thinkers, namely the Newtonian, argued in the strongest possible terms for a material order that was moved by spiritual forces outside of matter, by a providential creator who maintained a system of spiritual forces that regulated and controlled nature (11). If European radicals were to keep the new science and to escape its ideological burdens, then pantheistic and materialistic explanations would have to be fashioned. Yet these would have to exist in harmony with the mechanical world picture and the new scientific discoveries.

Enlightenment radicals searched for their philosophical foundations in two intellectual traditions. They embraced aspects of the new science while attempting to salvage and to revitalise purely naturalistic explanations of the universe which had largely flourished during the late Renaissance. In the late sixteenth and early seventeenth centuries, at the height of the religious controversies provoked by the Reformation and Counter-Reformation, these naturalistic arguments had been put forward by radical thinkers whose style – although not necessarily whose goals – were remarkably similar to the behaviour of eighteenth-century radicals. To establish the historical background to the Radical Enlightenment we must examine the naturalism of these late Renaissance reformers while simultaneously assessing the use to which the discoveries of the Scientific Revolution could be put by thinkers whose political goals and religious beliefs differed profoundly from those of the major scientists. In short we must understand how a pantheistic view of the universe, replete with mystical overtones, could be made compatible with mechanical explanations of nature, in themselves so apparently incompatible with it.

From a purely philosophical point of view the incompatibility of these traditions appears irreconcilable. Historically, however, the scientific rationalism of the seventeenth century owed much to a wide spectrum of Renaissance philosophising. Indeed, we now know that it is no longer possible to separate science from magic in the sixteenth and seventeenth centuries as neatly and surgically as had once been the case. In that period even the use of the term 'scientist' is less appropriate than that of 'natural philosopher' to describe the exponents of the new learning.

The conceptual roots of the Scientific Revolution lie in Renaissance Neo-Platonism and it is in that tradition that we find the bridge between the new science and pantheism. Neo-Platonism emphasised the existence of a universal system of spiritual hierarchy within nature, and this reality lay beneath the appearances of things. One thrust of this vision was to lead to the discovery of mechanical forces, invisible yet capable of mathematical expression. Western scientists operating in this tradition could argue for the existence of the invisible forces operating on nature, for, as in the case of Newton, the existence of a law of universal gravitation that operated on the atomic structure of matter, from the smallest terrestrial objects to the planets themselves. Equally, the Renaissance *magus* could argue for the existence of spiritual forces in the universe which could be comprehended and controlled by the human spirit in harmony with those forces.[3]

This so-called 'dark side' of Renaissance humanism, that is the search for an immediate comprehensive understanding of nature, encouraged magical and animistic speculations, in conjunction with the extreme individualism so characteristic of the magician. This aggressive self-confidence found expression in the formulation of bold and ingenious theories about the historical origins of true wisdom, locating it in pre-Christian times. The paganising and anti-Christian tendencies within this magical Neo-Platonism were all too clear, and its devotees went on, in some cases, to embrace Cabalistic learning or to search the supposedly ancient writings of the Egyptian priest, Hermes Trismegistus, for the key to this ancient wisdom, for *gnosis*, an immediate and direct comprehension that would unlock the secrets of nature (12, ch. 8).

This Hermetic tradition, that takes its name from Hermes, came to rest during the Renaissance upon two texts, the *Corpus Hermeticum*, and the *Asclepius*. They were revived in the West when the Florentine humanist, Ficino, translated the *Pimander* (that is, the *Corpus Hermeticum*) into Latin and published it in 1471. The *Corpus Hermeticum,* although a collection of philosophic aphorisms dating from the second century AD, was believed until the mid-seventeenth century to be the sayings and magical wisdom of that ancient Egyptian priest, Hermes. In the *Corpus* magic, astrology, alchemy, mystical and number symbolism mix easily with natural philosophy, with a distinct understanding of the physical world. That mixture, as we shall see, could dissolve, and very gradually the magical elements of this pagan naturalism fall by the wayside, leaving a pantheistic and materialistic philosophy of nature, with strongly magical overtones, as well as the crucially important belief that there is a pure wisdom, a *prisca*, that is, pagan in its roots, universal in meaning, and anti-Christian in its religious and political implication.

The dedication of Enlightenment radicals to the spread of the new science, from which they sought to extract weapons against the prevailing Christian orthodoxy precluded an interest in, and more precisely entailed a repudiation of magical beliefs and practices. Some went so far as to suggest that the founders of the major religions, Moses, Jesus and Mohammed, had in fact invented those practices in order to beguile a gullible populace (see chapter 6). The women and men subsequently accused of magical practices, witches, heretics and reformers, were cruelly abused by a clerical élite that had fallen victim to its own beliefs. The repudiation of magic on the part of Enlightenment radicals occurred simultaneously with their adherence to a pantheistic naturalism that had once been the prevailing philosophy of Renaissance adepts and *magi*. This extraordinary blending of science and mysticism makes historical sense only if we realise that seventeenth-century science at its very origins possessed certain magical associations.

Although the exact relationship between the origins of modern science and the Hermetic tradition is still hotly debated by historians, certain affinities seem to be certain. Two of the earliest and most important prophets of the Scientific Revolution, the English philosopher and proponent of scientific investigation based upon our experience of nature, Francis Bacon (1561–1626), and René Descartes (1596–1650), the most important mechanical philosopher and mathematician of the next generation, knew the Hermetic and magical tradition and received inspiration from its reforming aspects. Yet both resolutely repudiated its gnostic tendencies, its penchant for secrecy and its lack of precision.[4] So, too, Robert Boyle (1627–91), the inventor of experimental methodology, elaborated upon the Hermetic doctrine that man was created to possess and to rule over nature; Boyle also repudiated the gnostic and anti-experimental tendencies within Hermeticism (9, 105–6).

Despite these polemics on the part of the Christian advocates and founders of the new science, or possibly because of them, by the late seventeenth century European freethinkers turned back to the disparate writings of various Renaissance naturalists and reformers. This revival, beginning in the 1690s, of the writings of Giordano Bruno (1548–1600), Lucilo Vanini (1585–1619) and, to a lesser extent, Tommoso Campanella (1568–1639), marked the first stage of this new onslaught against orthodoxy and heralded the beginning of the Radical Enlightenment.[5] The radicals seized upon the pagan naturalism of the late Renaissance and found in it powerful justification for a pantheistic and materialistic explanation of the mechanical universe. Two aspects of late Renaissance Hermeticism were to resonate in the literature produced by the internationally connected freethinking circles of the early eighteenth century: its vitalistic and pantheistic conception of nature and that aggressively irreligious and mocking tone commonly used by late-sixteenth-century reformers like Bruno. His writings, more than any other, capture the spirit adopted by early eighteenth-century radicals.

Bruno lionised the pagan deities, assembled them at banquets, applauded their open sensuality and used them as mouth-pieces for his reforming philosophy. Within the Hermetic tradition, the pagan deity, Mercury, was in fact believed to be a Roman representation of Hermes, and Minerva, the goddess of wisdom, assisted Mercury and Jupiter in the work of reforming the heavens (12, 220, 326–7). Both deities figure prominently in Bruno's pagan imagery, and early in the eighteenth century they return as standard bearers for the Knights of Jubilation, that secret society of republicans and pantheists who will figure so prominently in the first generation of the Radical Enlightenment. Then, as with Bruno, this championing of the pagans was part of a larger attempt to fashion an anti-Christian stance that sought to repudiate traditional ethics as well as to undermine the orthodox concept of the transcendent deity.

For Bruno and for other late Renaissance Hermetists, in contrast to the relative freedom enjoyed by their eighteenth-century admirers, this pagan symbolism was a deadly serious business; personal survival was at stake. During the sixteenth century, the use of commonly recognised but elaborately complex symbols provided a mnemonic device whereby the reformer could communicate his intentions while arousing the least opposition from censors or from the Inquisition. In the eighteenth century, these symbols were to recur as decorative and artistic devices used on the frontispieces of subversive literature.

In the sixteenth century, the guardians of orthodoxy were not slow to catch on to the meaning of these symbolic devices, despite the precautions. In 1576 Bruno, a Dominican monk in Naples, found himself charged with heresy by the Neapolitan Inquisition, and he fled to Rome where the Roman Holy Office took an equally dim view of his presence. Thus began perhaps the most peripatetic philosophical career in early modern history. Bruno lived and preached his doctrines in Geneva, where he developed an intense dislike for orthodox Calvinists, in Toulouse, Paris, London, Oxford, various German cities; finally and fatefully he made his way back to Venice.

At every turn, Bruno sought out aristocratic and court circles with access to Renaissance princes, such as Henry III in France and Elizabeth I in England. His behaviour, as well as his writings, confirm Bruno as a utopian reformer who wanted to reinstitute the pagan wisdom of the ancient Egyptians, and to use this *prisca* as the foundation for a new religion of nature. He strove for a universal revival of learning led by princes rather than clerics, and for an end to the struggle between the forces of Reformation and Counter-Reformation. Bruno's willingness to seek secular patronage for his reforms presages the behaviour of various eighteenth-century radicals who latched on to one or another court circle generally in the Netherlands and sought there to win converts to their reforms.

Bruno's new religion of nature rested upon a pantheistic understanding of the universe. His infinite universe contained innumerable worlds, and its matter was eternally in motion. Bruno was the first philosopher to speculate seriously about the possibility of life on other planets, and he believed nature to be one vast continuum wherein all life is constantly created and transformed.

The mystical and magical aspects of Bruno's thought did not obscure his anti-Christian bias, nor did they undermine the coherency of his natural philosophy. Likewise his flirtation with court circles did not render mute his outspoken republicanism. He praised the Roman Republic not because it had been favoured by fortune but because its citizens had been truly virtuous (13, 40). In Bruno's thought we find the three themes that will be consistently presented in the writings of eighteenth-century radicals: pantheistic materialism, the search for a religion of nature, and republicanism.

In Bruno's *Spaccio della bestia trionfante* (Paris, but actually London, 1584), his best-known work during the eighteenth century, the pagan deities laugh and talk among themselves, debate about the merits of, and indulge in, sensual pleasure (although Bruno appears to be uneasy about female sensuality), and discuss with great concern the necessity for intervening in the human realm in order to reform it. Sophia 'vulgarly known as Minerva and Pallas' is enjoined by Jove to enforce civilised behaviour among mortals. Indeed, eighteenth-century reformers could not fail to identify with Bruno's exhortations:

> that the potent be sustained by the impotent, the weak be not oppressed by the stronger; that tyrants be deposed, just rulers and realms be constituted and strengthened, republics be favoured . . . that the poor be aided by the rich; that virtues and studies, useful and necessary to the commonwealth, be promoted, advanced, and maintained, and that those be exalted and remunerated who profited from them; and that the indolent, the avaricious, and the owners of property be scorned and held in contempt.(13, 144–5)

Among his contemporaries, Bruno made a few converts but it is doubtful that he established a sustained tradition of followers either before or after his death in 1600 at the hands of the Inquisition. Most of his Italian works had been published in England during his lifetime but they became quite rare until John Toland gathered them up and instigated their translation and circulation. That enterprise once again involved a court circle, this one centred in The Hague around Prince Eugène of Savoy, the great military leader of the Allied forces during the War of Spanish Succession (1701–13). Eugène's librarian collected just about every known work by Bruno, and indeed acquired Toland's own manuscript copy of Bruno's *Spaccio*. As we shall see in future chapters that early eighteenth-century revival of Bruno was part of a larger campaign, republican and freethinking in focus.

Throughout the seventeenth century, rumours circulated in Germany that Bruno had established a secret society of followers (12, 312–3). There seems at this stage in historical research, no substance to those rumours, but we must recognise that the dangerous and heretical doctrines that Bruno derived from the Hermetic tradition encouraged secrecy and caution. In the early 1600s, the publication of a variety of reformist manifestoes by a group calling themselves the Brethren of the Rosy Cross, or the Rosicrucians, echoed Bruno's ideals. They may also reflect the reformist programme of his contemporary, the Elizabethan mathematician and *magus*, John Dee.[6] Again, the Rosicrucian phenomenon of the seventeenth century, yet another example of revulsion against religious warfare, gave expression to the search for a universal religion, justified by a pantheistic philosophy of nature and both were tied to a utopian and reforming programme (14). By the early eighteenth century, the radical reformers, Toland and his friends, whom we can identify with the early years of European Freemasonry in The Hague, are the same circle wherein, predictably, Bruno's writings, in particular the *Spaccio*, were circulated.[7] Indeed, eighteenth-century Freemasonry was intended by some, although by no means the majority, of its participants to be an actual attempt to establish the natural religion sought and proclaimed, although never practised in a communal and ritualistic sense, by Bruno, Dee, and various Rosicrucian idealists.

It would be mistaken, however, to imagine that a continuous historical chain, yet to be discovered, exists between Bruno, through the seventeenth-century Rosicrucians, to the radicals of the early Enlightenment. Such an underground history would wrongly presume that secret societies were in fact established prior to Freemasonry and that they survived against all odds throughout the 1600s. Rather, there exists an intellectual tradition that bore fruit at various critical times in European history and, as we now know, made an essential contribution to the Enlightenment. That should be a sufficient tribute to its various adherents, and especially to Bruno. He was finally arrested in Venice in 1592, having been betrayed by his aristocratic employer who thought that he was withholding secret wisdom from him. Both the Venetian and Roman Inquisitions tried him on charges they had nurtured for many years. For eight years he languished in a Roman prison; in 1600 he was burned at the stake for heresy. In his final hours he refused to recant.

Controversy still rages about the precise role played by the new science and by magic in the thought of Giordano Bruno. He was among the very first philosophers to accept and champion Copernican heliocentricity. A similar controversy extends to Newton, whose profound interest in alchemy has raised the question of the indebtedness of his science to his knowledge and practice of the magical and Hermetic tradition.[8] Both disputes highlight the interrelationship between magic and science in the early modern period, yet neither concern us directly.

We have been looking at late Renaissance Hermeticism from the perspective of eighteenth-century radical reformers. They seized upon the naturalistic philosophers of the sixteenth-century because in their writings could be found an adulation of pagan, pre-Christian morality, and because in their vitalistic and magical philosophies could also be found, or so it was believed, a philosophy of nature compatible with materialism. Just as it is no longer possible to dismiss the magical philosophies of the late Renaissance as simply anti-scientific, so too the radicals of the Enlightenment, although hostile to the Christianised version of the mechanical philosophy that triumphed with Newton, were aggressively favourable towards science while at the same time searching for a natural philosophy that would release it from its Christian moorings. Late Renaissance naturalism, with its strongly animistic tendencies, when grafted on to a materialistic reading of the mechanical philosophy, provided the escape route that enabled the enlightened to keep the new science without its philosophical and religious foundations.

Bruno was not the only sixteenth-century source from which Enlightenment radicals drew. Aside from the Hermetic version of Renaissance naturalism one other classical tradition possessed strongly naturalistic tendencies. By relying upon the explanations for natural events given by Aristotle, especially as interpreted by the twelfth-century Arab philosopher, Averröes, it was possible to offer explanations of natural phenomena, of the workings of the universe, that seemed to reduce the providential God of orthodox Christianity into yet another natural phenomenon. That sort of Aristotelianism, coupled with a belief in magic and in the wisdom of the pagan philosophers, could put a philosopher of the late sixteenth century into extreme personal difficulties.

The Neapolitan philosopher, Lucilio Vanini, although a very different thinker from Bruno, met his same cruel fate. Temperamentally Vanini and Bruno were remarkably similar: assertive, combative, eager to make inroads into court circles yet in the end contemptuous of established authority. Vanini, like Bruno, travelled widely, to England and France most notably. In the writings of both men traces of magical belief recur. In his search for an understanding of nature, Vanini was drawn to astrology as well as to the writings of the ancient philosophers, particularly Lucretius and Empedocles. Both emphasised the material nature of the universe and sought in matter the principle of life or motion.

Vanini's pronouncements on the relationship between God and nature were at moments clearly pantheistic and of course heretical.

> Man should live according to natural law alone, because nature, which is God (because it is the principle of movement), has engraved this law in the heart of all men: as for all other laws, men should regard them as so many fictions and enticements, not invented by some malevolent genie . . . but by the princes for the education of their subjects, and by the priest with an eye to honours and riches.[9]

Statements such as these encouraged disaffection from established religious and political authority, at the same time implying that in nature men would find for themselves a personal morality.

The exact nature of Vanini's thought is to this day not fully understood, but his ability to make contradictory statements did not save his life. He too was burned at the stake in Toulouse in 1619. In the early eighteenth century his name was revived in clandestine materialistic literature, and also more openly in biographies and apologies emanating from Enlightenment radicals in the Netherlands. Vanini, along with Bruno, was transformed in the minds of eighteenth-century radicals into yet another pagan naturalist and pantheist, a martyr for the true wisdom of the ancients.

Although eighteenth-century radicals drew heavily from the Italian naturalists of the late sixteenth century, there were also other sources, closer to home, that were found to be compatible. By the early sixteenth century the paganising tendencies within Renaissance thought had spread to northern Europe, and had permeated aristocratic and court circles in France. Decades before Bruno and Vanini, French Protestant reformers like Calvin had spied these subversive influences among educated men and strongly condemned them.

One of Calvin's targets was the writer and poet, Bonaventure Des Périers (1500–44) who in 1537 published a curious and somewhat opaque work entitled *Cymbalum Mundi ou dialogues satyriques sur differens Sujets*. In 1711 one of Toland's friends in the Netherlands published an edition of the *Cymbalum* and in his preface Prosper Marchand made clear his admiration for the work and its author (see pp. 168–9).

To understand the significance that this book must have had for Marchand and his circle we must place it in the context of late Renaissance naturalism and the Calvinist response to it. Calvin attacked Des Périers and his philosophy as an impious atheism, and Des Périers was regarded by contemporary Calvinists as a Protestant who had once seen the light but had abandoned Protestantism for the philosophy of the pagans. The *Cymbalum* is a satire that was interpreted by its author's contemporaries as a thinly veiled assault on Protestantism, on Luther in particular, and also on Catholicism. Published only a year after the first edition of Calvin's *Institutes* (1536) and written by a man who had been involved in Reformation circles at the court of Margaret of Navarre (the sister of King Francis I), the *Cymbalum* established Des Périers as a notorious freethinker and atheist.[10]

In a tone of mockery and jest that resembles Rabelais, with whom the author was acquainted, Des Périers satirises human folly through the eyes of Mercury. He had taken a trip to earth where he observes the absurdities of the human condition, ranging from greed to the practice of alchemy. In the *Cymbalum* Minerva is the only pagan deity with any sense; she sends a message to the flamboyant Mercury telling him to chastise earthly poets for squabbling among themselves and to get down to the serious business of writing about love.

For the eighteenth-century French Protestant refugees who are the focus of this present study Des Périers appealed as an indigenous libertine, in touch with Renaissance paganism but also a proponent of a style of anti-establishment humour made famous by Rabelais. This style was also described by Calvin and others as 'Lucianique', that is in the manner of the ancient Roman, Lucian, who mocked all religions, including Christianity and its founder.[11] Indeed, Toland and his friends also admired Lucian, and it would easily be possible to devote a whole chapter, if not a book, to the classical origins of the Radical Enlightenment. Here it must suffice to recognise the important sixteenth-century antecedents, and to proceed from there to the Scientific Revolution of the seventeenth century. It was primarily in that natural philosophical revolution that eighteenth-century radicals found justification for their pantheistic materialism.

By the 1620s in England, France and the Netherlands that intellectual transformation was well underway, and its leading publicist was the English Lord Chancellor and loyal servant of James I, Francis Bacon. Bacon was inspired by the intellectual goals of the Hermetic tradition, its search for the secrets of nature, and its proclamation of a universal learning. Yet Bacon repudiated the *magus* as a cultural ideal and in its place proclaimed the cautious natural philosopher who experiences nature, collects its artifacts and cautiously attempts to formulate laws about its behaviour, all in the service of mankind.

In *The Advancement of Learning* (1605) Bacon called for a systematic and empirical examination of nature, and he argued for a new programme of learning specifically intended to improve the human condition. Although Descartes and a few other French thinkers knew and admired Bacon's programme, his writings about the social meaning of scientific inquiry made their greatest impact after his death; in the revolutionary context established by the English Civil Wars and the Puritan ascendancy. For that reason, our treatment of the Baconian contribution to the Scientific Revolution and to the Radical Enlightenment must await our discussion of the interaction of natural philosophy and the English Revolution in the next chapter.

During the first half of the seventeenth century, the natural philosopher who spoke most directly to his age and who offered an entire methodology and natural philosophy based upon mechanical principles was René Descartes. Just as the religious wars of the late sixteenth century had made urgent the utopian dreams of Bruno, they also led other thoughtful and disillusioned individuals, such as the French philosopher, Montaigne, to embrace scepticism as the only civilised and humanistic response to religious hatred and doctrinal warfare. If men cannot know ultimate truths then they will be less likely to burn one another and to create political discord in defence of religious convictions. For Montaigne scepticism enabled him to give allegiance to a tolerant prince, such as Henry IV (1596–1610) of France, who offered the possibility of stable government where religious interests would bow to monarchical interests.

While Descartes seems to have supported those political goals, he rebelled against this fashionable scepticism as an end in itself. Coming to maturity in the generation after Montaigne, Descartes sought a methodology that transcended doubt and made possible the discovery of a totally new science and natural philosophy based upon mechanical principles. Such a programme of learning, he believed, would not only rout the sceptics it would also lay a new foundation for Christian orthodoxy – one to which even the French Protestant minority as well as the sceptics and libertines would give their assent. The latter group appeared ever more visible during Descartes's lifetime. By the mid-seventeenth century Paris sported even more aggressive coteries of libertines, among them Cyrano de Bergerac, who spoke, and cautiously wrote, against Christian orthodoxy. From the point of view of the increasingly ambitious French monarchy and its architects, Richelieu and Mazarin, the libertines constituted a dangerous and subversive subculture to be watched carefully and, if need be, prosecuted.

By contrast, Descartes's intentions were decidedly orthodox. Yet his philosophy, as we shall see, was capable of being used by eighteenth-century materialists, however far their motives may have been from his original intentions. This most influential thinker had been educated at one of the finest schools of the Counter-Reformation, the Jesuit school at La Flèche. Yet as a young man Descartes realised that even the accumulated wisdom of the Jesuits could not insure against scepticism. He came to doubt all that he had learned, with the important exception of mathematics. And in that science he believed he could find the rudiments of a methodology that would yield certain knowledge and thereby defeat the sceptics and freethinkers.

To search audaciously for a universal science based upon a new methodology requires a unique psychology. Descartes believed himself to be the prophet of the new science, and his mission came to him in a dream he experienced during the night of 10 November 1619. Some years later in the *Discours de la méthode* (1637) Descartes describes his dream and proclaims a new methodology, derived from mathematics, through which men may arrive at the first principles of a universal science. Predictably from what we know about Descartes's sense of personal mission, that search begins with the self. Having rejected all previous knowledge as either untrue or uncertain Descartes asserts that knowledge of the existence of his own mind, and therefore of himself, is the only certain knowledge – 'I think therefore I am.' He has fundamentally disassociated his mind from the material world around him, and indeed from his own body. Using the instrument of his intellect, 'the natural light of reason', Descartes refuses to accept any statement or observation as true unless it is presented to his mind as 'clear and distinct' – as clear and distinct as would be any mathematical theorem. Out of this solipsistic position Descartes must find an exit, and he does so through his clear and distinct idea of God. Because he possesses such an idea, which he reasons could only have been implanted by an infinite and perfect being (nothing in human experience yielding such an idea), Descartes asserts God's existence. Such a being to be God could not create an elaborate hoax; the world outside of our mind must exist, because God created it, and it is knowable. Note that Descartes establishes God's existence solely because the idea of God lives in his mind.

The application of Descartes's methodology to the investigation of reality depends, of course, upon an act of will. He (and by implication anyone who would follow his method) must constantly exercise control over his thoughts, rejecting the unclear, the imprecise, while at the same time keeping his mind attentive. This methodology enabled Descartes to make enormous strides in the development of co-ordinate geometry and that success, in turn, assisted in the widespread acceptance of his philosophy. In the Cartesian system the willed imposition of order upon reality depends upon the individual's power to control his thoughts. In so doing he is imposing an order and logic where there may not be one; he is in effect controlling nature. A. J. Krailsheimer puts it succinctly: Descartes 'is making a claim for human self sufficiency of the most radical kind' (15, 35).

Descartes's philosophy rested upon two assumptions of immense consequence for the development of Enlightenment thought. First, individuals can achieve complete mastery over their own intellectual processes and, of course, by implication over the world around them. Cartesianism asserted the right of thinking men in possession of clear and distinct ideas to impose their will, to order and control society as well as nature. Secondly and in consequence, Cartesianism encouraged the aggressive assertion of the self, whether in intellectual matters, in the running of government or the ordering of society, or even in the pursuit of material interests. Of course, reason must guide these masterful intellects as they seek to impose order on the world around them.

In the first instance Descartes's philosophy was used, as he intended it, to support the authority of the church (even though some churchmen entertained grave suspicions about its orthodoxy), and it also served to justify the growth of absolutist and mercantilist forms of government. By and large, Cartesianism proved compatible with the interests of Christian princes and churches, although in the universities of Europe both Catholic and Protestant theologians occasionally opposed it. Their commitment to scholasticism often prompted that opposition, although by the 1660s in England Protestant theologians sympathetic to the mechanical philosophy were uneasy with the Cartesian approach. As we shall see their fears were well founded.

Cartesian individualism was capable of receiving an interpretation at variance with the needs of established authority, and one with direct bearing on the history of the Radical Enlightenment. Descartes proclaimed men to be the masters and possessors of nature and this call to freedom also inspired the critics of established authority. Two generations after Descartes's death a young French artist, Bernard Picart, who will figure in subsequent chapters, saw him as a symbol of intellectual freedom in the face of religious persecution. Faced with the prospect of conversion to Catholicism or flight, the young and promising Picart, whose father was a talented and successful Parisian artist and engraver, drew inspiration from both Descartes's philosophy and his life. In the early eighteenth century Picart actually contemplated a migration for religious freedom to Sweden because his hero, Descartes, had spent time there, been graciously received by Queen Christina whom he counselled, and had died there. In the end Picart went to the Netherlands, as had the young Descartes. He had feared that the silence imposed upon Galileo in Italy by the church (1633), might also be brought to bear against him.

Descartes was more than a symbolic hero for the Radical Enlightenment; his philosophy possessed distinctly materialistic implications. He had argued that the world around us – physical but by implication human and social as well – is composed of matter in motion, the universe is filled with atoms whirling in space governed by mechanical laws. Although Descartes asserts that those laws possess a real existence separate from their discoverer, they can also be understood as the construction of the human mind as it imposes order and logic on the world around. In anchoring his methodology solely on the willed operation of the human mind, in effect Descartes drastically separated mind from matter. This separation was so complete that in trying to explain the human body's connection to the mind Descartes was left asserting that mind only physically joins body in a concrete way at the pineal gland, a small gland at the back of the neck which we now know to be a vestigial eye that serves no useful purpose.

Cartesian dualism left open the possibility, eagerly exploited by those searching for new and unchristian explanations of nature, that all reality, including humanity and human thought, could be explained through a purely materialistic philosophy. If all external reality can be understood in terms of matter in motion, and since thought and will appear as forms of motion or change, why cannot the processes of the mind be explained in terms of the mechanical laws of motion? Instead of searching for an escape route from Cartesian dualism through the rather weak assertion of a conjunction in the pineal gland, eighteenth-century materialists such as La Mettrie (1709–51) and d'Holbach (1723–89) asserted that the mind perceives mechanical laws precisely because it participates in, rather than simply comments upon, the physical processes of the material order (see pp. 262–3).

One of the Descartes's earliest followers, Henri Le Roy (1598–1679), sometimes known as Regius, a professor at the University of Utrecht, did in fact assert that thinking might be a property or mode of matter. Descartes firmly attacked that interpretation and he himself contrived throughout his life to assert the primacy and independence of the mind. His Christian followers also adhered to this position and indeed the roots of an immaterialist or idealist philosophy such as we find in the writings of the early eighteenth-century English philosopher and Anglican bishop, George Berkeley, a great opponent of the radical materialists, can be found in Cartesianism. Yet by separating matter from spirit so drastically, Descartes unintentionally opened the door to a mechanistic materialism. Indeed, his own mechanistic analysis of the nervous system of animals, whom he regarded as soulless, possessed dangerous implications for human beings. If animation can be explained solely as the operation of corpuscular matter according to mechanical laws, then what role, if any, does spirit or soul play in the operation of human nature?

But that question was elicited over time, and largely by freethinking coteries intent upon looking at traditional philosophical problems in unorthodox ways. Within governmental and clerical circles during the seventeenth century in France, Cartesian explanations were enlisted to justify and explain the social and political order best suited to the interests of absolute monarchy. The idea of reason, with Descartes as its primary exponent, became by Richelieu's time 'a source or sanction for power, both political and philosophical'.[12] The imposition of reason entailed, as we have seen, an act of will initiated by the self-controlled thinker – by the self-interested man dedicated to the imposition of order and control.

Certain seventeenth-century French Cartesians, such as Jean Silhon, a close admirer of Richelieu and friend of Descartes, became a supporter of absolutism, arguing that reason was intended to promote the power of the state and not to criticise it.[13] Just as mind imposes order on to physical reality so too the state, embodied in the will of the prince, endeavours to impose reason and order over its unruly subjects. Late in the seventeenth century the Cartesian and Jansenist, Pierre Nicole, believed that a state organised according to Cartesian principles would truly give glory to God and possibly even exercise justice and charity in a society made essentially corrupt by human sinfulness.

In Descartes's philosophy, the mechanical interpretation of nature provided a model for the organisation and power of the early modern state. This statement will hold true for Newtonianism as stated by Newton's personal followers, as well as for the philosophy of Leibniz. Although their version of the mechanical philosophy differed in profound and important ways, yet the basic assumptions, first articulated by Descartes, will remain constant. All saw matter as separate from spirit, or soul, and governed by mechanical laws of motion capable of mathematical expression. Matter, or physical nature, could be explained by the human intellect, by the light of reason imposed by self-willed individuals. Despite the alternative uses to 'which their philosophies were put, the major seventeenth-century proponents of the mechanical world picture were quite willing to see their scientific principles and methodological insights enlisted in the ideological service of strong and authoritarian forms of government and in support of Christian orthodoxy. Descartes's ethical prescriptions called for conformity to all existing laws and institutions, for constancy in the pursuit of one's goals and for self-control over the passions.

But philosophers, like lesser mortals, do not always see obtained that which they advocate. During the early eighteenth century, Cartesianism was also enlisted in a modified form by the critics of established authority. Indeed, recent historians have emphasised the Cartesian origins of eighteenth-century materialism and scientific naturalism. They have stressed the ideological role of Descartes's insistence, revealed most forcefully in his *Recherche de la vérité par la lumière naturelle* (published posthumously in 1701) that his methodology, and hence his universal science, were available to the average mind provided it could grasp his technique of right reasoning (16, 29–30). These universalist claims closely conform to the goals of the Enlightenment, especially as they were articulated by the materialists. They envisioned nature as all-embracing, the single organising principle of life which when recognised by reasoning people, obviated the necessity for organised Christian worship and for the authority of the clergy. Guided by the Cartesian method of reasoning, anyone could arrive at knowledge about nature and society and deduce the simple, basic laws at work in the universe. Throughout the eighteenth century, Cartesian deductive reasoning remained a goal, even among materialist philosophers who accepted Newtonian physics and experimentalism (16, 159–60). That apparent dichotomy will make greater sense once we discuss the ideological and political affiliations of the Newtonian vision.

It is sufficient to recognise that one legacy of Cartesian dualism was that it enabled eighteenth-century radicals to retain Descartes's mechanical understanding of nature without recourse to his God. But the sources of radical materialism were never simply or perhaps even predominantly Cartesian. One of the earliest works to draw out the materialistic implications of Descartes's philosophy, Montfaucon de Villars's *La Suite du Comte de Gabalis* (written much earlier than its date of publication, 1708) noted the similarity between Cartesianism and the pantheistic speculations of Giordano Bruno (16, 53). The ground had been prepared for the materialist reading of Descartes by the late sixteenth-century naturalists, and in the course of the eighteenth century the indebtedness of radical thinkers to both traditions will sometimes render them almost indistinguishable.

There were other, less technically philosophical, roots for eighteenth-century radicalism. Pantheistic beliefs that saw humans as a part of nature also lived on within popular culture and had found expression among extreme Reformation sects that sprang up in Europe as early as the 1530s.[14] Some of these sects such as the Anabaptists and later the Mennonites, who were to befriend the young Spinoza, survived in northern Europe well into the eighteenth century and beyond. In England, the religious radicals of the seventeenth century, such as the Levellers and Diggers, likewise espoused pantheistic and materialist visions of humanity nature and society. During the English Revolution of the 1640s, long before Enlightenment radicals drew forth the materialistic implications of Cartesianism and introduced yet another dangerous implication of the mechanical philosophy, the materialistic arguments of these sects burst upon the political scene and in the context of revolution and social dislocation graphically revealed the implications of materialism when articulated by angry men in possession of a social and religious programme.

Although many of these mid-century revolutionaries journeyed to the Continent, in particular to the Netherlands, the radical sectaries of the English Revolution appear to have had no direct influence on the thought of French-speaking radicals of the early eighteenth century. Rather at its very beginning the Radical Enlightenment was comprised of a coalition of English republicans, far more moderate than their Leveller predecessors, but nevertheless aware of the philosophical and political radicalism of the English Revolution, and of a coterie of French Protestants exiled in the Netherlands and intimately acquainted with the writings of Descartes. In their collaboration, philosophical radicalism of popular and revolutionary origin merged with the new science of high culture to produce a unique and compelling attempt to subvert the established order.

Precisely because of the revolutionary implications of materialism made explicit during the English Revolution, the implications of Descartes's thought became a vexing question for late-seventeenth-century Christian philosophers and *virtuosi* intent upon integrating the new science with establishment Christianity. Among mid-century English natural philosophers and scientists who experienced the disorder unleashed by the radical sectaries and by political reformers with strongly materialist tendencies, the basic mechanical principles of Descartes's philosophy were repudiated and new mechanical principles put in their place.[15] That philosophical revolt, initiated by the so-called Cambridge Platonists and by various Christian *virtuosi*, was immensely important in creating the intellectual context for Newton's scientific and natural philosophical achievements and as such will concern us in Chapter 3.

The Radical Enlightenment certainly had important roots in the English Revolution, but it also had equally vital links with Continental versions of the new scientific methodology and its various philosophies of nature. Before turning, therefore, to the relationship between Newtonianism and the origins of the Radical Enlightenment, two major interpreters of the mechanical philosophy first articulated by Descartes require our attention. Both Benedict de Spinoza (1632–77) and Gottfried W. von Leibniz (1646–1716) grappled with the implications of Cartesianism, and each produced philosophies so profoundly at variance with it as to be openly antagonistic. Towards the end of his life Leibniz waged open war with the young, first generation of the Radical Enlightenment, while it, in turn, adopted Spinoza as one of its heroes. Leibniz's almost desperate attempt to avoid the materialistic implications of Cartesianism and at the same time to reconstruct the intellectual and political foundations of orthodox Christianity brought him into confrontation not only with the radicals but also with the first generation of Newtonians. His reactions to both groups will serve to focus our discussion of the early decades of the eighteenth century.

In contrast, Spinoza's critique of the Cartesian philosophy became one major source for the Radical Enlightenment. By the early eighteenth century 'spinozism' denoted a multitude of intellectual heresies, yet all possessed a common thread. Spinozism brought together all philosophy, ancient and modern, that possessed a tendency to unify, divinise or animate the universe, also more generally, that offered a deterministic philosophy of man and nature (17, II, 334–5). While the major scientists of the seventeenth century had emphasised the freedom of the human will to search for power and control over nature, the radicals of the eighteenth century often embraced determinism. They saw humans as a part of nature, as participants in a larger scheme wherein, of necessity, they always choose to do good, once 'the good' is clearly perceived. The religious and political conclusions of both positions were widely divergent: free will justifies obedience to established authority and the existence of eternal damnation, determinism sanctions a constant tendency to seek improvement and reform while rendering the notion of damnation for one's sins into an absurdity. In the thought of Spinoza, radicals found a major philosophical source in support of both materialism and determinism (19, ch. 7).

In 1709 the English radical, John Toland, equated spinozism with pantheism, the term he had in fact invented.[16] This pantheistic materialism in turn found expression during the early Enlightenment in a multitude of published treatises and clandestine manuscripts, many written or circulated by the radicals, and it became the intellectual centrepiece of their programme. It is the philosophical link that runs through European radicalism from the English Revolution to the French Revolution. Of course, it predates Spinoza, but in the eighteenth century contemporary opponents of this materialism likened it to his thought and indeed condemned him as its source. Predictably the radicals knew Spinoza's writings, in particular the *Tractatus Theologico-Politicus* (1670), and drew ideas from it where it suited their purpose. Of all the major seventeenth-century philosophers Spinoza was the least involved in wordly affairs, yet ironically his name, as well as his philosophy, became the most embattled.

Spinoza was born in Amsterdam in a family of recently immigrated Portuguese Jews. His father was a merchant, and like other well-to-do merchants of his time, sent his son to be educated by the philosophically learned physician, Francis Van den Ende. That fact alone attests to the remarkable degree of assimilation possible for the Jewish community in seventeenth-century Amsterdam.

Very little is known about the young Spinoza before 1661, the date of his first extant letter. According to an early and unsympathetic biographer, John Colerus, a minister in the Lutheran Church at The Hague, Spinoza's teacher, Van den Ende 'sowed the first seeds of atheism in the minds of those young boys'. Whatever else Van den Ende may have taught, he gave Spinoza a firm foundation in Latin, and that coupled with Hebrew, opened the young Spinoza to the world of classical and mediaeval philosophy, pagan, Christian and Hebraic. Yet it was a far more contemporary philosopher, Descartes, who opened Spinoza's mind to its intellectual power, 'at last, having light upon the works of Descartes, he read them greedily; and afterwards he often declared that he had all his philosophical knowledge from him. Spinoza was charmed with that maxim of Descartes, which says, that nothing ought to be admitted as true, but what has been proved by good and solid reasons.'[17]

Spinoza never took 'all his philosophical knowledge' from Descartes, but he was captivated by Descartes's insistence that only the individual mind with the natural light of its own reason can arrive at truth, and that truth should be expressed by logical maxims in imitation of geometrical propositions. Spinoza's first published work, *Principia Philosophiae Cartesianae* (1663), a summary of Descartes's *Principia Philosophiae* (1644), was one of the few works Spinoza ever published in his own name. His reading in ancient and modern philosophers inspired him with 'one purpose – to bring to its logical conclusion the reasoning of philosophers throughout history in their effort to reduce the universe to a unified and uniform whole governed by universal and unchangeable laws' (20, I, 33). Just as did Descartes, Spinoza searched for a universal science but he embarked on his journey with one daring assumption out of which his philosophy evolved.

Spinoza believed that there is no such thing as a finite substance. All philosophy begins with a definition of being or substance, and traditional Christian philosophy distinguished two types of substance, that of God who is perfect, infinite, immaterial and eternal and that of his creation, of finite beings, material, transient, dependent. Without this dualism Western philosophy, as adopted by the mediaeval scholastics, could not explain the existence of an immaterial God, separate from creation, who in turn created, by an act of will, a hierarchy of beings. Human beings occupy a unique place in creation, traditionally conceived. They possess free will and can aspire to eternity with God or they can violate his laws as explicated by the church and condemn themselves to an eternity of misery in hell. Human volition imitates divine, yet each is an attribute of separate substances that are real but distinct.

Spinoza abolished the dualism between God and the world, between the immaterial and the material, between matter and spirit. There is only substance for Spinoza; it is illogical, and contradictory, he asserts, to posit two kinds of substance. Spinoza identifies God with the wholeness of nature, and in abolishing the dualism of traditional Christian thought his purpose was not 'to abolish the materiality of the world, but rather to abolish the immateriality of God' (20, I, 80). Spinoza took Descartes's methodology and with it abolished the extreme duality Descartes had posited between matter and mind or spirit. Spinoza provided the metaphysical foundations for rendering nature into the totality of existence; matter in effect becomes spirit and out of that paradox it is possible to postulate a new religious vision where nature is not simply animated, it is, in effect, sacred. The intellectual odyssey that began in the seventeenth century with Cartesianism could lead to an entirely new foundation for Western religion.

The social and political implications of Spinoza's philosophy derive from his conviction that human kind is part of nature, not simply, as in traditional Christianity, that it occupies a unique place in nature. In contradiction to the self-interested man of Descartes, or of the English political philosopher, Hobbes, who is 'of a purely egotistic nature' and whose self-preservation could exclude the well-being of others, the self-interested man of Spinoza's vision 'is an expanded self of which the need of the society of others is a constituent part' (20, II, 247). It follows logically from Spinoza's assertion that nature or substance is the totality of all things, that in society reason and not authority *per se* should guide human action, and that social equality represents the expression of a metaphysical reality. Toleration and concrete freedom of speech are essential for the development of human thought, for our struggle to understand our role in nature requires that we communicate our ideas to other people. Finally, freedom of will is an illusion; as a part of nature man, like God, participates in a determined cosmos, 'the future is implicit in the present'.[18] Rulers who imagine that they impose their will and shape the future live in delusion. Spinoza's philosophy inevitably humbles the great.

Partly as a result of his lived experience in the Netherlands and partly by the logic of his metaphysics Spinoza gave his support to the republican form of government, and indeed he favoured a democratic rather than the prevailing oligarchical system for the Dutch Republic. Yet he may have supported the oligarchic anti-Orange republicans, the followers of John De Witt (d. 1672) who in Spinoza's time opposed the claim of the House of Orange to make Prince William III of Orange (later to become William III of England) the elected stadholder of most provinces of the Dutch Republic.

William's support, like that of his Orange successors in the eighteenth century, came from widely disparate elements within the republic. Some old aristocratic families, the Calvinist clergy, the rural gentry, and probably the great mass of the population, who saw William as a symbol of unity and strength against foreign aggression and against the self-interested rule of the commercial oligarchy, all gave their support to the Orange cause. Throughout Dutch history, Orangism could rally the old rural aristocracy but it also possessed a strongly populist and volatile base.

The backers of De Witt, on the other hand, controlled the province of Holland, the commercial and financial heart of the republic, and drew support from some quarters in the Dutch navy, from religious dissenters and intellectuals and from an alliance with France. To his loyal supporters, De Witt, one of the finest political leaders of his age, represented the cause of religious toleration, support for the new science, and the government of secular-minded laymen in opposition to a theocratic clergy.

Spinoza was 'no mere ideologist' of this oligarchic cause.[19] His political ideas display strongly democratic tendencies and his vision of a republic transcended time and place. That vision would inspire his eighteenth-century followers and admirers, although their political allegiances would be Orangist and to that extent different from those legend claims Spinoza to have given to De Witt and therefore, by implication, to the ruling Dutch oligarchy. The European wars of the early eighteenth century forced some radicals and Spinozists to re-assess their relationship to the House of Orange and out of that experience emerged a tenuous coalition. Yet eighteenth-century republicans and pantheists, active in the Dutch Revolution of 1747, saw themselves, quite rightly, as loyal to the maxims of Spinoza. In the *Tractatus Theologico-Politicus*, a much more widely read work than the dense and geometrically precise *Ethics* (1677), Spinoza proclaimed an ideal that would inspire European radicals throughout the eighteenth century:

> Seeing that we have the rare happiness of living in a republic, where everyone's judgement is free and unshackled, and where each may worship God as his conscience dictates, and where freedom is esteemed before all things dear and precious, I have believed that I should be undertaking no ungrateful or unprofitable task, in demonstrating that not only can such freedom be granted without prejudice to the public peace, but also, that without such freedom, piety cannot flourish, nor the public peace be secure.[20]

Throughout the eighteenth century, clandestine manuscripts, often published and disseminated by the freethinking circles that comprise the main subject of this book, alluded to Spinoza or claimed to repre-sent 'L'Esprit de Spinoza'. Many of these tracts and their originators avowed a pantheistic view of nature only distantly related to the philosophical rigour and metaphysical subtlety of Spinoza. At moments there is more mysticism than logic in some of these tracts; yet the simplicity of their language reveals that they were intended for a mass but literate audience. Eighteenth-century pantheistic material-ism, in its vulgarised form, can sometimes sound like what a university student once called 'the toad stools turning into grand pianos' philoso-phy of nature. Yet it would be a futile task to argue that the pantheism and republicanism of the Radical Enlightenment bears no significant relation to the spirit of Spinoza. Of all the major seventeenth-century natural philosophers whose vision of scientific knowledge was entwined with the political realities of that age, reforming radicals of the Enlightenment saw only Spinoza, however they 'misunderstood' him, as one of their own.

The first orthodox assaults against Spinoza and his heretical philosophy came from two disparate, yet as we shall see, not unrelated quarters. The earliest printed attack took the form of a piece of French political propaganda. When Louis XIV's armies invaded the Netherlands in 1672 (an act which led to the murder, by a bitter and enraged and pro-Orange crowd, of the former Grand Pensionary, De Witt), the French tried to weaken Dutch resistance and to arouse the ire of international Protestantism against them, by arguing that the Dutch were not truly Protestant, but heretics. *La Religion des Hollandais* (Paris, 1673), claimed that Spinoza's philosophy had made deep inroads in the Netherlands, and by implication that the absolutist monarchy of Louis XIV should be seen as the European-wide saviour of Christian orthodoxy (17, I, 19). The second attack was contained in a Dutch pamphlet that accused De Witt of heresy by claiming that he owned a copy of Spinoza's *Tractatus Theologico-Politicus*.

In both cases, one pro-French and the other pro-Orange, the political propagandists were attempting to discredit their opponents by tarring them with the brush of spinozism. Throughout the eighteenth century that accusation was to remain a dangerously potent one, and the fear of its being made goes a long way to explaining the extreme secrecy adopted by European pantheists. In the 1670s neither of those tracts appear to have had a measurable impact on the course of events, but from that time onwards Christian thinkers all over Europe were seriously alarmed by what they knew, or thought they knew, about Spinoza's heretical philosophy.

Within European academic circles, the first attack against Spinoza came from Leipzig, from the university scholar and teacher of Leibniz, the Aristotelian, Jakob Thomasius (17, I, 38). Both master and pupil were deeply interested in the philosophy of Descartes and spied in Spinoza a dangerous and wayward follower. Throughout his life Leibniz would remain deeply engaged with, and grow increasingly antagonistic to the letter as well as the spirit of Spinoza's teachings (21, 134–51, 214).

In the late decades of his politically active life, when Leibniz was an adviser and historian to the Hanoverian dynasty, he knew of, and actually conversed with, leading radicals of the early Enlightenment, in particular with the extreme Whig, John Toland. Toland and his friends merely confirmed what Leibniz had known for many years, that Christian piety was under assault from intellectual as well as political quarters.

The central motivation for Leibniz's diverse political, philosophical and scientific activities had been his desire to place Christian theology on a new and invincible foundation (22, 15–16, 144). Two intimately related principles guided Leibniz's extraordinary energies. He sought to expound a version of the new mechanical philosophy that would assert the essential unity of the physical and spiritual universe, and secondly, in the political sphere, he sought to re-establish the unity of Christendom through an ecumenical revival of ecclesiastical hegemony and the mediaeval concept of a Christian empire. He corresponded for many years with the French theologian and adviser to Louis XIV, Bossuet, among others, in an attempt, as the first step in this revival, to unite his own Lutheran Church with the still dominant Catholic Church. Leibniz's dreams for a unified Christendom extended to support for missionary efforts in China and North America and even to plans for a campaign against 'our archenemy in the East', the Turks.[21]

Leibniz's philosophical beliefs were likewise tied to his political and ecclesiastical goals. A mechanical view of nature that would find support from all Christians would provide an agreeable solution to the divisive theological issues, such as transubstantiation, that separated Catholics from Protestants. In many ways Leibniz's own version of Christianity was remarkably Catholic; yet he resisted conversion to Rome for reasons that were both political and intellectual.[22]

As a member of the disunified German empire, and more particularly as an adviser to the Hanoverian dynasty, Leibniz knew all too well the dangers posed by French absolutism. In 1672 when a French invasion, possibly of the empire, seemed imminent Leibniz hurried to Paris to try to persuade Louis XIV's advisers to embark upon an alternative invasion in the East for the purpose of capturing Egypt. This plan would crush the threat from the Turks, divert French designs on the Netherlands and in northern Europe in general, and allow for the possible conversion of the infidel. Little attention was paid to his scheme and instead France invaded the Netherlands as planned.

Throughout his life Leibniz's plans were seldom taken seriously by any political authority. Yet his political concerns, as well as his intellectual ones, were central to his age and coincided, almost precisely, with those of the radicals. Both feared French absolutism and both sought, in the basis of many different ideologies, to build a northern European alliance against it. Both Leibniz and the freethinkers of the early Enlightenment believed passionately in the republic of letters, in an international community dedicated to the search for truth in accord with commonly agreed-upon scientific and philosophical principles. That the methodology of the new science bore application to the improvement of the human condition was a belief shared equally by radicals and Christian philosophers alike. Scientific knowledge, they believed, would engender a generation of reasonable men who would repudiate the search for absolute power and by their actions imitate the harmony of the universe.

Leibniz laboured for many years to persuade one or another European prince to support his plan to establish a universal scientific academy, which might be secret in its early years, but which would seek to establish a universal science based upon the new mechanical philosophy and upon the study of *theologia mystica*. Leibniz's unfulfilled plan undoubtedly had much in common with earlier Rosicrucian schemes, common in central Europe. They called for the establishment of (and even claimed in some cases to have established) a fraternity, international in scope, which would search for a universal wisdom, co-ordinate a revival of the arts and sciences, and seek to institute concrete educational reforms. The Moravian educational reformer, Jan Comenius (1592–1671), had brought such a scheme to England in the 1640s and that ideal had fired the imagination of a coterie of young reformers and philosophers, not the least of them being Robert Boyle.[23] Leibniz's academy, possibly inspired by those earlier efforts, was intended to have official backing, preferably from within the Holy Roman Empire.

Through this academic institution Leibniz hoped to harness his intellectual energies and political expertise into the service of a revived Holy Roman Empire, centred in Vienna. In this spirit, Leibniz wrote his important *Monadology* (1714) at the request of Eugène of Savoy,[24] whose service to the empire led him to Vienna where his court became a centre for reformers and visionaries, just as it had been only a few years earlier in The Hague.

The strangely charismatic Eugène attracted a variety of visionaries from Leibniz to radicals in the Netherlands, in particular the circle of Toland and his friends. Late in his life Leibniz journeyed to Vienna in an effort to win Eugène's support for his reforms, and possibly to secure a place for himself at court. Other concerns may also have motivated that visit. Leibniz knew perfectly well that Eugène's circle at The Hague had been a centre for libertines, freethinkers and radicals who saw in him their hope to defeat militarily the French search for European hegemony. Some of them may even have believed Eugène to be a friend to republicanism (2, 60–5). In turn Leibniz may have been seeking to dissuade Eugène from embracing, or simply from encouraging, their heretical and subversive schemes.

One of the important treatises that expresses the spinozism and republicanism of Eugène's admirers in The Hague was circulated during the eighteenth century as the earlier mentioned clandestine manuscript, 'L'Espirit de Spinoza', more commonly known as the *Traité des trois imposteurs*. As a guide to the beliefs of the Radical Enlightenment the tract is unsurpassed and as such it will merit analysis in a subsequent chapter. From the moment its existence became public knowledge, Leibniz was concerned about its influence. Almost as if he knew or suspected that it came from the very circle associated with Eugène's entourage in The Hague, Leibniz wrote to Vienna to express his concern. He even enclosed a copy of a blatantly atheistical Latin treatise that also had the phrase 'religious imposters' in its title. Contemporaries, even the astute Leibniz, often confused the *Traité* with that other Latin work which may have been by Vanini's early eighteenth-century admirer, Arpe. That Leibniz should have been so concerned about this work, and that he should have connected it with Eugène's court, alerts us to the fear aroused by the political allegiances of the radicals. Little did Leibniz know that Eugène already possessed in his library an exact copy of the real *Traité* which undoubtedly came into his hands through the Marchand–Toland circle, possibly from its originator, Jean Rousset de Missy.[25]

Leibniz's life-long obsession with spinozism may have stemmed in part from his recognition of the curious similarity between his own political goals and the ideals of the radicals. Just as did Leibniz, various European radicals throughout the eighteenth century would attempt to ingratiate themselves with the imperial court in Vienna. The pattern that began with Eugène in The Hague continued well into the reign of Maria Theresa (see pp. 202–5). The fear of French absolutism and support for its antidote, the alliance of England, the Netherlands and Austria, inspired a variety of reformers, from Leibniz through two generations of radical republicans. Yet the similarity of their ideas did not prevent them from formulating widely disparate solutions. Leibniz's plan for an international academy dedicated to *philosophia nova* and *theologia mystica* was one such solution and it foreshadows by a few decades the establishment of Freemasonry in England and on the Continent. As we shall see, the very radicals who gathered around Eugène's court at The Hague played a vital role in the spread of that institution throughout northern Europe and also quite possibly to Vienna. But in the hands of radical reformers, Freemasonry offered a 'new philosophy' and a 'mystical theology' intended to displace the Christianity of Leibniz and to abolish traditional monarchy, however 'reformed' by Leibnizean principles.

Leibniz has been so often seen simply as one of the supreme 'rationalists' in an age of reason. That he should have entertained fantasies about the establishment of a secret academy dedicated to a universal wisdom, the *theologia mystica* as he called it, provides yet another example of the close intertwining of magic and science, even as late as the early decades of the eighteenth century. The mysticism of radical pantheism loses its novelty when we realise that there were strongly mystical elements in the thought of such a major exponent of the mechanical philosophy. These beliefs, including Leibniz's private dedication to astrology, have often been ignored because of their apparent incompatibility with the mechanical philosophy (21,

156–65). But Leibniz's version of the new science sought to define matter primarily in terms not of extension but of force and movement, and to locate the origin of force in a vast spiritual universe, and ultimately therefore in God. This spiritualised version of the mechanical philosophy could easily include an apparently mystical vision. Just as we have ignored Newton's alchemy, which also complimented his belief in spiritual, immaterial forces at work in the universe, so too we have rendered Leibniz's almost utopian search for theodicy into an excessively rationalist mode of thought.

But to ignore these mystical tendencies within the new science is to miss the central dilemma posed by Cartesianism and by the radical materialism and pantheism so easily derived from it or made to be compatible with it. By the second half of the seventeenth century, the implications of this Cartesian rationalism, its proclamation of the self as the sole determinant of truth, and its materialism, were painfully obvious to Christian philosophers on both sides of the Channel. Just as did the materialists, Leibniz and his followers resolutely adhered to a mechanical interpretation of nature, with one crucial difference. They located the origins of force outside of matter, in spiritual energy that derives ultimately from God. In Leibniz's words: 'I hold that even if individual effects in nature can be explained mechanically, nevertheless even mechanical principles and their effects, all order and all physical rules in general, arise not from purely material determinations but from the consideration of indivisible substances and especially of God . . .' (22, 145). The escape route from materialism had magical implications, just as the pantheism of the radicals had magical origins and mystical overtones. Whether acknowledging God or nature as the source of life and motion, by the late seventeenth century both Christian mechanists and pantheists embraced an understanding of the universe deeply indebted to the new science.

By the 1670s, the threat posed to Christian theology by the materialistic implications of the mechanical philosophy coincided with an equally dangerous political crisis. Leibniz and various English philosophers, along with Continental freethinkers and English republicans, perceived the danger posed to Protestantism and the maintenance of a balance of power in Europe as coming from the excesses of absolute monarchy, in either its Bourbon, or, from the English perspective, its Stuart variety. Each group proposed widely divergent solutions to meet an international crisis that threatened to plunge Europe back into an era of religious, political and civil wars.

Yet despite the severity of the situation, Christian philosophers could not agree upon any formula that would achieve Christian unity. While it might have been expected that Leibniz, the great spokesman for European Protestant unity, could have made common cause with liberal Anglicans in England, by the early eighteenth century a serious rift had developed between him and the followers of Isaac Newton, and they had become the intellectual leaders of the English church. As we shall see, this internecine warfare only served to encourage the radicals whose emergence as an international presence had contributed to the quarrel in the first place.

The differences between Leibniz and the Newtonians often sprang from simple national rivalries between England and Hanover (not to mention personal jealousy between these two great thinkers). Leibniz was one of the chief advisers to the Elector of Hanover, George, the future king of England as provided by the Act of Protestant Succession (1701). English ministers and churchmen feared the eventual institution of a Hanoverian clique at court that would direct English policy in favour of its own international interests. But the distrust for Leibniz was not only political, it was also philosophical.

While occasionally praising the virtues of a republic, Leibniz subscribed to the ideal of an absolute monarchy guided by reason and not by the dictates of greed and power. He eschewed the varieties of contract theory that had been developed by English political theorists in response to their revolution. Indeed, Leibniz detested those theories in large measure because Hobbes, whose version of the mechanical philosophy was decidedly materialist, had made so much of the notion of the contract between king and subject (23, 23). After 1689 the freethinkers and materialists were to enlist Hobbes in their struggle against the form of constitutional monarchy established by the Revolution Settlement. Their use of Hobbes's ideas, although in contradiction to his intentions, further convinced Leibniz that the English mechanical philosophers either directly or indirectly had encouraged the growth of materialism and irreligion. Despite the fact that the Newtonians bitterly attacked the radicals, Leibniz nevertheless accused Newton's followers of encouraging irreligion and believed, moreover, that their contemporary John Locke (1632–1704) had also by his writings encouraged the growth of atheism.[26] Leibniz repudiated Locke's sensationalist psychology as well as his contractual theories of government, while the radicals did indeed borrow certain of Locke's ideas despite his disavowal of their interests and intentions.

In contrast to the English contractualists, Leibniz believed that sovereignty meant simply 'internal control' and influence in European affairs, and that it was best embodied in a monarch who would reign with supreme reason and virtue. He even decried the decline of Stuart absolutism because it removed from the European scene a necessary check on the unbridled absolutism of Louis XIV. Leibniz's political thought displays a nostalgic longing for the irrevocably shattered ideal of a unified *Republica Christiana*, in fact a revived Holy Roman

Empire. Such a goal was anathema to the nationalistic and Protestant interests of English churchmen and court politicians who had also become after 1689 the advocates of strong constitutional monarchy. It is little wonder that when George I accomplished the Hanoverian Succession in 1714 Leibniz was ignored and left behind in Hanover to get on with the writings of its official history. The English Whig courtiers and Newtonian churchmen would not have had it any other way.

Leibniz's quarrel with England's intellectual leadership extended beyond political theory to natural philosophy. Leibniz was convinced that Newton had not offered a sufficient explanation for how gravity operated in nature. He bitterly accused Newton of reintroducing 'occult qualities', that is magic, into the mechanical philosophy. Leibniz's retreat from Cartesianism, which had been motivated by theological as well as scientific reasons, led him to a study of dynamics. Out of this he became convinced that the essential character of matter is not extension but force. His mathematical reasoning led him to assert that individual substance includes within it all that can be predicted of it, just as the circle by definition entails its circumference and diameter. Within every substance is displayed a harmony and universality reflective of a larger cosmic order. Because matter is infinitely divisible, and is therefore nothing but an aggregate of its atomic parts, substance, the real unity, must derive from that which is immaterial. Leibniz posited the existence of what can be described as non-material atoms, monads, discrete substances that embody both individuality and universality – 'every created monad represents the whole universe'.[27]

In his search for an escape from the materialistic implications of Cartesian dualism, Leibniz proclaimed a universal harmony in nature that was derived entirely from spiritual forces distinct from matter. Because of this heavy reliance on spiritual principles of force, Leibniz's natural philosophy bears comparison with Newton's in that both thinkers relied upon an incredibly rich and baroque ontology to save their systems from materialistic consequences. Both emphasised force in the workings of nature, and both were in dialogue with, and in opposition to, Cartesianism. Yet any comparison of their thought is easily strained.

Leibniz simply posited universal harmony in the universe. It had been placed there by a great 'clockmaker' God who structured and synchronised nature from all eternity. As a result of this postulate, Leibniz never felt compelled to search scientifically or empirically for the universal laws of motion. Furthermore, he was horrified by Newton's apparent retreat from the mechanical philosophy, by his refusal to provide a purely mechanistic explanation for gravity. Indeed, Newton at one stage in his thought probably believed that gravity was the will of God operating in the universe. He further believed that at moments the motion of the universe would run down, the system would want 'a reformation' and God would have to intervene to put it right. This extreme providentialism, so basic to the Newtonian synthesis and its determining characteristic throughout the eighteenth century, defied Leibniz's belief in the harmony and perfection of the universe. It brought the world dangerously near to being an imperfect creation that seemed in constant need of repair.

It is little wonder that in 1715 Leibniz wrote to the Anglican churchman and close friend of Newton, Samuel Clarke, to inform him that 'natural religion itself, seems to decay [in England] very much. Many will have Human Souls to be material: Others make God himself a corporeal being'.[28] Leibniz laid the blame for this decay squarely upon English churchmen and natural philosophers, in particular upon Newton and his followers. This famous Leibniz-Clarke correspondence must have delighted the materialists and freethinkers. Indeed, its editor was Pierre Desmaizeaux, a great friend of the Commonwealth men, Toland and Collins, and one who rightly deserves a place in the early history of the Radical Enlightenment. While Collins quarrelled bitterly with the Newtonian Clarke, who was an early and penetrating adversary of the radicals, Desmaizeaux, whose sympathies lay with his friends, published Clarke's confrontation with Leibniz. Collins advised him, 'Let not the collection of Leibniz's and Clarke's Papers etc. now printing in Holland wait for my reply to Dr. Clarke.'[29] Fascinated by the new science, Desmaizeaux edited the quarrels of the Christian *virtuosi* while privately belonging to an international circle of freethinkers and materialists.

By the early eighteenth century that international coterie had thoroughly confounded Christian philosophers like Leibniz and the Newtonians and had even put them at one another's throats. The new science and mechanical philosophy, which they had laboured so hard to integrate with Christian belief and to put in the service of the state, was being used to enhance purely naturalistic and materialistic explanations of the universe. The perpetrators of this subversion were also politically dangerous men who would disestablish churches and weaken the power of kings and courts. Leibniz encountered this subversive activity first hand when in 1701–2 he had personal conversations with John Toland who had turned up in Hanover with the delegation that brought from Parliament the Act of Succession. Toland was representing the republican faction of the Whig Party and he reported back to one of its leaders, the Third Earl of Shaftesbury.[30]

Much to the consternation of his associates back in England and of observers in Hanover, Toland largely kept his own counsel during this foray on to the Continent and he used the opportunity to preach pantheism. He carried with him his rare copy of Bruno's *Spaccio della bestia trionphante* and a draft version of his pantheistic *Letters to Serena* (1704) which was eventually dedicated to the Queen of Prussia, Sophie Charlotte. Both Toland's copy of Bruno and a French manuscript version of the *Letters* turn up in the library of Eugène of Savoy. Journeying on to Berlin, Toland met again with Leibniz who was on a diplomatic mission representing Hanoverian interests to the queen. Leibniz distrusted his political intentions and regarded him as an informant on the court and its negotiations. He also instantly perceived the materialistic tenor of Toland's thought, describing it as revolving 'almost on the doctrine of Lucretius, that is to say, on the coming together of "corpuscles" ' or atoms. Leibniz likened Toland's materialism to that 'of Hobbes, i.e., that there is no other thing in nature but its shapes and movements'. In opposition to Toland, Leibniz argued that 'I believe that above matter, above that which is purely passive and indifferent to movement, it is necessary to seek the origin of action, perception and order' (11, 231 2).

This initial confrontation between Leibniz and Toland was to be repeated throughout the eighteenth century as European churchmen, as well as moderate advocates of the Enlightenment, took issue with the extreme philosophies put forward by reformers far more radical than they. The Leibniz–Toland dialogue also illustrates the materialistic interpretations to be extracted from the new science, whether derived from Descartes, Hobbes or Spinoza. A mechanical rendering of the natural world when blended with the naturalism that we find in late Renaissance philosophers like Bruno and Vanini equipped European radicals with a dynamic philosophy of nature, in effect with the foundations for a new religious vision. In the history of Western thought we have now arrived at that moment when Nature could in effect be worshipped.

By the 1690s, these radical stirrings were evident in parts of northern and Protestant Europe as the reaction against French aggression spread and gained momentum. The driving force behind this political and religious radicalism came from England, from a political structure and constitutional order established by revolution. It was the crucible of that mid-century upheaval against crown and church, and its resolution in the Revolution Settlement of 1689, which established the political and intellectual environment that nurtured the Radical Enlightenment. There the new mechanical understanding of nature, in its Newtonian form, first triumphed. That moderate version of the Enlightenment, found to be so compelling by many Continental reformers, coexisted however, often hostilely, with an alternative vision.

Within English republican circles, the philosophical legacy of the

Scientific Revolution, and its late Renaissance antecedents, was fused with a revolutionary tradition hostile to courts and established churches. The mechanical philosophy made it possible to conceive of the universe as matter in motion without the need to postulate a separate and eternal Creator. Republicanism converted the resulting philosophical pantheism into civic religion, and the dynamism of that credo gave coherence to the Radical Enlightenment throughout the eighteenth century. The Christian opponents of republicanism and materialism, who were also the heirs of the English Revolution, had laboured throughout the second half of the seventeenth century to suppress that radical impulse. Their accommodation to the revolution, and their concomitant hostility to the radicals, must be understood before the Enlightenment, in either its Newtonian or Radical phases, can be properly understood.

Notes: Chapter I

1 Cf. G. H. R. Parkinson, 'Spinoza on the power and freedom of man', in E. Freeman and M. Mandelbaum (eds), *Spinoza. Essays in Interpretation* (La Salle, III.: Open Court, 1975), p. 9.

2 Cf. J. R. Jacob, 'Boyle's atomism and the restoration assault on pagan naturalism', *Social Studies in Science*, vol. 8 (1978), pp. 211–23.

3 D. P. Walker, *Spiritual and Demonic Magic from Ficino to Campanella* (London: Warburg Institute, University of London, 1958).

4 Paolo Rossi, *Francis Bacon: From Magic to Science*, trans. S. Ravinovitch (London: Routledge & Kegan Paul, 1968).

5 Campanella is only mentioned occasionally in the freethinking literature, and given the limitations of size and space, I have excluded him from this account of the intellectual background of the Radical Enlightenment. But he was not forgotten by the radicals.

6 See Peter J. French, *John Dee. The World of an Elizabethan Magus* (London: Routledge & Kegan Paul, 1972).

7 Some evidence for Bruno's influence in seventeenth-century England does exist; see Daniel Massa, 'Giordano Bruno's ideas in seventeenth century England', *Journal of the History of Ideas*, vol. 38 (1977), pp. 227–42.

8 Cf. Karin Figala, 'Zwei Londoner Alchemisten um 1700: Sir Isaac Newton und Cleidophorus Mystagogus', *Physis*, vol. 18 (1976), pp. 245–73; B. J. T. Dobbs, *The Foundations of Newton's Alchemy or 'The Hunting of the Greene Lyon'* (Cambridge: Cambridge University Press, 1975).

9 M. X. Rousselot, *Oeuvres philosophiques de Vanini* (Paris, 1842), p. 227. Vanini's major works were published in Latin in 1615–16. For his life see Adolphe Baudouin, *Histoire critique de Jules César Vanini* (Toulouse, 1904); and [David Durand], *The Life of Lucilio Vanini . . . with An Abstract of His Writings. Trans. from the French to English* (London, 1730); *La Vie et les sentimens de Lucillo Vanini* (Rotterdam, 1717).

10 Cf. Lucien Febvre, *Origène et Despériers ou L'énigme du Cymbalum Mundi* (Paris: Droz, 1942); Lionello Sozzi, *Les Contes de Bonaventure Des Périers. Contribution à l'étude de la nouvelle française de la Renaissance* (Torino: Giappichelli, 1965); W. Spitzer, 'The meaning of B. Des Périers' *Cymbalum Mundi*', *Publications of the Modern Language Association*, vol. 66, no. 2 (1951), pp. 795–819.

11 Christopher Robinson, 'The reputation of Lucian in sixteenth-century France', *French Studies*, vol. 29 (1975), pp. 385–97.

12 L. Marsak, 'The idea of reason in seventeenth-century France: an essay in interpretation', *Journal of World History*, vol. 11 (1968), p. 409.

13 See J. Silhon, *De la certitude des connoissances humaines où sont particulièrement expliquez les principes et les fondemens de la Morale et de la Politique . . . de l'Imprimerie Royale* (Paris, 1661); this interpretation is taken from Lionel Rothkrug, *Opposition to Louis XIV: The Political and Social Origins of the French Enlightenment* (Princeton, NJ: Princeton University Press, 1965), pp. 56–60.

14 George H. Williams, *The Radical Reformation* (Philadelphia, Penn.: Westminster Press, 1962), pp. 321–2, 599, 609. Cf. Lewis S. Feuer, *Spinoza and the Rise of Liberalism* (Boston, Mass.: Beacon Press, 1968), pp. 54–7, to be used with caution.

15 M. Nicholson, 'The early stages of Cartesianism in England', *Studies in Philology*, vol. 26 (1929), pp. 356–74; Sterling P. Lamprecht, 'The role of Descartes in seventeenth-century England', Columbia University, Department of Philosophy (ed.), *Studies in the History of Ideas*, vol. 3 (1935), pp. 181–242.

16 J. Toland, *Origines judaicae, sive Strabons de Moyse et religione judaica historia* (The Hague: chez Thomas Johnson, 1709), p. 117.

17 John Colerus, *The Life of Benedict de Spinoza, Done out of French* (London, 1706), pp. 3, 7. For Van den Ende's activities as a revolutionary, see Feuer, *Spinoza*, pp. 19–20. The French edition of Colerus was published by Thomas Johnson.

18 Robert J. McShea, *The Political Philosophy of Spinoza* (New York: Columbia University Press, 1968), pp. 37, 134–6.

19 McShea, *The Political Philosophy of Spinoza*, p. 27.

20 B. de Spinoza, *The Chief Works of . . .*, trans. R. H. M. Elmes (New York: Dover Publications, 1951), *Tractatus Theologico-Politicus*, preface, p. 6.

21 Jean Baruzi, *Leibniz et l'organisation religieuse de la terre d'après des documents inédites* (Paris: F. Alcan, 1907); A. W. Ward, *Leibniz as a Politician. The Adamson Lecture, 1910* (Manchester: University of Manchester, 1911).

22 W. H. Barber, *Leibniz in France: from Arnauld to Voltaire. Study in French Reactions to Leibnizianism, 1670–1760* (Oxford: Clarendon Press, 1955), pp. 15–16, 25.

23 H. Trevor-Roper, 'Three foreigners and the philosophy of the English Revolution', *Encounter*, vol. 14 (1960), pp. 3–20.

24 C. G. Ludovici, *Ausführlicher Entwurf einer vollständigen Histoire der Leibnitzischen Philosophie*, Vol. 2 (Leipzig, 1737), p. 344. I owe this reference to G. Tonelli.

25 ÖN, Vienna, MS. Cod. 10 450*, ff. 15–16, Leibniz to 'Monsieur', possibly Eugène's librarian, 30 April 1716 with manuscript entitled 'De imposturir Religionum breve compendium'. For Eugène's copy of the *Traité*, ÖN, Vienna, MS, Cod. 10334, f. 29 *et seq.*, 'L'Esprit de Monsieur de Spinosa'. Leibniz enclosed a copy of Rousset de Missy's *Réponse* written about the *Traité*; see pp. 219–21.

26 Stephen Nicholas Jolley, 'Leibniz's Critique of Locke with Special Reference to Metaphysical and Theological Themes', PhD dissertation, Cambridge University Library (1974), pp. 14, 28–9. Leibniz got a somewhat biased account of English affairs in a lengthy correspondence with Thomas Burnett of Kemnay (1656–1729). Cf. Nicholas Jolley, 'Leibniz on Locke and Socinianism', *Journal of the History of Ideas*, vol. 39 (1978), pp. 233–50.

27 Gottfried W. von Leibniz, *Monadology and other Philosophical Essays*, trans. Paul and Anne Schrecker (New York: Bobbs-Merrill, 1965), p. 158.

28 S. Clarke, *A Collection of Papers which Passed between the Learned Mr Leibniz and Dr Clarke* (ed. Pierre Desmaizeaux) (London, 1717), p. 3. For a discussion of the purely philosophical issues separating Leibniz and Clarke, see C. D. Broad, 'Leibniz's last controversy with the Newtonians', in his *Ethics and the History of Philosophy* (London: Routledge & Kegan Paul, 1952), pp. 168–91.

29 BL, MSS ADD. 4282, f. 150, 17 June 1718; for Desmaizeaux and the radicals see
    BL, MSS ADD. 4286, ff. 108–90. For Desmaizeaux's contact with Newton see
    Karin Figala, 'Ein Exemplar der Chronologie von Newton aus dem Besitz von
    Pierre Des Maizeaux in der Bibliothèque de la Ville de Colmar', *Verhandl. Naturf.
    Ges. Basel*, vol. 84 (1974), pp. 646–97; and A. Rupert Hall and Laura Tilling (eds),
    The Correspondence of Isaac Newton, Vol. 7: 1718–1727 (Cambridge: Cambridge
    University Press, 1977), pp. 99–101, 133–6, *et seq.*; cf. Robin Attfield, 'Clarke,
    Collins and Compounds', *Journal of the History of Philosophy*, vol. 15 (1977), pp.
    45–54; K. Figala, 'Pierre Desmaizeaux's view of Newton's character', *Vistas in
    Astronomy*, vol. 22 (1978), pp. 477–81.
30 PRO, Shaftesbury MSS 30/24/45, ff. 41, 52a, 60, 71–2, 108, 304 (signed 'you know
    who' but definitely by Toland); Hertfordshire Record Office, D/EP/F 29, 'Diary of
    Sarah Cowper', pp. 152–3 *et seq.*

CHAPTER 2

The Legacy of the
English Revolution

The radical mind of the eighteenth century extracted from the Scientific Revolution a reverence for and understanding of nature that rendered the God of traditional Christianity superfluous. Pantheism was never, however, intended as an arid philosophical exercise, or even primarily as anti-clerical and anti-Christian arrogance. Its meaning was rooted in history, in the desire for political reform and social change. Throughout the eighteenth century, radical reformers from the Commonwealthmen of the 1690s, through our coterie of Orangist Freemasons in the Netherlands, to d'Holbach and his Parisian coterie emphasised two themes: they opposed the excessive power of kings, courts and ruling oligarchies, and they wished to disengage established churches and their clergy from the business of government, and from the power they exercised over the minds of ordinary people. That cluster of ideas first achieved revolutionary expression in England from 1640 until 1660.

At this point we are concerned not with the narrative of that revolution but with its impact upon the intellectual leadership of the generation that came to maturity during it. They bequeathed to the Enlightenment essentially two contradictory traditions: the first, and by far the more predominant, repudiated the radicalism of the Puritan sectaries and republicans and offered in its place a moderate and liberal Christianity, wedded to the new science, and supportive of strong monarchy within a constitutional framework. The English scientist and religious thinker, Robert Boyle (1627–91) became the major spokesman of that tradition, and as such he and his moderate Anglican associates require our attention. A second, equally vital tradition, also emerged from the political experience and thought of the revolution. From the profoundly disparate writings of Thomas Hobbes (1588–1679) and James Harrington (1611–77), as well as from the lived experience of the Commonwealth period (1651–60), early eighteenth-century English radicals extracted a political legacy that was essentially republican, and seen to be in conformity with a pantheistic and materialistic understanding of nature. By the early 1700s both traditions derived from the mid-century revolution had crystallised into disparate versions of a new international culture, designated in retrospect by the title, 'Enlightenment'. As that culture found its first mature expression in England after 1689 the moderates of the English Revolution became the Newtonians, the exponents and promulgators of English science and its concomitant religious and political values. The neo-Harringtonian Commonwealthmen evolved into the pantheists, materialists and republicans, the radical opponents of Christian orthodoxy, established church and court-centred government.

The experience of revolution and its attendant social upheaval – the first of its kind in the highly centralised national-states of early modern Europe – forced thoughtful people, of whatever religious persuasion, to take stock of their most basic assumptions about man and society and about God's exact relationship to his creation. As we have seen in the previous chapter, early modern Europeans related their perceptions of human history to a larger cosmic, or natural, order. The English Revolution impelled natural philosophers such as Boyle, and certain of his lesser-known contemporaries like John Wilkins, Walter Charleton, and the mathematician and tutor of Isaac Newton, Isaac Barrow, to formulate a mechanical vision of the universe that emphasised at every turn the providential role of the Deity as the source of order and harmony imposed through laws at work in nature and capable of being imitated in society. They repudiated materialistic explanations of natural events in part because they feared and detested the kind of social order that would be established if men came to believe that they, and not God and his appointed representatives, could master the course of history. But the moderate assault on the philosophies of the radicals and the materialists only began in earnest after 1649 and the regicide of Charles I.

In 1642 when Parliament and this Stuart king faced one another with their respective armies, many Protestant reformers, who would later recoil in horror at the threat from the radicals, believed themselves to be on the verge of a new and golden age – a millenarian paradise. Their dreams were abated by Continental reformers such as Samuel Hartlib and Jan Comenius, who arrived in England in the 1630s bringing with them the Hermetic reformism so commonplace within the Holy Roman Empire. These European idealists made common cause with English reformers long schooled in Puritan religiosity and deeply intent upon reforming the flamboyant Stuart court and its established church.

The Puritan vision united various strands in late Renaissance and

Reformation English thought. English Protestants who looked to the Continental and not to the Henrican version of the Reformation perceived their place in history in boldly millenarian terms. Put quite simply, they believed literally in the Scriptural prophecies about the final days and the end of the world. God directs the course of human affairs, just as he directs the course of nature. At some point in time, one that could be determined by careful scholarship or even possibly by a gnostic illumination, history and nature would synchronise as God destroyed the world in a cataclysmic upheaval that would precede the institution of a thousand-year reign of the saints, the millennium. Millenarianism made urgent the Puritan craving for reformation and renewal. English Puritanism was heavily tinged by the militant Protestantism of Continental Calvinism, but gone from this mentality was any distrust for the new learning, in particular for the new science.

English Puritans seized upon the writings of Francis Bacon as their guide to the new scientific spirit and its empirical methodology. They interpreted Bacon not as the humanist he was but rather they emphasised the millenarian and reformist aspects of his thought. They laid claim to his programme for the advancement of learning, in particular scientific learning. Although Bacon (d. 1626) had been decidedly opposed to the Puritans in his own time, by the 1630s he had been enlisted in their cause.

This linkage between the advocacy of science and English Puritanism has vexed students and historians ever since Robert K. Merton published in 1938 his claim that the rise of modern science was inextricably linked to English Puritanism (29). After decades of argumentation, few historians now doubt that the fortunes of the new science, and most important the desire to render it socially useful, were linked in the period from 1640 to 1660 with the cause of the Puritan Revolution. Various historians have shown that Puritan reformers during the 1640s embraced the cause of science in the service of social reform. Their Baconian schemes for classification and improvement, often inspired and assisted by Hartlib and his friends, extended to universal education, medicine, not for the rich but for 'a physical regeneration of the nation' (30), the new mechanical philosophy, chemistry, mechanics and architecture. Bacon's utilitarian vision of science, his belief that men must experience nature in the service of God and for the sake of mankind, fused with Puritan chiliasm to place science as a central concern in the political and social reforms advocated by Puritan leaders, both in and out of Parliament (31).

The early 1640s must have been an exhilarating time for social reformers as well as for natural philosophers and scientific experimenters sympathetic to the parliamentary cause. From that period we can trace the inspiration for the founding of the Royal Society (1663), presaged by Robert Boyle's so-called 'Invisible College' of the 1640s but derived, in an institutional sense from meetings held at Gresham College, London in the 1650s and attended primarily by Boyle, Jonathan Goddard, John Wilkins, Christopher Wren, Henry Oldenburg, John Evelyn and Sir Robert Moray, among others. Likewise the reformers of the 1640s proposed new colleges, grammar scholars and academies, technological innovations in every thing from mining to banking, a central 'office of address' for the communication of useful knowledge, and the ideal of a physician for every parish in the country (30, 90–6, 259).

Within the context established by revolution and civil war, modern science at its very origins was perceived in terms of its social usefulness and linked to a larger vision of reform and enlightenment. When we analyse the uses to which scientific knowledge and naturalism will be put by eighteenth-century radicals, we shall be struck by the similarities between their educational goals and the Puritan reformism of the 1640s. In both cases science was perceived as *praxis*, that is both sets of reformers saw in the new science a model for all types of learning, in particular for knowledge about the injustices and abuses perpetrated by established churches and governments. Unlike their Puritan predecessors, however, the radicals of the Enlightenment seldom gained access to political power. In its absence they waged a vast propaganda campaign. As journalists, publishers and promoters of clandestine literature they sought to use scientific learning and methodology to reform people's minds, while at the same time whenever possible they ingratiated themselves into the corridors to political power.

The analogy between the Radical Enlightenment and the intellectual goals of the Puritan Revolution must not be overdrawn. Once the centre of the Radical Enlightenment shifts from England to the Netherlands, and then finally to France, and the English Commonwealthmen of the early eighteenth century fade in prominence, Continental radicals of the later period seem only dimly aware that there had once been a time in European history, in England during the 1640s, when the power of kings and churches had been shaken to its core. As with the pagan philosophies of the late Renaissance and the Rosicrucian schemes of the early seventeenth century and their relation to the radical phase of the Enlightenment, the revolutionary reforms of the English Revolution, in some cases instituted and then abandoned, established a tradition but not a continuous history. In eighteenth-century Europe the opponents of absolute monarchy and established churches will also champion the new science not simply as a new approach to the natural world but also as a methodological model for a programme demanding profound social reform.

In any analogy between the English Revolution and the Radical Enlightenment, one other essential difference must be stressed. The Puritan reformers of the 1640s, whether moderate or radical, were millenarians who drew inspiration from the Christian meaning of history. By the 1690s and the early stirrings of the Enlightenment in England, the radicals have abandoned that particular vision of a future paradise and substituted in its place a universalist religion of nature. When John Toland edited the works of the great Puritan republican, Edmund Ludlow, he quietly obliterated the Christian millenarian passages (28). Pantheism rendered the apocalyptic impulse into a secular utopianism.

Even a partial understanding of why English radicals of the early Enlightenment abandoned the Christianity of the Puritan revolutionaries requires that we return to that mid-century upheaval. The Puritan schemes for social and intellectual reform during the 1640s largely failed, and in that failure lies the origin of the moderate, Newtonian Enlightenment. In the 1650s the new science and its mechanical vision of nature was linked to a reaction against the extreme reformers, many of them drawn from the lower ranks of society (32). They came to prominence in the late 1640s and dared to challenge property rights and to propose the institution of social democracy. In response to that threat natural philosophers such as Boyle and his moderate associates offered the new science and liberal Christianity as an antidote. They articulated a theoretical programme designed to insure social stability which, as we shall see, was repeated and refined until well into the eighteenth century and which Continental reformers, intent upon checking the abuses of the *ancien régime* without recourse to revolution and its excesses, found immensely appealing. For eighteenth-century radicals, on the other hand, the formula, conceived in reaction against republican schemes, always fell short of their ideals. For them political reform could only be achieved if both the defeated Puritanism and the triumphant Anglicanism of the English Revolution were abandoned forever.

Some historians of ideas have almost invariably described the crucial period from 1640 to 1660 as simply a monolithic time-span characterised solely by revolutionary upheaval. In failing to distinguish between the heady idealism of the 1640s and the reaction to extremism of the 1650s they have been left having to explain the failure of the social and educational reforms of the 1640s by recourse to 'wicked politicians'. They have also blamed opportunistic doctors, lawyers and academicians, as well as Cromwell and his parliamentary followers, for failing to instill order in a Commonwealth, soon to fail, to be replaced in 1660 by what those historians regard as a cynical and reactionary monarchy. But that is only half the story of the failure of the Puritan vision. The other, and from the perspective of the background to the Radical Enlightenment, the more important reason for that failure lies in the changed social and political perspectives of the leading scientists and Christian thinkers. In the period after 1648, Boyle, Wilkins, Evelyn and their associates experienced grave misgivings about the course of the revolution and gradually they came to support a restoration of monarchy and a new vision of the social meaning of science.

In the case of Robert Boyle, the leading scientist of his age prior to Newton, it is possible to document this social and intellectual transformation. As J. R. Jacob has argued, it occurred precisely when Boyle adopted a Christianised version of the mechanical philosophy, one that repudiated the pantheistic materialism of the radical sectaries (9). At the same time he came to perceive his version of the natural order as a new and vital support for orthodox Christianity and the established church.

Boyle was the youngest son of the powerful Earl of Cork, an Elizabethan adventurer whose fortune rested upon his Irish estates. For men of his caste the English Civil Wars coupled with rebellion in Ireland brought devastation to his lands and interests. As a result his heirs were forced to abandon their easy assumptions about birth and privilege, and to adopt a new ethic, one adjusted to a fortune determined by the exigencies of war and revolution. The young Boyle's religious sensibility was intensely Protestant, Scripture-based and rooted in his own early conversion experience. Boyle thought frequently about the necessity of 'infused Grace from above' for salvation. In his youthful adherence to the doctrine of predestination, Boyle was a Puritan, although he never engaged in Puritan polemics against the established church.

The English Revolution not only forced Boyle to renounce the aristocratic ethic of his caste, it also led him to discover the extraordinary opportunities for the reform of learning presented by the Puritan ascendancy. He espoused the work ethic coupled with millenarian piety as the means to all reform, social, scientific and religious. Boyle looked to the new science and its systematic methodology for nothing less than the foundation upon which his country, torn by civil wars and sectarian conflict, could achieve a religious consensus in preparation for the establishment of the millenarian paradise. The bridge between Boyle's vision of the peaceable and stable kingdom and his science was his active faith in a providential God.

Unlike the God of Descartes, with whom Boyle was familiar, and unlike the random chance prescribed by the pagan atomist, Epicurus, as the guiding principle at work in the universe, Boyle's God operated in a mechanical, atomistic universe as the source of motion, order and design. Only with the operative notion of the providential God could

Boyle maintain a mechanical philosophy in harmony with his Christian religiosity; and clearly he was intent upon keeping both. Boyle's belief in providence derived from his own personal struggle to establish an ethic based not upon inherited privilege but upon work and striving and from his conviction that God did in fact reward men who followed his precepts. Boyle gradually moved away from the doctrine of predestination, in other words from Puritanism and what he saw as its divisive doctrines, and argued instead for salvation based upon work and piety. He took from the Protestant Reformation its central notion of God's will, reinforced by his personal experience of struggle and success amid the turmoil of civil war, and bequeathed it to the final phase of the Scientific Revolution as well as to the Enlightenment. Out of the lived experience of revolution Boyle refined his understanding of Divine Providence and carried it 'so far that he read the pattern not only into human affairs but also into the ordering of the universe' (9, 103).

The ordered, mechanical corpuscular universe envisioned by Boyle and by many other of his mid-century associates, Wilkins, Evelyn and Barrow, operated according to the laws of motion. Matter, atomic or corpuscular in nature, obeyed the laws of force that operated in a vacuum. Although motion appears to be a property of matter, in fact matter in its natural state is inert, only the laws of force give it movement, and force in the universe derives from spiritual agencies and ultimately from the will of God. By separating matter and motion so dramatically and by rendering matter as naturally inert – 'brute and stupid' as Newton would later describe it – the English natural philosophers of mid-century salvaged the mechanical philosophy from its materialist implications. In direct response to the materialistic pantheism proposed by the radical sectaries, by philosophers such as Winstanley[1] and by political leaders such as Lilburne, Boyle and his associates performed an intellectual feat that enabled them to keep the mechanical philosophy – the central achievement of the Scientific Revolution – and to reconcile it with Christian doctrine and the maintenance of an established church.

The Puritan millenarianism of the 1640s had convinced Boyle and his associates that order and design prevades the 'world natural' as well as the 'world politick'. If men would only embark upon a programme of experimental learning – in other words apply the work ethic to nature – then Bacon's dreams will be realised beyond his greatest expectations. Boyle and his associates believed that men could become the priests of nature, but only through experimentation, work, disciplined education, mutual communications, and only under the guidance of providence. Their version of the enlightened man not only permitted him to investigate nature, but it also insured that he would serve God and his established representatives.

The English Revolution nurtured alternative versions of social reform to be sought by enlightened people who would worship at a very
different altar from that prescribed by Boyle and his associates. In its
armed conflict with Charles I, Parliament was forced to recruit a new
army, drawn from many social groups, yet unique in its composition.
Dedicated Puritans, some aristocratic but most drawn from the lesser
gentry, commanded an army whose rank and file in many cases
belonged to the radical Puritan sects that had sprung up (it seemed at
times from nowhere and yet from everywhere) during the 1640s. Some
had their roots in the antinomian and Anabaptist phase of the Continental Reformation, others appear to have been indigenously English
with a history that may yet be proven to stretch back to the four-
teenth-century Lollards.

The radicals of the English Revolution, with names that barely
denote their ideals – Levellers, Diggers, Ranters, Muggletonians,
Familists and Quakers, to name only the major groups – held the base
of their political power in the lower ranks of the New Model Army. By
1647 they constituted, in the eyes of the landed gentry, moderate
Puritans and intellectual reformers, such as Boyle and his circle, a
grave threat to their most cherished plans for reform and stability. Like
their own, the philosophies and ideals of the radicals rested upon a
millenarian sense of history. The kingdom of Christ on earth was close
at hand. Before its arrival the Scriptural prophecies would find fulfil-
ment. For the radical sectaries, many of whom were 'masterless men'
in possession neither of property nor feudal obligations, Scripture
foretold the institution of a democratic order where property would be
redistributed, or as the Diggers would have it, held in common, where
priests would yield power to lay preachers, and where the spirit of God
would infuse the lowly and make them the wise and virtuous
inheritors of a new and godly order. The radicals further denounced
the authority of national churches, whether Anglican or Presbyterian.
In their place the spirit of God would work great changes in the elect,
however lowly their station or meagre their book learning.

This political-religious vision embraced the cause of science and the
new learning. Like Boyle and his friends the radicals also wanted to see
a 'great instauration' of learning and the implementation of scientific
programmes and medical learning in the service of the people. They
too praised the 'mechanical arts', indeed many of them were the
'mechanics', those skilled craftsmen whose usefulness Boyle and his
associates so often praised. But unlike the moderate reformers, the
radicals embraced a vision of nature that derived in large measure from
the magical and Hermetic traditions. For them nature itself was alive,
infused with spirit. For philosophers such as Winstanley, nature is in
effect God, and this pantheistic materialism proclaimed the equality of

all people through nature as well as the usefulness of the popular sciences – alchemy, astrology, herbal medicine and the magical arts. As we shall see again in our discussion of the intellectual achievement of the Radical Enlightenment, pantheism could constitute the philosophical foundations for democratic belief (see Chapter 7).

In the 1650s, the moderate Puritan scientists and Christian reformers posited their priesthood over nature, based upon experimentation, classical learning, and their version of the mechanical philosophy in direct opposition to the pantheism of the radicals and their extreme version of the social usefulness of a science derived from, but intended to sophisticate, the sciences of the people (9, 114–15). The mechanical vision of the universe bequeathed to the Newtonian Enlightenment achieved its earliest formulation in the context of revolutionary upheaval. Of course the technical scientific problems posed and answered by Boyle and his associates cannot be explained by the dialectics of revolution. But their natural philosophical understanding of the universe, a legacy essential to the Newtonian achievement, was intended, in the first instance, to serve as a new anchor for Christian belief in a revolutionary era. That mechanical and experimental philosophy only achieved focus and precise articulation in the period after 1647 when it seemed for a time that the radicals might achieve even a modicum of their desires.

In the late 1640s and early 1650s, Boyle, Evelyn, Barrow, and other moderate scientists grew increasingly disaffected from the Puritan cause. They had entertained the possibility of a republic or common-wealth in the mid-1640s but the regicide (30 January 1649) shattered their dream of a godly commonwealth and by the mid-1650s we can see the emergence of a new consensus among a scientific and intellec-tual élite increasingly destined for power should monarchy be restored. The doctrine of predestination has been quietly abandoned – for reasons that appear increasingly to have been social.[2] If lowly men could designate themselves as elect, then by a curious irony this most repressive of religious doctrines could sanction social levelling. In place of predestination the moderates posed the work ethic with its scientific corollary – experimentation. Republicanism with all its radi-cal associations has also been abandoned, and within the scientific community from Boyle to the circle of Oxford mathematicians rep-resented by John Wallis and Matthew Wren, monarchy of some form appeared to be the only godly solution.[3] For them, however, monarchy must be sanctioned by divine and providential authority, and not by *de facto* theories of contract. As we shall see, the major theoretician of royal authority during the 1650s, Thomas Hobbes, rested his under-standing of sovereignty on just such a theory. His political writings, also based upon a mechanical and materialistic understanding of nature, came to haunt the moderate supporters of church and monarchy and exercised a powerful influence during the early decades of the Radical Enlightenment.

By 1660 and the Restoration of monarchy in England and by 1663 and the establishment of the Royal Society under royal charter, the social vision of scientific learning that prevailed during the 1640s, that search for the 'great instauration', had given way to an increasingly entrepreneurial notion of scientific practice. Scientific learning became the work of great and enterprising minds at work in isolation, while the social purpose of science was linked solely with discoveries to improve trade and commerce, to build empire abroad and to promote material prosperity at home. We should not imagine, however, that the moderate idealists of the 1640s who fashioned a mechanical and experimental philosophy more accurate in its methods than anything proposed by Descartes and more compatible with the Christian definition of matter and spirit than the rival materialism, had become by 1660 broken and disillusioned men.

During the ensuing decade Boyle, Wilkins, Evelyn and Oldenburg (although he was suspected of heterodoxy) in the Royal Society, and Isaac Barrow at Cambridge, became the intellectual and even organisational leaders of the new scientific learning. They used the new mechanical philosophy as the foundation for a broad and tolerant Anglicanism, which found little favour among the restored Anglican hierarchy but which seems to have had considerable support among the educated laity, particularly in London and its environs (11, ch.1). They were described at the time by friends and foe alike as 'latitudinarians' and their position attracted a bevy of young Anglican clerics, Simon Patrick, John Tillotson, Thomas Tenison, Edward Stillingfleet and John Moore. Latitudinarianism, or simply liberal Anglicanism, will figure prominently in our discussion of the Newtonian Enlightenment, in the English origins of that philosophical version of the Enlightenment. Also important in that intellectual history were the so-called Cambridge Platonists, Henry More and Ralph Cudworth, contemporaries of Boyle and Barrow, who sometimes quarrelled with the new scientists on minor issues but who basically shared their mechanical philosophy and their religious liberalism. More as well as Barrow influenced the young Isaac Newton in the 1660s when he was a student at Cambridge.

During the English Revolution the mechanical philosophy of nature essentially derived from Descartes, and various pantheistic philosophies derived from the magical and Hermetic tradition merged for a time, but eventually came to clash with an empirical approach to learning inspired by Bacon. The arbitrators of these various traditions, *virtuosi* like Boyle and Wilkins, mathematicians like

Barrow, philosophers like More and Cudworth, grappled with these approaches to the natural world within the context of political revolution. At every turn they rejected mechanistic explanations that hinged upon the power of matter unassisted by spiritual forces separate from the natural order. To their mind, scientific materialism, whether mechanistic or pantheistic in its inclination, justified atheism, social levelling, political disorder, in short the turning of 'the world upside down'.

These liberal Anglican opponents of materialism knew that at least one version of that 'atheistical' understanding of nature flourished among educated men, some of whom belonged to the highest ranks of the political nation. Their textbook, as churchmen and *virtuosi* might imagine it, was nothing less than the major political treatise to be occasioned by the revolution, Hobbes's *Leviathan* (1651). While materialism of a strongly pantheistic variety expressed a philosophy common within republican circles, whether lowly or even gentlemanly (33, 126), materialism of a totally mechanistic variety was imbedded in Hobbes's analysis of the natural order as well as of the political order (35).

Deeply influenced by the mathematical way of Descartes, Hobbes saw the universe as matter in motion, defined by its mathematically measurable attributes and moved by forces inherent to it. Hobbes leaves little doubt that he saw these mechanical operations as the sufficient explanation of natural phenomena – without recourse to supernatural agencies or providential oversight. Equally alarming, however, was Hobbes's attempt to apply these mechanical principles to the social actions of men.

Hobbes's thought displayed to his contemporaries as well as to recent commentators the fundamental unity of his science-based materialism and his political theory (34, 78–9). Because he analysed men as mechanisms in motion, as essentially self-moved matter, he could postulate their political morality as springing from their actions or motions, that is from their desires, passions and repugnances, and not from any outside source, any higher or supernaturally endowed ethical standard, other than themselves. Spiritual forces derived ultimately from God play no part in Hobbes's materialism. As a result, the traditional explanations of political obligation – that it is based upon reason or obedience to God's will – play no part in his political theory. The political meaning of Hobbes's stark rendering of the mechanical philosophy, which he spelled out at great length in *Leviathan*, added yet another dimension to the socially dangerous implications of a mechanical version of nature left un-Christianised.

But there was another, equally dangerous, threat posed by the teachings propounded in *Leviathan*. For Hobbes, religion is 'feare of power invisible, feigned by the mind, or imagined from tales publiquely allowed' (36, 124). In short, religious belief springs from perpetual fear, nothing more, nothing less. As a result 'the Gods were at first created by humane fear', and in the world of human politics, as distinct from the Kingdom of God (about which Hobbes would have us know very little), the purpose of religion is that it 'teacheth part of the duty which earthly kings require of their subjects' (36, 170, 173-4). Religion springs from public necessity and its purpose is to impose public order and to alleviate fear of 'powers invisible', of 'a whole kingdome of Fayries, and Bugbears'. Hobbes personally advocated absolute monarchy and he praised the social value of religious belief enforced by a priestly caste, in short of civic religion, but he based'both prescriptions on the nature of man, on human solutions to human problems that arise from the passions, from matter in motion.

Hobbes was an extreme embarrassment to the royalist camp. Although a firm supporter of absolute monarchy, his ideas about political obligation and particularly about the origin and purpose of religious worship quickly found favour in freethinking and radical circles.[4] Although the career of Hobbes's philosophy during the Restoration remains somewhat opaque, in the very early decades of the Radical Enlightenment we find Hobbes being championed by Commonwealthmen like Anthony Collins. He is also the only English political theoretician of the revolution singled out for special citation in the most virulently pantheistic and republican tract of that period, the *Traité des trois imposteurs*. The radicals simply stripped Hobbes of his royalism; they championed his notion that political obligation arises from the necessities of politics, from *de facto* obligations intended to secure peace and stability, and if necessary imposed by revolutionary action. But it was his materialism, and in particular its implications for established religion and churches that most delighted his radical readers. They, too, saw the necessity for civic religion, for some Freemasonry would constitute such a creed, but its 'priesthood' would be lay and not clerical. Enlightenment radicals would attempt to replace the fear of supernatural powers, postulated according to Hobbes because man 'cannot assure himselfe of the true causes of things', with the scientific study of natural causes and effects. Nature would replace God as the source and explanation of human endeavours; and the need for stability and community demanded in turn that civil society itself become the object of common worship.

All of these uses to which Hobbes's theories were to be put, could only have been dimly imagined by the liberal Anglican churchmen and *virtuosi* of the Restoration who were in the forefront of the widespread and virulent campaign waged against Hobbes's theory of government. One historian has aptly described the campaign as 'the hunting of

Leviathan'. It mattered little that Hobbes had in fact advocated strong monarchy as the only solution to political disorder, indeed as the only alternative to revolutionary chaos. To his mind men's passions moved so violently and inexorably that only the heavy hand of authority would restrain human rapaciousness. In his obsession with greed and the self-interest of men, Hobbes has been seen by some modern commentators as the first major interpreter of the market society, in effect of emergent capitalism (34). Although this approach may over-simplify Hobbes, his contemporary Christian scientists and polemicists would probably have sympathised with it. The term 'capitalism' was certainly alien to their language but the experience of the market place, and hence of competition, was not alien to their daily lives. The Anglican clergy were inordinately concerned with social order, yet their prescriptions, consciously pitched at commercial society, were based upon the cosmic order proclaimed by the providential version of the mechanical philosophy. Their sermons and writings make clear their belief that greed and self interest, of a commercial nature, threaten the social order and necessitate the obsessive concern which they shared with Hobbes for the maintenance of order and stability.

Ironically Hobbes and his Christian and scientifically minded critics offered similar dire assessments of the dangers inherent in unbridled self-interest, in uncontrolled and unrestrained social and economic action. Yet they offered profoundly different formulae as solutions. Hobbes would have men make a contract and establish over them-selves a ruler who would control all, except their property. Christian *virtuosi* and liberal Anglican churchmen who wanted to make Christ-ianity relevant to the needs of the commercial and propertied élite, also used their mechanical understanding of nature to fashion a model for society and government. Providence governs both realms through laws of nature, and obedience to political authority stands in imitation of that cosmic system. Although the full political implications of this emphasis on the rule of law and on providentially directed harmony would not be evident until after the Revolution of 1688–9, the sermons and tracts of Restoration churchmen and their scientific associates laid the foundation for an acceptance of constitutional monarchy, sup-ported, of course, by an established church. Latitudinarian Christian-ity also laid great emphasis on the notion that self-interest can be made 'sober', that is useful and rewarding, through the practice of Christian virtue and restraint. God rewards industry; good works are profitable. In the ordered, mechanical universe proclaimed by Boyle and incor-porated into the Newtonian vision, men of property can pursue their interest without recourse to the necessity of an absolute sovereign.

But if Hobbes's formula was unacceptable, so too were the varieties of republicanism also proposed during the 1650s. The radical sectaries of the army met with political and ideological defeat, but they were not the only republicans with access to the printing presses during the Commonwealth period. In a utopian treatise dedicated to Cromwell entitled *The Commonwealth of Oceana* (1656), James Harrington laid the foundations for a body of political thought and sentiment that permeated the Anglo-American understanding of government until well into the late eighteenth century (38). Harrington articulated a vision of the republic that rested on the virtues and independence of the small land owner who bears arms in support of a state responsive to his needs and governed by a frequently elected Parliament. Harrington would not eliminate kings or aristocrats, far from it. His monarch would be governed by laws, while his aristocracy would be not the feudal nobility of the past but men of landed property forced to share their power with all men of property, however meagre their independent holdings. Harrington permitted aristocracy because he was in fact a democrat. He vested political power in the hands of the 'yeomanry or middle people'; his objective was 'that of bringing individuals, as free and non-dependent agents, into the processes of decision and virtue' (33, 53, 69). Leadership would come from men of greater property whose leisure permitted them to cultivate their minds; reason and not naked self-interest would govern their actions in Parliament and that institution rested on the will of the larger citizenry.

In Harrington's version of the republic, king, aristocrats and commons enter into a form of government that bears greater resemblance to the American Constitution than it does to anything devised as a result of the English Revolution. His emphasis on the independence and rights of the small property holder, on the rule of reason and virtue, his condemnation of standing armies and the unbridled executive power that would control them, rendered his thought unacceptable to the supporters of strong monarchy, constitutional or otherwise. Likewise his disdain for established churches and their natural allegiance to court and king placed his theories beyond the pale of enlightened Anglican thought, during the Restoration and beyond.

Harrington's vision of the republic was revived, however, in the 1690s during the first decade of the Radical Enlightenment. The Revolution of 1688–9 spawned a new generation of English republicans, politically more astute and tempered than their Commonwealth predecessors in the sense that they now perceived Parliament as a viable institution, one which they sought to manipulate (37). For them it would be a tool that would bring the new constitutional order into the hands of those lesser men of property and virtue whose suspicion of courts, placemen, bishops and their cohorts, had only been heightened by James II's attempt to institute absolutism.

Of the various legacies bequeathed by the English Revolution to the

European Enlightenment the republicanism of Harrington rang most true to its radical faction. For the so-called Old Whigs of the 1690s, whom J. G. A. Pocock has rightly called 'the first intellectuals of the Left', *Oceana* embodied not a call to action but a utopian symbol (38, 477). In 1699, John Toland edited, with a little help from his republican friends, the political writings of Harrington and dedicated the work 'to the Lord Mayor, Aldermen, Sheriffs and Common Council of the City of London', to Sir Robert Clayton, among others, who was also one of Toland's Masonic friends. Clayton had recently fallen into disfavour with court Whigs(39, 20; 40, 54, 59n). In the political turbulence of the 1690s, the republican faction of the Whigs, among whom Toland was regarded by the court as an 'incendiary', may have been seeking favour with London financiers like Clayton as well as with disaffected Tories like Harley. Years later Toland would claim that Harley 'encouraged me to reprint Harrington's *Oceana*, tho neither of us imagin'd the model it self to be practicable' (33, 141).

This post-1689 revival of Harrington's writings, part of a larger project to reissue much of the republican writings of the 1650s, signalled the birth of a new genre of republican thought, one that has been described as 'neo-Harringtonian'. At root this tradition of English and eventually American thought can be traced back to Machiavelli and his discussion of the nature of the Florentine republic. In the pages that follow we shall repeatedly encounter that tradition, not as a history of political theory, vital as that may be, but in the history of political action and religious thought. The Enlightenment, in both its moderate and radical forms, began in England but achieved intellectual maturity in Europe, in Continental states in possession of neither a parliament nor a two-party system comparable to that initiated, on the level of political ideology and occasionally political action, by eighteenth-century Whigs and Tories.

What we find in the European version of the Radical Enlightenment is a coherent tradition of political opposition to absolute monarchy, established churches and ruling oligarchies. At moments in that tradition, for example during the Dutch Revolution of 1747, we shall find republican theoreticians articulating political ideology that almost certainly derived from their knowledge of English republicanism or more precisely from their personal acquaintance with the Commonwealthmen of the early eighteenth century. In the first decade of the eighteenth century, Toland and Collins actively promoted their understanding of the English Constitution and the necessity for its continuing reform along republican lines, among French Protestant exiles who rose to political prominence in the Netherlands. The links between the English Revolution and its republican legacy and the various revolutions of the eighteenth century on the Continent, are more immediate and direct than had hitherto been suspected.

But ideas and intellectual traditions are molded by the crucible of historical action. Harrington's utopian vision of the balanced constitution, ruled neither by kings nor oligarchs, of the republic of reason, resonated throughout the writings and the revolutionary actions of European radicals. They may not have always seen themselves as the heirs of Machiavelli and his Renaissance version of republicanism – they often associated him with evil princes – but they were republicans none the less who looked to England for forms of government and for political traditions that could inspire a political and intellectual struggle characterised first and foremost by the politics of opposition, whether to established oligarchical, or monarchical or ecclesiastical authority.

One other common thread unites the republican tradition from its most comprehensive articulation in England during the 1650s to its lived experience in the Netherlands during the course of the eighteenth century. At this point we should be comfortable with the notion that ideas about physical nature and about the polity worked in tandem throughout much of this period. From Harrington onwards we can trace a consistent tendency on the part of republican thinkers to explain the ordered universe not by reference to an imposed, supernatural order, administered as it were by God's self-styled representatives, kings, oligarchs and the like, but by recourse to the notion that spirit lives in nature, in people as in all objects. This pantheism, with its roots as we have seen in the Hermetic and neo-Platonic tradition, can be found in the natural philosophy of Harrington himself.[5] By the early eighteenth century, however, it had become central to the way thinkers operating in a republican tradition formulated their arguments for a secular order decreed by the interests and necessities of ordinary men in search of a balanced and representative system of government. Their position makes perfect sense once we realise that the entire theoretical structure of legitimate political authority, with the divine right of kings as it most extreme expression, had been formulated for centuries around the notion that power comes from God, from a spiritual force separate from the realm of mundane, human concerns. It could be argued that the repudiation of that metaphysic had to occur before Harrington's country squires and ultimately their neighbouring craftsmen and shopkeepers could justify their claims for a share in the distribution of political power. Pantheism and republicanism were remarkably compatible, and in the thinking of political radicals who had given up any hope of reforming the established churches, they were necessary corollaries.

Because of its revolutionary associations, from the 1650s onwards, the republican legacy engendered critics and virulent opponents. The new scientists were in the vanguard of that opposition; they were after all the priests of a new understanding of the natural world and they struggled, with notable success, to integrate this new science with the traditional metaphysics of the Christian churches as well as with their vision of a society that would be both ordered and yet supportive of industry and learning. After 1660, Boyle and his associates threw their weight behind the restored monarchy, and the Royal Society (1662) became both a scientific enclave as well as a home for Anglican spokesmen intent upon showing the benefits for industry and empire to be derived from science supported by effective court-centred government. Sprat's *History of the Royal Society* (1667) stands as the ideological *tour de force* sponsored by the society to justify the compatibility of science and religion, and the usefulness of both in maintaining social stability while advancing trade and industry.

Once the role of science in late seventeenth-century England is perceived in these social and ideological terms, then the relationship between Newton's science and the origins of the Enlightenment assumes greater complexity. The old adage, derived haphazardly from Pope, that said let Newton be and all was light, requires qualification. Newton was the greatest scientific mind of his generation and therefore it is essential to realise that he subscribed to the version of the new mechanical philosophy, with its concomitant social and political meaning, first articulated by the Anglican natural philosophers, that is by the Cambridge Platonists, by Boyle and his associates. On the crucial level of matter theory Newton repudiated both the Cartesian definition of matter as extension and, in his words, 'the vulgar notion (or rather lack of it) of body . . . in which all the qualities of the bodies are inherent' because if 'we cast about we find almost no other reason for atheism than this notion of bodies having, as it were, a complete, absolute and independent reality in themselves' (47, 142–4). Both Descartes's philosophy and those 'vulgar' philosophies that place spirit inherent in bodies lead, in Newton's opinion, directly to atheism. Newton's philosophical definition of universal gravitation required active principles, spiritual forces, at work in nature but not inherent in it. Because Newton believed in the God of Boyle and the Cambridge Platonists he subscribed to an intensely providentialist faith that was also millenarian. He could postulate that gravity acted on bodies at a distance and that, contrary to the dictates of harmony and order, the universe might someday require a 'reformation', that it would in effect run down. Leibniz and various Continental mechanists were horrified by this retreat into what they imagined to be an occult philosophy (Chapter 1, pp 56–7), but Newton's highly spiritualised version of the ordered universe was totally compatible with the Anglican version of the mechanical universe articulated within the context of the English Revolution.

In a variety of manuscripts, most to this day unpublished, Newton refined and elaborated upon his understanding of God's relation to his mathematically ordered universe. In one particularly revealing exposition, almost certainly written between 1704 and 1706, Newton summarised his natural philosophy in such a manner as lay bare his debt to the neo-Platonic tradition and his own highly spiritualised account of motion in the universe:

> . . . it seems to have been an ancient opinion that matter depends upon a Deity for its laws of motion as well as for its existence . . . These are passive laws and to affirm that there are no other is to speak against experience. For we find in ourselves a power of moving our bodies by our thought. Life and will are active principles by which we move our bodies, and thence arise other laws of motion unknown to us. And since all matter duly formed is attended with signes of life and all things are framed with perfect art and wisdom and nature does nothing in vain; if there be a universal life and all space be the sensorium of a thinking being who by immediate presence perceives all things in it, as that which thinks in us, perceives their pictures in the brain: these laws of motion arising from life or will may be of universal extent.[6]

Without these spiritual agencies derived from the great mathemetician, as Newton addressed the deity, his universe could not subsist. This manuscript was written precisely at the time when Newton's metaphysical system of the world was under heavy attack from radical Whigs intent upon articulating a materialistic rendering of the mathematically ordered universe. While Newton penned these private manuscripts, his close friend, Samuel Clarke, took to the pulpit against Hobbes, Spinoza, Toland and Collins.

The impact of Newtonian science on European thought, after the publication of Newton's *Principia* (1687), owes much to his post-1689 friends and associates. From the perspective of history, however, that triumph would be unimaginable without the intervening Revolution of 1688–9. While English moderates had cast their lot with the restored monarchy in 1660, by 1685 it was clear that Stuart rule entailed royal Catholicism and the prospect, at least in the minds of the suspicious, of royal absolutism. By 1687 those suspicions had found plenty of verification in James II's attempts to install his placemen in the counties, the courts and the universities.

The ensuing revolution, although made almost inevitable by the refusal of the Anglican clergy with the latitudinarians in the foreground to give any support other than passive obedience to James II, nevertheless quickly bypassed the church's leadership and its interests. The constitutional settlement, the Bill of Rights (1689), the Toleration Act were all the work of Parliament. The effect on the church's morale was close to devastating and it was only the ascendancy of Anglican moderates, with their commitment to limited toleration, constitutional but court-centred and church-supported monarchy, as well as to Newtonian science, that saved the day, in both a political and ideological sense.

In the aftermath of the Revolution of 1688–9, liberal Christianity wedded to the new science was offered to an English and eventually to a European audience as a binding social philosophy capable of reconciling diverse Protestants and of sanctioning a stable social and constitutional order, born in revolution but intent upon repudiating revolution as an instrument of change. Newton's mechanical universe controlled by mathematical laws and rules of right reasoning, its hypotheses about the relationship between matter and spirit clearly evident, became the natural model for the triumph of the Whig constitution. It was a powerful metaphor which, as we shall see, attracted many followers as well as many opponents.

Contemporary radical Whigs, such as Toland, seized upon this Newtonian concept of the ordered universe and tried to graft it on to their materialism. Why not argue that Newton's laws work because spirit is inherent in matter, that gravity is proof of the force and power of nature? As early as 1704, the proponents of a far more radical Enlightenment tried, never with great success, to graft the new science into their programme. In response, Newton's followers thundered back at them; yet the radicals remained unmoved. In private letters, circulated within a Whig club called 'the college', a circle to which I shall return, Collins told his fellow Commonwealthman, John Trenchard, that Clarke had been put up to writing by the clergy 'a great many whereof know not upon [such] weak foundations the matters of the greatest consequence to them stand'. Collins believed that he could outwit his Newtonian adversary despite Clarke's claim 'of his having caught me at an advantage now that the dispute turns upon points of Mathematicks and Natural Philosophy'. Collins addressed the central issues: '. . . they all depend on ye Question of the Infinite Divisibility of matter which though some former jumbled mathematicians thought had such difficulties attending it as would not be resolved.' He went on to assert that now, as a result of Newton's science, it was possible, more than ever in the past, to assert the infinity of matter.[7]

But despite their self-confidence, efforts on the part of philosophical radicals to find what appeared to be actual scientific proof for pantheism would take many decades and come not from the new physics but from zoology and the life sciences in general. As a result the radical Whigs and their Continental followers took up an ambiguous, and somewhat tortured, posture towards Newtonian science. They championed its mathematical exactness, promulgated Newton's laws in their French-language journals, but searched nevertheless for arguments to repudiate the natural philosophical foundations upon which Newton's science rested. Despite its brilliance, the Newtonian light was filtered through a variety of tinted glasses and found selectively useful and enlightening by friend and foe alike only when rendered supportive of more human, less abstract, issues. In the hands of Newton's followers it lent vital support to the Anglican church and its interests; the radicals used the new science in general against the old theology, both Catholic and Protestant, but in their hands science was constantly molded to accommodate the search for purely naturalistic explanations of the human and natural orders.

The European Enlightenment begins in 1689, and the various political and ideological legacies of the English Revolution, far more than Newton's science *per se*, shaped its contours for decades. One other intellectual, equally important, tradition emerged from that revolutionary context, and it was embodied in the political and philosophical writings of John Locke (43). In response to the scepticism of his age, as well as in dialogue with the necessities of the new scientific inquiry, Locke articulated an epistemology, what is sometimes called his sensationalist psychology, that found favour among both moderates and radicals. In the *Essay concerning Human Understanding* (1690) he argued that 'reason is the proper pledge [of truth or error]; and revelation, though it may consenting with, confirm its dictates, yet cannot in such cases invalidate its decrees'.[8] Relying on sense knowledge, its data in turn compounded and analysed by the reasoning mind, Locke sought to lay the methodological foundations for the accumulation of purely natural knowledge about people and nature. Of course, Locke quickly maintained, and believed, that Christianity was compatible with this new psychology.[9] If its mysteries and doctrines were not always verifiable through the senses, they were at least reasonable. But Locke's argument was easily wrested from its Christian moorings and made to support a variety of natural religions. Among the leading spokesmen of that purely naturalistic interpretation were the radical Whigs, Toland and Collins, both of whom knew Locke well, possibly too well, for his public comfort.

In the 1690s, a high-ranking Anglican clergyman, Francis Gastrell, confronted Locke with this uncomfortable truth: 'Sir, you are highly considered and much quoted etc. by the Socinians, deists, Atheists, and the bold spirits of this Country etc. You do not approve them, but you ought therefore to disapprove them, for it seems to me that you cannot count the praise of such people to your honour . . .'[10] Locke never launched a broadside against his radical followers in large measure, I would suspect, because they were his political allies; they were the radicals of his own Whig party.

In the personal and political involvements of Locke and the radicals during the first decade of the Enlightenment its radical and moderate phases were as closely allied as ever they would be. Locke definitely sided with the court and its Whig administration yet he firmly supported toleration and the abolition of censorship, as well as a variety of fiscal and social reforms. He was both a beneficiary and an architect of England's new-found prosperity. That his epistemology could be used to argue against all claims for the existence of an invisible, supernatural realm must have been troubling, but given his other interests, hardly pressing. The church, and even for a brief moment, Newton, had the gravest suspicions about Locke's orthodoxy. At one particularly paranoid moment Newton thought him to be a Hobbist, that is one who would justify political legitimacy solely according to the dictates of power and necessity. Yet Locke never defected from the camp of the Newtonian Enlightenment. He did, however, leave behind an arsenal of ammunition for the radicals.

In the Netherlands during the Revolution of 1747 we will find Rousset de Missy, an heir to the radical Whiggery of the 1690s, proposing to bring out hurriedly another edition of the French translation of Locke's most important political treatise, *Two Treatises of Civil Government* (1690). It was intended by Rousset to justify this Dutch revolution just as it would be used, decades later, to justify the American Revolution. As a supporter of the Orangist cause Rousset and his patron, the great Whig lord, William Bentinck, found in Locke's theory of government justification for government based upon the 'consent of the people' and, if need be, upon revolutionary action (see p. 236). Both concepts related to Orangist claims to express the popular appeal of the Prince of Orange and popular support for his bid to resume power as stadholder. Locke's emphasis on contract as the foundation of legitimate government could also be used to justify a larger overhaul of the political machinery of the Dutch Republic and to validate an attack upon the excessive powers of its urban oligarchy. Locke's *Two Treatises*, originally drafted between 1679 and 1682 as an assault on the conceptual foundations of absolute monarchy, was enthusiastically taken up by the eighteenth-century English exporters and foreign practitioners of revolution. His arguments were seldom, if ever, sighted by the post-revolutionary Whigs in justification of the events of 1688–9 (42). Having secured their properties and prerogatives, their church and constitutional monarchy, they sought not to encourage political reforms and revolutions but largely to prevent them (45).

Out of the crucible of the English Revolution was born a new mechanical understanding of the natural world that was linked to a specific social ideology. This scientific legacy with its emphasis upon experimentation and its rejection of pantheistic and materialistic explanations of the physical universe was resolutely anti-Cartesian and anti-spinozist; it was also anti-magical in its repudiation of the popular sciences. Its prescriptions for the organisation and pursuit of scientific knowledge were individualistic and competitive rather than communal and socially beneficial in orientation. And finally the political burden of Newtonianism was more obviously monarchist than republican in its insistence upon the providential and supernatural origins of order in the physical and moral (and therefore in the political) order.

The Newtonian and moderate version of the Enlightenment, so powerful in the early decades of the eighteenth century, requires further elaboration and inspection. For radicals can only be such in juxtaposition to less extreme prescriptions for ordering and explaining the world. In the early eighteenth century, Europeans looked to post-revolutionary England, more than to any other society, for guidance as they sought alternatives to religious and political absolutism. In consequence of their revolutionary heritage, English theoreticians offered two conflicting formulations of the physical, moral and political universe. It is to that majority report that we must now turn.

Notes: Chapter 2

1   Christopher Hill (ed.), *Winstanley: The Law of Freedom and Other Writings* (Harmondsworth: Penguin, 1973), pp. 42–59. For an interpretation emphasising Winstanley's theism see Lotte Mulligan, John Graham and Judith Richards, 'Winstanley: a case for the man as he said he was', *Journal of Ecclesiastical History*, vol. 28 (1977), pp. 57–75.

2   For new evidence on the preaching of 'good works' in Cambridge in the 1650s, see Spencer Research Library, University of Kansas, MS. A. 41, Charles North's notes on sermons by Cudworth, Arrowsmith, *et al.*

3   On Wren see J. G. A. Pocock, 'Contexts for the study of James Harrington', *Il Pensiero Politico*, vol. 11 (1978), pp. 20–35.

4   Quentin Skinner, 'The ideological context of Hobbes' political thought', *Historical Journal*, vol. 9 (1966), pp. 286–317. James Jacob is currently studying the transformations affected on Hobbist theory by radicals during the Restoration.

5   On Harrington see Wm. Craig Diamond, 'Natural philosophy in Harrington's political thought', *Journal of the History of Philosophy*, vol. 16 (1978), pp. 387–98.

6   ULC, MSS ADD. 3970, f. 619^r.

7   Spencer Research Library, University of Kansas, Collins probably to Trenchard, MS.G.23, 9 May 1707; discussed in Margaret Jacob, 'Newtonianism and the origins of the Enlightenment: a reassessment', *Eighteenth Century Studies*, vol. 11 (1977), pp. 1–25.

8   John Locke, *Essay concerning Human Understanding* (New York: Dover, 1959) Vol. 2, p. 423.

9   See John C. Biddle, 'John Locke on Christianity: His Context and His Text', PhD dissertation, Stanford University, 1972.

10 As reported by Burnett to Leibniz and quoted in Stephen Nicholas Jolley, 'Leibniz's Critique of Locke with Special Reference to Metaphysical and Theological Themes', PhD dissertation, Cambridge University Library, 1974, p. 42.

CHAPTER 3

The Newtonian Enlightenment and Its Critics

The Newtonian achievement in science and natural philosophy sponsored one powerful version of enlightenment. This philosophic enlightenment, first visible in England by the 1690s, came to dominate much of eighteenth-century thought and certain assumptions were basic to it. The physical universe can be understood through mathematics and experiment, and by reference to mechanical laws emanating ultimately from a supernatural being. That being might be the Christian God of Boyle and Newton, or the remote deity found, for example, in the writings of the French *philosophes*, Voltaire and d'Alembert, or an amalgam of the two such as we find in the Masonic literature of the eighteenth century.[1] That originally British social institution offered the God of Newtonian science, the Grand Architect, as a supernatural entity that could be worshipped by either Christians or deists. In general the adherents of the Newtonian Enlightenment can be identified as proponents of the new science and natural philosophy who insisted on the existence of a supernatural being separate from nature, and who also held to the concomitant social assumption that the deity imposes order in nature and society, his function resembling that of the strong, but not arbitrary, monarch. In other words, in this period the refusal to accept a purely naturalistic or pantheistic rendering of the universe carried with it very real political implications and assumptions; without the postulate of a deity – however remote – it seemed that there could be no order in nature or society, and that inevitably, therefore, strong yet enlightened monarchy offered the only viable form of political organisation in the various nation-states of Europe.

By contrast, and often in direct opposition to this Newtonian vision, the radicals of the eighteenth century argued for nature as the only force in the universe. The political corollaries of eighteenth-century pantheism, so capable of being extracted, as we have seen, from sources as disparate as Spinoza and Bruno, followed logically: the advocacy of a civic religion dependent solely upon man's participation in the natural order and not derived from a series of rules or laws articulated and administered by an ordained clergy and, of course, the assertion of republican principles of government based upon *de facto* theories of political obligation and upon the notion that any man, if educated to it, had the right to attempt to mould government to his interests. Yet despite the antagonism of their respective visions, radicals and Newtonians during the first half of the eighteenth century could, and did, make common cause: in their opposition to French and Spanish absolutism and in their hatred for authoritarian and repressive attempts by state churches to persecute dissenters and to control all forms of publication.

Crucial differences of belief and political filiation distinguished the radicalism of the early Enlightenment from the Newtonian understanding of nature and society, whether articulated by the English churchmen who were Newton's close associates or by Voltaire who abandoned their Christianity and argued for a deistic version of Newtonianism. Here we shall examine that Newtonian Enlightenment as found among the major Newtonians, from Newton through Voltaire. In the chapters that follow we shall then focus on the institutionalisation of that Newtonian creed within British Freemasonry, and how, in turn, that society offered an unprecedented opportunity, unintended by its founders, for furthering radical objectives.

During the early eighteenth century, by comparison with the influence exercised by the proponents of English science, the radicals struggled to be heard: but they were successful. In England they were often to be found on the fringes of the now triumphant Whig Party; they were republicans of a sort who resorted to polemics and subterfuge, and sometimes secrecy, to press their cause. In northern Europe, more generally, the radicals can be found among Protestant refugees who fled north to escape persecution in France. In Paris some coteries of aristocratic intellectuals existed whose flirtations with spinozism and materialism approximated the creeds of the exiles whose experience of flight and relative freedom within the Dutch Republic gave urgency to their journalism and propaganda-making. As we shall see, the combined force of this English–Dutch radicalism paved the way for the later, the so-called High Enlightenment of the post-1750 period. Its characteristic materialism and republicanism gained ground in this later period only after having been nurtured during the first half of the century in a largely clandestine culture that circulated and published, whenever possible, a pantheistic literature that was largely anonymous. Only the 'public face' of the Enlightenment in its earliest phase was Newtonian, yet it too, like its radical counterpart, was a by-product of the English Revolution.

The Revolution of 1688–9 undid more than the Stuarts. In removing the threat of royal absolutism in the person and policies of James II it also established a constitutional monarchy, a Bill of Rights and religious toleration for Protestant dissenters. The effects of the revolution were equally profound for intellectual life. With the collapse of the church courts and with the ascendancy of Parliament, some of whose members possessed religious and political views closer to Hobbes than to the Anglican Church, a new generation of radicals believed, if only briefly, that a new day had dawned in England. Exiled or imprisoned for their radical activities during the 1680s, Major Wildman, a Leveller during the 1650s and John Hampden, a descendant of the Civil Wars radical, also returned to join in the work of reforming the new order. For a brief moment in the early 1690s it seemed as if the revolution might be pushed in a truly republican direction and concomitantly that the church's moral authority, already severely damaged by the settlement, might be displaced by new forms of religious belief, by a religion of nature without mystery and possibly even without God. As one contemporary observer described the political situation in 1693: 'There is a strong party in the Nation that endeavours to make the Crown Elective that they may sink Our Kings by Degrees to be Dukes of Venice and the Prince that yields to them will soon find them his enemies and the Monarchy Party noe good friends.'[2]

This new enthusiasm in the ranks of the ungodly was quickly perceived by pious observers. One such irascible churchman, Humphrey Prideaux, Dean of Norwich, complained that toleration 'hath almost undone us ... I find the Republicarians in these parts sedulous to promote atheisme, to which end they spread themselves in coffy houses and talk violently for it'.[3] In the face of the threat posed by the radicals as well as by the Hobbism to be found without the ranks of the political nation, the church mounted its offensive. Immediate and direct assistance came from the scientific leaders of their respective generations, Boyle and Newton. In 1691 just before his death, Boyle, the *doyen* of English science, lent his prestigious name and provided an annual stipend for a suitable podium, a church lectureship, from which the Christian religion would be proved 'against notorious Infidels, namely, Atheists, Theists, Pagans, Jews, and Mahometans ... and which would be used to answer such new Objections and Difficulties, as may be started, to which good Answers have not yet been made.'[4] Boyle left this lectureship under the administration of his close friends, John Evelyn and Thomas Tenison, and they in turn chose, among the early lecturers, the first Newtonians, Richard Bentley, John Harris, Samuel Clarke, William Whiston and William Derham.

Through their efforts, Newton's natural philosophy became the cornerstone of a liberal, tolerant and highly philosophical version of Christianity, a natural religion based upon reason, as its followers liked to say, that came dangerously close to deism but that managed, in Newton's own lifetime, never to slip over that particular ledge. Perhaps the major reason why the early Newtonians remained aggressively Christian, or more precisely Anglican, derived from the active role that Newton took in the promulgation of his natural philosophy. When Boyle was in his last illness and the terms of his will establishing the lectureship were known to his intimates, a close friend of Newton, the Scottish mathematician David Gregory, recorded in a memorandum dated 28 December 1691, a revealing glimpse at Newton's sense of what his philosophy might achieve:

> In Mr Newtons opinion a good design of a publick speech (and which may serve well at ane Act) may be to shew that the most simple laws of nature are observed in the structure of a great part of the Universe, that the philosophy ought ther to begin, and that Cosmical Qualities are as much easier as they are more Universall than particular ones, and the general contrivance simpler than that of Animals Plants etc. (48, III, 191)

From the date and contents of Gregory's memorandum it appears likely that Newton was referring to the projected Boyle lectures. His description of the 'publick speech' and the contents of 'ane Act', that is, a college speech, thesis or disputation, closely resembles the contents of lectures given in 1692 by Bentley. Newton, in effect, suggested that his discoveries in celestial physics would serve the argument from providential design better than that reliance on the 'contrivances' in animals and plants used by John Ray in his *The Wisdom of God Manifested in the Works of the Creation* (1691). In January 1692 Newton may also have suggested Richard Bentley as the first Boyle lecturer, and earlier in July 1691 Bentley had already received instructions via another liberal churchman, William Wotton, on how to understand the *Principia*. Wotton took a keen interest in the Boyle lectures, as did his patron and leader of the church party, Heneage Finch. In the autumn of 1692 Bentley developed his version of Newton's philosophy and used it as the underpinning for his social vision. Before publishing those sermons, Bentley consulted with Newton and the first of Newton's four replies began with the now famous words: 'When I wrote my treatise upon our Systeme I had an eye upon such Principles as might work with considering men for the beliefe of a Deity and nothing can rejoyce me more than to find it usefull for that purpose' (11, 156). By way of assistance to Bentley, Newton may have written an account of his system of the world; a manuscript version of that draft survives among Newton's unpublished papers.[5]

On the basis of Newton's interest in the Boyle lectures, we must conclude that this foremost English scientist was, in a social and ideological sense, a Newtonian. He condoned the social vision articulated by Bentley, Clarke and others; he lent the prestige of his achievement to what became in their hands an enlightened philosophy, in support of sober self-interest, of man's domination over nature, and of the pursuit of practical, material interests – in short, an ideology that could justify commercial capitalism and empire. This is not to say that social factors and political interest can account for Newton's scientific achievements, for his mathematical genius or his philosophical insights into the structure of physical reality. But it is to say that, with his consent, his science served a precise ideological function in the early decades of the eighteenth century. It was used to shore up the newly reconstituted monarchy and established church as the bulwarks of order and stability; only strong government, centralised and co-ordinated by court, placemen and bishops, would make the pursuit of interests possible. The cosmic order and design explicated in the *Principia* became, in the hands of Newton's early followers, a natural model for a Christian society, providentially sanctioned, reasonably tolerant of diverse religious beliefs provided they did not threaten the stability of the polity (hence the exclusion of Catholics and anti-Trinitarian heretics with their propensity, or so it was imagined, for purely rationalist explanations of supernatural phenomena), yet in need of no further political reform beyond that embodied in the Revolution Settlement.

Yet despite these powerful arguments for political and ecclesiastical oligarchy which thundered from the pulpits and the press, a weapon to which the clergy turned with increasing regularity, the radical reformers remained unconvinced. By 1700 the struggle between the Newtonians and their freethinking opponents reached critical proportions, and Newton's friends increasingly looked to him for guidance. Associates wrote to Newton's closer friends and urged, 'For God's sake keep Sir Isaac Newton at work, that we may have the chymical business, his thoughts about God'.[6] Churchmen outside this inner circle of Newtonians wrote to insiders begging them 'to hint anything briefly by Sir Isaac Newton . . . in confutation or dislike of any late Undertaking or Hypothesis in Philosophy . . . I shall have occasion to make use of it, when I'm glancing at yet Uncertainty and Precariousness of some Attempts in Philosophy' (11, 158–9).

In the face of this resurgence of 'irreligion', Newton's closest friends, Richard Bentley, Samuel Clarke and William Whiston, took to their pulpits and in their sermons and writings preached primarily to a London-based and prosperous – often mercantile – audience. They extolled the virtues of self-restraint and public-mindedness, while at the same time assuring their congregations that prosperity came to the virtuous and that divine providence permitted, even fostered, material rewards. The same providence that generates the mechanical laws at work in the universe oversees the workings of society and government, and men must see to it that they conform their political and economic actions to the stability and harmony decreed by supernatural authority. While tolerating doctrinal differences among Christians themselves, reasonable people must acknowledge a vast cosmic order, imposed by God, and attempt to imitate it in society and government. In Boyle lectures that were read and admired by thinkers as diverse as Samuel Johnson and Jean-Jacques Rousseau, Samuel Clarke exhorted:

> . . . even the greatest Enemies of all Religion, who suppose it to be nothing more than a worldly or State-policy, do yet by that very Supposition confess thus much concerning it . . . For the practice of moral Virtue does as plainly and undeniably tend to the natural Good of the World; as any Physical Effect or Mathematical Truth, is naturally consequent to the Principles on which it depends, and from which it is regularly derived . . . [Just as] that most universal principle of gravitation itself, the spring of almost all the great and regular inanimate motions in the world . . . is . . . an evident demonstration that [the world] depends every moment on some superior being for the preservation of its frame . . . and [this demonstration] does . . . give us a very noble idea of providence.[7]

Clarke argued that religion reinforced by science plays a vital role in state policy. It preaches social order and political stability; in other words, that men should not be 'extremely and unreasonably solicitous' to change their stations in life, or that they should not become, in the words of Bentley, 'men of ambitious and turbulent spirits, that [are] dissatisfied . . . with privacy and retirement'.[8] The natural rulers should be allowed their positions and stations; they, of course, must practise a moral virtue which is conducive to harmony because God's providence sees to it that it does. There can be no doubting the absolute necessity for social stability and no doubting that the moral laws ordained by God for its attainment are universal and guaranteed to work. The physical order explicated by Newton proclaims order and stability, but this order comes not from matter or nature but directly from God whose will operates in the universe either directly or through active principles. The 'world natural' stands as a model for the 'world politick' and Newton's explanation of the first provides a foundation upon which the government of the second should rest. Without that model what refutation could work against the republicans or the Hobbists, whose prescriptions rested upon observed behaviour and upon the experience of political revolution?

In the most influential and consistently republished lectures ever delivered during the eighteenth century, the Newtonians soothed and assured their congregations, yet simultaneously exhorted them.

Wealth, leisure and power in the hands of the natural rulers of society fulfilled the providential design, yet all had to be used with moderation and in the service of a liberal and tolerant Christianity. Social harmony and political stability complement an ordered universe explicated by Newton where matter is dead or lifeless, its motion controlled by the will of God; in short, as Clarke explained 'there is no such thing as what men commonly call the course of nature, or the power of nature. [It] is nothing else but the will of God producing certain effects in a continued, regular, constant, and uniform manner.'[9] The Newtonians succeeded, as had the Cambridge Platonists before them, in proclaiming the providential and interventionist God who allowed the ordered universe to operate according to discernible laws of nature.

In the hands of Newton's friends and followers, science had become a powerful weapon in the support of Christian natural religion, and it was therefore in alliance with the interests and needs of the Anglican Church, as those interests were perceived by the moderate ecclesiastical establishment that came to prominence after 1688–9. Bishops and archbishops such as John Tillotson, Thomas Tenison, William Lloyd, Simon Patrick and William Wake, lay leaders like Heneage Finch and his brother Daniel, and church intellectuals such as Pepys, Evelyn and Newton, approved the spirit, if not the content, of the Boyle lectures and rewarded the young Newtonians.

Once we perceive the social and political meaning of Newtonian science and natural religion, a meaning rooted in the experience of the first of the great modern revolutions and in the rejection of republican and democratic forms of government, we can see why European radicals from the English Commonwealthmen of the 1690s through their Continental followers down to, in an attenuated sense, Blake and Coleridge, rejected the Newtonian understanding of nature. They turned instead to pantheistic explanations of man and nature because they were searching for a new and, from their perspective, a more humane social order, and for a truly representative system of constitutional government. In historical and ideological terms, Blake had understandable reasons for seeing Newton as one powerful symbol of a social and cosmic order from which he was alienated, a system 'with cogs tyrannic'. For Blake, with his unique vision, Newtonians were the true 'materialists' in that they subjected people to the rule of an impersonal and mechanised nature divorced from the human order.[10]

As we have gained greater perspective on the strengths and weaknesses of Western liberal thought, we have gradually readjusted our understanding of the version of Enlightenment derived from the Newtonian synthesis. Some years ago one of the great interpreters of that synthesis, Alexandre Koyré, hinted at the social meaning of the Newtonian Enlightenment when he commented in passing on

'The Significance of the Newtonian Synthesis':

> . . . so strong was the belief in 'nature', so overwhelming the prestige of the
> Newtonian (or pseudo-Newtonian) pattern of order arising automatically
> from interaction of isolated and self-contained atoms, that nobody dared to
> doubt that order and harmony would in some way be produced by human
> atoms acting according to their nature, whatever this might be – instinct for
> play and pleasure (Diderot) or pursuit of selfish gain (A. Smith). Thus
> return to nature could mean free passion as well as free competition.
> Needless to say, it was the last interpretation that prevailed.[11]

What Koyré may not have perceived was that free competition and not
free love came to prevail in modern, capitalist society, in part because
the early Newtonians consciously argued for 'sober' self-interest in a
cosmically ordered market society, and pitted the natural philosophy
and science of Newton against contemporary philosophies of freedom,
sexual or otherwise. Diderot got his materialistic and libertine ideas
about nature and passion not from the Newtonian tradition, as some
historians have argued, but partly from the freethinking tradition that
had long remained underground but which first surfaced most dramatically in England and the Netherlands during the last decades of the
seventeenth and the first decades of the eighteenth century (16,
81–95).

It now seems plausible to argue that the Newtonian legacy upon
which some Enlightenment thinkers unquestionably did build, not
least of them Voltaire and d'Alembert, did not nurture, and indeed
may even have been intended to inhibit, the libertine and pantheistic
modes of Enlightenment. The simplistic assumption that at every turn
the Newtonian natural philosophy fostered the intellectual revolution
which is at the foundation of so much of modern thought and belief
requires serious evaluation and modification. The ideological dimension of Newtonianism, once understood, forces that re-evaluation.
This process must also be accompanied by an historical search for the
identity, as well as for the scientific, religious and political values, of
the earliest organised proponents of materialism and republicanism on
both sides of the Channel. Once the extent of that movement is
rediscovered along with its debt to the English Revolution then the
Newtonian version of the Enlightenment looks increasingly like a vast
holding operation against a far more dangerous rendering of Enlightenment ideals. Of course, proponents of both versions wrote for a
sophisticated and literate audience, largely urban-based, and enjoying
one of the most stable and open forms of government available to any
contemporary European.

By the 1720s, the Newtonian Enlightenment was firmly established
within the intellectual circles of the British ruling élite, much to the

amazement of the young and impressionable Voltaire. In 1726 he encountered that Whig oligarchy – Disraeli called them a Venetian oligarchy – whom J. H. Plumb has described so aptly: '. . . certain men of property, particularly those of high social standing either aristocrats or linked with aristocracy, whose tap root was in land but whose side roots reached out to commerce, industry and finance' (46, 69). Their concept of government rested upon the notion of a strong court buttressed by a standing army and by 'placemen' – servants of the crown who did its bidding in Parliament, in county elections, at the offices of customs and excise, at any place where patronage and influence might bring services or gain.

Of course, financing this vast machinery of bureaucratised government required credit and taxes, and gradually the former took on increasing importance as oligarchs, as well as thousands of businessmen, in London and the counties invested in the Bank of England and the National Debt.[12] By the 1720s, in the Britain ruled by Walpole and his band of loyal Hanoverians, a symbiotic relationship had developed between capitalism and government financing, between court and placemen, between ministerial independence from Parliament and the existence of a standing army. In the words of J. G. A. Pocock, 'with the aid of the invested capital, the state was able to maintain larger and more permament armies and bureaucracies – incidentally increasing the resources at the disposal of political patronage – and as long as its affairs visibly prospered, it was able to attract further investments and conduct larger and longer wars' (38, 425). For the Whig oligarchs and their friends it was truly a very comfortable world.

By the 1690s, however, a visible and vocal opposition existed to criticise the power and assumptions upon which those comforts were to rest. We can identify two main forms of political opposition and with them concomitant philosophical and religious beliefs. The first, which we shall discuss here only briefly as it is not the focus of this book, can be described as Tory, piously Anglican, strongly supportive of parliamentary institutions yet violently anti-radical. This Tory opposition is often hard to distinguish from 'country' opposition in the period after 1714 and the brief collapse of the Tory Party as an organised force – yet adherents were numerous and widespread and may even have constituted, at certain elections from 1714 to 1760, the majority of the eligible electorate. The adherence of this Tory sensibility to the welfare of the church separated it most significantly from that second form of opposition to court Whiggery, the freethinking and radical Whigs. At moments attempts were even made to forge alliances between the Tory Party and that radical and disaffected fringe – Harley may have tried such a courtship late in the 1690s and during the reign of Anne.[13] But luckily for court and oligarchy, political principles, and we would add religious convictions, outweighed the exigencies of the moment.

By the 1740s, Tory disaffection led its intellectually gifted camp to question the most basic tenets of liberal Anglicanism. Tory thinkers became increasingly convinced that the Newtonians, and possibly even Newton himself – although few, if any, of his contemporaries outside his circle knew what we now know about his ideological involvements – had, by their avowal of the new mechanical philosophy as the foundation of natural religion, effectively undermined all religion. Ironically they believed that the Newtonians had opened the door to the radicals, to the atheists, deists and spinozists (50, 122). This anti-Newtonian thrust within Tory Anglican thought received its most elaborate explication in the voluminous writings of John Hutchinson (1674–1737) and his many followers (51). Although primarily given to natural philosophical explanations of the universe, this anti-Newtonian movement also displayed strongly mystical and spiritualising tendencies. It sought to keep aspects of Newtonian science while finding in nature proof for doctrines as diverse as the fall of man and the Trinity.

Throughout the eighteenth century, the anti-Newtonianism of the devout may have been much more widespread than has as yet been imagined. Methodist preachers could be found who 'bitterly inveighed against Newton as an ignorant pretender who had presumed to set up his own ridiculous chimeras in opposition to the sacred philosophy of the Pentateuch'.[14] If any thread united such disparate religious positions as those of the Hutchinsonians and the 'enthusiastic' Methodists it was in fact their opposition to establishment culture and its liberal and Newtonian spokesmen.

The Tory or 'country' opposition, in particular its Christian and God-fearing element, of whatever sectarian persuasion, were convinced that the radicals were the quintessential symbol of a corrupt age. Ironically, given what we know about the polemics between the Newtonian Enlightenment and the radicals, Tory critics of both believed that the radicals were really the wayward children of their science-deceived elders – an historical misinterpretation that has made its way into the school books. True, the radicals were decisively in favour of the new science, while by mid-century many Christian thinkers had actually drawn away from it, convinced that the Newtonians had spawned an age of irreligion and libertinism. But given what we now know about the dialectics of the English Revolution, it no longer makes sense to accept that Tory interpretation of the role of Newtonian science in eighteenth-century thought. The Newtonian Enlightenment did not spawn a radical foil; if anything, the relationship could be said to have been reversed.

Without dwelling unduly on the anti-Newtonian, country sensibility

a few examples should suffice to contrast its adherents with the Newtonian leadership that by the 1720s dominated British cultural life at
court and in the fashionable London pulpits. George Cheyne
(1671–1743), for example, was one of the finest doctors of his age who
became an early convert to the Newtonian natural philosophy and who
wrote a long treatise (*The Philosophical Principles of Religion*, 1705,
1715) in support of natural religion based upon Newtonian principles.
Indeed, Cheyne was so convinced of the argument that he believed
divine providence to have designed the waters at Bath as the means by
which the English might cope with their weather and diet.[15] Apparently Cheyne knew whereof he spoke; he had been a 'Free-liver' and
suffered from extreme obesity for many years. He then became a
pioneer for clean living, careful diet, and an expert on gout.

By the 1730s, Cheyne was convinced that the body politic was
severely ailing and he traced its disease to 'spurious Freethinkers,
active Latitudinarians, and Apostolic Infidels'.[16] As Cheyne grew
increasingly disaffected from the ruling Whig oligarchy he spoke more
and more bitterly about liberal divines and freethinkers, and turned
towards Methodism.[17] At precisely the period of his political disaffection, Cheyne also grew sceptical of the new science with its emphasis
upon induction and calculation. In his search for physical well-being in
man and government, Cheyne abandoned the Newtonian synthesis
and opted for an increasingly spiritualised understanding of nature and
for a contemplative, almost mystical and millenarian version of Christianity.[18] In the face of the corruption he universally perceived, Cheyne,
the young Newtonian, became the disaffected and anti-establishment
Methodist. Faith in science during the eighteenth century depended
upon many variables, not least of which were its ideological uses.

The rule of the liberal and Newtonian hierarchy in the church
inflamed the clerical (as well as lay) opposition to Whig rule. Unlike
the latitudinarians, few, if any, of the opposition clergy ever emerged
out of the political and ecclesiastical wilderness in order to become
effective spokesmen against the prevailing order. After 1688–9 the
Newtonian and Low Church clergy had taken over leadership of the
church and by the 1720s and 1730s Walpole was said to have had his
pope in Edmund Gibson, Bishop of London, while the liberal Newtonian, Benjamin Hoadly, who had learned his science from Samuel
Clarke, incited the Tory opposition by arguing for the subordination of
church to state. Hoadly was rewarded with a bishopric for his efforts in
support of the Whig interpretation of ecclesiastical government. On
the other hand, alienated Tory and anti-Newtonian churchmen such as
the Hutchinsonian, George Horne (1730–92), generally kept their
opinions to themselves. Only in 1790 did he finally obtain high
ecclesiastical office as Bishop of Norwich; in the interim he confined

his opinions on current events and the state of the church to his private diary.

Horne's diary is therefore a valuable guide to his conscience, and it reveals that he believed that 'Arianism and Deism . . . have darkened the sun'. In a moment of self-pity he bitterly recorded 'these [are] poor gentlemen the Hutchinsonians because they'll never get any preferment. The bishops . . . all entered into a league never to promote them . . . [yet] we are not of the numbers of them who preach Christianity for gain or take orders because we are likely to get more by that than by anything else.'[19] Horne was convinced that the Whigs and liberal churchmen had invented pernicious political and religious principles, 'religion of nature [is] a chimera', while Whig principles almost invariably lead to republicanism.[20] In Horne's assessment, the radicals were everywhere; he observed 'a presbyterian who said that man was not born for serving kings – so chopping his neck with his hand'.[21] Horne knew 'ranters' in his own time (a radical sect of the 1650s) who true to their naturalistic doctrines make everything god, which 'is the dregs of the old corrupt heathen philosophy'.[22] If Horne's observations were true to a larger reality, perhaps we can better understand why the guardians of the Whig constitution enforced some of the most repressive legislation against disruptive elements ever to be devised in the history of English criminal law (49).

Despite this catalogue of woes induced by the spectre of popular radicalism, Horne reserved enough animosity to list tersely the many failings of John Tillotson, Archbishop of Canterbury after the Revolution (1691–5), who more than any other archbishop in his century had shifted the church's thinking towards religious toleration, constitutional monarchy and the new science. Well after 1750, Horne condemns Tillotson as if he were alive and well and accuses: he 'denies the divinity of Christ . . . denies the eternity of hell torments . . . speaks of the Old Testament as not good nor relating to Christ . . . makes Christianity good for nothing but to keep societies in order the better that there should be no Christ than that it should disturb societies'.[23] Horne had discerned, as had many of his alienated lay and clerical contemporaries, the social (but not necessarily the spiritual) message that lay at the heart of Newtonian natural religion. That its spokesmen were perceived as putting their blessings on a corrupt and godless society merely confirmed opposition attempts to find alternative forms of science and Christian worship.

Just as Anglican Tories, like the Hutchinsonians, looked to non-mechanical systems of nature upon which they could rest their understanding of what a Christian society should be like, so too did the radicals espouse alternative, but purely naturalistic, explanations upon which they rested their opposition politics. Yet because the radicals basically approved of the Revolution of 1688–9 and its constitutional settlement, although always believing that it had not gone far enough in the direction of parliamentary rule, their relationship to the ruling Whig oligarchy was in fact far more complex than that of the alienated Tory opposition. From the 1690s onwards, the Tories pressed the charge that the Whig Party was infested with irreligion, with libertines, atheists and deists, and the charge was not without merit. When we follow the pamphleteering or political careers of leading radicals such as Anthony Collins, John Toland, Barnham Goode, Joseph Morgan, and their friends (see p. 161–2), or even of radicals on the Continent, we find at various moments close contacts with English ministerial government or with Dutch 'Whigs' (as they called themselves) such as William and Charles Bentinck. The Radical Enlightenment first achieved cultural and social cohesion in the 1690s around the fringes of the Whig Party and the association was never entirely shaken. The radical Whigs were vitally instrumental in spreading a republican version of the 'Whig' revolution on to the Continent. Heirs to a revolution they felt had not gone far enough, they were not only intensely ideological but also political men; but they were also occasionally 'down and out'. In consequence of these sometimes conflicting needs and interests they took employment and favours from various Whig ministers. If that employment appears to tarnish their idealism then it simultaneously renders them into flesh and blood.

This relationship between the Radical Enlightenment and Whig government in England, and between the radicals of the Enlightenment and the northern Protestant alliance against France, must be stressed. Often, as official pamphleteers, spies, agents and messengers, the radicals were in fact advancing their own views as well as forging vital links in the publishing enterprise that lay at the heart of the Enlightenment and that sought to undermine both church and state in France. We can see this process at work in John Toland's missions to the Continent during the reign of Anne, and in Rousset de Missy's activities as a Freemason and agent for the Austrian government during the 1740s and 1750s (see pp. 231–2). Both were serving masters who used them as pawns in a larger political and diplomatic game, yet both imagined, I am sure, that their republican and pantheistic ideals put them one step ahead of their employers' intentions. A similar ambiguity governed the radicals' use of the new science. They were simultaneously among the first journalists to bring Newtonian science into the French-speaking world; indeed Newton sought out the services of the literary journal published by the associates of Toland and Collins in the Netherlands.[24] At the same time as they were propagating Newton's discoveries they were circulating one of the most pantheistic and heretical manuscripts ever devised during the eighteenth century (see pp. 217–20). Newtonian science spread on to the Continent in tandem with Whig interests, but the agents in that process used both to serve causes very different from, and in some cases antithetical to, the programme advanced by Newtonian church-men and court Whigs.

In Hanoverian England, the government remained firmly in control of church and state but ever vigilant against all forms of overt opposi-tion. Systematic efforts were made by various governments from the 1690s until well into the 1740s to guard against the radical flank and to spy upon, and if necessary to prosecute, the promoters of materialism, republicanism and the religion of nature. Radical Whigs had their uses provided they did nothing to antagonise the church or to promote sedition. When they did, they received little mercy from the guardians of social religion and political stability.

In the intellectual and political world that Voltaire came to know, the Newtonians were well entrenched at court, at the Royal Society and in various cultural movements, not least of which was Free-masonry. In the last years of Newton's life (d. 1727) the leading clerical Newtonians of the earlier period, Richard Bentley, Samuel Clarke and William Whiston, became less prominent. New names appear as close associates of Newton and as leaders in the Royal Society. In this new generation Henry Pemberton (1694–1771), Jean Theophile Desaguliers (1683–1744), Martin Folkes (1690–1754), Brook Taylor (1685–1731) and Sir Hans Sloane (1660–1753) stand among the scientifically gifted and politically active. Pemberton was educated in Leiden under the great physician and chemist, Boerhaave, from whom he probably learned his Newtonianism. His willingness to defend that system against the Continental followers of Leibniz brought him to Newton's attention and by 1725 he was supervising the production of the third edition of the *Principia* (1726). Although various London Freemasons were involved in its actual production, and indeed in the general dissemination of Newtonian science, Pemberton, unlike Desaguliers, Folkes and Taylor, does not appear to have been a Mason.[25]

The writings of Pemberton and his Newtonian colleagues repeated themes made famous by the great Boyle lecturers. Yet this next gener-ation of Newtonians toned down the polemics aimed at freethinkers which had been so characteristic of the earlier period. The accomplish-ment of the Hanoverian Succession in 1714 had engendered a mod-icum of political complacency. Dedicating his exposition of Newton's philosophy to Walpole whose government embodied reason as it did his 'masculine perspecuity and strength of argument', Pemberton claimed that Newton had read and approved the greater part of this treatise.[26]

Pemberton's *A View of Sir Isaac Newton's Philosophy* (1728) is a much more straightforward and succinct account of Newton's philosophy of nature, his definitions of matter, space, time, the vacuum, and the law of universal gravitation, than that found in the Boyle lectures. Christian apologetics have been de-emphasised in favour of a general, but constant, emphasis on the power of the deity, on a straightforward explanation of Newtonian physics. Whenever Pemberton enters into polemics, it is against the materialists: those who assert that gravity is essential to matter (as did Toland and his friends); those who would assert the eternality of the world; those who deny the supremacy of God in every aspect of creation.[27] In Walpole's era, a fashionable Newtonian and providentialist 'deism' replaced the doctrinal exactness of the early Newtonians. Their natural religion became an ethical system (seldom dwelt upon at any length) which was buttressed by Newtonian explanations of the universe. There is no evidence to indicate that Bentley, Clarke or Newton disapproved of this fashionable extrapolation. Nor should they have. This natural religion, so broad as to accommodate Protestants and even 'deists' of whatever doctrinal persuasion, at every turn asserted God's providential, if somewhat impersonal, relationship to his creation. It was a tested bulwark against materialism in philosophy as well as against political radicalism. By 1730, most observers declared that church and monarchy rested more securely than they had in previous decades; or rather that the seeds of destruction lay in internal corruption and not in the schemes of the radicals.

By far the most famous transmitter of the Newtonian Enlightenment to a European audience was the great French *philosophe*, Voltaire (53, 59–60). His *Lettres philosophiques* (1733), an immensely popular paean of praise to English government, mores and science, linked the achievements of Newton to a milieu of intellectual liberty such as only existed in England. Through Voltaire's writings, among others the Newtonian synthesis we have just described captured the mainstream of Enlightenment thought and became a vital tradition from which other philosophes, like Diderot, only dissented after careful thought and extensive reading in the largely clandestine literature of materialism. Although always the darling of Continental enlightened circles, whether deist or materialist, because of his caustic wit and bitter satire against churches and censors, Voltaire, for most of his life from the perspective of the Radical Enlightenment, must be classified as a moderate, as a Newtonian and a monarchist (54).

Voltaire's greatest achievement in relation to the Newtonian tradition was to wrest it from its specifically English moorings and to offer English science and society as a universal model for enlightenment. From his cosmopolitan stance as an alienated French writer bitterly hostile to the privileges of a moribund aristocracy and familiar with the Dutch republic, but most especially with London society where he lived for three years, Voltaire extracted from Clarke and Pemberton, as well as from personal conversations with Bolingbroke, a unique understanding of the Newtonian synthesis (55). In his hands Christian doctrines disappear entirely as a necessary corollary of explanations of physical phenomena; Newtonian metaphysics (although Voltaire generally eschewed the word) become sufficient. As we have come to expect, with Voltaire's Newtonian vision was integrated with certain basic religious and political assumptions. Voltaire insisted upon the existence of God, but in his hands that concept becomes largely impersonal, its function could be described as simply social. The deity maintains order. After a youthful flirtation with republicanism, and one that may well be directly related to his acquaintance with radical circles in the Netherlands,[28] Voltaire won universal acclaim in Walpole's London as a poetic and enlightened promoter of strong monarchy and enlightened but court-centred government. Voltaire was probably the first non-Christian of the Newtonian Enlightenment (although his intellectual mentor, Bolingbroke, would have been a candidate for that dubious public honour had he only subscribed to the ideology of court Whiggery and been frank about his deism). He shared the radicals' contempt for established churches with power independent of the state, yet steadfastly refused to subscribe to any of the intellectual or political alternatives proposed in the radical literature. Like so many of the major *philosophes* – among whom Voltaire stands unsurpassed in importance – he advocated monarchy in contrast to what he assessed as an impractical republicanism, and he insisted upon a Newtonian explanation of the universe which in later years he directly posited, as had the Boyle lecturers, against the panteists and materialists (58).

As a young man in Paris, Voltaire had suffered under the capricious power of aristocracy and learned to distrust its privileges and institutions. Yet he also frequented libertine and freethinking circles there, and he was already well on the way to becoming a *philosophe* before his extended travels to the Netherlands and England (59, 123–38, 511). From his earliest thoughtful years, he knew the literature of naturalism and materialism – as well as its circulators – but ultimately he resisted the force of its arguments. When he made his way north in 1722, stopping in Brussels briefly, he was immediately assimilated into enlightened circles there, and possibly through the followers of Eugène of Savoy (among them the exiled French poet, Jean-Baptiste Rousseau), who adorned intellectual circles in that now Austrian-administered city, Voltaire was put in touch with republican publishers in The Hague. He carried with him a manuscript copy of his epic poem on the life of Henry IV, *La Ligue*, and he was in search of a publisher for a work that, in praising religious toleration, could find neither favour in Gallican circles nor a publisher in Paris.

Perhaps inevitably, given what we now know about the early years of the French-speaking Enlightenment in northern Europe, Voltaire was put in touch with publishers at the heart of the Radical Enlightenment, the close associates of Collins and Toland. Among the few names we can associate with Voltaire's visit to The Hague in 1722 are Charles Levier, Prosper Marchand and Bernard Picart. Levier tried to arrange a subscription edition for *La Ligue*, or *La Henriade*, to use its eventual and more famous title; Marchand helped on the financial side, and Picart was asked by Voltaire to do the engravings for the volume.[29] The venture fell through in part because of the difficulty in securing a Parisian publisher. As we shall see in subsequent chapters, Marchand, Picart and Levier belonged to a secret and Masonic society, brought the infamous *Traité des trois imposteurs* into circulation, and all were freethinkers, if not pantheists. What else, we might well ask, did Voltaire get from them besides a commitment to publish his poem? Unfortunately there are few records from this early period of Voltaire's Continental travels, but one curious piece of evidence is worth assessing. An anonymous poem dated 1726 and deposited in the Bibliothèque Nationale in Paris maliciously accuses Voltaire of having attended services at a synagogue during his stay in the Netherlands. It claims that he played at a 'culte secret' where rabbis practised a 'pantomime indiscret' (57, 29–31). A most improbable legend has it that Voltaire attended services at the Amsterdam synagogue in 1722, but no other evidence exists for Voltaire, or any other non-Jew for that matter, having been allowed to attend a Jewish service at that time, whether reverently, or irreverently, as one biographer has rashly claimed.[30] Could it be that Voltaire attended a ritualistic meeting of the 'Knights of Jubilation' as Marchand, Picart and Levier called their secret society? It is at least plausible that contemporaries knew of the existence of such secret groups with their own private rituals and, in turn, easily and maliciously confused them with Jewish groups or sects. We shall probably never know if Voltaire attended a meeting of this clandestine circle. Certainly he stayed on fairly close terms with Marchand, although the latter along with some of his friends, grew over the years, as did so many 'little men' of the Enlightenment, to regard the mature Voltaire as 'impudent'.[31] Likewise Marchand, the Protestant refugee, took a dim view of Voltaire, the historian's, glorification of French monarchy.

Almost certainly, Voltaire got his first taste of republicanism, both theoretical and practical, from this early trip to the Netherlands (57). Indeed the course of Enlightenment thought might have been very different had Voltaire not ventured forth from The Hague, which he seems to have enjoyed, and four years later made his way to Hanoverian London. In 1726, he was graciously received by Walpole's government, to which he was introduced through the highest diplomatic channels, and there he conversed with the leading Newtonians and became a protégé of the regime (60). His epic, La Henriade (London, 1728), dedicated to George I, fitted precisely with the reigning political ideology of court and ministerial government, and with the king's new political strategy of trying to render Anglo-French relations cordial and of making the French pro-Hanoverian and anti-Jacobite. In fact Voltaire went through Walpole's most trusted government ministers at the secretaries of state office in an effort to obtain the support of George I for a subscription edition of La Henriade. His close relations with these lofty councils of government has led some authors to speculate whether Voltaire before his arrival may have acted at some point in its pay, possibly as a spy. The subscription list for La Henriade did in the end, however, cut across differences in political philosophy, as did Voltaire's many personal links with opposition and anti-Walpole oligarchs and writers.[32]

The political philosophy that Voltaire would hold throughout most of his life was basically embodied in this first major poem (58). Written before his arrival, but its text altered in one or two places to suit the imagined prejudices of its English audience, the poem expresses ideals that Voltaire's experience of English political life only seemed to confirm. The text is a paean to tolerant and enlightened monarchy, to the strong, even absolute king, such as was Henry IV (1598–1610) of France, whose path, Voltaire claims, was guided at every point by divine providence. He equates civil disorder with magic and religious fanaticism and in the poem he renders the assassin of Henry IV into a magician.[33] Likewise, his plea for order in society and government relies upon the metaphor of the ordered universe:

> Amid a Blaze of pure and lasting Fire,
> The Highest fix'd before the Birth of Time
> His starry Throne, Stability the Base.
> Beneath his Feet is Heav'n; the Aethereal Orbs
> Declare him to the wond'ring Universe,
> By radiant Circles regularly whirl'd
> Puissance, Love and Knowledge infinite
> United and divided from his Essence.[34]

Voltaire, the poet, yearned for what Voltaire, the natural philosopher, found in the Newtonian understanding of the universe. As we shall see, he readily embraced the social metaphor of order and stability easily extracted from the new science. And Voltaire, the poet, condemned the disorder he equated with the radicals of the English Revolution ('ces peuples de Sectaires,/Trembleurs, Independants, Puritans, Unitaires'); he bemoaned Charles I's fate. That particular passage was especially added for the English publication of his French text, but in his zeal to please, Voltaire got the politics a little wrong. His English translator removed the Puritans 'whose character [the author] seems not to be acquainted with, there being as little Phanaticism in Puritanism, as in primitive Christianity'.[35] In Hanoverian England, the moderate Dissenters had long since been ideologically, but not legally, countenanced.

Once in England, Voltaire embraced Newton's system of the world and natural philosophy like a religious convert embraces a new faith. Indeed, throughout his life that cosmic system possessed an almost religious intensity; it lay at the foundation of Voltaire's understanding of the world (61, 119-84). During his three-year stay, Voltaire conversed with Samuel Clarke, among other Newtonians, carefully read his Boyle lectures aimed against Spinoza, Hobbes and Toland, and then violently repudiated the system of Descartes. His reasons for doing so, which he committed to paper a few years after his departure from England, were precisely those of the Newtonians: Descartes's science is not only wrong, but his natural philosophy leads directly to materialism and atheism. One might have expected a French anti-cleric like Voltaire to repudiate Cartesianism because of the use to which Catholic polemicists like Malebranche had put it. Certainly that element is present in his rejection, but when Voltaire attacks Descartes's system it is precisely for its materialistic tendencies: 'With regard to the pretended infinity of matter, that idea hath as little foundation as the vortices . . . But what are we to understand by an infinite matter? For the term *Indefinite*, used by Descartes, either must be explained by this, or it signifies nothing at all. Do they mean, that Matter is essentially infinite in its own Nature? If so then Matter is God.'[36] Elsewhere, Voltaire makes it clear that all materialism, whether that of Descartes or of Toland, denies human freedom, and his understanding of the meaning of freedom comes directly from Samuel Clarke.[37] In the crucial area of matter theory and its social implications, Voltaire stands as heir to the Anglican Newtonians.

Voltaire's deism rested on the assumption that 'God the General in the Universe gives different Orders to different Bodies'.[38] Without those orders there can be no order. Many decades after his conversion to Newtonianism, Voltaire watched with alarm the spread of pantheistic and materialistic doctrines. The salon of the Baron d'Holbach, in conjunction with the publishing enterprise of Marc-Michel Rey in Amsterdam, poured forth a collection of anonymous and largely materialist tracts from the earlier, clandestine period of the Radical Enlightenment. The most notorious and famous tract from the collection was, of course, the *Traité des trois imposteurs* (1768), originally brought into circulation by the Knights of Jubilation. In a short poem written in 1769, Voltaire, still loyal to the philosophy of his youth, attacked its anonymous author as an 'insipid writer . . . as a poor enemy of the supreme essence'. God's system is necessary 'it is the sacred bond of society . . . if God did not exist, he would have to be invented'. Voltaire warns that kings can only be brought to fear God, and that the oppressed can look to heaven for revenge.[39] Voltaire rightly perceived that the anonymous author, or authors, of the tract sought to tear down not only Christian metaphysics but also the very foundations of monarchical authority. Voltaire acknowledges that he, too, has seen great injustice and fanaticism even in his time, but the only antidote he will countenance is toleration, the rule of law and justice administered by strong kings and sanctioned by the God of order, by Newton's God.

The Newtonian Enlightenment, as first articulated by Newton's followers and especially as translated by Voltaire, offered one powerful application of scientific ideas. By the 1730s, Newton's system, and the sanction that it gave to British constitutionalism, had many worshippers. For Voltaire, faith was a matter both private and polemical, but it was not in his nature to give ritualistic expression to his beliefs. Only late in his life did he allow himself to worship in a new temple, to be initiated into a Masonic lodge. But many of his early friends and associates in both England and the Netherlands were members of that new fraternity, which in turn spread rapidly throughout eighteenth-century Europe.

Freemasonry was one of the most extraordinary phenomena of that 'rationalist' age, and its rise is directly linked to the triumph of a new scientific culture, to the Newtonian version of enlightenment. Yet as we have seen, this new science could be given many interpretations, some of them directly antithetical to the Christian metaphysics of Boyle and Newton. Likewise, the English Revolution left a complex legacy, and the interpretation of government offered by its Whig victors was easily challenged by its republican reformers. Predictably, then, both English science and the English Revolution, despite the interpretations offered by their apparent heirs, are central to the history of the Radical Enlightenment and so, too, is Freemasonry. Within that institution the radicals found the makings of a new religion, just as the Newtonians used it to give expression to their new faith in the wondrous powers of the Grand Architect.

Notes: Chapter 3

1   For d'Alembert see Thomas L. Hankins, *Jean d'Alembert. Science and the Enlight-*

enment (Oxford: Clarendon Press, 1970), pp. 3–6; esp. 102–3. Cf. John N. Pappas, *Voltaire and D'Alembert* (Bloomington, Ind.: Indiana University Press, 1962), pp. 121–3.

2 ULC, MS. Sel.3.238, no. 359. Reference supplied by Mark Goldie.

3 *Letters of Humphrey Prideaux . . . to John Ellis, Sometime Under-Secretary of State, 1674–1722* (London, 1875), pp. 154, 162.

4 Eustace Budgell, *Memoirs of the Lives and Characters of the Illustrious Family of the Boyles* (London, 1737), appendix, p. 25.

5 I. B. Cohen, 'Isaac Newton's *Principia*, the Scriptures and the Divine Providence', in S. Morgenbesser, P. Suppes and M. White (eds), *Philosophy, Science and Method. Essays in Honor of Ernest Nagel* (New York: St Martin's Press, 1969), pp. 523–48.

6 Archibald Pitcairne to David Gregory, 25 February 1706; UL, Edinburgh, Gregory MSS Dc.1.62, f. 97. Pitcairne also believed ultimately that 'metaphysics can never prove a deity . . .'

7 *A Discourse Concerning the Unchangeable Obligations of Natural Religion and the Truth and Certainty of the Christian Religion* (London, 1706), pp. 152–3.

8 A. Dyce (ed.), *The Works of Richard Bentley* (London, 1838), vol. 3, p. 24.

9 *A Discourse . . .* in Richard Watson (ed.), *A Collection of Theological Tracts* (London, 1785), vol. 4, p. 246; a more accessible edition.

10 Kathleen Raine, *Berkeley, Blake and the New Age* (Ipswich, Suffolk. Golgonooza Press, 1976), pp. 6–7; cf. Thomas McFarland, *Coleridge and the Pantheist Tradition* (Oxford: Clarendon Press, 1969), pp. 107, 266–7.

11 Alexander Koyré, *Newtonian Studies* (Chicago, Ill.: University of Chicago Press, 1965), p. 22.

12 See P. G. M. Dickson, *The Financial Revolution in England: A Study in the Development of Public Credit, 1688–1756* (London: Macmillan, 1967).

13 Angus McInnes, *Robert Harley, Puritan Politician* (London: Gollancz, 1970), pp. 40, 83–4.

14 Bernard Semmel, *The Methodist Revolution* (New York: Basic Books, 1973), p. 20.

15 See George Cheyne, *An Essay on the Gout, With an Account of the Nature and Qualities of the Bath Waters* (London, 1720).

16 George Cheyne, *Dr Cheyne's Account of Himself and of His Writings: Faithfully Extracted from His Various Works* (London, 1743), p. 21.

17 *An Essay on Regimen . . . Serving to Illustrate the Principles and Theory of Philosophical Medicin, and Point Out some of Its Moral Consequences* (London, 1740), pp. xiv–xv; Charles F. Mullett (ed.), *The Letters of Dr. George Cheyne to the Countess of Huntingdon* (San Marino, Cal.: Huntington Library, 1940), *passim*.

18 *An Essay on Regimen*, pp. viii, pp. 206–8, 227–36.

19 'Commonplace Book 1 of George Horne, Bishop of Norwich'. Owned by Sir Robert Arundel, but now in the possession of the ULC, MS. ADD. 8134, f. 2. Made available by the kindness of Christopher Wilde. Probably written in the 1750s. For further evidence of tension between Hutchinsonians and Newtonians see Walter Wilson, *History and Antiquities of Dissenting Churches and Meeting Houses in London . . .* (London, 1808), vol. 2, p. 90.

20 'Commonplace Book', ff. 29, 42–3.

21 ibid., f. 70.

22 ibid., f. 100.

23 ibid., f. 111.

24 E. F. MacPike (ed.), *Correspondence and Papers of Edmond Halley* (Oxford: Oxford University Press, 1932), p. 128.

25 J. R. Clarke, 'The Royal Society and early Grand Lodge Freemasonry', *AQC*, vol. 80 (1967), pp. 110–19. Of the 200 known Masons (and the lists are by no means complete) based in London in the 1720s, one out of four were FRS.

26 *A View of Sir Isaac Newton's Philosophy* (London, 1728), dedication. The subscription list is heavily Whiggish.

27 *A View*, pp. 22, 180–1, 406–7.

28 G. Desnoiresterres, *Voltaire et la société française* (Paris: Didier et Cie, 1867), vol. 1, pp. 252–5, but without the information we now possess. For Voltaire's expression of republican sentiments, T. Besterman (ed.), *Voltaire's Correspondence* (Geneva: Institut et Musée Voltaire, 1953), vol. 2, no. 294, 26 October 1726; also very useful on this early period, H. T. Mason, *Pierre Bayle and Voltaire* (Oxford: Oxford University Press, 1963), pp. 4–6.

29 Besterman (ed.) *Voltaire's Correspondence*, vol. 1, pp. 119, 123.

30 O. R. Taylor, 'Voltaire. *La Henriade*. Édition critique avec une introduction et des notes', *Studies on Voltaire and the Eighteenth Century*, vol. 38 (1965), pp. 30–1, 38–47.

31 See Besterman (ed.) *Voltaire's Correspondence*, vol. 5, no. 1,170 on Marchand keeping letters for Voltaire. Marchand and d'Argens were in frequent communication, Cf. J. Fransen, 'Correspondance entre le Marquis d'Argens et Prosper Marchand', in *Mélanges de philologie offerts à Jean-Jacques Salverda de Grave* (Groningen: Wolters, 1933).

32 Francis Crowley, 'Voltaire a spy for Walpole?', *French Studies*, vol. 18 (1964), pp. 356–9; René Pomeau, 'Voltaire en Angleterre: Les enseignements d'une liste de souscription', *Annales publieés par la Faculté des Lettres de Toulouse, Littératures*, vol. 3 (January 1955), pp. 67–76; cf. Ragnhild Hatton, *George I. Elector and King* (Cambridge, Mass.: Harvard University Press, 1978), p. 291, technically Voltaire dedicated it to the queen. On Marchand's later antagonism toward Voltaire, see C. Berkvens-Stevelinck, 'La tolérance et l'héritage de P. Bayle en Hollande dans la première moitié du xviiie siècle', *Lias*, vol. 5 (1978), pp. 266–9.

33 Voltaire, *Henriade. An Epick Poem. In Ten Cantos. Translated from the French into English Blank Verse* (London, 1732), pp. 12–13, 108–9.

34 ibid., p. 227

35 *La Henriade de Mr De Voltaire* (London, 1728), p. 124. The English translation (1732), pp. 100–1, altered the text. The pirated edition, *La Ligue ou Henry Le Grand. Poème épique* (Geneva: chez Jean Mokpop, 1723), does not have this passage. Cf. Mr de Voltaire, *An Essay upon the Civil Wars of France, Extracted from Curious Manuscripts* (London, 1727), for praise of Milton, p. 108; for praise of government, pp. 122–3.

36 *The Elements of Sir Isaac Newton's Philosophy*, trans. John Hanna (London, 1738), pp. 182–3.

37 Voltaire, *Traité de Métaphysique (1734)*, ed. H. Temple Patterson (Manchester: Manchester University Press, 1957), pp. 17–19.

38 *The Elements*, p. 236n.

39 Voltaire, *Oeuvres complètes, Nouvelle édition* (Paris: Garnier Frères, 1877), vol. 10: 'À l'auteur du livre des trois imposteurs', pp. 402–5.

CHAPTER 4

The Origins of
European Freemasonry

There is simply no adequate account, in English, of the origins of European Freemasonry. Here we can only trace the barest outline of its history in England, emphasising its significant debt to the Newtonian Enlightenment as well as its early infiltration by pantheists and republicans. Although it may be said that the Newtonian Enlightenment gave birth to speculative Masonry, there was also an important and decisive contribution made by the radicals. The Freemasonry of the eighteenth century is commonly called 'speculative' to distinguish it from the masonry of the old 'operative' guilds. By 1717 and the official establishment of the Grand Lodge in London few, if any, of those latter sorts of masons can be found on its extant membership lists.

For disillusioned Christians, Freemasonry had within it the potential of becoming nothing less than a new religion – and in the hands of philosophical radicals a natural religion based upon belief not in the power of providence but in the power of nature. It provided ceremonies and rituals – some drawn from the original masonic guilds and some undoubtedly invented and improvised during the early eighteenth century – which were open to a variety of religious interpretations (see appendix, pp. 287 et seq.). Likewise its essentially social nature, reinforced by the trappings of secrecy, gave an extraordinary sense of community to men who were disaffected from church or chapel.

Alternatively, among Christian and Newtonian promoters, led in particular by Jean Theophile Desaguliers, organised Freemasonry served as a social nexus that promoted specific cultural and ideological goals: stability under a strong, but constitutional monarchy, social mobility under aristocratic patronage, religious toleration, Baconian experimentalism and, of course, dedication to the cult of the new science. With the exception of social mobility, all of these goals are elaborated upon in an official constitutions of 1723 (reprinted in the appendix). It remained throughout the eighteenth century the document to which all official lodges subscribed. The practitioners of the 'royal art', as Masonry was called, worshipped the God of the new science, the Grand Architect, as he was called, as a powerful symbol of order, regularity and stability. Perhaps inevitably the science of Newton gave birth to a new form of religiosity, although one that was singularly protean in character.

In the early Hanoverian period the spread of organised Freemasonry first in Britain and then on the Continent cannot be separated from the ascendancy of the Whig oligarchy and the growth of British influence on the Continent. In England that hegemony entailed not only economic domination and political influence, but also control over the fashionable cultural institutions. The Whigs who came to dominate the Royal Society and the new Grand Lodge of London, established in 1717, never intended to exclude Tories loyal to the Hanoverian succession. Rather these institutions embraced elements within the opposition while being kept (and not without a struggle) firmly in the government's camp. They, in turn, became social and intellectual forums that were imitated in provincial cities throughout the course of the century. In the case of Freemasonry, however, that uniquely British institution not only spread rapidly from London into the provinces, but also into almost every European urban centre.

If we look closely at Freemasonry in northern Europe, particularly in the Netherlands, the Holy Roman Empire and Austria, among Britain's allies in the first half of the century, we find within the lodges a social milieu enamoured of British constitutionalism, stability and prosperity, encouraging of enlightened and strong central government, and also dedicated to religious toleration. The official establishment of Freemasonry in The Hague, that is of a lodge affiliated constitutionally with the Grand Lodge, was the direct work of the Newtonian Desaguliers and the British grand master, the Duke of Richmond (80). Established in November 1734, its master was Vincent La Chapelle, a member of a London lodge and the *chef de cuisine*, first to the British ambassador, Phillip Stanhope, Earl of Chesterfield, and then to William of Orange, later to become William IV, Stadholder of the United Provinces at the Revolution of 1747.[1] That lodge and those founded immediately on its head were heavily Orangist, and within a year the anti-Orangist States of Holland and West Friesland interrogated the Masonic leaders. In December 1735 they were instructed to cease their assemblies and Dutch Freemasonry became illegal, but this prohibition did not impede its rapid growth.[2] The close links between British interests and the Orangist Party (84) make reasonable the assertion that Dutch Masonic membership, in these early years, generally approved of the Anglo-Dutch alliance.

Masonry continued to grow despite its official condemnation and at the Dutch Revolution of 1747 prominent Masons played central roles in the restoration of the stad-holderate (see pp. 233–39).

By the same token where we can find evidence of Masonic member-ship in the Austrian Netherlands in the period prior to 1750 it was among individuals closely tied to the Viennese government (83, 51), hostile to the power of the Jesuits, and sympathetic to the Northern alliance against France. In the Austrian territories, Masonry may have descended from the entourage of Eugène of Savoy, some of whose earliest admirers can now be shown to have been Masons (see pp. 179). Likewise Francis, Duke of Lorraine, representative of Charles VI, Emperor of Austria, was initiated into British Freemasonry at Walpole's country estate, Houghton Hall, in 1731(79). At Francis's coronation as Holy Roman Emperor in 1745 a Masonic ceremony occurred amid the proceedings and various Dutch and Belgian dig-nitaries were initiated.[3] It should be stressed that in this early period known Belgian Freemasons were favourably disposed to Austrian rule because they saw it as reforming and opposed to the extraordinary power accorded the Jesuits in that territory. By the middle of the eighteenth century prominent Austrian officials there, such as the Comte de Cobenzl, were also Masons, and he in turn gave encourage-ment to liberal journalists who delighted in goading the religious authorities (86, 13, 155–6, 186). Just beneath the surface of this world of court culture and officialdom, and often in its service, we find our world of philosophical and political radicals (88). Not surprisingly many of them were Masons. That originally British institution, trans-mitted clandestinely by the radicals and later officially by Whig politicians, provided the social milieu of the Radical Enlightenment on the Continent.

The major portion of this discussion of Freemasonry will be devoted to its official posture and representatives. However, before continuing that discussion we should substantiate our discovery of its important and radical underside. That aspect of this international movement can be traced back to the War of Spanish Succession (1701–13), to the political intrigues of the Commonwealthmen, John Toland and Anthony Collins, on the Continent. In greater detail in the next chap-ter I shall be arguing that they played a fundamental role in estab-lishing Freemasonry in the Netherlands, both north and south. The process of recruitment into Masonic lodges, those peculiarly English forms of socialising, appears to have been launched during the course of these two men's various forays on to the Continent, either as spies or agents, or simply as promoters of their version of the Protestant cause (28, 44–5). In Belgium their contact was one Lambert Ignace Douxfils (*fl.* 1710–53), who was a spinozist and who became secretary to the pro-Viennese and enlightened Duc d'Arenberg (1690–1754) (89, 38, 47). In the Netherlands, the early leadership of official Dutch Freemasonry, particularly in Amsterdam, owed much to the pantheist, Jean Rousset de Missy, and later one of his associates Henri du Sauzet, became a lodge officer. The young Rousset was, of course, Collins's and Toland's translator and he was also a life-long friend to Prosper Marchand, whose link with Toland is revealed in the latter's unpublished manuscripts. The recruitment of philosophical radicals continued well into mid-century with the membership in an Amsterdam lodge of the Abbé Yvon, that renegade French cleric who wrote the important articles on materialism for Diderot's *Encyclopédie*. From its inception this new, ostensibly most harmless, cultural and social institution housed intellectual radicals, who, as we shall see in Chapter 7, were also capable of revolutionary action. Official, organised Freemasonry was never intended by its Whig and Newtonian promoters to encourage pantheism and republicanism, but the radicals with their reforming ideals and utopian dreams could not be easily contained. Knowing as we now do that European Freemasonry at its genesis housed these radical elements and that its spread was linked to the fate of 'the Protestant empire', we can now perhaps better understand why it was perceived as dangerous and subversive by religious authorities in almost every Continental country, but particularly in southern and Catholic areas.

In England the creation of official Freemasonry entailed a sharp repudiation of the republican tradition inherited from the English Revolution. The Newtonian and Whig leadership of the Royal Society, whose authority had been enhanced by Newton's own presidency, guided the Grand Lodge in its formative years. Whig control over the Royal Society resulted from a political struggle in which Sir Hans Sloane, Desaguliers and Martin Folkes emerged as victorious. At the same time, over a fourth of early Masonic membership also belonged to the Royal Society, with Desaguliers as the most active and prominent leader in both camps.[4] Other Newtonians, such as the young and brilliant Brook Taylor, were also Freemasons and he may have been instrumental in transmitting that institution to France.[5] Taylor belonged to the Bedford Head Lodge in 1725, as did Martin Folkes, although their initiation into the 'Masonic science' was certainly prior to that date.

Taylor's career and his Masonic activities serve to illustrate the tone of intellectual life under the Whig ascendance. Although a supporter of the government, Taylor was not inhibited from maintaining a close intellectual relationship with Henry, Lord Bolingbroke, the Tory opposition leader who had been forced to flee to France in 1715 because of his sudden conversion to Jacobitism. Bolingbroke provides the rare example of a Newtonian who was also a deist and an opponent of the court (55). For disparate reasons both assisted in the spread of Newtonian ideas into France; Taylor, in typical Newtonian fashion, attacked the non-experimental nature of the reigning French Cartesianism and also laid emphasis upon the threat it posed to natural religion.[6]

Perhaps Taylor's closest friend was Lord Paisley (James Hamilton, 7th Earl of Abercorn, d. 1744), a Whig oligarch with a strong interest in both science and music who in 1726 became grand master of the Grand Lodge in London.[7] Indeed, Paisley, Desaguliers and Taylor established the charitable funds so characteristic of British and later European Freemasonry (78, 60). This circle commonly exchanged philosophical and scientific treatises,[8] and it may be assumed that these scientific discussions extended to the actual lodge meetings. Taylor's major philosophical work, *Some Reflections relating to the First Principles of General Philosophy,* reveals his profound concern to establish a fully rational and coherent natural religion based upon Newtonian principles. A mechanical philosophy such as Descartes's was insufficient to the task of defeating atheism and materialism.[9] For Taylor, only the providential universe proclaimed by Newton stands worthy of belief and adoration. Men like Taylor and Desaguliers insured that the official Masonry of the Grand Lodge was piously Christian and vaguely Protestant. As a result, eighteenth-century England provides little evidence that Freemasonry was ever perceived as a threat to the established institutions of either church or state. If anything, the opposite relationship became characteristic. Anglican ministers often preached at Masonic feasts and funerals, and Masonic inscriptions can be seen to this day on burial plaques in local parish churches.

Yet no other social institution of the European Enlightenment has provoked greater controversy at the time, as well as among historians of the eighteenth century. In some places on the Continent, Masonry was perceived as subversive of monarchy, social hierarchy, the Catholic Church and indeed all forms of organised religion. Apart from its radical underside, British Freemasonry also transmitted uniquely English forms of social behaviour such as the easy socialising of aristocrats and bourgeois gentlemen that so impressed Voltaire, or a belief in constitutional monarchy and Newtonian as opposed to Aristotelian or Cartesian philosophies of nature. As such it was antithetical to monarchical absolutism, to the hegemony of the universities and their official teachings, and to the old clerical and aristocratic estates with their social and legal privileges.

Yet even in Catholic Europe those tensions were at first minimal – despite the papal condemnation of Masonry in 1738 – until well into the final decades of the century. After the French Revolution, and beginning most prominently with the writings of the Abbé Barruel, Freemasonry became the target for a vast and largely paranoid literature that attempted to lay blame for the revolution on the Masonic lodges. Unquestionably the Masonic lodges and prominent Freemasons did play a political role in the revolution, but it would be naïve to imagine that they had conspired to bring it about. History simply does not work that way. Yet in our effort to avoid paranoia it would also be naïve to imagine that Masonic lodges, in various parts of Europe at various times in the eighteenth century, possessed no discernible political ideology and interests.

In the twentieth century, British Masonic historians have tried to play down the political involvements of their now somewhat anachronistic society. They argue that in the eighteenth century Freemasonry represented the advent of universalist, non-political ideals, in effect, 'the end of ideology'. Yet the Masonic constitution itself hardly supports such an interpretation, nor does any of the other evidence currently available. In both its Newtonian and radical manifestations, eighteenth-century Freemasonry, at its origins, possessed decidedly political overtones. Unfortunately the evidence for why that should be so is still scanty, but we must nevertheless try to piece together a story. Here emphasis will be placed upon those early fragments that reveal political tendencies and intellectual interests, but an equally useful history of early Freemasonry should be written solely from the point of view of social history and the formation of exclusive male fraternities.

During the 1650s, the Masonic guilds of operative Masons participated in the democraticising tendencies that swept through many guilds in that revolutionary age. The rules governing apprenticeships were relaxed and many guild members won a share in the government of the various trade companies. At the Restoration, however, these gains were lost and by the early eighteenth century there was to be a distinct weakening of the guild system as free market principles came to dominate the labour market (64, 338–46; 65, 176). Gradually many guilds became purely social and ceremonial institutions and their power to control wages, the labour force and the quality of goods all but disappeared. Only in the case of the Masonic guilds, which must have always emphasised the unique architectural and mathematical skills of their members, do we find the emergence of a new and extraordinary historical role.

By the 1670s, many operative and artisan masonic lodges in Scotland as well as in England began to admit non-masonic gentlemen into their lodges, probably for economic reasons. The masons were in need of fresh capital for their lodges and building projects; the gentlemen, who could be anything from prosperous shopkeepers to local gentry, willingly accepted this honorary membership in an 'ancient' society that possessed distinctive intellectual traditions and a vast body of lore, not to mention a mythological history (68). The masons had been the architects of the great cathedrals, the palaces of kings, as well as the fortifiers of towns and cities. Seventeenth-century masonic manuscripts from the operative guilds stress this 'ancient' history and as late as the 1690s make mention of a secret mathematical wisdom descended from Hermes. In this tradition, possibly rooted in popular culture and artisan craft, as well as in the scientific literature of the late Renaissance, we once again encounter a version of the Hermetic tradition.

Freemasonry provides one link between Renaissance Hermetism, with its strongly naturalistic tendencies, and the early stages of the Enlightenment in England. Gradually the Hermetic lore would be replaced by the 'magic' of Newtonian science, just as the artisans would be displaced from this 'speculative' institution. Yet both would leave their mark, in a mysticism that could easily lend itself to the worship of nature, in a dedication to the study of mathematics, and of course in ceremonies and rituals for the installation of grand masters and the initiation of apprentices, in aprons and emblems such as the square and the compass – all of which harkened back to a world of mechanics and craftsmen.

The importance of this ostensible link with the past should not be underestimated. Part of the appeal of Freemasonry in the eighteenth century lay in its claim to being in contact with a universal and ancient wisdom made manifest in the mathematical and architectural skills displayed in those early artisan achievements. By the late seventeenth century, the membership records indicate that this originally artisan society could become a social nexus that bridged profound class differences. A new form of socialising came into being and eventually it captured the imagination of thousands of educated Europeans, titled and most notably the untitled and the mercantile.

By the time this process was well underway in England, at the formation of the Grand Lodge in 1717, few artisans were actually left in the fashionable London lodges that had grown quite rapidly after 1689. Their artisan lore and wisdom, as well as their ceremonies, had been subsumed into a speculative and closed world where all brothers 'meet upon the level'. Within this egalitarian atmosphere the aristocratic leadership of the lodges became embourgeoised, while the illusion of equality must have pleased the largely mercantile rank and file, some of whom probably had artisan and 'mechanick' origins. Undoubtedly this link with the guild tradition proved a significant factor in Masonry's rapid spread on to the Continent.

The private lodge established by the English Commonwealthmen in The Hague around 1710 will figure prominently in the social world of the Radical Enlightenment in the Netherlands. Significantly it was composed largely of publishers and booksellers who were members of the booksellers' guild in that city. Many of them were also Huguenot refugees whose intellectual odyssey had led them to question traditional Christian doctrine. Early Masonic lodges, however inchoate and unaffiliated, could capture the imagination of town and city guildsmen, as well as of independent craftsmen who had moved from the protection of the old artisan guilds to lives as independent entrepreneurs. This pattern holds true for England, it would seem, and it may also hold for European Freemasonry in the early years. There also appears to be a significant similarity between Masonic rituals and myths and those used by the secret guilds of French craftsmen, called *compagnonnage*.[10] It seems altogether probable, however, that in the course of the eighteenth century the *compagnonnage* borrowed from the Masonic tradition, rather than vice versa.

Despite these links with artisan confederations, by the 1720s the membership lists of various London lodges were heavily bourgeois, although many lodges did include, and indeed sought out, aristocratic leadership. The lodge of the St Paul's Head Tavern on Ludgate Street, for instance, had 107 members in 1730 and its records include their occupations. With the exception of three attorneys-at-law, one or two 'Esqs.' and 'Gents', most were businessmen engaged in everything from pharmacy and banking to distilling, surgery and wine selling.[11] For these practical men of affairs the Hermetic tradition supplied a universalist ideology based upon the glorification of ancient learning which was vaguely mystical in the telling but immensely practical in application. Business contacts and applied mathematics, not to mention good food, drink and song, became the stuff of social cohesion, and to this combination of esoteric philosophy, merry-making, and useful practice one can easily see why devotees of the new science, shrewd businessmen, and possibly even aristocrats with practical interests, were drawn in increasingly large numbers. By the 1720s, the official constitution of the Grand Lodge condemned the protective practices of the old masonic guilds and asserted that modern Freemasons would never 'encourage any such confederacy of their working Brethren' (63, 36).

To understand this process by which practising masons were replaced by non-masons we must go back to the mid-seventeenth century. The earliest records indicating the initiation of non-masons into English and Scottish lodges date from the 1640s and significantly for this story, concern two important practitioners of science and magic, Elias Ashmole and Sir Robert Moray. Ashmole, a royalist with strong interests in alchemy and number mysticism, was admitted to a lodge at Warrington, Lancashire, in 1646.[12] A few years earlier, in 1641, Sir Robert Moray became a devoted Mason and eventually master of his lodge in Edinburgh. At the time, Moray was general quartermaster to the Scottish army and in the service of Charles I.[13] Ashmole had strong interests not only in the Hermetic tradition but also in the Rosicrucian manifestoes that were published in Germany during the early years of the Thirty Years War. Likewise, he believed that alchemy might provide the foundations for a universal and practical learning, Baconian in its utility, Hermetic in its origins (14, 196–7). Moray appears also to have had strong interests in alchemy. Both men became founding members of the Royal Society, with Moray attending more of the early meetings than any other member. Early in the history of speculative Masonry, in fact by the 1640s, long before the process of transforming Masonry into a gentlemen's club became commonplace, certain political and intellectual characteristics appear visible. Both Moray and Ashmole were politically well-connected royalists and worth cultivating; their membership would have been useful in times of political uncertainty. By the 1720s, official Masonry seems almost completely consumed by the search for political allegiances, only now three generations later these will come almost entirely from powerful Whig oligarchs.

The information about Ashmole and Moray fits what we know about Masonry, science and politics after 1717. The evidence for the other political involvements of Freemasonry prior to that date is tantalising, but less clear. One of the few references (1676) to Masonry during the Restoration links it to the 'Green Ribbonned Cabal', claiming that the 'accepted Masons' dined with the notorious Green Ribbon Club, a semi-clandestine society of 'Whigs' who advocated the exclusion of James II, a Catholic, from the throne and who possessed strongly republican tendencies.

A search through the membership records of the Green Ribbon Club indicates no obvious Masonic affiliations, yet certain of the practices of late seventeenth-century Whig clubs imply a compatibility with later Masonic practices. The Green Ribbon Club liked to dress up in priests' vestments for their ritualistic pope-burnings.[14] The habit of wearing priest-like ceremonial garb – on far less provocative occasions – was (and still is) part of Masonic practice. Similarly, Whig clubs in general display a tendency to eat and drink in self-consciously libertine proportions and the records of even respectable and court-centred Whig clubs, like the Kit-Cat, display a tolerance for religious heterodoxy.[15] Some contemporaries in the 1690s called the Whigs and their Rose Club, 'Rosicrucians' (39, 215). Tory clubs in the same period display none of these heterodox or ritualistic tendencies. Where they can be found at merry-making it is church and queen that Tory clubmen predictably salute.

It seems probable that by the late seventeenth century urban Whig culture provided a congenial environment for the cultivation of heterodoxy. Likewise, the Hermetic overtones contained within the lore of operative Masonry may have won the attention of those disillusioned with church or chapel. In their search for good fellowship, as well as for totally naturalistic explanations of the world around them, some men were drawn to the masonic guilds. Alternatively, the transformation of operative Masonry into speculative may have been one of the by-products of the Whig exclusionists' search for artisan allies after 1679. All of these factors contributing to a certain filiation between the artisan guilds and Whiggery may explain why even the official histories of speculative Freemasonry acknowledge that the earliest known lodge in London, of a totally speculative variety, was headed in the 1690s by the former Whig exclusionist, Sir Robert Clayton (d. 1707).

Clayton was a wealthy London merchant, a money-lender and an exclusionist who also had business dealings with John Wildman, the Leveller, and one of the few important radicals of the 1650s to survive politically into the 1690s. Clayton also appears to have been uncooperative with the Whig junto after 1689.[16] Little is known about Clayton's lodge although its membership may have included some very prominent post-1689 Whigs: John Methuen, Lord Chancellor of Ireland; John Freke; Locke's friend and correspondent, Edward Clarke, MP for Somerset;[17] the Whig pamphleteer, Thomas Rawlins; John Toland, a radical Whig and pantheist; and William Simpson, a Baron of the Exchequer. All of these names conform closely to a Whig coterie of the period known as 'the college' which may have started with John Locke, Freke and Clarke but which grew to include Toland, Tindal, Thomas Rawlins – in short, Whigs of a radical or Commonwealth variety.

Throughout the eighteenth century, English Masons claimed Locke as one of their own, and the eighteenth-century portrait gallery of the Grand Lodge includes him as well as Clayton and one of our radicals in the Netherlands, Bernard Picart (75). Both of the latter deserve a place in that gallery but the evidence for Locke's Masonic membership – one letter of 1696 of very dubious origin – hardly qualifies him. The importance of Clayton's circle and its filiations with Masonry lies in its simultaneous links to the radical faction of the soon-to-be-triumphant Whig Party during the post-1689 period.

After 1689, that faction grew increasingly discontented and increasingly irreligious. William Stephens, one of its associates, attributed its disillusionment to the failure of the revolution to produce a truly parliamentary form of government and in *An Account of the Growth of*

Deism in England (London, 1696) he lamented, 'the late happy Revolution . . . came on too soon, and was cut off too short . . .' In their disappointment the radical Whigs increased their attacks against the church while at the same time their enemies perceived 'that they may sink Our Kings by Degrees to be Dukes of Venice'.[18]

Among the intellectual leaders of this faction and its most philosophically and radically innovative member was John Toland. Private letters to Toland indicate that he was part of Clayton's intimate circle, and I would argue that his familiarity with Masonry through Clayton led him, in turn, to establish a private lodge in The Hague, evidence for which comes from his manuscripts (see appendix, pp. 268–9). This 1710 meeting record, indicating the presence of a constitution and grand master, reveals that Prosper Marchand, Michael Böhm, the Gleditsch brothers, Charles Levier, Bernard Picart, a M. de Bey, and a variety of 'devil-may-care gentlemen' belonged to this secret society. Other manuscript records in Marchand's papers also indicate that his club was self-consciously Masonic, in that Marchand employed the word *Maçon* in a speculative sense in a treatise that he wrote for his 'brother', de Bey (see pp. 158–9). Toland's lodge qualifies as the earliest private Masonic lodge on the Continent, although it must be stressed that it never attained official standing when British Freemasonry was transmitted to the Netherlands by the leaders of the Grand Lodge in 1734. Some of its early members and associates, however, play a very decisive role in that later history.

Knowing as we now do about the active role played by radical Whigs in early Masonic lodges in London and in the spread of that movement on to the Continent, perhaps we can now more easily understand why the Masonic Constitutions of 1723 insisted as the first rule that no member should be 'an irreligious libertine or a stupid atheist'. The early Masonic fragments, where they can be linked to political culture, indicate a closer filiation with Whig rather than with Tory circles and, of course, that brought with it a radical faction given to heresy and republicanism. These early fragments also suggest a strong link with the new science of the Royal Society, as well as a gradual social amalgamation of prosperous, independent craftsmen with segments of the mercantile community.

Up to this point in our discussion of the origins of European Freemasonry, its egalitarian and even radical tendencies have received emphasis. But the earliest records also reveal a traditional and hierarchical side of Masonry in its transitional period, and given the royalist ideology of official British Freemasonry it would be worthwhile to highlight that equally early and more powerful tendency. As we shall see in the remainder of this chapter, official Masonry and its prominent leaders were anything but subversive.

One of the earliest references to speculative Masonry in European literature comes from a mid-seventeenth-century Scottish poem praising both Masons and the Stuarts:

> For we be brethren of the rosie cross;
> We have the mason-word and second sight,
> Things for to come we can foretell alright . . .
> But for King Charles, his honour we are bold.[19]

As the lines reveal, Masonry, from its earliest history, was linked to the Rosicrucian myth and to its ideal of universal learning. In the first half of the seventeenth century in England, that myth was also tied to royalist culture of a Protestant variety. The architectural style pioneered in that period by Inigo Jones, and revived in the eighteenth century by Scottish and English devotees of what became known as the Palladian style, had been heavily patronised by James I.[20]

Like official Freemasonry in the eighteenth century, the Palladian style had definite royalist associations, and indeed the revival of Inigo Jones in the 1690s was started by Tories with a nostalgia for the Stuart past. The eventual triumph of Palladian architecture, with its Masonic associations, owes more to the great Whig oligarchs who built the Palladian mansions of the eighteenth century, not least of them Walpole's own Houghton Hall in Norfolk. The royal style of the seventeenth century became the court Whig style of the eighteenth, and into this sensibility both Freemasonry and dedication to Newtonian science and geometrical regularity fitted very comfortably.

Throughout the eighteenth century, Masonry was often called the 'royal art'. Even among European radicals with Masonic affiliations we can observe a tendency to be drawn to powerful figureheads, whether they be Eugène of Savoy, William IV, or even Maria Theresa. At crucial moments, this desire for influence and perhaps social status could, however, break down to such an extent that during the Dutch Revolution of 1747 we find Rousset de Missy, to his peril, siding with the artisan reformers in Amsterdam who wanted a full-scale assault on oligarchical privilege (see pp. 237–9). In general the secret world of the Masonic lodge embraced the fashionable élites and offered no opposition to established institutions; this was nowhere truer than in British Freemasonry.

Before any social institution dedicated to the cult of Newtonian science could take root, it would have to have been judged by the established church as posing no threat to its hegemony. Certainly the old operative lodges appear never to have aroused suspicion. In 1689, Edward Stillingfleet, soon to become Bishop of Worcester, regarded the 'Mason word [as] a Rabbinical mystery' and appears to have seen in this guild tradition no threat to established religion.[21] Yet during the Restoration, as we have seen, there were hints that some Masons at least might have been drawn to the cause of exclusion. In 1698 an anonymous pamphlet accused the Masons of being the Antichrist and warned Londoners 'mingle not among this corrupt People lest you be found so at the World's Conflagration' (67, 34–5). That pamphlet very possibly reflects the infiltration of the new speculative Masonry by irreligious men in search of alternatives to the established church. In general, however, that infiltration never gained ascendancy during the first half of the eighteenth century, in large measure because the Newtonian leaders of speculative Masonry saw to it that it did not. When speculative Masonry finally appeared with the formation of the Grand Lodge and in the publication of *The Constitutions of the Freemasons* (1723) it was aggressively royalist, with its leadership predictably drawn from two quarters: Newtonian scientists coupled with Whig oligarchs and their placemen.

The Revolution of 1688–9 transformed the Whigs from an opposition and even persecuted party with republican tendencies into the new leadership of the political nation. In the 1690s, a split within the party emerged which isolated its radical republican faction and transformed the mainstream of the party into placemen, servants of the crown, promoters of the Bank of England, advocates of a standing army, and firm supporters of a limited toleration for the Dissenters that was tied to the maintenance of an established church controlled by the state. Likewise, as we have seen, the revolution brought the latitudinarian and increasingly Newtonian faction within the church into power, in the bishoprics as well as in the important London pulpits. By the time of the Hanoverian Succession (1714), Whigs and Newtonians had made common cause over a variety of issues, including the achievement of the succession itself, and most important for our purposes, over the usefulness of liberal Anglicanism as the ideological support for court-centred and ministerial government. And Masonry provided an ideal vehicle for the transmission of that ideology. Here was a society dedicated to the 'royal art' yet religiously tolerant, while at the same time progressive, as well as committed to the spread of the new mathematical and natural philosophical learning. In Hanoverian England, Whiggery provided the beliefs and values, while Freemasonry supplied one temple wherein some of its most devoted followers worshipped the God of Newtonian science.

Despite the importance of Freemasonry for the Enlightenment, of whatever variety, this originally British institution has received scant attention from British academic historians. Even one of the finest, most comprehensive biographies produced by the current generation of English scholars, J. H. Plumb's *Sir Robert Walpole* (London,

1956–61), never once mentions that Walpole was a Mason or that important servants of his government and some of his diplomatic agents were also. This is a particularly unfortunate gap in the historiography of the eighteenth century, not only for intellectual but also for political history. By way of a corrective, it is now possible to offer some new information about the lives of prominent early Hanoverian Freemasons and to illustrate the range of their political and intellectual involvements. Here we shall focus, of course, on Desaguliers and his associates, in particular the Rev. James Anderson, but we shall also try to include lesser-known figures especially from the world of politics, notably one Charles Delafaye, an official in the Secretary of State's office. These were minor men, participating in the birth of a new and eventually important cultural institution; hence they are all the more fascinating.

Desaguliers was a Huguenot refugee who became after 1717 the guiding force in British Freemasonry (69). He had arrived in England as an infant, received a good education at Oxford (MA, 1712) while taking holy orders in the Church of England (70). Throughout his life he combined a career as a cleric, which he tended to neglect, with a passionate interest in Newtonian natural philosophy, mechanics and Freemasonry. The exact date of Desaguliers's initiation into the lodge that met prior to 1717 at the Rummer and Grapes in Channel Row is unknown, but it probably occurred in 1713 when Desaguliers moved into the district. That lodge, in turn, became the Horn Tavern Lodge (in New Palace Yard, near Westminster Hall), the most dynamic and important of all the early lodges.

Desaguliers's introduction to Newtonian science is easier to date. At Oxford he studied with John Keill, a follower of Newton, and Desaguliers's expertise was sufficient for him to take over Keill's course of lectures in his absence. Through Keill, Desaguliers moved immediately into the circle of Newton's friends, and they socialised at the Royal Society as well as more personally as Newton was godfather to one of Desaguliers's children. Almost all of Desaguliers's other social connections were with fellow Masons, and in 1716 he became chaplain to the Earl of Carnarvon, later the Duke of Chandos, and eventually in 1737 grand master of the united English and Scottish lodges (71, 103, 152).

Desaguliers earned his living in London by giving courses in Newtonian science which he illustrated not mathematically but mechanically, using machines or devices to demonstrate the basic physical laws. Among the mathematically inept who could afford to take his course (generally at a charge of two guineas), Desaguliers's approach became very popular and he travelled about England and the Netherlands repeating his courses and experiments. After becoming a fellow of the

Royal Society in 1714, he quickly moved into a position of leadership and became curator of experiments, an office he held until a year before his death. The published and unpublished records of the society are filled with details about Desaguliers's useful experiments in mechanics, most of which were intended to perfect or to develop labour-saving devices.[22] As a relatively young man, Desaguliers joined the select company of Bentley, Clarke, Whiston, Keill and Roger Cotes, that first generation of Newtonians who championed the moderate version of Enlightenment. Indeed, Desaguliers embraced the latitudinarian natural religion of Bentley and Clarke. He was so convinced of its validity that he believed it possible to argue the truth of Christianity without recourse to arguments from revealed religion, which he believed could all too easily be attacked by freethinkers. Desaguliers arranged for the publication of an English edition of a work by the Dutch pastor and philosopher, Bernard Nieuwentyt (1654–1718), who had spent many years in polemics against spinozists and materialists.[23]

The link between Desaguliers and Nieuwentyt indicates the similarity of their intellectual concerns and the common identity of their internationally active enemy. Nieuwentyt wrote against his spinozist contemporaries in the Netherlands. Yet the English translator of his work, John Chamberlayne, told John Toland, whose *History of the Druids* had offended the Whig Lord Chancellor, the Earl of Macclesfield, that Nieuwentyt's *The Religious Philosopher* was intended as its antidote.[24] Nieuwentyt's work attacked those who 'think they are able to convert most things that occur to them in the World to their own Advantage, and to render them subservient to their own Necessities and Pleasures'. Such freethinkers and libertines acknowledge only 'the unknown Laws of Nature or Necessity' and are more concerned with the nature of the gods than with the existence of God.[25]

Throughout his life Desaguliers, like his other Newtonian contemporaries, brought the burden of Newtonian science to bear against the radicals of the Enlightenment. Indeed, Desaguliers's contribution to the early history of English Freemasonry may have been vitally important in setting that movement officially in opposition to 'stupid atheists and irreligious libertines', as the Masonic constitutions described them, as well as in aligning it with court Whiggery and the Royal Society.

Desaguliers's particular version of Newtonianism relied heavily on practical mechanics, and indeed his inquisitive attitude towards workmen and their skills closely resembles the interests of Boyle and the first generation of English mechanical philosophers. He believed that philosophers can learn by observing skilled craftsmen who, he asserted, often do not understand that they are imitating mechanical principles. Freemasonry, with its roots in the mechanical and artisan crafts, would naturally appeal to mechanically minded Newtonians like Desaguliers.

Although Desaguliers may have enjoyed watching and learning from artisans, his social loyalties lay with the aristocracy. He managed to preach at court and to become chaplain to Frederick, Prince of Wales, who appears also to have been a Mason. He spent years in the service of the Duke of Chandos and did the water-engineering on his huge country estate. He was fiercely nationalistic, regarding the French and Italians as 'Fops'. Desaguliers's joy at the coronation of George II spilled over into a poem, the truth of which he thought served 'to excuse the badness of the poetry' (72, vi).

The Newtonian System of the World, the Best Model of Government merely put into bad verse what the Newtonians had been preaching from the 1690s. Desaguliers extolled the British monarchy as the guarantor of liberty, rights and privileges – harmony and love bind all and 'attraction is now as universal in the political, as the philosophical world':

> What made the Planets in such Order move,
> He said, was Harmony and mutual Love.
> The Musick of his Spheres did represent
> That ancient Harmony of Government

Only strong monarchy secures the value of money, yet kings must be bound by the 'Almighty Architects unalter'd Laws' (72, 17). The principle of attraction binds sun and planets, monarch and his ministers, yet 'His Powers, coerc'd by laws, still leaves them free,/Directs but not Destroys, their Liberty/ . . . And reigning thus with limited Command/He holds a lasting Scepter in his Hand.' Newton's philosophy provides the foundation for the worship of limited monarchy, for the overthrow of foreign philosophies like Descartes's with their atheistic implications, and for the maintenance of order and stability. It is little wonder that Whig oligarchs and their placemen flocked to Masonic lodges whose spokesmen offered so much confirmation to their self-esteem and insured the cosmic significance of their activities. Hogarth, himself a Mason, caught an aspect of Desaguliers in one of his engravings. In *The Sleeping Congregation*, with a title that tells all, Desaguliers was widely reputed to resemble the preacher.[26]

Desaguliers received vital assistance in the creation of speculative Masonry from another clergyman, also with a craving for aristocratic society, the Rev. James Anderson, DD (1680?–1739). He was a Scots Presbyterian educated in Aberdeen who in 1710 made his way to London and the Presbyterian congregation in Swallow Street. His detractors called him the 'Presbyterian Bishop' and indeed his early sermons strike an ecumenical chord while at the same time being aggressively royalist. In the course of exonerating the Presbyterians of the English Revolution, Anderson blamed the regicide of Charles I (1649) on the radicals of the army; he also preached unflinchingly for the Hanoverian succession.[27] He warned against freethinkers, Unitarians, Jacobites, and most forms of political or intellectual deviation. The first Masonic constitutions (1723), although the work of various hands, appeared under Anderson's name. Anderson also wrote political propaganda for Whig policy aimed at a Masonic audience, but little of it appears to have survived.[28]

In their Masonic lives and writings, Anderson and Desaguliers display common themes that recur within the history of the institution they laboured so hard to create: a strongly Protestant and latitudinarian religious vision that could be Anglican or conservatively Dissenting; a dedication to strong monarchy and the Hanoverian succession; a willingness to allow the state to control the church and thereby to maintain religious peace; a propensity for aristocratic fellowship and patronage (Anderson made the historical reconstruction of aristocratic genealogies his major scholarly enterprise); and finally in the case of Desaguliers and his Royal Society and Masonic friends, a strong commitment to Newtonian science.

Under the guidance of Desaguliers and Anderson, Masonic lodges became places where gentlemen, whether lowly or titled, could receive a minimal instruction in mathematics, listen to lectures on the new science,[29] or make up for what they did not know in science by participating in a movement that claimed to be descended from the earliest practitioners of applied mathematics – the masonic 'architects' who constructed the ancient temples, the mediaeval cathedrals, and practised the 'royal art' in the loyal service of generations of English kings. One historian of eighteenth-century education has argued, quite rightly, that some scientific societies which were often synonymous with Masonic lodges or sponsored by them, played a vital role in the diffusion of scientific knowledge in both England and the Netherlands (103, 158–9).

Indeed, the first encyclopaedia of the eighteenth century, Ephraim Chambers' *Cyclopædia* (London, 1728) which was the cause, but not the inspiration, for Diderot's *Encylopédie*, can probably, unlike the latter venture (see pp. 256–9), be described as a Masonic project. Chambers (1680?–1740), it is believed, belonged to the Richmond lodge and was for a time its master.[30] He had been apprenticed to the globe-maker and printer, John Senex, who along with Desaguliers, the Rev. James Anderson, and Francis Sorrell had been among the non-aristocratic leadership of the early Grand Lodge (78, 52–7). Senex encouraged the young Chambers's desire for learning and was also one of the publishers for the 1728 first edition of his *Cyclopædia*(104). Senex specialised in publishing scientific works, whether technical or intended for the natural philosophical instruction of the layman. He printed the first galleys for the 1726 edition of the *Principia*(48, VII, 288) as well as the 1719 edition of s'Gravesande's *Mathematical Elements of Natural Philosophy* and the 1718 translation of Nieuwentyt's *The Religious Philosopher*, both edited or translated by Desaguliers.[31] Although Senex's name does not appear on the title-page as the publisher of the 1726 *Philosophiae naturalis principia mathematica*, the names of the printers for the Royal Society, William and John Innys, do. There is a Mason, J. Innis (his name was spelled interchangeably in the early eighteenth century), who was a member of the King's Armes Lodge at St Paul's Churchyard in 1726 (78, 32) and that churchyard fronted on to the district of the printers and booksellers where Innys had his business. His shop was also the site of Newtonian lectures given by Benjamin Worster, a friend of Desaguliers, during the 1720s (103, 142).[32]

The evidence strongly suggests that not only was Chambers's venture assisted, but that it may also have been inspired by his Masonic affiliations. The *Cyclopædia* gave considerable attention to Newtonian science and also contained one of the first accounts of British Freemasonry, which was widely cited by Continental journals. In the generation after the great Boyle lectures, it played a significant role in spreading Newtonian science to a wide and literate audience on both sides of the Channel.[33]

Confirmation for the role of Freemasonry as an educational force, particularly in mathematics, comes from lodge records made even in towns remote from the major urban centres. We would expect lodges in London or Amsterdam to attract members with decisive intellectual interests and to cater to those needs during the time set aside at every lodge meeting for instruction. But in lodges as far away as Sluis, in Zeeland in the southern Netherlands, members were instructed that knowledge of geometry and architecture distinguishes 'the true Masons from the ignorant'. Freemasonry was an 'institution which has as its object to recall men to their primitive equality and to reassert among Masons the bonds of society and humanity by undercutting the distinctions of birth, rank and occupation'. Within this egalitarian environment, part of the Mason's obligation was self-instruction, assisted by lessons given in the lodge by an orator. Furthermore, Masons had a particular obligation to see to the education of their children. These practical rules and scientific activities were mixed with a heady dose of memorised rituals and 'catechisms':

Q. What form does our lodge have?

A. A long square.
Q. Where is it situated?
A. Exactly from the East to the West.
Q. Why?
A. Because all edifices consecrated to the divine cult must be there.[34]

That European Freemasonry possessed this distinct dedication to education and mathematical instruction, must owe a great deal to the
scientific interests of its early founders.

The leadership provided by Desaguliers and Senex (who served as
his grand master); the Rev. James Anderson; Nathaniel Blackerby, a
prominent London merchant (78); Charles Delafaye, an official in the
office of the Secretaries of State (102, 74) and an active Masonic song
writer; and by the Duke of Montague, was also resolutely Whig (72,
passim). That is not to say that Tories such as the writer John Arbuthnot could not play active roles in the intellectual and social preoccupations of their lodges, provided of course that these brothers supported
the Hanoverian Succession. It is to say, however, that the leadership
gave its active support to Walpole's government and, as we shall see,
that the mythological history and official constitutions of British
Freemasonry self-consciously argued for ministerial and court-centred
government based upon the constitutional settlement of 1689.

It should be kept in mind that Walpole was himself a Mason, and
that his home, Houghton Hall, was the scene of at least one lodge
meeting, the initiation in 1731 of Francis, Duke of Lorraine. That
initiation occurred precisely at a time when Walpole was seeking to
cement Austrian–English relations, all for the purpose of preventing a
European war. Towards the end of his life Walpole allowed himself to
be painted wearing the insignia of the Master of the Grand Stewards'
Lodge (79).

Freemasonry proved useful at the courts of Europe, and that diplomatic and ceremonial function fitted well with the royalist posture of
its constitution that idealised the culture of the old Stuart court and
even, with the exception of James II, the Stuarts. This adoration, that
defied historical events so blatantly, undoubtedly reflected a willingness to compromise with the Scottish branch of Masonry, which had a
strong emotional identification with the Stuarts and hence possibly
with the Jacobite cause. With the establishment of the Whig administration in Scotland after 1715 and the abortive Jacobite rebellion, a
few new offices were added to the king's payroll, and among them was
one that bore the title, 'the king's mason'. These offices represented an
attempt to gratify one or another interest group and clearly the Masons
were among those so favoured.[35]

Scottish Freemasonry may have played a distinctive role in the spread of Freemasonry on to the Continent, and indeed the first Masonic lodges in France that can be identified in the 1720s were led by Jacobite aristocrats who had fled to France in the service of the Stuarts. As a result, the exact relationship between French Freemasonry and the early Grand Lodge in London remains obscure. The Jacobite cause was totally antithetical to the principles of Desaguliers and his friends, and indeed one attempt by the Jacobite Duke of Wharton to take control of the movement in the early 1720s was firmly thwarted. Similarly, French Freemasonry in its early decades gave great prominence to its aristocratic leadership and, of course, remained strongly monarchist, although Jacobite, in direct contrast to the Hanoverian Masonry of the Grand Lodge that in turn permeated Protestant Europe.

The historical links between French and British Freemasonry may in fact lie in the traditional British aristocratic orders such as the Knights of the Bath and the Order of the Garter, rather than in any direct implantation from the Grand Lodge. During the late seventeenth century, wherever we find a literature glorifying and explaining those orders it was almost always by royalist Masons. Ashmole wrote a history of the Order of the Garter, while Randle Holmes (1627–99) wrote an extraordinary encyclopaedia listing all the symbols by which men delineate their social position. He was also a Freemason and his work gave special emphasis to the aristocratic orders and even described the bathing ceremony by which a Knight of the Order was literally christened in his office.[36]

In the 1720s, just at the time when we find official Masonry publicly espousing the ideals of court Whiggery, we also find Walpole's government making strenuous efforts to revive both the Knights of the Bath and the Order of the Garter. Within government circles, it was put about that 'when King James II came to the Crown he did propose to convert the Order of the Bath into a kind of religious order for the defence of the Roman Catholic Religion . . . that design not only failed but . . . the Order itself was discontinued at that time.'[37] Both before and after his exile, James II may very well have used these orders to reward aristocrats loyal to his principles–certainly the Whigs believed that he had done so.

As speculative Freemasonry emerged as a significant cultural institution after the Hanoverian Succession is it not conceivable that rival lodges were established in France by Jacobite aristocrats? They would have been familiar with ceremonial orders, and therefore predisposed to imitate Masonic ceremonies as they learned them from Masonic and Jacobite visitors such as the Duke of Wharton, who appears to have been the first grand master of French Freemasonry (96, 11–17). Its early sensibility, as well as some of its rituals, seem heavily indebted to the older aristocratic orders and indeed gossip within Jacobite circles about the Duke of Wharton emphasised not the Masonic character of his activities but his use of regalia traditionally associated with the Order of the Garter. One of his exiled associates thought that Walpole would try to harm Wharton's interests, possibly his estates in England, because of his public use of those symbols: 'He should have care however of appearing in his star and garter on that occasion if he intends to continue in Paris; complaint from W[alpole] on that head, may easily procure an order that will grieve him.'[38] Most probably this is a reference to Walpole's concern, which would have been conveyed through his elaborate system of Continental spies and agents, that an English aristocratic order, now rendered loyal to the Hanoverians, should not be sullied by Wharton's Jacobite activities. It is also possible that the Pretender was busily at work creating his own knights of the bath or the garter.

Although French Freemasonry and the Grand Lodge did establish formal relations in 1734, these were often strained by political and intellectual differences. European Freemasonry was never a monolith and where in the period prior to 1750 it did act as an umbrella for freethinking causes, the Masonry was generally English and Dutch and not French. No better illustration of the aristocratic but Jacobite, anti-materialist yet anti-Newtonian, character of French Freemasonry can be found than that of the career of its most prominent intellectual leader, Chevalier Andrew Michael Ramsay (92, 233–49).

Ramsay (d. 1743) was bitterly opposed to both the Newtonian and radical versions of Enlightenment, in effect to all forms of natural religion, and sought to ground enlightened culture on the ancient theology of true Christianity. In contrast to the 'precarious Hypotheses in the Newtonian and in the Cartesian Scheme' and above all in the 'endeavour . . . to undermine Spinosism' (96, 192–3), Ramsay offered a Christian Enlightenment, mystical yet mathematical in character and openly Masonic (93). His piety was quietistic and he emphasised the mysteries and dogmas of true Christianity. Yet his commitment to toleration and open intellectual discourse made him a Jacobite with whom the Whigs could deal and in 1730 he was admitted to the prestigious Horn Lodge in London.[39] While Ramsay embraced the encyclopaedic and Baconian aspects of the Masonic mind, his goals were resolutely Christian and combative against those of the French philosophes. In 1737 he delivered an oration calling for a new encyclopaedia to carry forth his ideals (94), and some historians have wrongly assumed that Diderot's *Encyclopédie* was its logical outcome. The ideological commitments of Ramsay and the *Encyclopédie* could not, however, have been further apart. The *Encyclopédie* does bear relation to European Freemasonry, but this is a topic best left for our conclusion.

There were social ties between French and British Freemasons, and of course the aristocratic leadership of both shared a nostalgia for the old aristocratic orders. Yet there is no concrete evidence to suggest that the Grand Lodge directly spawned the French movement. In the face of French–British rivalry during the eighteenth century, Free-masonry, despite its universalist goals, managed only an occasional bridge. This was undoubtedly because in England Freemasonry emerged as a uniquely Hanoverian social institution, an embodiment of the Newtonian Enlightenment and officially dedicated to the ideology of court Whiggery.

Finally, to illustrate this Hanoverian character, we should venture further into the world of English Masonry, survey its official publications and meet a few of its members. Anderson's *Constitutions* (1723), published by Senex, stands as an extraordinary example of political propaganda. According to its author, Queen Elizabeth, because she was a woman, and because she was also jealous of all the assemblies of her subjects 'slighted the Masons, but James I revived the movement and gave it artistic expression in the architecture of Inigo Jones' (63, 38). Charles I was a Mason 'but was unhappily diverted by the Civil Wars. After the Wars were over, and the Royal Family restored, true Masonry was likewise restor'd' (63, 40). Charles II encouraged the Masonic art but under James II 'Free-Masons in London much dwindled into Ignorance, by not being duly frequented and cultivated'. As a result of the Revolution of 1688–9, the condition of the Masons steadily improved and finally (in 1717) 'the Freeborn British Nations, disintangled from foreign and civil Wars, and enjoying the good Fruits of Peace and Liberty . . . reviv'd the drooping Lodges of London . . . so that the whole Body resembles a well-built Arch: several Noblemen and Gentlemen of the best Rank, with Clergymen and learned Scholars' having come together to establish the Grand Lodge (63, 47).

Empire and court are idealised in the official Masonic literature. The 'royal art', as Masonry was called, of course supposedly had its origin in ancient times, indeed Adam 'must have had the Liberal Science, particularly Geometry, written on his Heart . . .' This art, in turn, passed to Rome

> which thus became the Centre of Learning, as well as of Imperial Power, until they advanc'd to their Zenith of Glory, under Augustus Caesar (in whose Reign was born God's Messiah, the great Architect of the Church) who having laid the World quiet, by proclaiming universal Peace, highly encouraged those dextrous Artists that had been bred in Roman Liberty, and their learned Scholars and Pupils, but particularly the great Vitruvious, the Father of all true Architects to this Day. (63, 24–5)

If we translate the official Masonic position into the language of eighteenth-century political discourse, it becomes clear that the new science and culture of the Augustans, although resting upon republican virtues, resolutely repudiates the republican and Harringtonian model of balanced constitutional government.[40] The proponents of Augustus – he also had many eighteenth-century opponents who labelled him and his government as odious and tyrannical – invariably favoured the dominance of king over parliament, of placemen over independent squires. In the clash between 'court' and 'country', British Freemasonry should be seen as a social and cultural institution intended by its leaders to ensure loyalty to the crown and its ministers.

And lest we doubt that political ideology failed to conform with political action, a search through Walpole's private correspondence, deposited at the University Library, Cambridge, should dispel all doubts. If we use as our guide the official membership list published in 1913 by the Quatuor Coronati Lodge, the still active British lodge dedicated to historical research, a few names on this probably incomplete list can in some very interesting cases be matched to correspondents of Walpole.

In that correspondence Masonry is seldom mentioned, and never by name, but various political projects do figure prominently in the correspondence of known Masons. In 1740, Nathaniel Blackerby wrote to Walpole on behalf of merchants in the city interested in protecting the wool trade.[41] His confidential proposal, which had been seen by only one other associate, described a plan whereby it would be possible to keep trade going and also therefore to employ the poor even in time of war. His proposal was intended to assist the government in its war with Spain while at the same time securing the interests of London merchants.

Throughout Walpole's vast correspondence various Masons turn up as foreign agents and spies for the government. Martin Bladen represented Walpole's government on a mission to Paris in 1719. M. La Roche, a French Huguenot and member of the lodge at Prince Eugène's Head coffee house in St Alban's Street, spied on the Jacobites in Paris and reported back directly to Walpole.[42] His fellow lodge member, Vincent La Chapelle, was of course the first Grand Master of official Freemasonry in the Netherlands.

French Huguenot refugees, or their descendants, seem to have been particularly attracted to Masonry and especially loyal to the movement; they often also made devoted servants of the government. David Papillon, a member of the Royal Society's inner circle, acted as a personal agent for Walpole, and probably as a spy, and his name turns up in the correspondents' list of the Grand Lodge of the Netherlands in The Hague. He also felt close enough to Walpole to recommend candidates for offices.[43] Indeed, the sinews of patronage noticeably intertwine the correspondence of prominent Masons. For example, the Duke of Richmond endorsed his fellow lodge member at the Horn Tavern Lodge, Sir Thomas Prendergast, for the position of post-master-general.[44]

Yet membership in a Masonic lodge was no panacea for the cares of this world. Ralph de Courteville, whom the opposition maliciously dubbed 'Court Evil' (105, 192), loyally served Walpole as a spy on the Jacobites and as a writer of Whig propaganda for the *London Journal*. Yet he was forever begging favours that often went unrequited. At one point he was both seriously ill and heavily in debt, and he informed Walpole that his bed was about to be confiscated.[45] Although the links between Masonry and court Whiggery were close, the former should never be imagined as a government-sponsored movement or as a sure guarantor of worldly success.

By far the most ubiquitous and prominent Masonic correspondent of Walpole was John, Duke of Montague (1688?–1749), who was grand master in 1721 and one of the guiding forces within Freemasonry. Montague was a Whig oligarch if ever there was one, but he also suffered from very severe financial difficulties. He seems never to have recovered his financial balance after the South Sea Bubble burst in 1720, but this did not inhibit his almost obsessive interest in gentle-manly, quasi-military or aristocratic societies. He badgered Walpole to speak to the king about new officers for the Band of Pensioners; he sent lists of vacant places in the Knights of the Bath; he wanted a fourth regiment of guards created, and he longed to be placed in charge of the Blue Regiment.[46] He sought to become governor of the Isle of Wight so that 'I then again may be a military Man, that being a Military Post'.[47] For some men, organisations such as Freemasonry may have provided a satisfying alternative to the discipline and camaraderie normally found only during wartime.

Not only did official Masonic literature stress its dedication to con-stitutional and strong monarchy, the publications of its intellectual leaders promulgated a distinct religious philosophy, one based in large measure on the natural religion preached by Newton's early followers. They had proclaimed the ordered, harmonious, and mathematically comprehensible universe guided by the providence of God as the model for society and government. Masonic literature, in turn, stressed social stability and glorified the Masonic lodge as the model for the stable and harmonious society.[48] Masons were model citizens, loyal to the king, never libertine or immoral, knowledgeable in the arts and sciences and in particular in mathematics and geometry, 'the mother and touchstone of all other sciences'.

The early Newtonians had argued for an ethic of restrained self-interest capable of engendering success in the market-place, while at the same time insuring its stability and conformity to the providential plan. In their hands, the mechanical universe became a model for capitalistic enterprise. Not surprisingly, Masons gloried in the fact that they were good at business; the new speculative Masonry was urban-based and heavily mercantile. In a pro-Masonic tract published in 1726, a son, newly arrived in London, tells his gentleman father back in the country that 'Masonry here is upon another footing to what it is in the country; it is not a dozen pots of beer, nor a dozen gallons of Wine'; it provides access to the court and 'no small advantage to a man who would rise in the world and one of the principal reasons why I would be a Mason' (67, 157–76).

To best illustrate this Masonic sensibility we should not turn to major Newtonians, like Desaguliers or s'Gravesande, nor to Whig oligarchs like Montague, but to a relatively unknown figure, a Mason who incidentally in the course of his high-placed government career assisted in the prosecution of known radicals, some of whom were also brothers in the craft (see pp. 173–4). The mentality of official Masonry – its taste for science, its craving for order and stability, its worldly mysticism, as expressed in fanciful rituals, passwords and mythology, its love of secrecy, and above all its religious devotion to higher powers, be they the Grand Architect, the king or the grand master – all found expression in the career of Charles Delafaye, Esq., FRS (d. 1762).

By the time Delafaye ended his long career of service to the govern-ment he had become an under-secretary of state. His father, Lewis, had been a Huguenot refugee who came to England in the late 1670s and who made a living as the official translator of the *London Gazette* into French and eventually as a government agent overseeing news-paper distribution. From these humble beginnings the Delafayes became devoted servants of the crown. Charles was brought into his father's office in the 1690s, spent some time in The Hague as an informant on Dutch political affairs,[49] and so began a long career as a devoted Whig bureaucrat who eventually became one of the most intimate and trusted members of Walpole's government. During the delicate interrogations of Jacobite spies Delafaye was one of the very few government members whom Walpole permitted to witness the proceedings, and he gave evidence against Jacobites at their trials (99, 117).

Delafaye was also an entrepreneur. Not content solely to distribute government-backed newspapers to individuals and coffee houses in London, Delafaye expanded his business and offered domestic and foreign journals at cut-rate prices to customers all over the British Isles. Through a network of other Huguenot acquaintances and with the extra perquisite of franking and therefore mailing privileges at the Secretaries of State's offices, Delafaye's business flourished.[50]

Eventually he devoted himself entirely to government service and, in his cherished leisure time, to Freemasonry. Richard Steele, who was also a Freemason, succeeded him as government gazetteer (77).

Delafaye belonged to the prestigious Horn Tavern Lodge at West-minster, one of the four original London lodges that gave birth to the Grand Lodge in 1717. The exact date of Delafaye's initiation prior to 1723 is unknown, but his lodge included among its membership Desaguliers, the Duke of Richmond, Nathaniel Blackerby, Lord Paisley, Sir Thomas Prendergast and Lord Waldegrave (78, 5–6). It possessed a distinctly cosmopolitan character, with some of its members serving as ambassadors and government agents àbroad. Among the foreign dignitaries admitted to the Horn Lodge were Montesquieu, as well as Chevalier Ramsay (98, 139–42).

Delafaye was no ordinary lodge member; his enthusiasm led him to compose Masonic songs which were widely printed during the eighteenth century, and circulated on both sides of the Channel. In one such creative effort, 'The Fellow-Crafts Song', first published with Anderson's *Constitutions* (1723), Delafaye extols the virtues of the craft and claims that it represents the resolution or end of all political ideology and all squabbling about religious differences:

> Hail masonry! thou craft divine!
> Glory of earth! from heaven reveal'd!
> Which doth with jewels precious shine,
> From all but masons eyes conceal'd . . .
> Ensigns of state that feed our pride,
> Distinctions troublesome and vain,
> By Masons true are laid aside,
> Art's freeborn sons such toys distain . . .[51]

Indeed, in the absence of full legal equality for the Dissenters, Freemasonry did provide a social nexus where, within the lodge, equality could be countenanced. In that respect, Freemasonry offered one uniquely English solution to religious controversy and was eagerly seized upon by Continental reformers.

But to imagine that Freemasonry represented the end of ideology would be to overlook the evidence that Delafaye, both in his life's work and in his personal letters to Walpole, provides. In 1734 Delafaye wrote to Walpole on behalf of a fellow lodge member, Thomas Meadowcourt (78, 23), who appears to have been seeking place and who had been accused, unjustly as both Meadowcourt and Delafaye protest, of having participated in anti-government riots in Oxford against the Excise Bill. What is important is Delafaye's characterisation of their beliefs as they found expression in the camaraderie that can only be associated with their lodge meetings. Delafaye wrote to Walpole, himself, as you will recall, a Mason, about Meadowcourt:

> I have been intimately acquainted with him about Fifteen Years and very often in his Company [lodges regularly met once or twice a month] with a little Knot of Friends in those unguarded hours when a man shows what he is, and never observed in him the least Tendency to any one Vice: for several years past he has taken to a vegetable diet and drinks nothing but water and a little Cyder. His Notions of Liberty and of the Happiness of our Constitution under the present Royal Family are very High, and he has very low ones, of the Divine Right of the Clergy, and the warmth of his Zeal has made him act, preach and write upon those subjects in such a way, as has created Enemys to him; the *Craftsman* [the opposition newspaper] once bestowed a whole paper upon him, which I thought rather did him honour, so little had it to say against him.[52]

Delafaye, Mason and civil servant, had built his life around two principles which, as the letter reveals, were to be discussed in private and which had an almost religious quality in their intensity: loyalty to the Hanoverian dynasty, as bound of course by the constitution, and the submission of church to state. In this latter principle, Delafaye must have sided with the latitudinarian position as articulated by Benjamin Hoadly. When he found time away from his demanding work in the Secretaries of State office, which must not have been very often, Delafaye 'showed what he was' (as he said of Meadowcourt) by worshipping at the Masonic Temple.

His life was a model of order and efficiency, to which his voluminous and meticulous correspondence attests, and this was in large measure assisted by his wife. As Delafaye told Thomas Robinson (1695–1770), British ambassador in Vienna and Lord Waldegrave's replacement, he depended heavily upon her domesticity – although he noted her occasional complaints on that score.[53] In what time he had left, Delafaye devoted himself to science. As he told the Duke of Newcastle, 'Your Grace knows my Inclination to Mechanicks'.[54] He was on good terms with the Newtonian doctors, John Freind and George Cheyne, and they were the only ones whom he would allow to treat him for the gout.[55] Scientific dilettantism provided Delafaye's escape from the cares of political life. To Robinson, Delafaye wrote: 'I can not help giving the preference to the *Arbor Vitae* before the political pamphlets being, as you know by troublesome experience [Robinson had procured Tockay vines and antimony for him in Vienna] I am a lover of Horticulture and Botany and not an Enemy to the Mathematicks, though by age and want of leisure, I cannot attend the practice of them so much as formerly.'[56] And to assist in the enterprise of science as best he could Delafaye badgered Robinson to procure 'for some friends who are virtuosos' items from abroad which they needed for their experiments.

It now seems reasonable to ask what precise role scientific thought played in the lives of men like Charles Delafaye. What did they think about their role in the world, about its relation to the cosmic order so carefully designed by the Grand Architect? Although scientific amateurs like Delafaye leave only hints about the meaning they extracted from the new science, his fellow lodge member, Desaguliers, did write a lengthy treatise on Newtonian science. Its subscription list was heavily Masonic, including Delafaye, and *A Course of Experimental Philosophy* (2 vols, London, 1734–44) was also published by the Freemason, John Senex. With a dedication to Frederick, Prince of Wales, the treatise proclaimed the purpose of the mechanical and experimental philosophy devised by Sir Isaac Newton: 'To contemplate the Works of God, to discover Causes from their Effects, and make Art and Nature subservient to the Necessities of Life, by a Skill in joining proper Causes to produce the most useful Effects is the Business of a Science . . .' The ordered universe proclaimed by Newton made enterprise possible, whether scientific or commercial. Much of Desaguliers's book describes useful mechanical devices, from Newcomen's steam engine to wooden railways intended to move stones from quarries to the waterside.[57]

At every turn, Desaguliers praises entrepreneurial efforts in science. He is enthusiastic in his belief that through these projects human energy can be channelled by machines, and that by the use of force, leavers, pulleys and mechanical devices of every sort, human labour can be made more efficient and profitable. He even assures his readers that five English labourers, as opposed to seven French or Dutch labourers, have been observed to equal the power of one horse. He urges investors to put their money into the development of new machinery, but he cautions them to be careful of 'boasting Engineers'.[58]

Desaguliers's vision of the mechanical philosophy was firmly rooted in his understanding of capitalist enterprise. His emphasis upon labour-saving mechanical devices was directed, with a prescience that foreshadows the industrial revolution, at their exact usefulness in augmenting the profits of industry. In discussing a machine to replace human labour in the cumbersome task of pumping water out of mines, pits or wells, Desaguliers explains that 'it must be a rich Mine indeed whose Profit can afford to keep 200 Men at this work'. Alternatively, he considers the application of horse power, but concludes 'it is plain to any body that though the Horses may be had cheaper than Men, yet that will be a very expensive way'. What is in fact needed for efficient and profitable industry, in this case for the removal of water, is for 'a

Philosopher to come, and find a means to bring down the End of the Beam, without Men or Horses, in this manner', that is, through the use of steam power.[59] The mechanical image of nature that lies at the heart of the Newtonian Enlightenment yielded a variety of compelling analogies. The providential order proclaimed by Newtonians such as Desaguliers could be imitated by art and science, through the application of mechanical devices in industry, through the exploitation of human labour in the service of those devices, or simply through the imposition of order in the machinery of the state. Devotees of the new science like Delafaye willingly put their labour into the service of that public machine with the knowledge that their actions possessed cosmic significance. Their dedication to the principles and practice of Whig government, coupled with their devotion to the cult of Newtonian science, gave them a new and powerful vision of their role as the masters and orderers of society and government – all in imitation of the Newtonian universe.

For some of the leaders and the followers of this post-revolutionary Enlightenment, its scientific vision must have conferred an enormous sense of power and dominion over nature, a vision of almost religious intensity. Undoubtedly there were, as we have seen, a variety of motives for joining the new Masonic lodges that sprang up so rapidly during the 1720s. But where we find dedicated Masons who articulated its official ideology there we also find a heady mixture of court Whiggery and Newtonian imagery. It is as if we have suddenly entered into a very private world where ritual and ceremony sanctioned a new social cohesion and where the Grand Architect could now be worshipped secretly by his most faithful and knowledgeable beneficiaries.

Yet the social world and ideology of official Masonry had its dissenters, on both sides of the Channel. If the new scientific culture of the Newtonians sanctioned a providential faith in king and church, that same science, re-interpreted, could also sanction a naturalistic faith in purely human institutions, in republics, and also in that same private world of brothers, lodges, secrets and ceremonies. Such was the social reality of the Radical Englightenment to which we must now finally turn.

Notes: Chapter 4

1   Dr S. K. Blom, 'Vincent La Chapelle', *Thoth. Tijdschrift voor vrijmetselaren*, vol. 28 (1977). Cf. Gemeente Archief s'Gravenhage, Inv. no. 1885. akte 29², 28 May 1735, a notarised statement by La Chapelle describing him as 'Chef d'office de . . . Prince d'Orange et de Nassau', on a book sale arranged with one Paul Crespin in London, witnessed by James Abercrombie. Kindly provided by B. Croiset van Uchelen. Cf. *Acta Historico-Ecclesiastica*, vol. 10 (Weimar, 1736), pp. 105 *et seq*.

2   Membership lists and a chronology of these events are contained in MSS Kronick Annales and Kronick de Louis Dagran, the Grand Lodge of the Netherlands, The Hague. The Masonic dedication to the House of Orange is also clear in a laudatory poem to William IV filled with Masonic symbolism in Gerrit van der Haar, '*T Leven van Willem Den IV Prins van Oranje en Nassau* (Amsterdam, 1752), 'Aanspraak aan Nederlant'. These Masonic archives are in French up to 1760.

3   MS. Kl. 1062, the Grand Lodge of the Netherlands, The Hague.

4   John Byrom, *The Private Journal and Literary Remains of . . . John Byrom*, ed. Richard Parkinson, Manchester, 1854–5: (Chetham Society), vol. 1, pp. 272–5; Harcourt Brown, 'Madame Geoffrin and Martin Folkes', *Modern Language Quarterly*, vol. 1 (1940), pp. 215–41; J. R. Clarke, 'The Royal Society and early Grand Lodge Freemasonry', *AQC*, vol. 80 (1967), pp. 110–19.

5   See *Contemplatio philosophica: A Posthumous Work, of the late Brook Taylor . . . A Life of the Author, by His Grandson, Sir William Young . . . with Letters . . .* (London, 1793). Taylor's French correspondents make constant reference to individuals later active within organised Freemasonry, e.g., Lord Waldegrave, John Arbuthnot; and also to s'Gravesande.

6   *Contemplatio philosophica*, p. 65.

7   See his [Anon], *Calculations and Tables relating to the Attractive Virtue of Loadstones* (London, 1729); and *A Short Treatise on Harmony . . .* (London, 1730). 'This treatise was wrote by Lord Paisley and revised by Dr Pepusch'.

8   *Contemplatio philosophica*, pp. 36–7.

9   The original title of the *Contemplatio;* see esp. pp. 69–73; on materialism, pp. 65–6.

10 On the subject of *compagnonnage*, see Chapter 5, n. 26.

11 Bodleian, Oxford, MS. Rylands, d. 9, ff. 119 *et seq.*

12 For the relationship between eighteenth-century Masonic symbolism and the alchemical tradition, see Ronald D. Gray, *Goethe, The Alchemist* (Cambridge: Cambridge University Press, 1952), pp. 49, 177, and *passim*. Cf. Elias Ashmole, *Memoirs of the Life of that Learned Antiquary . . . Published by Charles Burman, Esq.* (London, 1717), p. 15. Printed for J. Roberts. Note the date of publication by a prominent Whig publisher. This text published from a copy made by Robert Plot, an associate of Ashmole.

13 D. C. Martin, 'Sir Robert Moray', in Sir Harold Hartley (ed.), *The Royal Society* (London: the Royal Society, 1960), p. 246. Cf. *The Lodges of Edinburgh (Mary's Chapel), No. 1, 1599–1949* (Edinburgh, printed for the Lodge, 1949), p. 8.

14 Magdalen College, Pepys Library, misc. 7, f. 484. Cited through the kindness of J. R. Jacob.

15 BL, MSS ADD. 40060, f. 1; and entry for September 1703 for reference to St Evremond and Bacchus. Cf. K. M. Lynch, *Jacob Tonson. Kit-Cat Publisher* (Memphis, Tenn.: University of Tennessee Press, 1971). By contrast see BL, MSS ADD. 49360 for a Tory club, 1709–14. The term 'brother' is used, but there is no ritual or hint of heterodoxy. Cf. David Allen, 'Political clubs in Restoration London', *Historical Journal*, vol. 19 (1976), pp. 561–80.

16 PRO, PROB 11/527, f. 105 for Wildman's will dated October 1670 but only proved in 1712. They had joint ownership in land in Hampshire. Wildman's will concludes that 'he so loved his God that he could serve no man's will and wished the liberty and happiness of his country and all mankind'. Information communicated by Henry Horwitz. Yet Clayton managed to vote with the court on certain issues when MP; I. F. Burton, P. W. J. Riley and E. Rowlands, 'Political Parties in the Reigns of William III and Anne: The Evidence of Division Lists', *Bulletin of the Institute for Historical Research*, no. 7, special supplement, 1968. There are Clayton MSS at the National Library of Wales but they do not apparently shed light on this period.

17 See Benjamin Rand (ed.), *The Correspondence of John Locke and Edward Clarke*

(Cambridge, Mass.: Harvard University Press, 1927).
18 ULC, Sel. 3.238, p. 359 (1693). Brought to my attention by Dr Mark Goldie.
19 Henry Adamson, 'Muses Threnodie', in Thomas H. Marshall, *The History of Perth, from the Earliest Period to the Present Time* (Perth, 1849). Cf. David Muriran, 'The Scots Tongue – the Folk Speech', *Folklore*, vol. 75 (1964), pp. 37–47, esp. p. 40, seeing the 'word' and its many imitations, e.g. miller's word, as a possible mnemonic device.
20 T. P. Hudson, 'The Origins of Palladianism in English Eighteenth-Century Architecture', D. Phil. dissertation, Cambridge University, 1974, pp. 146–7, 296–8.
21 UL, Edinburgh, MS. La. III.545, f. 19, 'The Commonplace Book of Robert Kirk' Cf. Robert Kirk. *The Secret Commonwealth* and *A Short Treatise of Charms and Spells,* ed. Steward Sanderson (published for the Folklore Society, 1976), pp. 88–9.

22 For example, Royal Society of London MSS R. B. C. 18, ff. 319–53; R. B. C. 18, f. 53 on an experiment developed by s'Gravesande in 1732; R. B. C. 12, f. 494.
23 Bernardus Nieuwentyt, *The Religious Philosopher,* trans. John Chamberlayne, prefatory letter by Desaguliers (London: John Senex and J. Innys, 1718), p. viii; J. Bots, *Tussen Descartes en Darwin. Geloof en Natuurwetenschap in de achttiende eeuw in Nederland* (Assen: Van Gorcum, 1972), p. 45. E. W. Beth, 'Nieuwentyt's significance for the philosophy of science', *Synthese,* vol. 9 (1955), pp. 447–53 sees the entire thrust of his thought as aimed against Spinoza; c.f. A. C. de Hoog, 'Some Currents of Thought in Dutch Natural Philosophy', D. Phil. dissertation, Oxford University, 1974, pp. 300–3.
24 BL, MSS ADD. 4295, f. 27.
25 *The Religious Philosopher,* p. vi.
26 Eric Ward, 'William Hogarth and his fraternity', *AQC,* vol. 77 (1964), pp. 1–20.
27 James Anderson, *No King-Killers. A Sermon Preach'd in Swallow Street, St. James' on January 30, 1714—15* (London, 1715). Only known copy is at the National Library, Edinburgh.
28 James Anderson, *A Sermon Preach'd in Swallow Street, St James' on Wednesday, January 16, 1711/12* (London, 1712); cf. W. J. Chetwode Crawley, 'The Rev. Dr. Anderson's non-Masonic writings, 1712–1739', *AQC,* vol. 18 (1905), pp. 27–41.
29 N. Hans, 'Holland in the Eighteenth Century "Verlichting" (Enlightenment)', *Pædagogica historica,* vol. 5 (1965), pp. 20–2. Cf. W. D. Hackmann, 'The growth of science in the Netherlands in the seventeenth and early eighteenth centuries', in Maurice Crosland (ed.), *The Emergence of Science in Western Europe* (New York: Science History Publications, 1976), pp. 100–1.
30 W. J. Songhurst (ed.), *Quatuor Coronatorum Antigrapha, Masonic Reprints of the Quatuor Coronati Lodge, No. 2076* (London, 1913), vol. 10, p. 122. The evidence is not conclusive as the membership list refers to 'Mr. Chambers'. N. Hans asserts that Chambers was a Mason; see in bibliographical essay item 103; 154. E. G. R. Taylor, *The Mathematical Practitioners of Hanoverian England* (Cambridge: Cambridge University Press, 1966), p. 143.
31 Bernardus Nieuwentyt, *The Religious Philosopher,* prefatory letter by J. T. Desaguliers (London, 1718).
32 John Nichols, *Literary Anecdotes of the Eighteenth Century* (London, 1812), vol. 1, p. 240. Cf. [Anon], *The Secret History of Clubs: Particularly the Kit-Cat . . . Vertuosos, Quacks, Knights of the Golden Fleece* (London, 1709), p. 19.
33 E. Chambers, *Cyclopædia* (London, 1728), vol. 2, p. 506 for Freemasonry; vol. 2, pp. 628–30 and vol. 1, p. 182, for Newtonian science and s'Gravesande; *Neueroffnetes Welt und Staats-Theatrum . . . in Europa* (Erfurt, January 1741), pp. 54–6. Chambers' account was picked up by Nathan Bailey, *Dictionarium Britannicum* (London, 1736). I owe the reference to Howard Weinbrot.

34 The Grand Lodge of the Netherlands, The Hague, MS. made by Frère Adolph van
    Schweinitz, 'Materiaux sur la Maçonnerie', MS. 62, f. 179; f. 4. As a prisoner of war
    in Dijon, Schweinitz became a Freemason and brought back these rules for his
    lodge in Zeeland. The manuscript is in erratic French with some parts translated
    into Dutch. The French for f. 179 reads:
    Demande: Quel forme avoid votre Loge? [sic]
    Réponse: un Quarré Long
    D.   Comment etoit Elle Située
    R.   Exactement de l'orient à l'occident
    D.   Pourquoi
    R.   Parce que tous les Edifices consacrer au
               Culte Divin [sic] doivent être ainsi.
35 P. W. J. Riley, *The English Ministers and Scotland, 1707–1727* (London: Athlone,
    1964), p. 259. Some contemporaries may have feared that Freemasonry had
    Jacobite tendencies; see Martin Balfertin (ed.), *Tom Jones*, Wesleyan edn (Oxford:
    Clarendon Press, 1974), bk 2, ch. 4, p. 85. I owe this reference to Howard
    Weinbrot.
36 *The Academy of Armory, or, A Storehouse of Armory and Blazon. Containing the
    several variety of Created Beings* (Chester, 1688), bk 3, pp. 55, 393.
37 ULC, Chol. 91, 43/1, 43/2.
38 Archives des Affaires Etrangères, Paris, 37 Quai d'Orsay; Angleterre, vol. 88, 3
    May, 1729, Atterbury to Sempill. The crucial 'star and garter' passage is incorrectly
    transcribed by Chevallier (see bibliographical essay 96, 12). On Walpole's
    installation into the Order of the Garter, see Edward Young, *The Poetical Works of
    Edward Young* (London, 1754), vol. 1: 'The Instalment, 1726'; his installation
    aroused much resentment. For references to Masonry, see also Alexander Pope,
    Dunciad, Twickenham edn (London: Methuen, 1945), bk 5, pp. 398–9; bk 4, p. 11;
    pp. 571–2 and notes, p. 473.
39 *Report on Manuscripts in Various Collections*, Historical Manuscripts Commission
    Reports, vol. 8 (1913), pp. 381–2, 'although he is of the Pretender's Party, I assure
    you he hates slavery as much as the greatest Whig in England'.
40 Ian Watt, 'Two historical aspects of the Augustan tradition', in R. B. Brissenden
    (ed.), *Studies in the Eighteenth Century* (Canberra: Australian National University
    Press, 1968), p. 73. For the career of Augustus, see Howard Weinbrot, *Augustus
    Caesar in 'Augustan' England. The Decline of a Classical Norm* (Princeton, NJ:
    Princeton University Press, 1978), pp. 112–16).
41 ULC, Chol. MSS 3072, 3 February 1740.
42 ULC, Chol. MSS 778, 734; for Martin Bladen, MP (1680–1746) see *DNB*; Chol.
    MSS 1178, 1371, 1454, 1864.
43 Chol. MSS 2587, 23 July 1736, 3303a; the Grand Lodge of the Netherlands, The
    Hague, Annales de Dagran, MS. Correspondence List, 1734–57.
44 Chol. MSS 2097, 9 December 1733.
45 Chol. MSS 3041, 3231, 2388, 1801, 1789; occasionally government propagandists,
    like de Courteville, spoke up against Augustus, see Weinbrot, *Augustus Caesar*, p.
    117.
46 ULC, Chol. MSS 2396e, 3092, 1507a, 2119.
47 ULC, Chol. MSS 2008, 5 July 1734.
48 Edward Oakley, *A Speech Deliver'd to the Worshipful Society of Free and Accepted
    Masons, at A Lodge held at the Carpenters Arms in Silver St., Golden Square, the
    31st December 1728* in the library of the Grand Lodge, The Hague, bound with
    Cole's Constitutions, ed. William J. Hughan (Leeds, 1897); Charles Bathurst, *A
    Speech Deliver'd to the Worshipful and Ancient Society of Free and Accepted
    Masons at A Grand Lodge, held at Merchant's Hall, in the City of York, on St. John's
    Day, December 27, 1726* (London, 1734); the Grand Lodge, The Hague, MS. 926:

'Various Tracts concerning Freemasonry, or the Royal Art by George Smith, A.B., Lector Mathematica of a Constituted Lodge at Amsterdam', 1757 – Smith was originally an English Mason. The most easily consulted work would be W. Smith, *The Free Mason's Pocket Companion* (London, 1736) and reprinted frequently. Cf. Wellins Calcott, PM, *A Candid Disquisition of the Principles and Practices of the most Ancient and Honourable Society of Free and Accepted Masons* (London, 1769) for an attack on Hobbes.

49 BL, MSS ADD 28900; whole volume filled with Delafaye's reports to John Ellis, Secretary of State, on Dutch affairs in the 1690s.

50 Michael Harris, 'Newspaper distribution during Queen Anne's reign: Charles Delafaye and the Secretary of State's Office', in *Studies in the Book Trade in Honour of Graham Pollard*, Oxford Bibliographical Society Publications, new series, vol. 18 (Oxford, 1975), pp. 139–51.

51 Smith, *The Free Mason's Pocket Companion,* and bound with it, *A Collection of the Songs of Masons* (London, 1734), p. 66; also found in W. Calcott, *A Candid Disquisition . . .* pp. 231–2.

52 ULC, Chol. MS. 2119, 5 June 1734.

53 BL, MSS ADD. 23786, f. 130, 20 October 1732.

54 BL, MSS ADD. 32689, f. 373.

55 ibid., and f. 464.

56 BL, MSS ADD. 23784, 28 December 1731; ADD. 23791, f. 143; BL, MSS ADD 23785, f. 266, 23 June, 1732; cf. ADD. 23790, f. 19, 9 January 1734 where he says he is nearly dying of the gout.

57 J. T. Desaguliers, *A Course of Experimental Philosophy* (London, 1734–44), vol. 2, preface and pp. 465–90.

58 ibid., vol. 1, pp. 254–7; vol. 2, preface, pp. vii–viii.

59 ibid., vol. 2, pp. 467–8.

CHAPTER 5

Radical Whigs, Masons and Knights of Jubilation

There is a mighty Light which spreads its self over the world especially in those two free Nations of England and Holland; on whom the Affairs of all Europe now turn; and if Heaven sends us soon a peace suitable to the great Successes we have had, it is impossible but Letters and Knowledge must advance in greater Proportion than ever. There are indeed inconveniences which for the most part attend all good Things and Liberty of Thought and Writing will produce a sort of Libertinism in Philosophy, which we must bear with. Those were far worse Libertys objected to us Protestants at the beginning of the Reformation than any that can be now objected. For as to Blasphemous Enthusiasts and reall Phanaticks we have a few or none very dangerous remaining; and as for Atheists or such as favour those Hypotheses in Philosophy, their manner and Phrase is both modester and more polite, and as such, less dangerous; for I am far from thinking that the Cause of Theisme will loose anything by fair Dispute. I can never . . . wish better for it than when I wish the Establishment of an intire Philosophicall Liberty.[1]

> Anthony Ashley Cooper, Third Earl of Shaftesbury to Jean Le Clerc in the Netherlands, 1706.

Men of a variety of political and religious persuasions, as we have seen, found meaning in the new science and by the early eighteenth century British Freemasonry gave institutional expression to this new scientific culture. The official Masonic lodges stand as a metaphor for their age. Ruled by grand masters drawn from the peerage, strictly hierarchical in structure yet curiously egalitarian at their meetings and banquets, governed by 'charges' or rules constitutionally enforced, yet indifferent to religious affiliation, the lodges mirrored a larger social and ideological consensus. Voltaire encountered that social cohesion during his 1726 visit and was captivated by it. Montesquieu went further and embraced its metaphorical expression; he was initiated at the Horn Tavern Lodge in 1730. But beneath this placid homogeneity lay another movement, one that was politically and religiously radical and intent upon subverting the prevailing order in church and state. Long before the arrival of the French *philosophes,* the Revolution of 1689 had spawned a new generation of republicans whose dedication to European Protestantism had established an international culture centred in England and the Netherlands. But the politics of opposition, even in those relatively open countries, brought with it the habit of secrecy. By the 1690s, radical Whigs, or Commonwealthmen as they were sometimes called, had formed private groupings, clubs and cabals that, in at least one instance, embraced the form of a Masonic lodge. In the ritual and ceremony preserved in artisan lore and out of the forms of guild socialising these dissenters from court and church constructed a new type of social gathering, one capable of sanctioning their private search for new systems of belief and even of worship. And almost inevitably these English radicals exported this nascent Freemasonry, along with the Commonwealth tradition, to the only Protestant republic in Europe.

In the previous chapters we have examined the philosophical and political ideas of the seventeenth century that nurtured the Radical Enlightenment. We have also depicted the largely successful Newtonian attempt to forge a coherent ideological alternative to pantheism and republicanism. Only after having explored aspects of this fashionable and established culture of Anglican churchmen, Newtonian scientists and court-appointed placemen are we now in the position to juxtapose radical culture to it and to explore that unique historical phenomenon. To do so, we must enter into this international and sometimes clandestine social world and meet its participants, many of whom came to maturity in England during the 1690s. From the perspective of history, it was there that the Radical Enlightenment first gained momentum. In late seventeenth-century England we find coteries of political men who display a unique mixture of republican politics and polemics practised within a parliamentary and post-revolutionary context. They combined political opposition with an astute interest in the new scientific learning as well as with the search for new principles of religious belief and even of religious worship. This insight does not deny the vitality of French libertinism in the same period nor does it obliterate the existence of republican schemes afoot even in that most tightly controlled kingdom in western Europe.[2] But it does, nevertheless, assert that just as the Enlightenment in its moderate and Newtonian phase first began in England, so too the Radical Enlightenment, as a coherent political, religious and philosophical tradition, took shape in a social and constitutional order forged by revolution (106, 8–9).

This new radicalism spread first and very rapidly to the Dutch urban centres, The Hague, Amsterdam and Rotterdam. Shaftesbury's letter which opens this chapter, reflects its growth and his enthusiasm for this new international culture. Yet as a Commonwealthman and a theist, Shaftesbury had grave misgivings about the libertinism and atheism he saw as vital to it. Although politically close to many of the central figures in the Radical Enlightenment, Shaftesbury was a freethinker who journeyed frequently to the Netherlands and who was closer intellectually to Pierre Bayle in Rotterdam and even to the liberal Protestant, Jean Le Clerc, than he was to Toland and his friends. Indeed Bayle (d. 1706), himself a victim of absolutism, was fascinated and repelled by the pantheism that captured the imagination of this new generation of freethinkers, many of whom he had befriended as young Protestant refugees. They, in turn, universally admired his *Dictionnaire* (1697) and indeed sponsored a new edition of it. This first encyclopaedia of the Enlightenment introduced them to a new scientific approach to learning and years later they would hail Bayle as their 'Patriarch'.[3] But the freedom of which Shaftesbury spoke led these angry republicans to embrace not the God of Calvin, as did Bayle, but rather nature as the principle of order and coherence in the world.

Although the Anglo-Dutch republican nexus lay at the centre of the Radical Enlightenment, by the turn of the century Paris also nurtured a variety of intellectual coteries that gave life to pantheistic philosophy and anti-monarchist theorising. We shall take a brief look at those Parisian coteries and their links with radicals in the Netherlands. Eventually we want to focus our attention on The Hague, for it is in the Dutch cities that we can trace a continuous social and intellectual history of radicalism beginning in the 1690s and extending to the 1750s. In 1710 at The Hague (if not slightly before) the English Commonwealthmen, Toland and Collins, participated in a secret society of French Protestant refugees which they undoubtedly had a hand in setting up. Designated by the delightful title, the Knights of Jubilation, this society was led by Prosper Marchand (1678–1756), editor of the 1720 edition of Bayle's *Dictionnaire*; Bernard Picart (1673–1733), the finest engraver of his generation on the Continent; Charles Levier, a publisher and writer; Michael Böhm, Gaspard Fritsch and G. Gleditsch, all publishers; and M. De Bey, who may have been an editor. Into their orbit gravitated the young and bitterly anti-absolutist Jean Rousset de Missy (1686–1762), who eventually became one of the leaders of Dutch Freemasonry and a highly placed servant of the House of Orange until his sudden exile in 1749 for revolutionary activities.

Every one of these refugees possessed an affiliation with the book trade, and this gave them access to the nerve centre of the European Enlightenment. Through their publishing firms and journals they disseminated heterodoxy, the new science, and republicanism to French readers within the republic of letters. In the course of their lives, these social connections, forged in secrecy, nurtured and promoted their intellectual and business interests. As purveyors of the printed word they, in turn, made contact with a new generation of mid-century publishers and authors who, whether purposely in the case of the publisher, Marc-Michel Rey, or inadvertently in the case of the zoologist, Abraham Trembley, gave new life to pantheistic explanations of the natural order (see p. 200). Marchand saw to the publication of Trembley's experiments on the self-generation of water polyps, while Rey extracted many of his publications from a largely clandestine literature that had circulated within this very radical circle in the period prior to 1750. Rey, in turn, became the leading publisher of the High Enlightenment who gave to the world works by Rousseau, Diderot and d'Holbach, as well as a vast body of materialistic and anti-Christian literature. He was tutored in intellectual matters by the scientist, J. N. S. Allamand and both, as we shall see, had a variety of associations with Marchand and others affiliated with this secret society, the true nature of which Rey and Allamand probably never knew, if indeed they knew of its existence. And to point ahead to the conclusion of this book, to the materialism that was so endemic to the later Enlightenment and its major propagandist and spokesman, the Baron d'Holbach, Rey was his major publisher and Toland was one of the most important influences on his thought. For the present, however, we must focus our attention on the early part of the century, on the radical Whigs in England, their shadowy links with Masonry, and their friends in the Netherlands, the Knights of Jubilation.

After 1690, the alliance of England and the Netherlands against France provided the political context that created this international culture. One goal inspired the advocates of this alliance: the defeat of France, and after the Treaty of Utrecht (1713), when military defeat was no longer possible, the gradual subversion of French absolutism. Of vital concern must also have been the establishment of links with like-minded reformers within France itself. Yet the evidence for such contacts prior to Louis XIV's death in 1715, let alone for the existence of comparable groups in this early period in Paris, is slim indeed. French censorship, police surveillance and the persecution of Protestants after the revocation of the Edict of Nantes (1685) has left us with an incomplete and ambiguous history for such subversive activities If the student could actually see a copy of a typical French police report, tracing the career of a publisher or intellectual suspected of subversion, the modernity of its thoroughness and its insidious blend of half-truths and spy reporting would facilitate an understanding of why Paris sported few enough radical circles.[4] Undoubtedly there is a history to be written about the contacts made by radicals in northern Europe with their counterparts in France, but such is not the focus of the present book. Here it must be sufficient to hint at possible influences but to concentrate on what we now know about radical coteries that were politically and intellectually active in the early decades of the eighteenth century and which had easy access to the printing presses in England, but especially in the Netherlands.

During the late seventeenth century most specifically republican attacks against the absolutist power of Louis XIV emanated from the Netherlands, from French Protestant refugees, the so-called Huguenots of the Dispersion (108, 65–8). In contrast, within the private Parisian academies that flourished by the late seventeenth century, political opposition to the regime tended to be *parlementaire* rather than specifically republican. These supporters of the provincial *parlements* – courts (not legislatures) with the privilege of dispensing royal justice and with the power of checking royal abuses – were often aristocratic and to that extent represented traditional social privilege and vested feudal interests. Most important for our story, however, these academies nurtured dissident philosophers such as Henri, Comte de Boulainvillier (1658–1722) and the Abbé de Saint-Pierre (114, 288), both of whom appear to have been in contact with radical circles in the Netherlands.

Some years ago, Ira Wade suggested Boulainvillier as the likely author of one of the central and originally clandestine texts of the Radical Enlightenment, the so-called *Traité des trois imposteurs* (The Hague, 1719) (5, 116–17, 124–35, 314–15). We now know that it came from the Knights of Jubilation, but its authorship will have to await our discussion of the text (see pp. 218–24). Here it is sufficient to note that the *Traité* came into existence not in Paris but in The Hague, at the hands of Charles Levier and Rousset de Missy, both French Protestant refugees in close and clandestine rapport with the English Commonwealthmen.[5] For our purposes, whether or not Boulainvillier authored an original manuscript on which the *Traité* is partially based, is not anywhere as important as the fact that it expressed ideas vitally important to these early Enlightenment radicals, who in turn put the text into circulation.

If, therefore, we were surveying the indigenous roots of the French Enlightenment it would be appropriate to lay great emphasis on those Parisian coteries of *parlementaire* opponents of Louis XIV. Certainly Montesquieu, a thinker more representative of the Newtonian than the Radical Enlightenment, benefited from their thought and probably knew members of those aristocratic academies (114, 293). His *L'Esprit des Lois* (1748) raised the *parlementaire* doctrine of balance of power to the level of a philosophical foundation for enlightened government. Yet even in the case of Montesquieu, we can see the influence of two of our radicals in the Netherlands. Montesquieu knew the thought of Jean Frédéric Bernard and Saint-Hyacinthe, both of whom were associates of Marchand, Picart, and their circle (98, 31, 135–7, 147).

In general it seems accurate to describe the *parlementaire* contribution to the radicalism of the early Enlightenment as having been religiously heterodox and philosophical rather than political. By and large, the fashionable and often aristocratic opponents of absolutism in France recoiled from either republicanism as preached by the radical Whigs or from the idea of rebellion. Their northern European counterparts, as the Dutch Revolution of 1747 will show, had no such inhibitions. Yet Louis XIV's agents watched this indigenous opposition closely and closed down their salons at the first hint of sedition. Indeed, the French government even tried to get the Dutch government to clamp down on opposition presses in its territories but only weak and ineffectual gestures were made in the direction of placating French demands (115, 44–5). The links between these Parisian circles and the centres of radical culture in the Netherlands may have been fairly extensive, but if so their means of communication remain to this day obscure.

At the heart of the early years of the Radical Enlightenment on the Continent lay the entourage of Eugène of Savoy at The Hague. It attracted radical Whigs and French Protestants, and indeed if ever they had access to European power politics, prior to the Orangist revival in the Netherlands during the 1740s, it was in those heady days after Eugène's brilliant military victories in the War of Spanish Succession. The Baron Hohendorf was the go-between of the court and the radicals, and his library (eventually moved to Vienna where it remains intact) contained just about every clandestine manuscript and subversive book, including works by Bruno and Des Périers, that can be traced to their door. Likewise, the separate and show-cased library of Eugène of Savoy amply represented the pagan naturalists of the late Renaissance, and in particular the nearly complete writings of Bruno.[6]

A variety of French poetry of a libertine and subversive character also made its way to the court at The Hague.[7] During the war this traffic to the nerve centre of the northern alliance against France must have caused considerable alarm, as extensive police reports from the last years of Louis XIV's reign seem to indicate. These reports also tell us that by the 1720s various Parisian cafés, such as the Café de Procope, had become centres of anti-government talk which sometimes spilled on to the streets. For example, a cleric named Gautier told his audience in the Luxembourg gardens that Moses had been a tyrant who invented a cult to keep his people in check – an idea that Gautier may have got from reading a clandestine copy of the *Traité*, wherein Moses is named as one of the three great imposters. Others spoke about the need for a Cromwell who would exterminate all oppressors (114, 341). At the Café de Maugis, lawyers, booksellers and journalists met in the 1720s to discuss the latest work attacking religion, while within academic circles professors, such as Camille Falconet, would be found who were active admirers of Spinoza (117, 15–16).

So it would seem that by the 1720s the outcroppings of radicalism that can be documented in Paris often point back to ideas emanating from clandestine literature written in the Netherlands or being circulated from there. This is never to imply that the majority of publishers in The Hague were radicals; most were simply businessmen. But there were important exceptions, and they in turn could find individuals on the trade routes to Paris will to do business with them. In a famous raid on the Rouen journalist, Bonnet, the French police seized copies of *L'Esprit de Spinoza*, as the *Traité des trois imposteurs* was sometimes called (116, 280). Any publisher in fact could get involved in the clandestine trade in forbidden books, if the price were right, but the Knights and their friends took risks, and most importantly, managed to work out through members of their secret society well placed in the post office, an elaborate system for by-passing French customs (see pp. 202–15). But sometimes, as in the case of Bonnet, the police were smarter than the publishers and booksellers.

Extensive police surveillance could not, however, prevent personal contacts between this *parlementaire* opposition led by groups like the Club de l'Entresol and visiting aristocrats such as the English Tory, Lord Bolingbroke. He had known Marchand and some of his friends in the Netherlands, endorsed their society, and he, in turn, received a warm welcome in Paris (114, 174–81). Bolingbroke brought with him a sophisticated understanding of the ideas of Locke and Newton, and indeed the *parlementaire* circles were among the first in France to champion the Newtonian Enlightenment while still discussing fervently the ideas of Spinoza.[8]

But this is not to minimise the political differences – nor the social and occupational ones – between these *parlementaire* coteries and radical groups in the Netherlands. One illustration of those differences comes from a letter by a harsh critic of French absolutism, the Abbé de Saint-Pierre to Prosper Marchand. The *Journal littéraire* (1713–22) edited by Marchand and his French and Dutch friends had called attention to Saint-Pierre's scheme for a universal peace and the establishment of a system for checking the rapacious militarism inherent in absolute monarchy. Gratefully Saint-Pierre, who had probably met

Marchand during his stay in Holland, tells him that he too is 'un Républicain de la république des lettres' and then, very carefully, Saint-Pierre has crossed out the word 'Républicain' and substituted 'citoyen'. Saint-Pierre would not dare to write about, or possibly to hope seriously for a world where kings would be figure heads – if they came to exist at all.[9]

In the late seventeenth century two transformations in the history of European monarchy coalesced the disparate proponents of pantheism and republicanism on both sides of the Channel. The first was, of course, the Revolution of 1688–9 in England which deposed James II and established William of Orange, Stadholder of the United Provinces, to be William III by Act of Parliament. The second began in the 1680s when the most powerful, as well as absolutist, of European monarchs, Louis XIV, sought to extend his territory and power even further by eradicating dissent at home while launching a new wave of military campaigns on the eastern frontiers of the Holy Roman Empire. Each, in different ways, galvanised the forces of opposition to established monarchical authority.

Spawned by the Revolution of 1688–9, the radical Whigs of the 1690s, with their roots in the English revolution of mid-century, developed friendships with anti-absolutist Protestant refugees in the Netherlands as well as with the small community of English republicans who resided there. As had previous generations of English radicals they made their way to the only Protestant republic in Europe where they congregated around the home of Benjamin Furly (1636–1714). A Quaker emigrant from Colchester whose father had been loyal to the Commonwealth and as a result imprisoned for his beliefs, Furly maintained a salon in Rotterdam, kept a splendid library of heretical books, and established his home as the *entrepôt* between English republicans, Dutch Dissenters, and French refugees (109) Locke resided there in the 1680s; Furly and Anthony Collins were good friends; the young Toland met and won Furly's approval in the early 1690s; and Furly and Shaftesbury conducted a warm and extensive correspondence.[10] They were the closest of these associates, and their bond rested on a commitment to the cause of international Protestantism as well as to free-spirited inquiry into religious doctrine and belief, together with a mutual hatred of French absolutism. Within Furly's circle could be found heterodox Whigs like Toland and Collins who embraced, unlike their less-daring associates such as Trenchard and Freke who merely entertained, ideas about God, nature, and therefore religion, that were materialistic; while in the case of Shaftesbury, we find a Whig who was aggressively anti-Church.

Under the impact of French military aggression all those issues took on sudden and dramatic importance in the Netherlands. Not only did the Dutch stadholder secure the throne of England for himself and his wife, Mary, James II's daughter, but after the revocation of the Edict of Nantes in 1685 the Netherlands was deluged by thousands of French Protestant refugees, a migration not unlike the one experienced by the Low Countries during the late sixteenth century. The Seven Years War (1689–97), led on the allied side by William III, coupled with fear of a French invasion, galvanised Dutch and Protestant political consciousness.

In this period the Netherlands was also probably one of the most sophisticated political cultures in Europe. Republican as a result of its experience of Hapsburg absolutism during the sixteenth century, the Dutch Republic by the late seventeenth century did recognise the claims of the Orange family to govern not as kings but as stadholders – protectors of the state. The Dutch legislative assembly, the States General, contained representatives from the various provinces and their ruling oligarchies and it was bitterly covetous of, and servile towards, local power. Throughout the seventeenth century, the oligarchs and their supporters, 'Patriots' as they called themselves, distrusted Orangist power and sought to check it at every turn. The 'Patriots' tended to represent urban and commercial interests that had generally sought an accommodation with the French colossus; peace was good for business. Yet these urban centres could also be violently Orangist. Supported by the Calvinist clergy and in reaction to these oligarchic regents, or in fear of French invasion, the populace would traditionally turn to the House of Orange. Such had been the violent events that led in 1672 to the brutal murder of John De Witt, the Grand Pensionary, and the installation of William as stadholder. Once again in 1747 French invasion would provoke a general call for the restoration of the stadholderate, only then, as we shall see, Whigs and republicans would have a special role to play in restructuring the government of the republic (see Chapter 7). All these social and political tensions were played out in cities that were by far the most cosmopolitan in Europe. By the late seventeenth century, it is estimated that well over 10 per cent of the population of Amsterdam was of foreign extraction while literacy rates in the Netherlands were among the highest in Europe.

The revival of militant absolutism produced in the 1690s a new intellectual climate throughout northern Europe. In this almost hysterical atmosphere of fear and religious hatred, some European Protestants looked for the second coming of Christ and the institution of a millenarian paradise, all presaged upon the defeat of Louis XIV. French Protestant refugees like Pierre Jurieu (110) as well as less directly threatened Anglicans like Isaac Newton looked to divine intervention to save Europe from Catholicism – from the Anti-christ and whore of Babylon as personified by the French king. In an apocalyptic mood in the winter of 1707 Newton and his close friend and millenarian, Fatio de Duillier, fantasised that 'King Louis shall be made a prisoner in the present war, and shall be kept betwixt an Iron Grate on one side and a Fire on the other'.[11]

In contrast to Protestant millenarianism, Louis XIV's policies triggered among Europeans of a less Christian temper another, equally urgent, mental revolution that gave birth to the Radical Enlightenment. One overriding goal, from the 1690s until well into the 1750s gives coherence to European radicalism: the subversion of French absolutism. Every political pamphlet, every social link, every clandestine manuscript we can trace to these circles on the Continent bears witness to this cause – the French monarchy, and its supporting institutions of church and aristocracy must be weakened. And from that perspective it was not difficult to advocate the destruction of all such 'corrupt and tyrannical' regimes.

In response to revolution at home and war abroad, the extreme Whigs succeeded in creating an extensive and extremely active political coalition. John Toland, Anthony Collins, Matthew Tindal and John Trenchard were at the intellectual heart of the radical Whig 'college' as its members described it, and they were its leading philosophical spokesmen. There was a close overlap between Robert Clayton's friends, who may have been in that early Masonic lodge and known members of the college: John Methuen, Lord Chancellor of Ireland and later ambassador to Portugal;[12] Edward Clarke, MP, Locke's great friend; John Freke; Sir Robert Molesworth, a landed gentleman with strongly Commonwealth views; William Simpson, a Baron of the Exchequer; and a host of lesser lights such as Thomas Rawlins and William Stephens who wrote Whig propaganda, and publishers such as John Darby and James Roberts who published it.[13] All had strongly republican tendencies although these could sometimes be subdued for a position within the government. They clubbed, feasted and perused books like Bruno's *Spaccio* at the Grecian Coffee House on Devereux Court in the Strand,[14] which became a veritable den of iniquity in the minds of pious churchmen who repeatedly attacked the 'deists and atheists' of the Grecian. This tension between the religious and scientific establishment and the radical Whigs could only have been exacerbated by the fact that the leaders of the Royal Society, including possibly Newton, used to take their coffee at that same house.[15] There, of an evening, the assembled could hear, or overhear, ridicule heaped upon the achievements of court Whigs like the Duke of Marlborough. His military performance was 'vilified and lessened' while, on every occasion, absent members would find that those present 'would drink your health at the college'.[16]

This college, like Clayton's lodge, may bear some relation to the group founded by Locke (d. 1704), Edward Clarke and Freke. Unlike Masonry, however, Locke's name is never associated with the college after its expansion, although he and Freke communicated regularly. Locke appears to have first come upon the idea of a 'college' in the Netherlands where in the 1680s he and Benjamin Furly established their own (109, 88–95). Just as Furly was a Quaker with freethinking tendencies so, too, not all the members of this extended college could be described as anti-Christian. Yet most knew Hobbes's writing, liked Collins's rationalistic attacks on the church and clergy, as well as on Christian orthodoxies, and consulted among themselves about the Newtonians who constantly attacked them. In a letter to Trenchard, Collins thought that the Newtonian Samuel Clarke was sadly misguided and that most philosophical explanations of the universe hung on 'the infinite divisibility of matter'. In other words, Collins was a materialist who grounded his beliefs on his understanding of the new science from Descartes to Newton. In a letter to Baron Hohendorf Toland also described Clarke as his most virulent critic. Although a key member of this circle, Toland did not always express philosophical views that met with its approval; yet he was never disowned. In 1701, Methuen sent his 'humble service to Mr Toland and Dr Tindall [the deist, Matthew]'. He added, 'I hope that the same colledge of politicians will be every night with us.' Four years later he seems to have lost interest in Toland's philosophising.[17] In contrast, Toland and Collins visited frequently and probably agreed on most philosophical and religious matters. Collins had a substantial country estate in Essex where he regularly entertained the impecunious Toland.[18]

Of all these radical Whigs, Toland strikes the modern reader as the boldest and most original in a philosophical and religious sense. He was also a truly international figure, at home on the Continent where he preached English republicanism and his own pantheistic materialism. There his ideas merged with an indigenous spinozism and republicanism, as well as with the campaign against French absolutism to permeate the beliefs of the first generation of the Radical Enlightenment.

Toland had found his intellectual footing during the 1690s in Rotterdam. He had been sent to the Netherlands as a student for the Presbyterian ministry, but he quickly gravitated towards liberal Christian as well as unorthodox freethinking circles. Le Clerc and Furly wrote enthusiastically to John Locke about Toland, describing him as 'freespirited and ingenious'. A few years later in England Locke shied away from Toland whom he appears to have regarded as dangerous and whose ideas, especially on Christianity, he sought to rebut in his magisterial *The Reasonableness of Christianity* (1695).

The extremity of Toland's position sprang from his rejection of Christian metaphysics, his unique and materialistic reading of the new science, and his refusal to accept the authority of either the established church or the Dissenting community. For Toland, as for all pantheistic materialists, God and nature are effectively one, and this position was stated most clearly in *Letters to Serena* (1704) and the *Pantheisticon* (1720). Bruno had a direct influence on Toland who read him as a freethinker, ignored his magical beliefs and imbibed his naturalism with its mystical overtones (11, ch. 6). We might well believe that Toland's unique reading of Bruno, which became so commonplace during the Enlightenment, vastly distorted the meaning intended by this martyr to the Inquisition. Yet the foremost modern commentator on Bruno, Frances Yates, has stressed that at heart his purpose was to invent a new religion, an alternative to the embattled Christianity of his age.

In this one respect Toland and Bruno (d. 1600) were kindred spirits separated by a century of history yet strangely allied in their quest for new, and inevitably more secular, forms of religiosity. For Toland was a deeply religious thinker, well schooled in the classics, theology and philosophy, familiar with the liberal Anglican tradition from Boyle to the Newtonians. Yet in one crucial respect Toland broke with that tradition: he was a Protestant for political reasons but he was not a Christian. He was a seeker after a new metaphysics, one that combined the new science with a naturalistic vision of the universe; in short he sought a universal religion complete with a new community and a new ritual. It is little wonder that Toland spied in Freemasonry a solution to his quest.

For some decades now a few historians have recognised that one of Toland's last published works, the Latin *Pantheisticon* was probably used or intended to be used as a ritual for Masonic meetings. Other such rituals were invented by known Masons among his contemporaries, and although such rituals were never taken up by the official lodges there is no reason to doubt the motives of their inventors. In 1711, Toland wrote to Baron Hohendorf, informing him that his liturgy was nearly complete[19] and it seems altogether possible that Toland had tried it out on his friends in The Hague where he lived from 1708 to 1710, and with whom Collins, among others, frequently socialised. A sample passage from the *Pantheisticon* should give us a flavour of this ritualistic civic and universal religion which, Toland claimed, resembled that practised by the ancient Egyptians and the Druids:

President: Keep off the prophane People
Response: The Coast is clear, the Doors are shut, all's safe

President: All things in the World are one, And one in All in all things.

Response: What's all in All Things is God, Eternal and Immense . . .

President: Let us sing a Hymn Upon the Nature of the Universe.[20]

The evocation of the Druids is important. In his *Critical History of the Celtic Religion*, dedicated to his fellow Commonwealthman, Lord Molesworth, Toland hypothesised that the Druids had presided over the indigenous Anglo-Saxon and Celtic pagan religion centred around the worship of nature, symbolised by the sun, and that it had been overcome by a bellicose Christianity.[21] Toland's religious myth had its political analogue: seventeenth-century English revolutionaries believed that the original Anglo-Saxons had been free born and self-governed and that the Norman conquest had imposed the yoke of tyranny.[22] The revolution would restore this ancient freedom and Toland was seeking, in the first instance, a restoration of this indigenous paganism.

If the institution of a republic of Druids seems a little far-fetched it should be recalled that Anglo-American radicals until well into the late eighteenth century held the Druids in high regard. Thomas Paine, quite possibly a Freemason himself, argued that Masonry was derived from 'the religion of the ancient Druids who like the magi of Persia and the priests of Helipolis in Egypt, were priests of the sun', while radical republicans in the new American republic were known to set up Druidical lodges.[23] In the 1760s the English deist and libertine author of *Fanny Hill*, John Cleland, wrote about 'the real secret of the Freemasons' and also claimed that their oath and religious beliefs originated with the Druids.[24]

In the early eighteenth century, the return to paganism, especially of an indigenous variety, seemed to offer a solution to the religious problem bequeathed by the English Revolution. Radicals in the 1690s who desired a republican version of the constitution, true religious toleration, social reform, a Parliament ruled by gentlemen in the interest of the people, had to recognise that those goals had been rejected in 1660 at the Restoration. As a result, they had to know why the Commonwealth had failed and why the restored monarchy had succeeded so effectively in imposing its will – almost, in the reign of James II, to the extent of instituting a Catholic and absolutist regime. The answer seemed to lie in religion: the Commonwealth had foundered on the shoals of religious disagreements. Similarly kings after 1660 had ruled – or failed to rule – only with the consent and assistance of the established church. Republicans like Toland knew that in religious consensus, in a civil and universal religion, lay the key to the reform of the old order. For them, republicanism and pantheism were of a piece, and Freemasonry provided one possible mode for its ethical and social expression. It is little wonder that Newtonian churchmen and Newtonian Masons attacked Toland and his friends with equal vituperation.

When Toland found his French Protestant friends in the Netherlands they proceeded to found a secret society remarkably similar in some ways to the one described by Toland in the *Pantheisticon*.[25] As the meeting record of the Knights of Jubilation, published for the first time in the appendix, shows (pp. 268–9), this little society also excluded the profane, the man 'of the world' just as the ritual of the *Pantheisticon* prescribed. This document provides the vital link between the radical Whigs and the first generation of Continental radicals, and one that leads to the Netherlands and its vast publishing industry.

The first record of this secret society comes from Toland's private manuscripts, and it recounts one meeting held in 1710 in The Hague during the time of Toland's residence there. This is an extraordinary document written and signed by Prosper Marchand, and without it vast sections of the Marchand manuscripts in Leiden would make little or no sense. Without knowing, as we now do, that Marchand belonged to this secret society, we could not understand references that occur throughout his correspondence with other members of 'Les Chevaliers de la Jubilation'. Why, for instance, would one Gaspard Fritsch sign many of his early letters to Marchand 'Le Grand Maistre'? Why would Marchand edit for publication the autobiography of one Charles Levier? The Toland manuscript reveals that they were 'brothers' in this secret society. And finally why would Jean Rousset de Missy, one of the founders of organised Dutch Freemasonry, write a series of long and intimate letters to Marchand that discuss pantheism, European politics and Freemasonry? Rousset's early association with the Knights again provides the key to that correspondence.

In short, the Knights of Jubilation manuscript is one of those precious historical documents which when pieced together with other records provides new insight into the history of the early Enlightenment, and one that forces an historiographical revision of our understanding of that movement. Basic to that revision is the question of the origins and social uses of European Freemasonry. In the previous chapter, I argued that Freemasonry could serve a variety of social and intellectual purposes which in England, and elsewhere, were largely supportive of established political authority. Yet European radicals in England and the Netherlands (and by implication in other European countries) could also find in the Masonic lodge a vehicle for expressing religious heterodoxy, indeed for constructing a new religious vision. Most significantly, English radicals like Toland played an essential role in transmitting that originally English form of social behaviour on to the Continent, decades before that process began in earnest. They laid roots that flourished in the period after 1730 when official Freemasonry, that is Masonic lodges affiliated with the Grand Lodge of London, took hold in various European cities and towns. It now seems increasingly clear that from its earliest formation as an international culture, the social world of the Radical Enlightenment, although not necessarily all of its adherents, was Masonic. This milieu reveals a living historical culture where the connections between religion, natural philosophy and politics take on a human reality, where ideas about nature, social equality, the new science, as well as the republican ideal produced a new kind of European (few in number to be sure) who worshipped the natural world in a new temple and who found in the brotherhood of the lodge a private, secret expression of an egalitarianism that in the course of the eighteenth century became, and remains to this day, so vital to the programme and ideals of Western reformers. In purely demographic terms, during the eighteenth century the Enlightenment had few adherents, and the Radical Enlightenment had still fewer. But in assessing the force or validity of reforming ideals, then or now, it would be most discouraging to rest one's faith or programme on a mathematical reckoning.

Can we establish definitively that this small secret society, whose membership and ideals have to be pieced together from a variety of manuscript sources, was Masonic? The manuscript from Toland's papers, given his own affiliations with Sir Robert Clayton and his liturgical writings, is highly suggestive of Masonry but not in itself proof of speculative Freemasonry. One way of interpreting the Knights of Jubilation might be to call them proto-Masonic and leave it at that. But that would be to write yet another version of 'whig' history, to read back in time, to 1710, a movement that was well under way by the 1720s and which was often copied by non-Masons from then onwards, men who had a dim idea of what Masonry was all about and who went off to establish societies in imitation of it. Were this document dated later, let us say 1720, we might see the Knights as one such society. Given the date, however, we must conclude that either Toland and his friends were groping towards a new form of social behaviour, the religious and political implications of which they barely understood, or that they were indeed self-consciously imitating Clayton's lodge, and trying therefore to establish this new form of social organisation and religious behaviour as a vehicle for expressing their political and religious ideals, their pantheism and republicanism, as well as for recruiting a good business network, one not without use in the publishing world and especially in the clandestine book and manuscript trade in which they were involved. The rituals of this early lodge, not to mention its anti-Christian stance, may have borne little resemblance to the version of organised Freemasonry established by Desaguliers, *et al.*, in 1717. But there must have been many attempts to devise new rituals, some based on the old artisan ceremonies, others of more individual origin, as a variety of non-Masons flocked to the early lodges. It is little wonder that the liturgies tried out by pantheists like Toland never gained acceptance.

The original manuscript states that the Knights of Jubilation possessed a grand master and a constitution, both essential to speculative Masonry, but other elements, from different traditions, are also present. This group of largely French refugees, all involved in the book trade as publishers and as members of the publishing guild in The Hague, are imitating rituals associated with French artisan guilds. Playfully one member is having to pay the 'guild' for the right to marry, a custom that may also be found among the semi-clandestine guilds called *compagnonnage*.[26] Similarly, the Knights of Jubilation may also have been in imitation of literary societies and academies that began to proliferate during the sixteenth century and that can be found in French provincial cities or in German Lutheran towns. The taking of aristocratic titles was commonplace in such groups whose composition was nevertheless heavily bourgeois. The tone of the document also sounds clearly Rabelaisian, recalling the coteries of French libertines that flourished in mid-seventeenth-century Paris. It seems altogether fitting that early Freemasonry would have subsumed elements from a variety of traditions, many of them far removed from the artisan guilds of English masons who first opened their doors to local gentlemen. It should also be added that the very title of this society, or 'order' as they would have said, may harken back to a society of the 1650s, *Les Chevaliers de l'Ordre de l'Union de la Joye,* to which the republican leader of the Netherlands, John De Witt, belonged and about which Toland and his friends may have heard.[27] In short, the manuscript in Toland's possession, with its obviously Masonic elements, is highly suggestive of a new, speculative version of that ancient craft, but it is not in itself conclusive. But there is other evidence.

Charles Levier, the 'joker' of the order (a similar figure, 'Le Terrible', survived as a regular officer within organised Dutch Freemasonry),[28] was a trusted friend of Anthony Collins. After he was forced to leave England briefly because of the furore caused by his *Discourse of Freethinking* (1713) the Knights were his closest social ties in the Netherlands. As his letters to Levier reveal, Collins belonged to their 'order' and met with other members on his journey through the Austrian Netherlands.[29] As we shall see, by 1712 the Knights had broken through what we might have been tempted to dismiss as their local or 'guild' structure; they had extended their network to Brussels and Antwerp, cities at that time in the war controlled by the allied powers (see pp. 203–5).

The international character of the Knights points once again in a Masonic direction. One of the great strengths of that originally British phenomenon was its exportability; unlike the old operative guilds Freemasonry possessed a universalist ideology. But it would be most comforting to find the actual word 'mason', in French *maçon*, used by this group in a speculative context. We would hardly expèct them to speak of *Francmaçonnerie* at this early date; indeed after some initial confusion with the translation of the term 'freemason' that word only appears in French translation in the late 1730s. In this early period, English writers simply referred to 'Masons' and there to associate them with drinking and merry-making as well as with scientific circles.[30]

The best evidence for the specifically Masonic character of the Knights, aside from the life-long Masonic involvements of some of its members and associates, comes from the manuscripts of Prosper Marchand. He was, of course, secretary to the order and as we shall see one of the leading *savants* of the Radical Enlightenment. In 1712, Marchand wrote a manuscript treatise for M. de Bey, one of the other officers of the Knights, entitled 'Idée d'une Logique et Rhétorique du sens-commun; ou Essai de quelques Règles Générales pour bien composer un Discours'. It explains that rhetoric and logic comprise 'the rules and precepts of an art and a science. They are not communicated to all the world. They are rather rewards only attained by continual and assiduous study, and by lengthy and profound meditations.'[31] The treatise goes on in a leisurely fashion to explain these rules and to use very selected and adapted portions of a poem by the seventeenth-century French poet, Boileau-Despreaux, *L'Art poétique* (1674), to illustrate the art of composition. What is so important about Marchand's exercise is its link with European Freemasonry.

Throughout the eighteenth century, Freemasons emphasised the necessity of their members' possessing skills in the seven liberal arts and especially in logic and rhetoric. Adopting the role of the pedagogue to his friend, de Bey, Marchand selects a portion of Boileau's poem that uses the French word *maçon*, addresses it to de Bey while applying the passage exclusively to achievements in the intellectual arts. Marchand has chosen from a host of illustrations used by Boileau to single out the Mason and to emphasise the notion of rising by degrees:

> For you therefore is given an excellent lesson
> Better be a Mason, if it is your bent,

A lauded worker in a necessary craft
Than a commonplace author, a banal writer.
In all other crafts there are degrees of excellence;
It is honourable to occupy the second place.
But in the dangerous craft of speaking and writing
There is no distinction between the middling and the bad.[32]

Marchand is telling de Bey that just as in Masonry there are degrees of achievement (from apprentice through to grand master), and although it is acceptable to be a lodge member and not necessarily a grand master, in the arts of speaking and writing nothing but the highest achievement is sufficient. To address de Bey in this fashion, pulling from Boileau's poem one of the few passages in seventeenth-century French literature that makes mention of a Mason, and to tie the notion of rising by degrees to excellence in the intellectual arts, qualifies Marchand's treatise as one of the earliest expressions of speculative Freemasonry. Most important, that expression is tied to the programme of Enlightenment.

Having established the Masonic character of the Knights, it seems appropriate at this point to introduce the full cast of characters who can be directly linked to membership in the Knights of Jubilation. As grand master we find Gaspard or Caspar Fritsch, a Protestant bookseller and publisher who had been born in Leipzig where his brother, Thomas, ran a lucrative publishing business. After 1706, Gaspard Fritsch opened a business in Amsterdam and Rotterdam with another Knight, Michael Böhm, and together they took over the book business of Reinier Leers (d. 1704). Leers had been one of the most important Protestant publishers of the late seventeenth century.[33] In the 1690s, he had taken in Pierre Bayle and supported him while he compiled his *Dictionnaire* (1697). Leers, along with a variety of other booksellers who often used the false imprint 'Pierre Marteau of Cologne', stands in a tradition of Protestant booksellers who were highly educated and who used their presses as propaganda tools in the bitter pamphlet war against French absolutism. Indeed, publishers like Fritsch and Böhm, in the vanguard of publishers of early Enlightenment works, and associated with this republican coterie (even after a personal falling out), possessed an intellectual tradition that harkens back to Leers and 'Marteau'. By the early eighteenth century that tradition included a keen interest in the new science, and it surfaced once again in this freethinking opposition to monarchy and national churches.

Fritsch corresponded for years with Marchand and those letters provide a lively portrait of their intellectual interests. Among the earliest is a letter from Marchand to Fritsch and Böhm sending greetings to one 'frère Jacobson' wherein Marchand announces that he has begun 'to copy the manuscript notes on the *Tractatus Theologico-Politicus* although he is having trouble with the Hebrew and Syriac characters'. A heavily annotated copy of Spinoza's *Tractatus* survives in Marchand's manuscripts,[34] and the conclusion presents itself: his circle constituted one of the largest and most intellectually active coteries of 'Spinozists' or pantheists, as they used that word, to be found in northern Europe during the first quarter of the eighteenth century.

In the lives of these Enlightenment publishers, there is much to remind us of an earlier period in the religious life of early modern Europe. During the sixteenth century various Protestant sects emerged that espoused extreme versions of Christianity, often to the horror of Luther and Calvin (121). In that radical Reformation publishers and booksellers played a major role far in excess of their numbers, and they were often congregated in the Spanish Netherlands. For example, Christopher Plantin built one of the finest and largest publishing businesses of the later sixteenth century. In Antwerp, he had the lucrative right to publish Bibles for the Spanish king; in secret he belonged to a radical sect, the Family of Love, and surreptitiously published works by its leaders (120, 5–16). The liberal beliefs and secret practices of this sect have often been seen as foreshadowing those of Freemasonry (118). Perhaps it is not accidental that one of the finest libraries in The Hague, to which the Knights supplied books, the library of Baron Hohendorf, Eugène of Savoy's adviser and close friend, also collected works by Plantin.[35] Over a century of semi-clandestine Protestant opposition, first to Spanish and then to French absolutism, would be represented in a collection of books that runs from Plantin, through 'Marteau', to the numerous works published by Fritsch and Böhm, Marchand, Picart, another of the Knights, and their friends.

The partnership of Fritsch and Böhm dissolved and Fritsch moved from Rotterdam back to The Hague in 1716. He and his brother in Leipzig, who was in partnership with Jean Friedrich Gleditsch (1653–1716), another Knight, built two of the largest publishing firms in northern Europe.[36] The two families were linked by intermarriage – a pattern common in the lives of these publishing families – although the Gleditsches lost contact with the Knights after 1716. The possibility remains, however, that one of them may have brought Freemasonry to Leipzig decades before that city became one of its centres during the 1740s.

At The Hague, Fritsch would have resumed contact with his fellow Knight and correspondent, Charles Levier (d. 1734), who was briefly in business with Böhm, and whose writings, entirely unpublished, as well as his publishing activities, should qualify Levier as a minor philosophe in his own right. He was one of the leaders of the Knights and a friend and publisher to another philosopher, Themiseul de Saint-Hyacinthe, and to the Whig historian, Paul Rapin de Thoyras.[37] Born in Picardy, Levier had fled to Rotterdam sometime before 1710. There he established a fairly secure publishing business that was continued by his widow. She occasionally published with Pierre Paupie, another publisher of Enlightenment works as well as of Chevalier Ramsay's 1737 Masonic oration on the necessity of a new encyclopaedia.[38]

Levier got his understanding of the English Revolution directly from Collins who informed him in a letter (which makes clear their personal friendship) that William of Orange came to

> re-establish the penal laws that King James had suspended (or if you please abolished) by his sole authority. But the Prince came to England in order to correct this error in another manner, namely to have the penal laws suspended or abolished by the legislative power that alone has the right to suspend a law, and which effectively suspended them by an act of parliament called the Act of Toleration, made in the first session of the Parliament of King William.[39]

This was a very 'country' and parliamentary reading of those events – no talk here of providential right or even of abdication. The Knights imbibed a Whig reading of that central political transformation, and they learned it from one of the leading radical spokesmen of that party.

Levier also knew Benjamin Furly, and most important, had access to his library. There Levier copied a manuscript, 'La Vie de Spinoza' that laid the foundations for the infamous *Traité des trois imposteurs*. At a later point I shall be arguing that Levier and Jean Rousset de Missy are in effect the authors of that clandestine manuscript. Aside from works by Bruno, Furly's library contained a variety of clandestine manuscripts and subversive tracts. He owned almost all the great republican and democratic works of the English Revolution including the writings of Gerrard Winstanley. When Furly's library was sold after his death in 1714, two of the Knights, Fritsch and Böhm, handled the sale and also laid claim to a variety of books by English republicans – Harrington and Tyrell, for example, as well as to a number of Exclusionist tracts (128).

This alliance of the Knights with the radical fringe of the Whig Party, an alliance forged at the height of the War of Spanish Succession, was undoubtedly intended to serve British interests in northern Europe. Whig policy, as well as Tory, demanded the creation of an Anglophile group or party in the Netherlands, and in their political activities the Knights and their Dutch associates contributed to that effort. When the wealthy art collector and spy for Walpole, Phillip von Stosch (101), left The Hague in 1721 on a mission for his English employers he entrusted Levier with his papers and belongings.[40] Even after Levier's death, one of Walpole's agents, Peter August Samson, wrote to his widow, also a publisher, to send greetings and regards from the 'maison d'Walpole'. That August Samson is the same person to whom Toland dedicated his *Adeisidaemon* published in The Hague in 1709. Levier also published Rapin de Thoyras's *Dissertation sur les Whigs et les Torys* (1717) which delineated the moderate Whig credo throughout much of the eighteenth century.[41]

Prosper Marchand, secretary of the Knights of Jubilation, and Anthony Collins were also on good terms, while Jean Rousset de Missy, Marchand's close friend, acted throughout much of his career as a propagandist for English and allied interests in Europe. Significantly for our story, Rousset's first published work was a translation of Collins's *Discourse* coupled with a rare work by Toland, *A Letter from an Arabian Physician* (London, 1706).[42] That early link between Toland and Rousset is vital for understanding the thought of this journalist and publisher who became, in 1747, a revolutionary. When Rousset was an aging man in his 60s, exiled from the Netherlands for his part in the Dutch Revolution, he still wrote enthusiastically to Marchand about 'le Panthéisme' (see Chapter 7).

There is no small irony in the perception that these European radicals, who supported English interests on the Continent, yet who were fiercely loyal to the Netherlands, their adopted country, unwittingly helped to promote the interests of an aristocratic and commercial oligarchy in Britain that had long ceased to practise the republican creed. Yet there is also irony in the fact that while Walpole's government persecuted radicals at home, it had little choice but to rely on them as spies and agents abroad. When British Freemasons officially tried to establish Freemasonry at The Hague in 1735, an act that was almost certainly political, they also unwittingly gave sanction to an institution that housed the most extreme forms of religious and political radicalism.

It should never be imagined that the Knights and their friends were simply agents of Whig foreign policy. They were freethinkers in every sense of the term and their writings, published and unpublished, make clear their convictions. Yet all belonged to the Walloon congregations, and their reasons, as refugees, should be clear enough. The churches gave them a social identity and the hint of irreligion would have destroyed their reputations and probably their businesses. When Bernard Picart, the 'illuminator' of the order and one of the finest engravers of his age, sought as a widower to remarry in The Hague his hopes were nearly dashed by objections raised by his prospective father-in-law. It appears that he distrusted the sincerity of Picart's devotion to Calvinism. For French refugees the Dutch cities must have been very small worlds; indeed the population of The Hague in this period was barely 35,000. It is little wonder that Marchand waited until his last will and testament to condemn the practices of organised religion – 'non seulement comme vaines et blâmables, mais même comme criminelles et condamnables, vue le grand abus qu'on en fait' (113, 252). In a private manuscript treatise Levier, also a member of the Walloon Church, makes clear the reasons for his seeking refuge in the Netherlands, for leaving his parents, friends, fortune, country 'and all that I hold dear in the world'. It has been 'in order to have the liberty to live according to the light of my conscience'[43] – a clear statement of his search for intellectual freedom and not for Protestantism *per se*.

Marchand and Levier must have been very close friends and evidence suggests that they remained so throughout their lives. The latter wrote a very curious and amusing 'autobiography'. Written as a long parody on the Jesuits, and claiming in effect to be the life of the saintly founder of the order, Ignatius of Loyola, Levier's text is really a thinly disguised life portrait. Marchand edited it for publication, and the central point of this 'life' is to depict Levier as the founder of a new order that is spreading all over the world. Les Inighistes, as the order is called, aimed at sanctity and piety but they were sometimes accused of being nothing less than a modern revival of paganism.[44] According to the autobiography this order met at 'Gaillardin', and of course that is exactly the meeting place described in the Toland manuscript.[45] The tone of mockery and joviality adopted by Levier also conforms to the tone of the meeting records and letters left by the Knights and their associates.

This curious work, I would suggest, is nothing less than a Masonic allegory expressing a long-nurtured antagonism against the Jesuits, the Catholic Church, the Inquisition and the papacy. Some years after Marchand published it, Rousset de Missy wrote in one of his many letters to Marchand that anyone could become a Mason, except a Jesuit.[46] Levier remained devoted to this new order throughout his life, as well as to the northern alliance against France, and he was, as we have seen, on personal terms with some of the leading Whig theoreticians of the early eighteenth century.

Can we discern a link between Levier's private beliefs and his public life as a publisher and bookseller? Happily the sale catalogue of Levier's shop inventory, compiled at his death, has been preserved and it reveals that he owned and sold almost every sort of freethinking and heretical work as well as the standard sources for Enlightenment culture.[47] He had a vast collection in seventeenth-century science, while under the category 'Theologia Scholastica', he or possibly his widow, has devilishly listed works by sceptics and heretics. He sold works by English republicans as well as by Hobbes and Machiavelli, and his shop contained in addition libertine manuscripts including *Les Amours pastorales de Daphnis et Chloe* (1718), an erotic work that also turns up in Baron Hohendorf's library. In Levier's shop the reader found the Enlightenment in all its facets, and if M. Levier were at its counter one could also meet one of its progenitors.

Yet of all the Knights of Jubilation, Marchand and his intimate friend, Bernard Picart, are the most famous and in intellectual terms their leadership within the society is most visible. Marchand, a French Protestant, established a good bookselling business in Paris during the 1690s. In 1709 he removed to The Hague for religious reasons, also quite probably because Louis XIV's repressive policies against small book dealers (whether in fact orthodox or not) could hardly have promoted Marchand's business. Yet those years in Paris were fruitful ones. From at least 1700 Marchand associated with Picart and both had businesses on Rue St Jacques in the Latin Quarter.[48] Picart was the son of Etienne Picart, an engraver and artist of some distinction, who in turn trained his uniquely talented son. By the 1690s, the younger Picart had already achieved a reputation in Paris but this fame did not inhibit his personal intellectual growth. The earliest extant engravings of this immensely prolific master display distinct philosophical interests that matured into a style particularly characterised by the use of pagan symbolism.

In the case of Picart, style appears to have reflected intellectual conviction. Although born a Catholic and already well on his way to a lucrative career Picart converted to Protestantism at the very time when Louis XIV's campaign against French Protestantism was at its height. Picart's intellectual odyssey only began with his conversion. By the early 1700s, if not before, his engravings and drawings depict philosophical themes later commonly associated with the Enlightenment. This originality was augmented by a technical proficiency acquired, in part, through his familiarity with the new science and technology, by the study of anatomy, and by the use of the microscope to perfect his engraving techniques. Among Picart's earliest engravings (1688–93, but unfortunately now lost) were an allegorical series on the life of Descartes.

Throughout the mature work of Bernard Picart certain iconographical keys appear with regularity and this ensemble of symbols and pagan figures bear direct relation to late Renaissance naturalism.[49] Minerva and Mercury reappear time and time again; Mercury in flight showering the earth with books, Minerva triumphant, Minerva as patron of the new science, Minerva surrounded by engrossed *putti* who delve mysteriously into half-opened books, gaze at partially covered globes, or play with the pots of the alchemist. Always in these philosophical engravings the square and the compass, the tools of the mason and the engraver, appear. In one engraving Apollo is taming nature in the form of animals and at the same time building blocks are falling into place, the mason's work completed for him by the harmonious sounds of Apollo's lyre. A matching engraving shows the sun imposing a similar harmony on the earth and nature.[50] By the early eighteenth century, this symbolism was widely understood by literate viewers who had access to handbooks that explained it. In one such popular guide, Minerva was identified with the government of a Commonwealth and with liberty. Dutch engravers of the sixteenth century had used her as just such a symbol of their struggle against Spain.[51] By the mid-eighteenth century, Dutch Masonic symbolism relied heavily on the figure of Minerva depicted in a style that harkens back to Picart.[52]

The Knights of Jubilation, as the notes of their meetings reveal, took Minerva and Mercury to be their standard bearers. Minerva is, of course, wisdom; and in the Hermetic tradition, as interpreted by Bruno, Minerva, like all the pagan deities, represents 'the virtues and powers of the soul'. The soul of every man is, however, a participant in 'a world, a universe' (12, 220). To inculcate these spiritual virtues, as clearly the Knights sought to do, in effect to reform one's soul, is a vital step in the direction of reforming and enlightening the world. How fitting that these publishers and booksellers, men of business and commerce, should take Minerva, who was also sometimes seen as the goddess of printing, on the one hand and Mercury on the other, as their standard bearers. Mercury is, in addition, a representation of Hermes Trismegistus as well as being the god of commerce.

Hermes was the great teacher of the ancient theology of the Egyptians, and as Toland explained in one of his tracts all the myths and fables of the gods were intended to cover over their pantheistic materialism.[53] Priests and princes purposefully took those myths, never intended to be taken at face value, and inculcated them as superstitions 'to keep the common people in good order'. By adopting Minerva and Mercury as one's standard bearers, while proclaiming reason and the new science (and, as we shall see, the Knights and their associates were among the important transmitters of Newtonian science on to the Continent), and while publishing and circulating pantheistic treatises, the Knights of Jubilation were attempting to restore the ancient wisdom as the cornerstone of a radical version of enlightenment and reform. They were also attempting to survive and profit in business and it must never be forgotten that in pre-industrial Europe capitalistic enterprise and political, religious and social reform were often entwined. Over the years Picart became the 'official' engraver of the Knights, and in books published by one or another of the members an engraving by Picart often adorns the title-page.

The decision to begin life anew in a different, although Protestant, country must have been made with some difficulty. In the 1690s, Picart journeyed to the Low Countries, made friends within Protestant circles, but returned home. By 1708, however, his first wife and all his children by that marriage had died, and he was in trouble with the authorities for an engraving in praise of Descartes.[54] Two years later and after some considerable difficulties in obtaining permission to leave France, Picart journeyed to Brussels and Antwerp, and then joined the Huguenot community in The Hague. Eventually he made his way to Amsterdam where he opened a shop at the sign of the star, and there he trained an entire generation of Dutch and English engravers, including John Pine, L. F. du Bourg, and J. Folkema. Hogarth also knew and admired his work. After the death of Louis XIV (1715), Picart was able to make a few surreptitious journeys back to Paris and he may very well have made contact with *parlementaire* circles there.[55]

In the Netherlands, Marchand and Picart resumed their business association and life-long friendship. Both became involved with friends and associates of Pierre Bayle, and somehow the task of putting out a new edition of Bayle's correspondence fell to Marchand. He also edited and, together with Böhm, another Knight, published, a new edition (1720) of Pierre Bayle's great *Dictionnaire* (1697), the original of a genre of Enlightenment encyclopaedias. Rivalry over which of Bayle's many admirers among these radical coteries on both sides of the Channel would succeed in putting out this edition led to a falling out between Desmaizeaux, Toland's editor, and Marchand. This tempest brewed in its teacup for many years and provides a good illustration of commercial rivalries at work to cause rifts in this freethinking and subversive world (131).

Even before Marchand's departure from Paris one aspect of the new scientific learning had shaped his intellectual life most profoundly, and that was the Baconian passion to investigate and classify. Recent research has shown that Marchand deserves a very special place in the history of the classification of knowledge. Independently and yet simultaneously with Gabriel Martin, Marchand perfected a system for the classification of books – and hence knowledge – that many years later would inform the method of classification used by Diderot and d'Alembert for that great work of the Enlightenment, the *Encyclopédie* (1751) (131, 2–16). Given what we know about Ephraim Chambers, and about Marchand and his associates, we can better understand why the scent of Freemasonry has laid heavily around the great *Encylopédie*. In one form or another the association will not go away despite the efforts of cautious scholars to point out that there is not a shred of solid evidence linking Diderot, or his four publishers, whose combined efforts brought out that extraordinary revision of Chambers' original encyclopaedia, to organised Freemasonry. In the last chapter, I shall be suggesting a new approach to reconciling that old conflict; suffice it to say at this point that Diderot's project was not directly Masonic but that for a number of reasons it had various Masonic associations.

So, too, did the 1720 edition of Bayle's *Dictionnaire*. Marchand edited and Böhm published it, while Picart did two of its highly symbolic engravings. His design for the title-page has been interpreted as Rosicrucian, although there the evidence is not conclusive; the frontispiece, however, is replete with the figures of Minerva and Mercury as well as the range of Picart's usual devices, the compass, the square, the cornucopia, etc. The cult of Minerva in the eighteenth century as a symbol of the Enlightenment, given one of its earliest expressions in Picart's engraving, at least partially owed its origins to the Knights and their literary society. It is not accidental, therefore, that in the course of the century the figure of Minerva when combined with certain symbols took on decidedly Masonic associations.[56]

Evidently the 1720 edition of Bayle's *Dictionnaire* was inspired by a very different set of assumptions about nature and religion from those that gave meaning to the life of its author. Yet the Knights' affection for Bayle and their desire to preserve his memory remained constant throughout their lives. In recent historiography, Bayle is sometimes excluded from Enlightenment studies and in juxtaposition his Calvinist faith receives emphasis.[57] The latter approach seems valid but the former assessment hardly conforms to contemporary opinion of his friends and admirers. Bayle's deep commitment to religious toleration and his free-spirited system of inquiry, coupled with his encyclopaedic tendencies, place him closer to the 'Masonic' mind than might have previously been suspected. He was a deeply religious thinker, and so, too, were the radicals. It is just that their versions of religion came to differ profoundly.

It seems reasonable to suppose that Marchand and Picart arrived in The Hague with an already well-developed set of intellectual interests at variance with official French culture and with orthodox Christianity. Marchand's early Baconian interests are well illustrated in his private manuscripts, and Picart's adoration for Descartes is well known. Luckily Marchand's index to his private library, begun in the 1690s, has also been preserved, and it reveals that he read widely in late sixteenth- and seventeenth-century natural philosophy, in Campanella, Bacon, Hobbes and Descartes. Later he would add Spinoza to his list of carefully perused authors. Indeed, Marchand's full library, when combined with his private one, reveals an intellectual odyssey that begins with Calvin, includes his contemporaries Rabelais and Servetus, proceeds to Vanini and Agrippa, and from the seventeenth and eighteenth centuries concentrates on libertine literature, the new science, Toland, Collins, Tindal, works on the Hermetic tradition, hieroglyphs and Freemasonry (not to forget a few mildly pornographic, yet philosophical pieces like Diderot's *Les Bijoux indiscrets*).[58] As a reader Marchand was prolific. As a writer, editor and journalist Marchand contributed decisively to the encylopaedic mentality of the early Enlightenment as well as to the circulation of heretical and naturalistic literature.

Aside from his work on Bayle's *Dictionnaire,* and his own posthumously published version of that work, edited by his friend, J. N. S. Allamand, Marchand wrote one of the first histories of printing. He received assistance in compiling the details of this history from many of his friends, especially from Jean Rousset de Missy and from the Dutch scientist, Willem Jacob s'Gravesande. Marchand's *History*, published by Levier's widow, is dedicated appropriately enough to Minerva, and its symbolic frontispiece was designed by the author himself.[59] Throughout the work Marchand emphasises the direct role played by printing and printers in the spreading of learning and enlightenment. The point has only just been emphasised and elaborated upon by contemporary historians. For Enlightenment publishers like Marchand, relatively free to pursue their professional and intellectual interests in the Netherlands, the link between publishing and the spread of the Enlightenment seemed self-evident and probably a source of enormous personal pride.

One of Marchand's earliest publishing ventures in this new environment reveals his debt to the naturalistic tradition so central to the Radical Enlightenment and discussed in some detail in Chapter 1. In 1711, Marchand edited and published the extremely rare, and in its time extremely heretical, *Cymbalum Mundi* (1537) by Bonaventure Des Périers. The title-page of Marchand's edition is adorned by a small engraving designed by Picart. At the centre is a large star surrounded by a constellation of seven smaller stars and the central star appears to symbolise the sun or light which is radiating on to the earth. Framing this central theme are two cornucopia yielding forth open books and tools, among them a ruler and compass, the tools of workmen such as masons and engravers. The words *Inter Omnes* appear at the top of the engraving, which if translated as 'among all men' carries the clear implication that the book contains a universal message worthy of illuminating all who read it.

The volume is introduced by a letter that had been written by Marchand to Picart in October 1706 when they were still in Paris and in it Marchand argues that despite its infamous reputation the *Cym-*

balum Mundi was neither impious nor atheistical. Marchand does admit that one of the author's secret intentions may have been 'to turn into Ridicule whatever is believ'd in Religion',[60] but in general Marchand simply claims that Des Périers's intention was 'to laugh indifferently at all the World'. He rightly places Des Périers into the naturalistic and satirical tradition of libertinism made famous by Rabelais, and Des Périers did apparently know people in Rabelais's circle. Marchand tells Picart that he agrees with Bayle, that instead of trying to convert the ancient pagans we should laugh at them. Yet Marchand is not simply laughing at Des Périers's account of Mercury's difficulties during a trip to earth, he is also laughing with Des Périers's satire on the alchemists and with the spirit of the book in general. In this work, Minerva is the only pagan deity with any sense; she sends a message to Mercury telling him to chastise earthly poets for squabbling among themselves and to get down to the serious business of writing about love. Suddenly, at the beginning of the eighteenth century, the naturalists of the sixteenth and seventeenth centuries, with their roots in the Hermetic tradition, have been reintroduced into European thought and turned into freethinkers and jesters at established religious authority. The message that Marchand, Picart and their friends took from Des Périers (which may not have been the one he ever intended) linked him to their ideals and made him one of the spokesmen for their little society.

Whatever their intellectual interests and energies before their arrival in The Hague, these Protestant refugees and *émigrés* acquired new resources and opportunities from their secret society. On a business level it could also obviously act as a hedge against the fierce competition that book dealers and publishers were always trying to control. Any good book business could also be tempted to stretch its market into clandestine literature, but given the intellectual interest of the Knights such activity must have almost been inevitable. Dutch law enforcement against forbidden books was from city to city almost non-existent, and book dealers who could move their wares about from place to place were particularly immune and therefore particularly free to enter the trade in forbidden books. Secrecy, rather than being seen as bizarre, should perhaps be understood as useful. When the Dutch authorities did attempt to crack down on the book trade and publishing industries, during the 1730–1 anti-libertine hysteria in the Netherlands, Picart, Rousset and many of their friends were closely interrogated by the Dutch authorities, but they escaped unharmed.

Certainly their tutor in the art of forming secret societies, Toland, had expressed cogent reasons for the practice. In 1709 at The Hague he published a treatise called *Adeisidaemon* (The Unsuperstitious Man) in which he advised secrecy as a means to an end, as a way of arriving at the true esoteric philosophy, the knowledge that God and Nature are One. He especially praised the Chinese mandarins for their caution and political expertise. Toland also addressed that work to Collins, and it was probably published by Thomas Johnson who went on to publish the literary journal edited by Marchand, Saint-Hyacinthe, s'Gravesande and their friends.[61]

This reference to the mandarins may help to elucidate the relation Toland and his friends in The Hague appear to have had to the court of Eugène and in particular to its gifted librarian, Baron Hohendorf. Both are mentioned in letters and indeed the Knights contemplated the dedication of books to one or the other.[62] In a political sense, could they have imagined themselves as an international Protestant intelligentsia, who if military events went the right way might some day find themselves as advisers to a truly enlightened and powerful reformer? The fantasy appears thoroughly possible and will be seen to be directly related to the later political involvements of these northern European radicals.

But military events did not proceed to the liking of the radical Whigs. A new Tory ministry sued for peace and although French ambitions in northern Europe were checked, they could hardly have been seen as destroyed. The war against absolutism now became a propaganda war while the subversion of established religion continued in the clandestine and anonymous literature that became increasingly more commonplace. These early contacts between the Commonwealthmen and the Knights of Jubilation appear to have lessened, or at least the evidence gives out after 1720. But the Radical Enlightenment should not be seen as a momentary phenomenon, as solely a response to the European wars of the late seventeenth and early eighteenth centuries. After the Peace of Utrecht (1713), to be sure, the geographical focus of our story shifts almost entirely to the Continent, more precisely to the Netherlands, and in the chapters that follow we shall trace the careers of these pantheists and republicans until their deaths – generally after mid-century.

But before crossing the Channel we should pause briefly in England to assess what legacy, if any, the radical Whigs left in their own culture. The triumph of Whig oligarchy after 1714 has tended to obscure their very existence, let alone their influence in a world rendered relatively serene by the absence of the abrasive party conflicts so characteristic of the late 1690s and the reign of Anne.

In assessing the intellectual achievement of the Radical Enlightenment in the English-speaking world (before concentrating our attention on a Continental arena dominated linguistically by French), it might be sufficient to point to the survival of Commonwealth ideals, well into the reign of George III, and to refer the reader to that excellent body of historiography that describes that process in England and the American colonies in great detail.[63] Yet it must be apparent that by the middle of the eighteenth century, England seems increasingly remote from the radicalism of the Enlightenment. That movement, whose principal roots can be traced to the post-revolutionary order of the 1690s, appears by the 1740s to have largely disappeared, and to have found its European home in the Netherlands, with small enclaves in Austrian territories and possibly in the Holy Roman Empire. The traditional explanation for that shift has been that England already enjoyed many of the liberties, and the religious liberalism, sought by the enlightened opponents of absolutism and state churches on the Continent. There is a small measure of truth in the argument that England barely experienced the Enlightenment after the 1720s, even in its moderate let alone its radical variety, because it was hardly needed. The difficulty, however, with that assertion is that it cannot embrace new evidence for the survival, tenuous though it may have been, of radical coteries directly in contact with the ideas and social world once frequented by Toland and his friends. That argument also vastly overestimates the liberality of the ruling order and ignores its strenuous efforts, begun in Walpole's time and continued throughout the century, to police and prosecute the press and to prevent a return to the relatively open years that followed the lapsing of the Licensing Act in 1695. From the perspective of Enlightenment propaganda England was a far more open society in 1705 than it became by 1735, if not well before.

Despite the most strenuous efforts on the part of the authorities to suppress them, radical coteries with international contacts can be found in England well into the reign of George II. Republicanism survived as more than an intellectual tradition; it also blended into the goals of philosophical radicals who were watched and prosecuted by the Secretaries of State Office. Indeed, one of the vigilant servants in that office who bent his efforts to weed out radicals was none other than our Freemason and devotee of the new science, Charles Delafaye. Perhaps one of the reasons for Delafaye's zeal came from his Masonry, for on at least one occasion he was in pursuit of radicals who were also themselves Masons. He had at his command the services of the Secretaries of State Office and its network of spies and informants whose major job was to control the opposition and Tory press.[64] Out of that essentially political motive came, however, the mechanism for controlling religious radicals in contact with the Commonwealth tradition. For example, when in 1730 the government seized the papers of Richard Franklin, the printer of the *Craftsman,* it also confiscated evidence on one Lacy, a Quaker, in the form of a poem against the government, 'to be had off the Booksellers or Mrs. Lacey who starves in Virginia St.'.[65]

The inner light doctrines of the Quakers bore no small resemblance to the pantheism of the freethinkers, and either combined with active opposition to the established government could spell trouble.

But there were more dangerous radicals around than poor Mr and Mrs Lacy. One Joseph Morgan, sometimes called John Morgan, because of his annoying and intentional habit of signing himself J. Morgan, possibly for safety's sake, was a Freemason.[66] In 1732 he published and dedicated to the Freemasons and their one-time grand master, Charles, Duke of Richmond, a journal that printed attacks upon present-day politicians that 'have so far forgotten the Good Old Cause so signally owned from Heaven, and are so besotted and degenerated into a self-seeking, slavish and enslaving Spirit . . . [that they] are gone back to Egypt, to wit, [to] the old wicked Foundation and Things of Monarchy . . .'. Morgan appears to have circulated around the fringes of the Whig Party, and he began his literary career with a useful and relatively unbiased account of Mahometanism that was subscribed to by Edward Clarke, Anthony Collins, William Morehead and Barnham Goode.[67] All had been associates of Toland; Morehead did the actual translation of Bruno's *Spaccio*, Collins and the college are central to this story, and Barnham Goode received from Toland in 1720 a long letter explaining his *Pantheisticon* and describing Collins to Goode as your 'fellow collegian' (11, 223, 245). Pope labelled Goode a dunce, but it would be more accurate to call him a marginal man, one of those radicals who had trouble surviving in a harsh world and who occasionally sold his services to Walpole and his government. Goode was also a university man who resigned his fellowship from King's College in 1700 so that he could marry. Later in his career he was publicly consoled for Pope's cruel attack by the known pornographer, Giles Jacob.[68] And to set the stage in preparation for our central character in the radical agitation of the 1730s, Count Radicati, we must add to this list Morgan's publisher and fellow Freemason, William Mears (78, 43, 155).

Alberto Radicati di Passerano (d. 1737) was a Piedmontese nobleman whose self-education, probably undertaken in reaction to the religious one he formally received, led him to embrace the Enlightenment. He made his way to England in 1730, if not before, fresh from combat with the Inquisition which he had tried to persuade the King of Sardinia to abolish. No sooner had Radicati arrived in England than he proceeded to write his philosophical works, which were in turn published in a piecemeal fashion through the services of William Mears and John Peele. In *XII Discourses, Political and Historical* (1730–1), the *Parallel between Muhamed and Sosem* (1732) and *A Philosophical Dissertation upon Death* (1732), Radicati established himself as a 'pagan philosopher newly converted' whose account of the Bible is, in his own words, as 'extravagant as impious'. His dissertation on death, by far the most outrageous of his works, openly describes his pantheistic materialism, and significantly for our story it was translated for Radicati by Joseph Morgan and published by William Mears.

The similarity between Radicati's materialism and Toland's pantheism is overwhelming. A few choice phrases from Radicati's *Dissertation* should make the point:

> By the Universe, I comprehend the infinite Space which contains the immense Matter, sowed, or interspersed throughout with most exiguous Vacuities, wherein, with an eternal Variation, are moved to and fro its most tenuous Particles ... This Matter, and this Motion are inseparable ... In short, Motion is to Matter as essential as is Heat to Fire. Matter then and Motion are of an eternal Co-existence, since it is not possible that they should be derived from Nothing ... This Matter, modified by Motion into an infinite Number of various Forms, is that which I call NATURE. Of this the qualities and attributes are Power, Wisdom, and Perfection, all which she possesses in the highest Degree.[69]

Radicati's philosophical treatise is nothing less than a hymn to 'the Goddess Nature', which advocates stoicism in the face of life's adversities, as well as an epicurean enjoyment of its pleasures, when available. And lest the similarity with Toland's philosophy be missed by readers, Mears advertised his complete works on the back pages of Radicati's *Dissertation*, along with treatises on rhetoric, science and the art of writing.

The response of the ecclesiastical and secular authorities was instantaneous. The Bishop of London, Edmund Gibson, who was called Walpole's Pope by his Tory enemies, wrote to the Duke of Newcastle, Secretary of State, and began a relentless campaign to have Radicati and his friends arrested and silenced. Newcastle dropped the problem into the lap of Charles Delafaye who took his time but who finally arranged for the arrest of Mears, Morgan and Radicati. Delafaye interrogated them and eventually released Radicati on the staggering bail of £400 while Morgan got off more lightly. Both were frightfully poor; indeed Radicati appears to have been near starvation, yet someone, who unfortunately cannot be identified, put up bail for them both. Mears languished in prison for a few months, but eventually he, too, was released after protestations that he believed not a word in the treatises he had published. Radicati would not, however, be silenced and despite the threat of prosecution he continued to advertise his works. Then almost predictably, given what we now know about the international character of the Radical Enlightenment, Radicati fled to

The Hague in late 1734 or early 1735. Indeed, the Dutch journalists had been among the few to give publicity to his writings, and in particular the *Bibliothéque raisonnée*, a journal with which Rousset de Missy was closely associated, had been one of those (106, 63–102).

Before we follow Radicati on to the Continent and briefly explore his social contacts and his valiant efforts to continue publishing despite poverty and a lethal attack of tuberculosis, we should inquire about the effectiveness of official repression in England. Were Gibson, Newcastle and his bureaucracy effective in stamping out this new outcropping of radical religion, whose doctrines, in the words of Gibson, were 'very terrible to civil government' (106, 63–102)?

Radicati's version of pantheistic materialism, so similar to indigenous English radicalism, may very well have been thought out before his arrival, but clearly he had found no difficulty in finding associates of similar persuasion. Indeed, during the 1730s English radicals led by one Samuel Strutt were busily maintaining that very tradition. In 1732, Strutt published *A Philosophical Enquiry into the Physical Spring of Human Actions, and the Immediate Cause of Thinking* and in its preface directed the reader to Toland's *Letters to Serena* for elaboration on the subject of the relationship between the material and the immaterial. Strutt once again took up the controversy with the Newtonians, in particular with the now deceased Samuel Clarke.[70] Strutt and some of his friends, a Mr Pits and the brothers White, had promoted their views in the London coffee houses, in particular at the Golden Lion in Fleet Street and at the Bull's Head at Ludgate Hill.[71] But their 'Deist club', as an observer called it, was not confined to London. Strutt had followers as far away as Wymondham, the Norfolk market town whose sole claim to notoriety rested on the fact that Kett's Rebellion began there in 1549. One of its local worthies, a Mr Stephen Gibbs, belonged to a circle that read Strutt's *Philosophical Enquiry* and that referred to its author as 'Father Strutt'.[72] That sort of irreligious use of clerical titles must have been fairly common in radical circles; we are reminded here of the Knights of Jubilation who often referred to members as 'our vicar'. But the circle in deepest Norfolk was matched by one in Cambridge led by Tinkler Ducket, MA, a fellow of Gonville and Caius.

The persecutions of Radicati and his friends were repeated in 1739 when Ducket was brought before the vice-chancellor of the university and accused of spreading atheistical notions that it was claimed he got from Strutt.[73] Ducket was also accused of trying to seduce a woman, and his defence rested on an avowal of repentance. He was expelled from the university. Ducket at least met a kinder fate than another freethinker as well as befriender of Quakers, the famous Thomas Woolston (d. 1733); he died in prison.

It is not possible to go on from here tracing the remnants of English radicalism into the mid-eighteenth century. Were such a history uncovered it might very well take us up to the 1760s and the followers of John Wilkes. Wilkes may have known that tradition well; he certainly supplied his close friend from their student days in Leiden, the Baron d'Holbach, with copies of pantheistic works from the earlier part of the century. But the Wilkes-d'Holbach link must wait for our final chapter, and our discussion of the relationship between the Radical Enlightenment and the so-called High Enlightenment. The major intellectual achievements of that earlier movement occurred primarily on the Continent, and we must return to its publishing heartland, the Netherlands and in particular The Hague.

Radicati struggled on there for a few years and he had no trouble finding publishers for his political and philosophical works. We would dearly like to know the names of his associates in that city – could they have been Marchand, Rousset de Missy and his friends? Everything about Radicati's thought, his 'naturalism' as he called it, his knowledge of Collins and Tindal, his possession of a codicil to the *Traité*, links him to their ideas. Certainly they knew some of the same people and had some of the same enemies. Radicati made a deathbed confession to the Walloon minister, Daniel de Superville, and he was an occasional contributor to the revived *Journal littéraire*. La Barre de Beaumarchais, a defrocked priest who wrote gossipy books about the republic of letters, thought that Radicati (whom he may have met) was odious; he also had some very unkind words for Rousset de Missy, whom he did know (106, 81–102, 95). Furthermore, Radicati's political writings extolled civic religion, a religion overseen by legislators.[74] He longed for Italian unification, if necessary under a strong sovereign who would undermine the power of the churches, and one wonders if this is not close to what the radical Freemasons in the Netherlands were searching for in their curious blend of republicanism, pantheism and support for the House of Orange – in opposition to the ruling oligarchies and the particularism of the States General.

In his last years, Radicati linked his beliefs to those of the Ebionites, an heretical Quaker sect led in England by E. Elwall who issued in 1726 *A Declaration against All the Kings and Temporal Powers under Heaven*. In Toland's manuscripts there is a letter from a 'true Ebionite' discussing aspects of his view of the gospels. Collins had instructed Marchand in the writings and doctrines of the Quakers, and years later Marchand praised them in contrast to Anglicans for whom he had little use.[75] Marchand also possessed at least one work by Elwall in his library. Many differences, to be sure, existed between freethinkers on either side of the Channel and the Ebionites, but both were heretics of the spirit intent upon new religious forms and upon obliterating the distinction between the world of spirit and its priestly overseers, and the human and material order.

Yet for all their similarities of thought and reading, in the end the Knights and Radicati parted company. Sick and dying, Radicati recanted his extreme pantheism and ended his life reconciled to the Reformed Church in The Hague. There is no evidence that Marchand, Rousset, or any of their associates, experienced a similar *crise*. Yet ironically they all died as members of the Walloon congregations that had received them as refugees. Marchand's last will and testament made clear his opposition to revealed religion, yet it is not surprising that he never renounced his affiliation, for practical and, I suspect, personal reasons. Absolutely central to the Radical Enlightenment is the search for the philosophical foundations of a new religion. Although these seekers had little use for the forms of organised Christianity with which they were familiar, it is hardly surprising to find that they maintained their social affiliations with the Huguenot churches, or that Radicati, alone and distraught, provides an example of someone who slipped back into a Christian fold sufficiently different from that of his birth, and itself a victim of the absolutism he so bitterly detested. And, finally, should we be surprised that an English secret society with Protestant and republican filiations appealed to French Protestant refugees long schooled to believe in election and the rule of the saints? Calvinist psychology, it would seem, could survive even after its theological underpinning had been obliterated.

By the second decade of the eighteenth century, post-revolutionary English republicanism, with its dedication to parliamentary forms of government and its distrust of monarchies and established churches, had been exported to the Netherlands, into the hands of French-speaking propagandists with access to the presses. Yet this new generation of philosophical radicals possessed no Parliament and their political experience had been shaped, and would continue to be so, by the spectre of French absolutism. Within that context, their intellectual and political odyssey unfolded in a variety of enterprises, in literary and publishing projects, some of them clandestine, in the institutional establishment of Freemasonry in northern Europe, and not least, in the political life of the Dutch Republic.

Notes: Chapter 5

1 PRO, 30/24/22/2, 6 March 1705/6.
2 Lewis S. Feuer, *Spinoza and the Rise of Liberalism* (Boston, Mass.: Beacon Press, 1958), pp. 18–21, to be used with caution; cf. Klaus Malettke, *Opposition und Konspiration unter Ludwig XIV. Studien zu Kritik und Widerstand gegen System und Politik des französischen König Während der ersten Hälfte seiner persönlichen Regierung* (Göttingen: Vandenhoeck & Ruprecht, 1976).

3 For Shaftesbury and Bayle, PRO, 30/24/22/4, ff. 32–3; 30/24/21, f.225. Yet Shaftesbury may have known something about the Masonic links, e.g., PRO, 30/24/46a/81, a manuscript entitled 'The Adept Ladys or The Angelick Sect. Being The Matters of Fact of Certain Adventures Spiritual, Philosophical, Political, & Gallant. In a Letter to a Brother. 1701/2'. For Bayle and the radicals, UL, Marchand MSS 2, Fritsch to Marchand, 17 January 1740; cf. Stanley Green, *Shaftesbury's Philosophy of Religion and Ethics* (Athens, Ohio: Ohio University Press, 1967); PRO, 30/24/45, ff. 575–6, 1712, Coste to Shaftesbury indicating that Prince Eugène has solicited a translation of Shaftesbury's *The Moralists*, part of *Characteristicks*; Pierre Rétat, *Le Dictionnaire de Bayle et la lutte philosophique au XVIIIe siècle* (Paris: Université de Lyon, 1971).

4 BN, Fr. N. A. 10782, f. 13 on booksellers circulating works by Rapin de Thoyras and Tindal; BN, F.M. MS. 184, ff. 44 *et seq.* records assembled by police on Freemasons in Paris; BN, Fr. MS. 22109, f. 43, 21 July 1749, a report on Rousset de Missy from someone in the Bastille; and in same volume, f. 60, dated 1752, on the distribution of the *Pantheisticon*; cf. J. P. Belin, *Le Commerce des livres prohibés à Paris de 1750 à 1789* (Paris, 1913) and Gustave Brunet, *Imprimeurs imaginaires et libraires supposés. Étude Bibliographique* (Paris: Tross, 1866).

5 The Harvard copy of the *Traité*, supposedly from the library of Eugène of Savoy, is listed as MS. fr. 1*. For a much more cautious assessment of Boulainvillier's 'spinozism' see Renée Simon, *Henry de Boulainvillier, Oeuvres Philosophiques* (The Hague: Nijhoff, 1973), pp. x–xiii.

6 Karl Otto Brechler, *Die Büchersammlung des Freiherrn von Hohendorf Generaladjutanten des Prinzen Eugen von Savoyen* (Vienna, 1928); Josef Stummvoll, *Geschichte der Österreichischen Nationalbibliothek* (Vienna: H. Bauer, 1968), p. 194; ON, Vienna, MS. Cod. 13966*, *Index Alphabeticus . . . Bibliotheca Ser. Principis Eugen*, including ten works by Bruno.

7 ÖN, Vienna, MS. Cod. 10243, poems by Ferrard, J. B. Rousseau, *et al.*, on libertine subjects (e.g. sodomy) and religion, also a variety of anonymous pieces mocking French court.

8 Cf. MSS of M. Perelle in BN, MSS Fr. 14708, ff. 41–7 for both strands. Perelle is also an interesting case because of his rampant misogyny.

9 UL, Leiden, Marchand MSS, letter from Paris, Palais Royal, 8 July 1714; cf. M. C. Jacob, introduction to Charles [Castel] de Saint-Pierre, Abbé de Tiron, *A Shorter Project for Perpetual Peace*, in B. W. Cook, S. Cooper and C. Chatfield (eds), *Peace Projects of the Eighteenth Century* (New York: Garland Library of War and Peace, 1974).

10 BL, MSS ADD. 4286, f. 142, de la Motte to Desmaizeaux on this subject, c. 1700; Margaret Jacob, *The Newtonians*, pp. 212–13; and the Furly–Shaftesbury correspondence in the PRO.

11 Margaret Jacob, 'Newton and the French Prophets: New Evidence', *History of Science*, vol. 16 (1978), pp. 134–42.

12 For the list of Clayton's known associates, see p. 151. Cf. Trinity College, Dublin, King MS. 750, ff. 128, 141, William King to Sir Robert Southwell suspecting Methuen of being unfriendly to the church's interests in Ireland. For the 'college' I have relied heavily on manuscripts at the Spencer Research Library, University of Kansas.

13 BL, MSS ADD. 4465 letters left for Toland with Mr Roberts, Warwick Lane.

14 John Timbs, *Clubs and Club life in London* (London, 1873), p. 357.

15 Larry Stewart, 'The Structure of Scientific Orthodoxy: Newtonianism and the Social Support for Science, 1704–1728', (Ph. D. dissertation, University of Toronto, 1978), p. 75.

16 Spencer Research Library, University of Kansas, MS. c. 163, 19 September 1704, Sir William Simpson to John Methuen; same to same, 25 September 1705.

17 ÖN, Vienna, MS. 10325, f. 134; Spencer Research Library, University of Kansas, Trenchard–Simpson Correspondence, 9 May 1707, Collins to Simpson. Simpson was Methuen's closest friend and intimate correspondent. Their correspondence is also at the Spencer. Spencer, MS. E 82, Methuen to Simpson, 6 December 1701; 6 February 1705. Methuen had a strong interest in Newton's scientific publications.

18 BL, MSS ADD. 4282, f. 127, Collins to Desmaizeaux.

19 BL, MSS ADD. 4295, ff. 19–20; cf. Albert Lantoine, *Un Précurseur de la Franc-Maçonnerie, John Toland, 1670–1722, suivi de la traduction française du Pantheisticon* (Paris: E. Nourry, 1927). Lantoine was himself a Mason. For Hohendorf, BL, MSS ADD. 4295, f. 20, 7 March 1711.

20 *Pantheisticon*, pp. 70–1 and 47, 95.

21 Toland's essay, probably written sometime after 1714, first appeared in P. Desmaizeaux, *A Collection of Several Pieces of Mr John Toland* (London, 1726); also in that volume *Cicero Illustratus Dissertatio Philologico-Critica* (1712) dedicated to the Baron Hohendorf and Eugène of Savoy.

22 Christopher Hill, *Puritanism and Revolution. Studies in Interpretation of the English Revolution of the Seventeenth Century* (New York: Schocken Books, 1958), pp. 50–122.

23 Philip S. Foner (ed.), *The Complete Writings of Thomas Paine* (New York: Citadel Press, 1969), vol. 2, pp. 832–3 from 'The Origin of Freemasonry'; and G. Adolph Koch, *Religion of the American Enlightenment* (New York: Thomas Y. Crowell, 1933, reprint 1968), ch. 5.

24 *The Way to Things by Words, and to Words by Things . . . On the Real Secret of the Free Masons* (London, 1766; reprint, ed. R. C. Alston, London: Scholar Press, 1968).

25 For Toland on the Continent, Henry L. Snyder (ed.), *The Marlborough–Godolphin Correspondence* (Oxford: Oxford University Press, 1975), vol. 2 pp. 1,059, 1,165. The court Whigs deeply distrusted Toland. Cf. *The Manuscripts of the Duke of Portland*, Historical Manuscripts Commission Reports, vol. 5 (London, 1897), p. 4.

26 On *compagnonnage*, see Agricol Perdiguier, *Mémoirs d'un compagnon*, intro. Alain Faure (Paris: François Maspero, 1977); Cynthia M. Truant, 'Compagnonnage: Symbolic Action and the Defense of Workers' Rights in France, 1700–1848', (PhD dissertation, University of Chicago, 1978), pp. 84–93. On the mythic level Masonry almost certainly influenced the *compagnons* and not vice versa. Printers did not engage in *compagnonnage* in this period.

27 Herbert Rowen, *John de Witt, Grand Pensionary of Holland, 1625–1672* (Princeton, NJ: Princeton University Press, 1978), p. 99.

28 See 'Kroniek Annales', unpublished records of the Grand Lodge in The Hague, written by Du Bois, as the 1758–9 membership list, with officers, of the lodge 'L'Indisoluble', The Hague.

29 Marchand MSS 5, 1; unfoliated, Collins to Levier, 1 October 1713, London; Marchand MSS 2, 11 September, Anvers, undoubtedly 1713 when Collins was *en route* to England. This last letter is extraordinary and only makes sense if we know that Levier wrote an autobiography modelled on the life of Ignatius of Loyola, and that members referred to one another as 'votre Père', or 'notre Vicaire' (p. 271). In the letter Collins talks of being with 'les Jésuites et je trouvais le Père du Sollier avec une femme dans le coin de leur grande salle . . . Je vous prie de faire mes complimens à vos Messieurs et de remercier Mr Böhm pour la lettre qu'il m'a donné au Reverend Père, et d'être assuré que je suis avec une sincerité parfaite . . .' Commonwealthmen were not in the habit of socialising with Jesuits. The letter indicates that a Mr Kuster made 'sa conversion à ses propres lumières'.

30 [Anon], *The Secret History of Clubs: Particularly the Kit-Cat . . . Vertuosos, Quacks, Knights of the Golden Fleece* (London, 1709), pp. 18–19; Françoise Weil, 'Un Franc-Maçon oublié: l'auteur des 'Nouvelles de la Cour et de la Ville'

1734–38', *Dix-huitième siècle*, vol. 10 (1978), p. 256, 'frey massons' and 'frimaçons' were common; Marchand MSS 2, De Beyer to Marchand, in 1750s where 'Franc-Maçon' and 'Franc-masson' are used interchangeably; and J. Fr. Boissy to Marchand, n.d. 'Je sai dans quelques villes on dit Maisonneur, mais ce mot n'est pas d'un usage général.'

31 Marchand MSS 61, f.2. This could be Jean Baptiste de Bey, a friend to the Marquis d'Argens and one Prévost. Information communicated by I. van Eeghen. See Sgard, *Dictionnaire des journalistes*, under Charles de la Motte; and Steve Larkin, 'Voltaire and Prévost: a reappraisal', *Studies on Voltaire and the Eighteenth Century*, vol. 160 (1976), pp. 11–37.

32 The original passage from the fourth song of *L'Art poétique* can be found in *Oeuvres de Boileau-Despreaux* (Amsterdam, 1717), vol. 2, p. 73. The original in Marchand's hand, MS. 61, reads:

> Pour vous donner encor un Précepte excellent,
> Soiez plutôt Maçon, si c'est votre talent,
> Ouvrier estime dans un Art Nécessaire.
> Que médiocre Auteur, et qu'Écrivain vulgaire.
> Il est dans tout avec Art des degréz differens;
> On peut avec honneur remplir les seconds rangs:
> Mais dans l'Art dangereux de parler et d'écrire
> Il n'est point de degréz du médiocre au pire.
> Qui dit froid Écrivain, dit détestable Auteur,
> Indigne d'occuper le Loisir d'un Lecteur.

33 A.M. Ledeboer, *De Boekdrukkers Boekverkoopers en Uitgevers* (Deventer, 1872), pp. 330–1.

34 Marchand MSS 2, 3 November 1711. For Marchand's heavily annotated copy of the *Tractatus*, Marchand MSS 77.

35 Karl Otto Brechler, *Die Büchersammlung des Freiherrn von Hohendorf Generaladjutanten des Prinzen Eugen von Savoyen* (Vienna, 1928), p. 7. Cf. on Plantin, Elizabeth Eisenstein, *The Printing Press as an Agent of Change* (Cambridge: Cambridge University Press, 1979), vol. 1, pp. 75, 99–100 *passim*.

36 A. Brauer, 'Johann Ludwig Gleditsch, Leichpredigt mit Lebenslauf, 1741', *Archiv für Geschichte des Buchwesens*, vol. 9 (1967–9), pp. 1,597–1,612.

37 UL, Leiden, Marchand MSS 2, Fritsch to Levier, 7 August 1714, and numerous other letters; Rapin and Saint-Hyacinthe letters are in Marchand MSS 2.

38 [Chevalier Ramsay], *Lettres de M. de V****, *avec plusieurs pièces de différens auteurs* (The Hague: chez Pierre Poppy [i.e. Pierre Paupie], 1738).

39 Marchand MSS 2, Anthony Collins to Levier, 1 October 1713, London.

40 Marchand MSS 2, F. Fagel to Marchand, 10 September 1722 'Voici une lettre que je viens de recevoir de M. Stosch . . .'

41 M. Rapin, *An Historical Dissertation upon Whig and Tory* (London, 1717); ambiguous about the republican Whigs, e.g. pp. 23–4 *v.* 89.

42 [Rousset de Missy], *Discours sur la liberté de Penser. Écrit à l'occasion d'une nouvelle Secte d'Esprits forts, ou de Gens qui pensent librement. Traduit de l'Anglois et augmenté d'une Lettre d'un Médecin Arabe* (London [actually The Hague], 1714).

43 UL, Leiden, Marchand MSS 65 'Varia Theologica excerpta . . .', ff. 33 *et seq.*, contains a long manuscript entitled 'Extrait d'une lettre écrite par Mr l'Abbé B*** à ***', dated 1712, not written in Levier's hand but his notations are so extensive as to constitute in effect a complete treatise in themselves.

44 UL, Leiden MS. 43 'Histoire de l'admirable don Inigo de Guy Pascoa, chevalier de la Vierge et Instaurateur de l'Ordre des Inighistes', published as the very rare, Rasiel de Selva [Ch. Levier], *Histoire de l'admirable don Inigo de Guipuscoa*,

180 THE RADICAL ENLIGHTENMENT

chevalier de la Vierge . . ., 2 vols (The Hague, 1736). I have used Marchand's own annotated copy. The section on paganism is ff. 179–82.

45 It is just possible that this was the home of one Mattheus Gaillard, bookseller at The Hague in 1710. Cf. E. F. Kossman, *De Boekverkoopers Notarissen en Cramers op het Binnenhof* (The Hague: Nijhoff, 1932), p. 185.

46 Marchand MSS 2, Rousset to Marchand, f. 36, item 8.

47 This very rare catalogue, *Catalogus Librorum Bibliopolii Caroli Levier . . . Die 20 Junii et Sequentibus, 1735* (The Hague, 1735) can be found in the Bibliotheek van de Vereeniging ter Bevordering van de Belangen des Boekhandels, Amsterdam.

48 On this period in the history of the book trade see L. Febvre and H. J. Martin, *The Coming of the Book* (London: New Left Books, 1976), pp. 155–8.

49 See Jean Seznec, *The Survival of the Pagan Gods: The Mythological Tradition and Its Place in Renaissance Humanism and Art*, trans. Barbara Sessions (New York: Pantheon Books, 1953).

50 For a list of his engravings see B. Picart, *Imposteurs innocentes, ou Recueil d'Estampes* (Amsterdam, 1734). See also MSS lists in the Prints Room, the Rijksmuseum, Amsterdam. Engravings that I have found particularly revealing can be seen in the Teylers Museum, portfolio 237, 'L'Histoire composant le grand Dictionnaire Historique'; portfolio 202, 'Monument consacré à la Postériorité en mémoire de la folie incroyable de la XX année du XVIII siècle'. From the Metropolitan Museum of Art, New York, see 'Erudit et Ditat', 1722; 'Vivitur ingenio cetera mortis erunt', 1728; figure of Apollo and animals, nos 16, 18, 1718. From the New York Public Library, Prints Division, Bernard Picart, *Collection de vignettes, petites, estampes et portraits*, nos 5, 8. Cf. Bernard Picart, *The Temple of the Muses; or, The Principal Histories of Fabulous Antiquity* (Amsterdam, 1733), this work belongs to a tradition of late Renaissance naturalism which glorifies the pagans. This English translation has a preface disclaiming any such intention; in the French edition of 1742 there is no disclaimer.

51 Herbert M. Atherton, *Political Prints in the Age of Hogarth. A Study of the Ideographic Representation of Politics* (Oxford: Clarendon Press, 1974), pp. 89–94; cf. Cesare Ripa, *Iconologia*, with an introduction by E. Mandowshky (Hildesham, NY: G. Olms, 1970). Ripa was widely available in a variety of translations.

52 J. J. Hanrath, P. H. Pott and B. Croiset van Uchelen (eds), *De Beoefening der Koninklijke Kunst in Nederland* (The Hague: printed privately by the Grand Lodge of the Netherlands, 1971), plate 24.

53 *Clidophorus; or of the Exoteric and Esoteric Philosophy* in *Tetradymus* (London, 1720), pp. 81–3.

54 In Marchand's MSS there is a copy of the death notice for Picart's first wife. On that engraving of Descartes and its career in the eighteenth century see Francis Haskell, 'The Apotheosis of Newton in Art', in R. Palter (ed.), *The 'Annus Mirabilis' of Sir Isaac Newton, 1666–1966* (Cambridge, Mass.: MIT, 1970), pp. 313–14.

55 For Picart see J. Duportal, *Bernard Picart, 1673 à 1733. Extrait de l'ouvrage, Les Peintures français de XVIIIᵉ siècle* (Paris, 1928); M. M. Kleerkooper and W. P. van Stockum, Jr., *De Boekhandel te Amsterdam voornamelijk in de 17th eeuw* (The Hague: Nijhoff, 1914–16), vol. 1, pp. 560–1.

56 J. J. Hanrath, P. H. Pott and B. Croiset van Uchelen (eds), *De Beoefening der Koninklijke Kunst in Nederland*, plate 24.

57 Peter Gay, *The Enlightenment: An Interpretation. The Rise of Modern Paganism* (New York: Vintage, 1966), pp. 17, 283–4, but also, pp. 290–5. Cf. E. Labrousse, *Pierre Bayle. Hétérodoxie et Rigorisme* (The Hague: Nijhoff, 1964), vol. 2, ch. 10.

58 UL, Leiden, Marchand MSS 21, II, dated 1696; UL, Leiden, Archief van Curatoren, Legatum Prosperi Marchandi, 159 pp.

59 W. Gs. Hellinga, H. de la Fontaine Verwey and G. W. Ovink, *Copy and Print in the*

Netherlands. An Atlas of Historical Bibliography (Amsterdam: North-Holland, 1962), pp. 171–8; cf. P. Marchand, *L'Histoire de l'origine et de premiers progrès de l'imprimerie* (The Hague, 1740).

60 A convenient English translation of this letter and the *Cymbalum* appeared in 1712, *Cymbalum Mundi. Or Satyrical Dialogues Upon Several Subjects* (London, 1712).

61 *Adeisaedaemon, sive Titus Livius a superstitione vindicatus. Annexae sunt ejusdem Origines Judaicæ* (The Hague, 1709).

62 Marchand MSS 2, Saint-Hyacinthe to Levier, n.d., f.2, 'Mais le baron d'Hohendorf que j'ay veu aujourdhui . . .'; mention here also of Douxfils.

63 One place to start is Alfred F. Young (ed.), *The American Revolution. Explorations in the History of American Radicalism* (De Kalb, Ill.: Northern Illinois University Press, 1976).

64 A good study is yet to be written on this system; one place to start would be PRO, State Papers Domestic, George II, General, vol. 50, nf. 264–8; cf. John Nichols, *Literary Anecdotes of the Eighteenth Century* (London, 1812), Vol. 1, pp. 289 *et seq.*, for a list of loyal as well as subversive printers and publishers; Herbert M. Atherton, *Political Prints in the Age of Hogarth* (Oxford: Clarendon Press, 1974), pp. 13, 45–7; Bertrand Goldgar, *Walpole and the Wits. The Relation of Politics to Literature, 1722–1742* (Lincoln, Nebr.: University of Nebraska Press, 1976), pp. 64–5; C. Realey, *The Early Opposition to Sir Robert Walpole* (Lawrence, Kans.: University of Kansas Press, 1931).

65 ULC, Chol. MSS 74, no. 41.

66 Harry Sirr, 'J. Morgan and his *Phoenix Britannicus*', *AQC*, vol. 19 (1906), pp. 127–36.

67 There is a John Morgan who asked for a private audience with Walpole in 1736, ULC, Chol. MSS; J. Morgan (trans. and ed.), *Mahometism fully Explained . . . Written in 1603 by Mahomet Rabadan* (London, 1723); subscribers' list in vol. 2.

68 BL, MSS ADD. 25711, a letter from Goode; a life of Goode in King's College MSS, *Skeleton ollegii Regalis*, vol. 4 (1875–9). Cf. BL, MSS ADD. 4295, f. 39; MSS ADD. 4465, f. 26; Phillip Frowde, Esq., *The Fall of Saguntum. A Tragedy* (London, 1727), a Whig play sponsored by Goode and Robert Ingram, Esq., probably Toland's great friend mentioned in his letters to Goode; Giles Jacob, *The Mirrour: or Letters Satyrical* (London, 1733), pp. 13–15; cf. the useful study of Pat Rogers, *Grub Street. Studies in a Subculture* (London: Methuen, 1972), pp. 338n–340.

69 *A Philosophical Dissertation upon Death. Composed for the Consolation of the Unhappy. By a Friend to Truth* (London, 1732: printed and sold by W. Mears, at the Lamb on Ludgate Hill), pp. 5, 8–9, 10–11.

70 *A Philosophical Enquiry*, pp. 17–18.

71 Richard Parkinson (ed.), *The Private Journal and Literary Remains of John Byrom* (Manchester: Chetham Society, 1854–5), vol. 2, pp. 323, 366, on conversations held in 1729. Byrom also had no difficulty locating Bruno's works during this period: vol. 2, pp. 396, 401; cf. vol. 1, p. 130, and vol. 2, p. 322 on Elwall.

72 ULC, MS. Ee.6.43, Ducket to Mr Stephen Gibbs, Wymondham, with mention of one Bob Pate (who went to London *incognito*), and a Brother Whitehead and Mr Windle.

73 ULC, MSS ADD. 2961, f. 6, *et seq.*

74 Albert Radicati, *Recueil de pièces curieuses sur les matières les plus intéressantes* (Rotterdam: chez la Veuve Thomas Johnson et Fils, 1736). A copy in the Houghton Library, Harvard, c. 1866.1.2.

75 Marchand MSS 2, Collins to Levier, Lincolns Inn, 5 January 1713; Marchand to d'Argens, Marchand MSS 2, 14 February 1737. My thanks to S. J. Larkin for bringing this letter to my attention. UL, Leiden, Catalogus van de UB 1741–90, lere Legatum Prosperi Marchandi, ff. 154–5.

CHAPTER 6

The Social World of the Radical Enlightenment, 1710–60

The alliance of extreme Whigs and Huguenot refugees and publishers, represented by the Knights of Jubilation, was forged during the exigencies of the War of Spanish Succession. After the Peace of Utrecht (1713), as peace returned to northern Europe, the salons and coffee houses of The Hague, especially the new one recently established by Marchand and his friends, turned their conversation to literary and intellectual matters. And probably in that same coffee house, the Knights of Jubilation established its new literary society and this extended coterie also adopted, as its extant minutes reveal (see pp. 270–4), the habits and forms of secrecy. On regular evenings its members, most prominent among them being Willem Jacob s'Gravesande, Themiseul de Saint-Hyacinthe, Albert-Henri de Sallengre, Justus Van Effen, Marchand and the still obscure M. Alexandre, gathered for convivial gossip, merry-making, and the reading of original literary exercises. From this same but increasingly influential circle, we can trace the evolution of a social world that came to encompass scientists, publishers, political leaders like the Bentincks, Freemasons, postal officials, and most important for this story, philosophical radicals. The inner circle of this literary society (135) published the *Journal littéraire*, a publication dedicated to the spread of enlightened ideas, in particular the new science, and to the maintenance of communication within the republic of letters (132). Other members, perhaps less philosophically gifted, plied their trade as publishers, doctors, lawyers, translators and writers.

All require introduction, however brief, but initially we should consider the exact relationship of this new literary society to the grand master and brothers who made up the Knights of Jubilation. If we were examining the projects sponsored by a Masonic lodge in, for example, the 1740s, then the establishment of an attendant literary society, often in conjunction with a small, private lending library, would have been a fairly commonplace practice, at least in northern Europe.[1] Its membership need not have been Masonic, although such societies were obvious places to look for promising and intellectually active candidates. Such an early example of this practice means, of course, that we have no guide posts for interpreting its exact character. As we explore the membership and records of this society and the life-long friendships there engendered, it should become clear that some of its members were more privy than others to its 'secrets'. The meeting records, or what has survived of them, indicate that this society was dedicated to 'the cultivation of the sciences', to the enjoyment and preservation of life-long camaraderie, and that it placed its proceedings under the protection of Minerva and Mercury – both of whom, but especially Minerva, were to assume particular symbolic meaning within eighteenth-century Freemasonry. Were all the members of this literary society actually Masons, did they also participate in the secret gatherings and banquets of the Knights? All we can do, in some cases, is to guess at the nature of the camaraderie between certain members of the literary society and various Knights of Jubilation. What is certain is that this literary society provides a social context for the Radical Enlightenment which stretches from those final years of the war until well beyond the Dutch Revolution of 1747, from Marchand and his friends to the intellectual centre of the Enlightenment in the Netherlands, to the home of Charles Bentinck in The Hague during the 1750s and 1760s.

Indeed, the fashionable salons and coffee houses of The Hague ranked with their counterparts in London and Paris as centres for the new enlightened culture. With access to streets lined with book dealers and publishers, its propagandists and philosophes, from Voltaire through Diderot and Rousseau, made their way to this small centre of international diplomacy which became in the course of the eighteenth century one of the publishing capitals of the world. There, around 1714, this new literary society spawned by the Knights opened a coffee house on the fashionable Korte Voorhout. It was consciously in imitation of coffee houses that s'Gravesande and Van Effen had seen during their journey to London, and every Friday evening the society assembled there for satiric conversation and merriment (see appendix). Perhaps this coffee house also served as an alternative gathering place to that once and very briefly provided by Eugène of Savoy's court where many of its members had turned up from time to time.

From our historical distance, some members of this literary society have faded into obscurity. For example, an active participant was one F. le Bachellé, a physician in Utrecht, who gave accommodation to the Whig propagandist and historian, Rapin de Thoyras. Le Bachellé voted conscientiously for or against new members and explained his failure to keep in touch with the society on one of his journeys because of his experience with lost letters and also his fear of hazarding 'the secret of the society'.[2] The membership of a medical man in this society of journalists conforms to a pattern that was their hallmark. Although men of letters engaged in writing, publishing and selling they were vitally interested in the new scientific learning of their day (133, 331–3).

The society had contacts all over Europe, again sometimes with figures now so obscure that their exact relationship to the Knights, and therefore to early European Freemasonry, may never be established. One M. Gibert in Paris kept them informed for some years about literary news and sent packets of books through their man in Brussels, Lambert Ignace Douxfils. Douxfils was also a vital member of the Knights and he became, in effect, the head of its Brussels chapter.[3] A. M. Loubier was proposed for membership but then his fate is never recorded. But other Parisian literati were affiliated with the society, among them, François Gacon, a poet of sorts and literary enemy of the embroiled café poet, Jean-Baptiste Rousseau.[4] Through Gacon, Fritsch and Böhm were able to pirate an edition of Rousseau's poems and to cash in on his libertine reputation. Many years later, Rousseau and Douxfils would become close friends, probably because of their mutual loyalty and clientage to Eugène of Savoy. These few Parisian ties do, however, point in the direction of the libertine salons mentioned in the previous chapter and indeed those members of the literary society or Knights themselves who were not French refugees, for example, Fritsch and de Sallengre, journeyed frequently to Paris. In addition to its dedication to French letters and language, the group was also powerfully drawn to English political ideas. Publishers specialising in English literature, Isaac Vaillant and Thomas Johnson, had some sort of affiliation with the society, and Jacques Boyd, who did a translation of Algernon Sidney, was definitely a member. It is not clear if the Whig historian, Rapin de Thoyras, belonged but certainly he was on very good terms with his publisher and Knight of Jubilation, Levier. The link with the Commonwealth tradition, clear between the Knights and Toland and Collins, appears to have been continued by their literary society.

Various Protestant ministers whose views were of a heterodox if not heretical cast also turn up as friends of the society. The French refugee, David Durand, who eventually made his way to England and a Whig chaplaincy, was on good terms with the Knights who published his life of Vanini. This biography is ostensibly critical yet very revelatory of Vanini's beliefs and aggressively sympathetic to his cruel martyrdom. From as far away as Marburg in the imperial territory of Hessen a

Protestant minister, Christopher Balber, wrote to Marchand urging him, Picart, Levier and de Bey to continue their activities, in particular their work begun by the publication of Des Périers's *Cymbalum Mundi*. Balber acknowledged that he was a minister who found not the Christian religion, but Christian theology to be an embarrassment.[5]

From these relatively unknown correspondents, who had somehow discovered this congenial literary and intellectual circle centred in The Hague, we can ascend into the inner core of the literary society and its most prominent members. Their major intellectual interest centred on the *Journal* whose tone was orthodox yet tolerant on religious matters. While giving ample space to the English freethinkers, the *Journal littéraire* is most important because it became one of the earliest vehicles for the dissemination of Newtonian science on the Continent. Credit for this achievement undoubtedly belongs to the young Dutch scientist, s'Gravesande (1688–1742), perhaps the chief editor of the journal and a leading member of the literary society.

After his education in Leiden, s'Gravesande began his professional career in The Hague as a lawyer with a strong interest in science. He was also devoted to the allied cause in the War of Spanish Succession, a loyalty not shared by every Dutchman, and he received the personal gratitude of Eugène of Savoy for his work in deciphering enemy codes.[6] These political and intellectual interests would have drawn him to Marchand's circle and its close contacts, through Toland and Collins, with English Whigs as well as with Eugène's court.

As an editor of the *Journal*, s'Gravesande found an outlet for his scientific interests and for a renewal of his English ties. As a student at Leiden, s'Gravesande had known the son of Gilbert Burnet, Bishop of Salisbury, and indeed this offspring was probably the M. Burnet admitted to the literary society. That link between Burnet and s'Gravesande provided Newton with an entrée to the editors; he personally saw to it that the *Journal* was used for the dissemination of his science and natural philosophy (48, VI, 8 June 1714).

S'Gravesande and Marchand developed a life-long friendship that included literary collaboration as well as research assistance for Marchand's history of printing.[7] S'Gravesande also married Anne Sacrelaire, probably the daughter of Isaac Sacrelaire, another associate of this circle. Given what we now know about Freemasonry and the Masonic character of the Knights the following questions become inevitable. Was s'Gravesande a Mason?[8] And what role did the literary society play in the intellectual formation of this most important Newtonian scientist in the generation after Newton?

S'Gravesande's intimate involvement in the most private meetings of this society is clear from the minutes. Saint-Hyacinthe proposed him for membership and s'Gravesande's loyalty seems never to have wavered. When we find him in close communication with English thinkers in this period it is with Desaguliers and John Arbuthnot, both Masons. In turn, s'Gravesande became for his generation the most important Continental exponent of Newtonian order and design, a representative of the Newtonian Enlightenment whom Voltaire held in the highest regard (134, 116–39). The conclusion seems inescapable: s'Gravesande embraced the Newtonian faith as mediated by the vehicle of Freemasonry, as well, of course, as by his own reading of Newton's writings and by his intellectual experiences during his trip to England in the entourage of the Dutch ambassador.

This social context is vitally important for illustrating the change that occurred within the Newtonian Enlightenment as it was transmitted on to the Continent, partly through the agency of Freemasonry. Gradually it began to lose its polemical character and the violent attacks of the early Newtonians on freethinkers, spinozists and atheists, gave way to the vaguely providentialist and mechanical ideology that Voltaire embraced so readily. Yet Newtonians like s'Gravesande had their anti-heretical or perhaps, given the freethinking character of the literary society, their defensive moments (133, 49, 64–89). At his 1717 inaugural lecture for the professorship in astronomy at Leiden, a post secured for him through Newton's intervention, s'Gravesande defended mathematicians from the accusation of atheism and irreligion, and he spoke out against 'those men who have never thought that their very existence and that of the things around them would not be possible without the effects of a powerful and a very wise Cause . . . and against those who are only occupied with religion as it is an object of their indecent railleries . . .'[9] This attack on certain kinds of indecent freethinkers was no doubt sincere, and possibly born of personal experience, although it should be remembered that a Dutch university position was so sensitive that its incumbent had to avoid even the hint of unorthodoxy. For example, Tyssot de Patot, the freethinking associate of Toland and his friends during those early years at The Hague was stripped of his teaching position at Deventer for having been accused of spinozism; he died in penury and obscurity.

Throughout his career and in his various expositions of Newtonian natural philosophy, s'Gravesande avoided the polemics so characteristic of the English, and generally clerical, Newtonians. For s'Gravesande his early and life-long association with freethinkers such as Marchand, Levier and Saint-Hyacinthe, rendered him a tolerant man and even opened him to the accusation, which was in all probability false, of spinozism (111, 182). His pupil and editor, J. N. S. Allamand, the intellectual mentor of Marc-Michel Rey, succeeded s'Gravesande at Leiden while maintaining cordial relations with Marchand.

Despite all these early radical associations, s'Gravesande embraced a providential and liberally Christian vision of the natural order. In refusing to succumb to pantheism perhaps his personal acquaintance with Newton and his English followers proved crucial. That providentialist faith survived and found expression at the early and nearly simultaneous death of s'Gravesande's two children, and there seems no reason to doubt its veracity in retrospect. Yet he must have accepted the fact that for some of his friends pantheism could provide a comparable strength. Given the intimate nature of the literary society, he must have known of the reconciliation they made between their materialism and Newton's science, that they had abandoned the Christian metaphysics that lay at its heart. In partnership with freethinkers far more radical than he would ever be, s'Gravesande explicated Newton's science to the European audience that perused the widely circulated *Journal*. He also remained vitally interested throughout his life in the world of the publicist and publisher and he assisted Marchand in the compiling of material intended for his history of printing.

Equally active among the *Journal*'s editors was the young Themiseul de Saint-Hyacinthe (1684–1746), originally a French Catholic with aristocratic connections, who as a soldier in the French army had been captured and imprisoned in the Netherlands in 1704. That period of confinement and solitude, coupled with his lively literary imagination, plunged Saint-Hyacinthe into a religious crisis from which he emerged as a deist with strongly materialistic tendencies. Although he returned to his native Troyes in 1706, Saint-Hyacinthe found in the Netherlands an intellectual and spiritual home to which he would return many times in the course of his life. He frequently allowed himself to pass for a French Protestant and in about 1711 he made contact with Marchand's circle and became especially close to one of its inner core, Albert-Henri de Sallengre, a Dutchman of French Protestant background.

Saint-Hyacinthe's military career, coupled with his disaffection from Catholicism and his sympathy for the Protestant cause, made him, some years after his death, the prime candidate for the authorship of a long and important clandestine manuscript, *Difficultés sur la religion,* more commonly called, *Le Militaire Philosophe* (London, but really Amsterdam, 1768). The publisher, Rey, with the assistance of the Baron d'Holbach and his atheist friend, J. A. Naigeon, sparingly doctored the original text that probably dates from 1711 to 1715, and published it – whereupon Voltaire put out the rumour that Saint-Hyacinthe wrote it. The manuscript ranks with the *Traité des trois imposteurs* as one of those early Enlightenment tracts that assaulted the credibility and authority of organised religion. It is resolutely not spinozist, although the author seems to know enough about Spinoza's ideas. The deistic posture of the tract, the frequent reference to ideas associated with Bayle, the disaffection from Catholicism and the mention of a military career, make Saint-Hyacinthe a strong, but far from proven, candidate for its authorship. Its author says, moreover, that he is old, but in this period Saint-Hyacinthe, like his friends, was decidedly young. Unfortunately I cannot bring new light to bear on this old problem of its authorship; the Marchand manuscripts do not address themselves to this manuscript. While they do enable us to trace the *Traité des trois imposteurs* directly to the Knights and their friends, *Le Militaire Philosophe* awaits further evidence, should it ever be discovered.[10] In assessing works like these, however, we would do well to think about the possibility of authorship by various hands. Secret clubs like that of the Knights, especially with literary and religious interests, were precisely those sorts of places where clandestine manuscripts could be outlined and their contents debated. Certainly this literary society, for example, provided a freethinker like Saint-Hyacinthe with vital social support throughout his life-long intellectual odyssey.

Indeed, the theme of fraternity runs through Saint-Hyacinthe's writings.[11] To another close friend, Levesque de Burigny, a materialist in the Cartesian tradition (16, 237–8), he described his circle of friends in the Netherlands in the most intimate terms and concluded, 'You know that this [living in a society of friends] has been my purpose during my entire life' (136, II, 300). Saint-Hyacinthe, in turn, made this literary society famous when with its assistance he authored a very humorous and mildly *risqué* satire on the pedantry of the universities and the pious proponents of ancient learning. That anonymous work can at least with certainty be traced to him.

Le Chef d'œuvre d'un inconnu (1714), supposedly by one Dr Matanasius but in fact by Saint-Hyacinthe, opens with a series of flattering encomia to its authors. Predictably among the adulators we find M. Alexandre, the secretary of the society, and Thomas Johnson, the publisher of its journal.[12] But there also is the previously unnoticed name of Henry St John, Viscount Bolingbroke, one of the leaders of the Tory Party in England, Secretary of State at the time (before his sudden conversion to Jacobitism) and a prime negotiator at Utrecht.

Bolingbroke's presence adds further weight to the contention that the Knights and their friends were indeed an Anglophile coterie. On this occasion, Bolingbroke may have been courting their favour in a desperate attempt to ingratiate himself with the loyal followers of Eugène of Savoy, the ally whose aggressive war effort against the French Bolingbroke had so ruthlessly undermined at the peace negotiations. Yet another possibility comes to mind: Bolingbroke was a bitter opponent of the court Whigs, and just at this time he rightly perceived that their success with the Hanoverian king, could his succession be irrevocably insured, would sound the death knell for Bolingbroke's political career. How fitting then that this supreme political manipulator should try his hand at a republican coterie, safely tucked away in The Hague but well connected with the opposition country Whig faction. Harley, the Tory minister, had kept Toland around as a pamphleteer and probably as a spy and, of course, in the Walpolean era the Tory opposition adopted country Whig principles by which it might embarrass the government.[13] Whatever Bolingbroke's motives, however, the personal link with this literary society appears not to have survived. Years later the Brussels member of the Knights, Douxfils, who remained attached to this coterie throughout his life, sent a jolly song to Marchand about the 'demi-libertines' and it mentioned, among this early circle, only Johnson, de Sallengre and Henri du Sauzet.[14]

The most recent biographer of Saint-Hyacinthe, after consulting the Marchand manuscripts (but without access to the evidence now available), concluded that he must have been a Freemason (136, 75, 258–65). In the 1720s, when Saint-Hyacinthe resided in England, he socialised with Desaguliers with whom he shared a passion for the new science, for 'l'ésprit géometrique'.[15] Also among his confidants in London was Pierre Desmaizeaux, the collaborator of Collins, the biographer of Toland, and the London correspondent for the *Journal*. Desmaizeaux has long been suspected of Masonic links (which in his case cannot be established definitely) and of belonging to a lodge, largely composed of French refugees, that met at the Rainbow Coffee House. Saint-Hyacinthe also maintained close relations with Chevalier Ramsay,[16] one of the architects of French Masonry, and with Montesquieu during his time in London. That latter association has been noted but never explained; Freemasonry provides one obvious explanation (98, 134–7).

A basically religious thinker, Saint-Hyacinthe, after flirting with various forms of Christianity, abandoned it for a deism that gave preference to the morality of the atheist over that practised by the idolator.[17] Indeed, by comparison with his 'frères' Saint-Hyacinthe displays the highest degree of personal struggle in his search for religious truth. Employing the sceptical methodology first advocated by Descartes, Saint-Hyacinthe came to see God as simply 'the architect'.[18] But a deistic understanding of God's relationship to nature had immediate implications for man and society. Saint-Hyacinthe argues that all morality is relative; this insight does not lead him to despair or nihilism but to an evocation of charity and friendship as the guiding principles of human behaviour. How many European thinkers, once loosed from the moorings of the Christian churches, found in the camaraderie of Masonry the roots of a new ethic and even of a new politics?

As early as *Le Chef d'œuvre,* Saint-Hyacinthe (and his literary associates who shared in the enterprise) praised the English system of government and condemned the absolutism of James II. In his later writings, Saint-Hyacinthe displays democratic tendencies, stating that he could not believe 'that there is any other considerable difference between Men, than what proceeds from education and habit'. He denied the existence of any significant difference between peasant and lord and argued without qualification that sovereignty resides in the people.[19] Saint-Hyacinthe probably never socialised outside of the bourgeois and aristocratic circles in which he travelled, yet Masonic camaraderie must have caused some men to question, however weakly, the very existence of class differences. In keeping with his radical associations, Saint-Hyacinthe was one of the first critics of Voltaire to recognise his 'court' posture and to attack his adulation of kings and their power. By the time of Voltaire's stay in England, Saint-Hyacinthe had made his way there and frequented refugee circles that gathered at the Rainbow Coffee House. From those early years of the Radical Enlightenment we can begin to see the formation of hostility to *les grands* of the new culture, men such as Voltaire was becoming, who made their way with ease from one liberal court to the next. Saint-Hyacinthe attacked *La Henriade* along stylistic lines, but his political antagonism is also clearly visible. He notes with irony that Voltaire's hero, Henry IV, had converted to Catholicism, but more important to Saint-Hyacinthe is Voltaire's failure to see that the English Parliament, far from being unique, was once the natural form of government throughout Europe. It is the ambition and avarice of kings that despoils the polity; all praise belongs to the revolutionary spirit of the English.[20] Saint-Hyacinthe appears to have learned his politics from a variety of sources, English 'country' Whigs primarily, but perhaps also from his contact with *parlementaire* and aristocratic clubs in Paris, such as L'Entresol to which Ramsay belonged.

Although a republican, Saint-Hyacinthe appears never to have embraced wholeheartedly the pantheism or materialism found among his associates (16, 237). Yet there are moments when he speaks of nature as an independent principle that 'Follows all the rules of mechanism with great exactness; and this is what enables her to make the best advantage of every thing'.[21] Certainly his religious views were dangerous and heretical enough. Even Levier, his publisher, toned them down on one occasion, much to Saint-Hyacinthe's annoyance. Yet because of 'the freedom with which certain matters are dealt in the book, it can only be printed in Holland', Saint-Hyacinthe remarked to Levier,[22] and that statement tells much about the palpable meaning of the republican state for religious radicals of the early Enlightenment. Despite his abandonment of Christianity, Saint-Hyacinthe stayed on good terms with s'Gravesande although he appears to have quarrelled with Justus Van Effen, another editor of the *Journal* and a prominent translator of English works by Shaftesbury and Defoe, among others, into Dutch (138). Van Effen's collaboration with the literary society was shortlived and years later Fritsch complained to Marchand about Van Effen's pompous manner (see p. 278). But in those early days Van Effen offered one of the first printed critiques of Bishop Berkeley, the English philosopher who posited an extreme idealism in reaction to the materialism of the freethinkers (137, ch. 3). While rejecting Berkeley's extreme position in religious matters, Van Effen was a liberal Christian, a member of the Dutch Reformed Church, and he closely adhered to the liberal Anglicanism found in the writings of Addison and Steele. Yet in the early 1730s, he turned violently against the French refugees and the libertine culture they had come to symbolise and joined the orthodox and partly homophobic backlash against it (139, 291). That bitter reaction against 'libertinism' began with a series of accusations against suspected homosexuals, men and women, and lead in turn to a number of interrogations of publishers and booksellers known for their freethinking publications. It culminated in the burning and public strangulation of men convicted of homosexuality.[23]

Among the Knights and their associates, Van Effen's liberal Christianity represented a distinct minority view. Historians have traditionally associated the origins of the Enlightenment in the Netherlands with that version of Christianity found in the writings of prominent Dutch theologians and philosophers like Limborch and Le Clerc (140). Both were in close contact with liberal Anglicans, the Cambridge Platonists and John Locke, for example. Like their English counterparts they were enthusiastic about the new science and indeed did much to publicise the Newtonian achievement. They were also bitterly hostile towards the freethinkers. Throughout the correspondence of the Knights there is no evidence to suggest that they received any encouragement from Le Clerc, despite their mutual interest in the writings of Pierre Bayle. Indeed, one of the few references to Le Clerc is a very negative one, indicating that among journalists the Knights regarded him as a devil to whom they, like the Indians, had to offer sacrifices.[24] The tension we have perceived between the Newtonian Enlightenment and the Radical Enlightenment in England seems to hold true for the Netherlands, where it might also be argued that the liberal and radical versions of Enlightenment sprang from different sources and existed in tension rather than in harmony.

Van Effen's gradual defection from the cause of the Enlightenment would tend to suggest such a tension and certainly none of the life histories of the other *Journal* editors or of the Knights offer a comparable example. Saint-Hyacinthe settled down to a quiet life as a bookseller in London. He married there yet maintained his contacts in the Netherlands and in Belgium. Throughout his life he was on close terms with Desmaizeaux as well as with Lambert Douxfils, who became an official Freemason and who will figure prominently in the Masonic side of this history. In 1741, Douxfils did another edition of a work by Saint-Hyacinthe and the Brussels copy of that rare edition contains a letter by Saint-Hyacinthe making oblique references to 'la constitution'.[25]

Saint-Hyacinthe's close Masonic ties with Douxfils and s'Gravesande included a life-long intimacy with the merriest of these journalists, Albert-Henri de Sallengre (1694–1723). Indeed the two were so close that works by Saint-Hyacinthe are often wrongly attributed to de Sallengre, who should perhaps best be remembered for his essay in praise of drunkenness. That eulogy, by one of the literary society's most active members, extols the virtues of good drink, good song and good company. Its ribald wit apparently offended key members in the society; for reasons that are not clear de Sallengre was eventually dropped from the editorial staff of the *Journal* (131, 94–5). In true libertine fashion he combined in that tract useful advice on how to treat hangovers with lists, intended for the encouragement of others, of some of the world's great drinkers. From his student days at Leiden he recalls professors who displayed a particular talent at the art.[26] De Sallengre may have met s'Gravesande there in that early period; both had studied philosophy and law at Leiden.

Those links with the university are worth stressing. Various enemies of Toland and his freethinking friends at The Hague, among them Elie Benoist, a Walloon minister at nearby Delft, attacked them by comparing this irreligious circle to those found among university students at Leiden.[27] Unlike English universities of the period with their emphasis on a clerical education and with their college system that safely locked students away every evening, Dutch universities, for students but not for faculty, were freer places where student life spilled into cafes and rooming houses and where medicine and law, along of course with theology and philosophy, were held in high regard. Dutch universities contributed a youthful environment that helped in the context of a war against absolutism to spawn the radicalism of the early Enlightenment.

There are moments in the minutes and correspondence of the Knights and their literary friends when laughter and good cheer pervade the proceedings. Mockery and jest not only make life more bearable, but in the hands of publicists they are also powerful weapons in any struggle against orthodoxy, religious, political or whatever. Both can have the effect of ritual, of making the sharers of the jest feel that they enjoy a special insight into the world, in this case its folly.

Good times and good company were combined by the Knights with an intellectual freedom that permitted heresy, if that were a member's bent. In that environment these prosperous businessmen (when things were going well) also worked at enjoying themselves as well as at intellectual self-improvement, at a self-imposed programme of enlightenment (see pp. 270–4).

It seems appropriate at this point to remark on one of the uses to which the Masonic lodge was put throughout the eighteenth century. Generally it became an outlet for 'the middling' sort of men where they could pursue their leisure and their intellectual interests without the necessity of playing conventional social and familial roles. That perception, of course, raises the question of the relationship between Masonry and the role and status of women in the eighteenth century. Since the issue has a direct bearing on the question of women's role in the Radical Enlightenment it will receive a separate and more extensive treatment (see pp. 206–8). Suffice it to say for the moment that the Knights clearly separated their intellectual preoccupations from their family life, despite the fact that many of them ran their publishing businesses as family concerns. Although it fell far short of our current egalitarian ideal, the Masonic lodge did offer a meeting place for men of similar mind, and it is hardly surprising to find political and philosophical dissenters coalescing around a particular lodge.

The discovery of these social ties and of their Masonic character illuminates the international character of the Radical Enlightenment. Marchand contemplated, and may have undertaken, a long visit to England, while de Sallengre was among the best travelled of this society. He, like Saint-Hyacinthe, was in contact with freethinking and libertine circles in Paris, while during his visits to England he stayed with Anthony Collins at his country estate in Essex. There in 1718 Collins, Toland, de Sallengre and Desmaizeaux socialised and discussed philosophy.[28] They may also have clubbed with another Commonwealthman, John Asgill (1659–1738), who had been for a time an MP in both the English and Irish Houses. Asgill had a bent for unorthodox philosophising which earned him the censure of the Commons, and which to this day renders him a most eccentric thinker. Briefly stated, he argued for the obliteration of all distinction between matter and consciousness – 'all life is motion'.[29] Out of this materialism, Asgill asserted that contrary to appearances men do not die but are merely translated from life to eternal life. Firm in his unorthodox convictions, if lacking perhaps an exact vocabulary, Asgill said that he would 'die of no Religion'. This aversion to organised religion and its rituals did not preclude membership in the Masonic lodge at the Three Tuns Tavern where Asgill served as warden of the lodge (78, 176).

Asgill's connections with the Commonwealthmen and his Masonic affiliations probably explain how, after 1717, de Sallengre was brought in touch with official and organised British Freemasonry. In this manner, the English translation of de Sallengre's essay on drunkenness became in 1723 the first book dedicated to the newly formed Masonic order. The translation was executed by one of Asgill's friends, the hack writer and Freemason, Robert Samber.[30] Given Samber's interests and his financial need, he was a good choice as translator for de Sallengre's mildly libertine meditation on what must have been a fairly commonplace activity of the Knights and their literary society. Aside from a variety of other translations, one of which was also dedicated to the Freemasons, Samber left various essays, published and unpublished, which tell us much about the early, somewhat inchoate, years of English Freemasonry and illustrate the Newtonian, Whig and freethinking *mélange* that characterised it. As the text in the appendix indicates (pp. 287 *et seq.*), Samber was deeply influenced by the Hermetic tradition, and held to definite magical beliefs while avowing his devotion to Newtonian science.[31] He claimed to be a Christian and a Freemason who composed Masonic rituals; he was also a libertine with a particular interest in venereal disease, and a seeker after a universal religion which his published essay on Freemasonry aptly illustrates.

These international comings and goings of the Knights and their freethinking associates alerted their opponents on both sides of the Channel and even brought official Freemasonry in England under suspicion. There one contemporary protested publicly that among the Freemasons 'the Divinity . . . is handled by some of these wretches with a most shameful buffoonry and contempt'.[32] Rightly, British Freemasonry was suspected of housing intellectual and political radicals, although little was probably known about their international ties that considerably predate Desaguliers's travels in the Netherlands during the 1730s when many official lodges were finally established. Given the elaborate nature of these interconnections our description of this social world must extend beyond the known frequenters of the coffee house on the Korte Voorhout.

Other intellectual associations of the Knights and their friends may in no sense have been Masonic but they were certainly subversive. In the Netherlands and as far away as Hamburg, Marchand, Toland and their friends maintained warm relations with disparate radicals and intellectual dissenters. Toland knew Tyssot de Patot (1655–1738) at The Hague and described him as 'a Gentleman of great wit and learning, to some of whose friends I showed my manuscript at The Hague in the year 1708' (142, 93). Tyssot wrote one of the earliest examples of an utopian genre of voyage literature which attempted to invent an imaginary terrestrial world and to contrast it with the failings evident in European society.[33] His violent attack on European religion was probably published by Thomas Johnson, and some years later a pirated edition appeared using a title-page engraving by Picart.

In Germany, the isolated Peter Friedrich Arpe, who was one of the extreme naturalists of his day, made early contact with this new circle in The Hague and Fritsch and Böhm became his publishers. Arpe wrote a very important and highly laudatory life of Vanini[34] as well as numerous works, as he described them, 'on fate, on divination, on holy writing, [and in] the defense of famous men falsely accused of magic'. He subscribed to the Hermetic tradition with its belief in a secret and lost wisdom but he offered another version of the myth of Hermes. Arpe claimed that 'there never was a Hermes, but rather that there were at various times famous men, who were called commonly Hermes, though their writings were attributed to one Hermes . . .'[35] Arpe postulated a long line of ancient and modern thinkers, among them Campanella, who had been in touch with this true and ancient wisdom.

In an extremely laudatory letter to Marchand, Arpe implies that he regards him as one of those gifted savants and in turn sends regards to Picart.[36] This letter also helps to clarify the confusion that has surrounded Arpe's career as the attributed author of various clandestine manuscripts. For some centuries Arpe has been a candidate for the authorship of the Traité des trois Imposteurs (144). One scholar rightly noted, however, that Arpe probably did not know French and his letter to Marchand, written in Latin, confirms this. Had he known Marchand's native language, Arpe would almost certainly have used it. Although Arpe did not write the Traité he appears to have authored an equally scurrilous and blasphemous Latin treatise on the three imposters which even Liebniz confused with the Traité. All of this recently uncovered evidence reveals that Arpe and the Knights were embarked upon a vast campaign of popularising the naturalism of the late Renaissance and its concomitant pantheism; it is no accident that two of the Knights became his publishers.

Hermes had other advocates in the Netherlands with whom some of the Knights or their close friends were familiar. Jacob Campo Weyerman (1677–1747) published in the 1720s a weekly paper, Hermes of Rotterdam, that gave publicity to freethinking and which gave considerable press to Toland who, it claimed, had established a sect in the Netherlands. Weyerman knew the writings of Bruno, and his name has often been linked to Dutch Freemasonry. In particular, Weyerman was rumoured to belong to Rousset de Missy's lodge in the 1730s, but evidence for this is not conclusive.[37] What is conclusive is that Rousset knew Weyerman who had died in prison. After Rousset's exile from the Netherlands, an alternative to imprisonment for his political involvements, he wrote of his experience to Marchand and explained that he had preferred to avoid the sad fate of Weyerman.[38] We should not be surprised at the extensive nature of the personal and intellectual links within the Radical Enlightenment; such a minority of like-minded men needed all the personal support and company they could find.

Links with freethinkers such as Patot, and later with the journalist Weyerman, meant that in those early years the Knights did make their way into Dutch society, although with the exception of s'Gravesande, hardly into respectable academic or Calvinist circles. The overwhelming preponderance of their associates were, however, of French extraction or at least used French as their official language. The literary society contained many such members and the Knights were not above admitting at least one journalist, Gabriel d'Artis (1650?–1730?) who was a decidedly orthodox Calvinist (111). But d'Artis had good connections in Berlin, and at some point business is business.[39]

Among this circle of French refugees who will provide a continuity between the Knights and the later Enlightenment were two associates, Jean Frédéric Bernard (1683?–1744) and Henri du Sauzet (1686/7–1754).[40] An early associate of Pierre Bayle, Bernard worked closely with Picart to produce one of the most fascinating anthologies of the early Enlightenment, Cérémonies et coutumes religieuses de tous les peuples du monde (Amsterdam, 1723). This magnificently engraved and illustrated anthology catalogued the practices and rituals of Christians and non-Christians without attention to the supposed veracity of Christian doctrine. The implication, which presaged the science of anthropology, was clear enough: all religions are the same and all fulfil similar human needs – but the editors would have added, not all of them ennobling. In the 1734 volume of this anthology Picart posthumously presented the first pictorial representation of Freemasonry (reproduced on cover), and the narrative treated it as simply another form of Western religion.[41]

Bernard was also a prolific writer who specialised in the clandestine. As a result the bibliography of his works is hopelessly confused. One of the few works believed to be his is a humorous satire, The Praise of Hell (London, 1760 for the English translation), in which the infernal regions are overcrowded with popes, bishops and kings. Among them is Machiavelli 'who first taught princes, that, to fix, establish, and perpetuate the sovereign power they claim over their subjects, they may with the utmost impunity violate all the laws of nature and humanity, and tyrannize over their subjects . . .' Alongside his anti-absolutism Bernard was outspokenly republican in an early published work that may pre-date his association with Picart or may have led to it.[42] These Réflexions . . . sur les mœurs de notre siècle are thought to have inspired Montesquieu's *Lettres persanes* (1721) (146), although it should be noted that despite these intellectual filiations between the radicals and Montesquieu, he himself remains resolutely a representative of the Newtonian Enlightenment as symbolised by official British Masonry in this early period. Despite tendencies to irreligion, Bernard brought up his own daughter Elizabeth (b. 1723) to be devout, and she in turn married the foremost publisher of the High Enlightenment, Marc-Michel Rey. They ran a family business in Amsterdam and indeed at mid-century Rey moved into this now aged coterie almost immediately upon his arrival in Amsterdam (see pp. 260–2).

Bernard also collaborated with Henri du Sauzet, another refugee who turns up in the early correspondence of the Knights. Du Sauzet had close business dealings with Fritsch and owned a unique collection of Picart illustrations (112, III, 105–8). He also associated with Rousset de Missy and together they were involved in promoting trade in clandestine manuscripts, in particular the *Traité*. Both men provide the link between the Knights and official Dutch Freemasonry in that they became leaders of that movement in the 1740s and 1730s.[43]

Indeed, of the many collaborators and associates of the Knights none is more important than Jean Rousset de Missy (1686–1762) (111). The life of John Toland embraced a unique mixture of radical Whig politics, and the search for civic religion based upon a pantheistic natural philosophy – all made palatable by new rituals and even by a new religion. In Rousset de Missy we find his spiritual heir. As previously indicated, Rousset's association with Collins and Toland can be dated from his first published work, a single volume containing French translations of Collins's *Discourse of Freethinking* (1713) and Toland's extremely rare *A Letter from an Arabian Physician . . . Concerning Mahomet's Taking Up Arms, His Marrying of Many Wives, His Keeping of Concubines . . .* (1706).[44] Toland's essay compared Christianity and Mahometanism, finding neither to be more nor less absurd. Rousset often gave his writings to Henri Scheurleer for publication and he, too, was an early associate of the Knights, but his exact relation remains unfortunately obscure.[45]

It seems safe to assume that Rousset had met Toland and Collins in The Hague where he had fled in 1704. His father had been imprisoned in Laon for his Protestantism, and throughout his life Rousset harboured a violent hatred of French absolutism, from which he generalised to a hatred of all absolutism as well as of ruling oligarchies and established churches. This hatred for the French system remained on the surface throughout his life; the larger political passion was to find expression in the *Traité des trois imposteurs* and in his revolutionary activity during the 1747 upheaval in the Netherlands (see Chapter 7).

Rousset must not be seen, however, in the romantic posture of a nineteenth-century revolutionary. As a good bourgeois, a member of the publishers' guild, and for a brief time as a schoolmaster to aristocratic children in The Hague, Rousset sought respectability in his newly acquired homeland. Yet his school must have been a centre for anti-French propaganda; it was closed briefly by the Dutch authorities after 1713 and because of pressure applied by the French government. Rousset was also an incredibly prolific journalist and author; a complete bibliography of his writings, many of them anonymous, may never be compiled. Most important for this narrative Rousset combined pantheism with reformist politics and with an intense dedication to European Freemasonry. From the earliest record of his membership (4 March 1735) in the newly established official Masonic lodge in The Hague, Rousset became one of the leaders of Dutch Freemasonry (8). He served for a time as grand master of the lodge, La Bien Aimée, in Amsterdam; only recently exploited Masonic records indicate that he was probably the single most important and energetic leader of a movement that became well established in the Netherlands by the 1740s. Throughout his life he maintained a close friendship with Marchand and Lambert Ignace Douxfils, that Brussels member of the Knights of Jubilation whom Rousset later described as one of his oldest friends. In nearly every letter sent to Marchand, Rousset also conveyed greetings to their grand master in The Hague: 'I pray you salute him for me by the fraternal number', that is, by the Masonic number (three).[46] Marchand could hardly have done so if he were not himself a Mason, nor could he have sent long descriptions to Rousset about Masonic artifacts, among them the Mason's cabinet, a partitioned box used by eighteenth-century Masons to store their regalia, writing paper, etc., and often adorned with a wood-encased globe of the world.[47]

From 1735 until Marchand's death in 1756, Rousset and Marchand conducted a long correspondence, and fortunately Rousset's portion has survived amid Marchand's manuscripts. Those letters provide one of the richest portraits now available for any eighteenth-century radical, and when combined with a variety of sources they add a new dimension to our understanding of the larger phenomenon of the European Enlightenment. In this later period the social world of the Enlightenment in the Netherlands was dominated by the home of one figure, Charles Bentinck (1708–79), the brother of William Bentinck. Both were the younger sons of Hans Willem Bentinck, Duke of Portland (1649–1709), intimate confidant and diplomatic adviser to William III (d. 1701), King of England and Stadholder of the Netherlands. The Bentincks became very important figures in Dutch political life in the 1740s. They played a crucial role in the restoration of the stadholderate in 1747 and in the installation of William IV, William III's cousin, as the possessor of that revived office. What has never been known about Charles Bentinck until now was that his self-conscious Whiggery, learned as a boy in England and from his tutors in the Netherlands, apparently included a dedication to Freemasonry.

Charles Bentinck was by far the most scholarly member of an otherwise supremely political family. He had been educated partly in Geneva by the French Huguenot refugee, Pierre Crommelin, and throughout his adult life Bentinck maintained a keen interest in the new science. He and his brother were the architects of the new, hereditary stadholderate, and both were immensely popular public figures (150). Their political intrigues and the role of their clients, this new generation of radical Whigs, in the Dutch Revolution of 1747 must await the next chapter; but here it can be noted that almost inevitably, as in England after 1689, where we find Whig oligarchs and Whiggish concepts of government, there too we shall find the radicals. At this point their social world, the context of their political and intellectual activities, needs to be established.

From shortly after his exile in 1749, Rousset de Missy, a devoted Orangist and, unfortunately for himself, a democrat, resumed an intense correspondence with his intimate friend in The Hague, Prosper Marchand. Almost every letter from Rousset ends with the invocation to give his regards to the grand master, to 'maître Charles', or more commonly to 'frère Charles'.[48] This brother is never identified by his last name, but we learn from the letters that he has a home in The Hague, that he frequently visited Voorburg, a small village just on its outskirts where William IV had acquired an estate called 'De Loo' and that he has access to the Princess Royal, as she was called, that is, to Anne, the widow of William IV and the daughter of the King of England, George II. Rousset appears to be doing some book business for 'fr' Charles, but more important it is this same brother who notifies Rousset when Marchand's final illness appears to have debilitated him. Charles Bentinck made just such a notification to J. N. S. Allamand, s'Gravesande's successor in Leiden, and he also arranged for Marchand to have a pension 'from the society'.[49] He was one of Marchand's closest associates in this later period of his life, as was M. de Bey,[50] a very old friend indeed, a Knight of Jubilation to whom in 1712 Marchand had written that tract on rhetoric and logic. It seems a reasonable conclusion, based on this circumstantial evidence, that Charles Bentinck was also a Freemason. Although his name does not appear on the official membership lists of the Grand Lodge in The Hague – a list acknowledged to be incomplete – the name of Charles's older brother, William, Graaf v. Bentinck (1704–74) does appear on the official membership register of Rousset's lodge, La Bien Aimée.[51] Both Bentincks were extremely close, and shared common political and cultural interests.

Charles Bentinck, as well as his less intellectually active, although gifted brother, William, who had studied with s'Gravesande, were among that small group of eighteenth-century aristocrats or sons of aristocrats, who sponsored and supported the new culture. William Bentinck brought the zoologist Abraham Trembley into his home as tutor to his children, and it was there at Sorgvliet in 1741 that Trembley made his startling discoveries about the self-reproductive powers of fresh-water polyps (52). That scientific discovery, so basic to the early history of zoology, was brought to publication by Marchand who may have been suggested as its agent by Allamand. Its importance for the history of the Enlightenment, as demonstrated by Vartanian, lay more in the area of philosophy and metaphysics than in zoology. Could Marchand and his pantheistic friends have been among the first to realise what so many European materialists seized upon, namely that the pious Trembley had unwittingly come upon a discovery that seemed to give scientific verification to the notion that matter is self-generating, that soul or motion is indeed essential to matter? The full implications of that discovery for the spread of pantheism must await the next chapter (see p. 248), but it is highly probable that Marchand responded as more than a disinterested agent when he arranged for Trembley's publication.[52] It is also altogether possible that Trembley's research may have been prompted, or at least encouraged, by the kinds of intellectual conversations that must have gone on in the Bentinck circle. Certainly he must have known Marchand and Rousset for they were a very intimate part of the Bentincks' fraternal world, and Charles Bentinck communicated Trembley's discovery to the Royal Society in London. Bentinck also carried on an extensive correspondence with the Genevan scientist, Charles Bonnet, and it reveals deistic views on religion and statements against theologians that were decidedly freethinking (151, II, 583–5).

The Bentincks never subscribed to anything so heretical as pantheism, or so we can suppose, but then probably neither did the Whig oligarchs back in England who kept the radicals in their various employments. Yet Charles Bentinck became a loyal supporter and follower of the great French *philosophe,* Jean-Jacques Rousseau (152). Rousseau was no materialist but he certainly held to some rather startling notions about the morally regenerative powers of Nature, and about human equality. In the 1760s and 1770s, Bentinck also made his home at Nyenhuis a centre for scientific and philosophical discussion; Rousseau, godfather to one of William Bentinck's grandchildren, David Hume, and Diderot, as well as Allamand, all dined there (as well as with the elder Bentinck) (153). The publisher, Marc-Michel Rey, sent to the Bentincks, via Allamand, his enlightened and undoubtedly self-interested plan for controlling and modifying the censorship of books.[53]

The social world of the Enlightenment in the Netherlands, in particular its international aspect, was heavily Whiggish and Masonic, and the coterie begun by, and including, the original Knights of Jubilation figures prominently in it. We shall probably never know the exact relation of that society to the evolution of organised Dutch Freemasonry. While Rousset's role was vital to it, other names with which we are now familiar are not present on the extant lodge registers. All that can be done, in the face of this incomplete evidence, is to postulate a history of private Masonic gatherings that begin in 1710 and that may have continued intermittently until the London Grand Lodge, quite probably as an extension of pro-Orangist government policy, helped to initiate the opening of that first official lodge at The Hague in 1734.[54] As fascinating as Masonic history may be for its *dévots*, what matters here is not that the student should grasp its most intricate details, but rather that he or she should realise its protean character, particularly in matters of religion and politics, as well as its role in creating a social context for enlightened ideas, whether deistic, pantheistic or republican. Thanks to the letters of Rousset de Missy to Marchand, we shall be able to assess its meaning in the lives of two pantheists – and it seems safe to assume that Marchand shared the views of his friend – when in the next chapter we examine their creed and its relation to ethics, Freemasonry, and the new scientific culture. And given what we now know about Freemasonry and the Orange Party, the egalitarian side of Masonic fraternity will also have to be taken into account when we assess the role of Rousset de Missy in the Dutch Revolution and its implications for the republican tradition. For strange as it may seem, given the parliamentary character of English republicanism, some of these idealistic Orangists, who were in contact with that tradition and who sought to restore what other Dutch republicans regarded as a quasi-monarchy, actually believed themselves to be republicans, to be searching for, in the words of Charles Bentinck to his brother, 'the resurrection of the Republic' (154, 102n). It remains a matter for discussion if the Commonwealthmen would have approved of their actions, if in other words, their actions can be related to the classical, 'old Whig' version of the republican tradition.

From a single manuscript in the private papers of John Toland we have moved very rapidly to the ideological and social connections between the radicalism spawned by the English Revolution and the first half-century of the pantheistic and republican Enlightenment on the Continent. Through that intellectual history we shall arrive at one of the important sources for the High Enlightenment. But en route we must sketch out the remainder of the social roots of the Radical Enlightenment that stretched, from at least 1711, into the Austrian Netherlands. Pantheism and republicanism have a continuous intellectual and social history that begins in England in the 1690s and that moves rapidly into the Netherlands, both north and south, and most important into the world of government officials and political activists.

One link in this chain requires that we return again to the Knights and address the question of Rousset's direct involvement in that earliest coterie. Was Jean Rousset de Missy actually admitted to the company of 'our devil-may-care gentleman' mentioned at the end of the 1710 meeting record? Is he 'Frère Jean' mentioned frequently in the other meeting records? Certainly he was in The Hague at the time; he was married there in the Walloon Church in August of that year. Fritsch's letter (see appendix, pp. 277–9) confirms that Levier and Rousset were on very close terms – they perused together the clandestine manuscript from Furly's library that provided the basis for part of the *Traité des trois imposteurs*. Then Rousset published anonymously a famous letter about the tract in de Sallengre's *Mémoires de littérature*, published by du Sauzet. In it Rousset linked the *Traité* with Bruno's *Spaccio* which he says Toland circulated on the Continent (see pp. 218–20). He also signed his letter in the name of Marchand's correspondent – Peter Friedrich Arpe – an obvious ruse. Furthermore, Rousset was on good terms much of his life with du Sauzet and Henri Scheurleer, his usual publisher; both figure in letters from Fritsch to Marchand. And not least, Rousset was also a devoted follower of Eugène of Savoy as well as a promoter of the Whig interpretation of the Revolution of 1689.

All the evidence points to Rousset's membership in the Knights, but the matter will probably never be proven absolutely. Firm historical evidence about secret heretical societies is not always easy to come by. What is certain, from Rousset's letters to Marchand, is that by the mid-1730s Rousset was an absolutely dedicated Mason and so, too, were Douxfils and Marchand. They also maintained a life-long friendship, and some of those letters have happily been preserved.

Since this triumvirate of Rousset, Marchand and Douxfils provides so much important evidence for the continuity between the Knights and official Freemasonry, as well as for much else, and because the most enigmatic of our cast of characters has been saved for last, we must pay some attention to Lambert Ignace Douxfils (*fl.* 1710–53). His exact dates are unknown, yet this journalist and editor, who was, of all things, the Commissioner of the Post in Brussels, belonged to this clandestine world from the earliest years of the Knights until his last letter to Marchand in 1753. In 1712, Fritsch wrote to Marchand, care of his publishing firm of Fritsch & Böhm, and referred to Douxfils as 'coadjutor and vicar of the order'; at other times he was called 'our friend and loyal vicar and cousin'.[55] In later years, as a fellow Freemason, Rousset addressed him as 'mon frère' and in fact he was taken in by Douxfils after his exile. The name of Douxfils runs like a leitmotive through the business and personal relations of the Knights and their associates in the literary society.

As Rousset's letters reveal, he and his Masonic friends had worked out a variety of special relationships with post offices, or more precisely with postal officials in certain key Dutch and Belgian cities. 'Frère Douxfils' took care of by-passing the censors in Brussels; 'frère Felbier' managed things in Antwerp. The Knights were using a system of agents and spies that had been installed by the Allies during the War of Spanish Succession. From about 1706, François Jaupain, the postmaster at Brussels and director of the Belgian postal system, was in the pay of the English government and his services, for which he was handsomely rewarded, continued well into Walpole's era. He, in turn, brought various other officials into this network, and reasonably we can suppose that Douxfils and Felbier were among them.[56] In a later period, Rousset also availed himself of the services of the Baron de Sickenhausen, who was director-general of postal services in the Dutch Republic.[57]

Government records in Vienna indicate that Douxfils and Felbier served as especially valued officers of Eugène of Savoy's post-1714 government in the Austrian Netherlands. Eugène had been rewarded for his military service to the Allies with the governorship of the southern Netherlands, an office he executed in absentia and partly through the loyal services of Baron Hohendorf whom he stationed in Brussels. Douxfils and Felbier figure in a very select company of officials loyal to the vastly unpopular new regime. As a reward for their services, these 'officers of the post' were given the rank of 'chefs de villes' in the Low Countries, and officers of His Majesty, Charles VI in Vienna, with all 'privilèges attendant'.[58]

Yet surely not all these officials could have been attracted to Freemasonry; that seems to have been the province of convivial men with intellectual interests and reforming instincts. Douxfils came from a family with social pretensions and some considerable education. He lived in great style but was plagued by debt and by a disreputable relative who went about the capitals of Europe posing as an aristocrat. This brother-in-law eventually married a woman who was to become Voltaire's mistress.[59] Indeed, when Voltaire went to the Netherlands in 1722, via a stopover in Brussels, it was probably Douxfils, a friend to the poet, Jean-Baptiste Rousseau, who put Voltaire in touch with Levier and Picart in The Hague. As discussed in the previous chapter, they tried, unsuccessfully, to publish Voltaire's epic poem, *La Henriade*.

Although probably born a Catholic in Namur, the Douxfils we encounter in Brussels was only enchanted by those works in philosophy which could be put side by side 'with those of the Voltaires and Spinoza'.[60] Although later in his life Douxfils, along with Rousset, developed a particular dislike for the 'impudent' Voltaire, in ideological terms Douxfils was a man of the Enlightenment and a spinozist. And that was a very dangerous intellectual posture to adopt in the Austrian Netherlands which was, by all accounts, one of the most clerically controlled and heavily censured territories in Europe. It is little wonder that Douxfils found in Freemasonry the camaraderie and freedom that he needed.

During a brief period in the War of Spanish Successsion, when the southern Netherlands was controlled by the allied powers, Douxfils ventured an attack on a prominent Jesuit. After the institution of Hapsburg authority, and the re-emergence of traditional clerical claims for a powerful and independent role in the state, he retreated into literary silence.[61] He devoted himself to the loyal service of Viennese interests, which were often perceived as being in conflict with the interests of the local nobility and clergy, whose extreme Catholicism and assertion of feudal rights differed markedly from the enlightened and centralising tendencies manifest in this absentee government. Douxfils's political involvements in the entourage of the Duc d'Arenberg, as well as those of his friends in The Hague, are all to be left for a subsequent chapter. What is especially important about Douxfils at this point in our story is his employment.

Douxfils started his career first as a minor official in the Brussels post office and then as its commissioner, an office with status and power over communications within the Hapsburg administration. The letters of the Knights and their friends, and those of Douxfils, make constant mention of packets of books, or packets of manuscripts, sent to him or received by him. Furthermore, as the correspondence reveals, they are writing frankly because the letters would be transmitted by friendly officials well placed in the post office. The conclusion presents itself: this secret coterie of shrewd businessmen with an interest in the circulation of forbidden books and manuscripts, especially in finding ways of getting that material into France, had their 'frères' in the very post offices that were the central link in communications between the Netherlands, north and south and, as we shall see, France.

Much intelligent history has been written about the transportation industry for clandestine literature into France, in particular about the small army of porters who were hired to carry it over the mountainous Western frontier from Switzerland.[62] That expensive and dangerous system did often succeed in by-passing border agents, the police and customs officers. But the heavily travelled and geographically open border between France and the Low Countries, and the obvious necessity for getting forbidden books from Amsterdam and The Hague through the Catholic and Austrian Netherlands, necessitated other, equally ingenious, systems of transportation. What better method than to have as one's agent a trusted official, completely in charge of the Brussels post office, who could be relied upon to transmit packets or cartons of books and to ensure their safe arrival at least to the border, if not beyond?

Frères Douxfils and Felbier, the commissioner of post in Antwerp, received and forwarded packets from Marchand, Rousset and their friends for decades. From as early as 1716, Douxfils in turn had a working relationship with M. Pajot, the director of the post at Lille, just across the French border, who received packets from him (as well as gifts for his services).[63] Indeed, Douxfils was so adept at gaining the services of French officials that even when the French army occupied Brussels (1746) during the War of Austrian Succession Douxfils used the services of the commissioners of the post for the French army.[64] If we accept the notion that the literature of the Enlightenment, much of it produced in the Netherlands, served to undermine the ancien régime in France, then it must be noted that corruption within its very bureaucracy helped to sow the seeds, or more precisely, dig the furrows, by which that very destruction was accomplished. Bureaucratic corruption (although undoubtedly in this instance on a smaller scale than the underground coach and porter systems of transportation) played its part in the work of the Enlightenment.

But what exactly did those packets and cartons mentioned by Douxfils and the Knights in their life-long correspondence contain? We can only surmise. Throughout his life Marchand received book orders for a variety of works, some quite 'harmless', others genuinely heretical, such as Voltaire's *Urania,* Toland's *Pantheisticon*, a life of Servetus, Diderot's *Les Bijoux indiscrets*, and, of course, older heretical works, such as Des Périers's *Cymbalum Mundi*.[65]

In one sense, Douxfils may simply have been transmitting material in such a way as to avoid the customs excise, that would have been good for profits. But from the perspective of the historical significance of his actions, we should keep it in mind that the Knights originated at least one of the most virulently pantheistic and materialistic clandestine manuscripts of the eighteenth century, the famous *Traité des trois imposteurs*, and that it somehow made its way all over France (not to mention Europe and the New England colonies). If Douxfils had a hand in that enterprise, and there is every reason to imagine that he played his part, he was truly taking quite a risk and that should be clear once we analyse the contents of the tract. It must wait, however, until we take one final look at the social milieu within which the manuscript originally surfaced.

There are people strangely, even glaringly, absent from this social portrait of the Radical Enlightenment both at its core and its periphery. Throughout these manuscript records, the letters and written works, published and unpublished, women are seldom if ever mentioned. Where they appear, as in the dedication to Minerva, or in Toland's dedication of his pantheistic *Letters to Serena* (1704) to the Queen of Prussia, which contained an affirmation of the intellectual capacities of women, or in Radicati's feminisation of nature, they are remote patrons or mythic and symbolic figures, never immediate intellectual companions. Occasionally Rousset de Missy, who, as he tells Marchard, thought that monogamy was contrary to nature, sends greetings to his friend from his wife 'of over forty years'.[66] In the early meeting records of the literary society there are literary exercises on the theme: 'Of the two, which is less grievous to a lover, the death of his mistress, or her infidelity?' The young gentlemen assembled concluded, upon careful reflection, that her death would indeed be preferable.[67] If these freethinkers spoke from experience, of mistresses that is, scant evidence survives to attest to it. Although Saint-Hyacinthe appears to have fathered an illegitimate child who was consigned to the Walloon orphanage (136, I, 52 and II, 219) he and his 'frères' were eventually and generally married, sometimes socialised together in couples, and seem to have taught their wives and children of both sexes enough about their publishing businesses so that, as in the cases of the widows of Levier and Thomas Johnson or the daughter of Bernard and wife of Rey, they could help with or take over the businesses.

The subject of the role of women in the Enlightenment, whether moderate or radical, is so vast and as yet so woefully unexplored that here we can only focus on one aspect of that complex issue. Assuming as we have that we are exploring one of the earliest forms of European Freemasonry at its origins and beyond, then the question inevitably arises, are women so absent from this intellectual life and social world because of its Masonic character? And if that is the case, as it appears to be, then what are the implications to be drawn from the exclusion of women from that movement and hence from one aspect of Enlightenment culture? One might answer simply by concluding that in European Freemasonry we find yet another example of the failure of Western egalitarian ideals to encompass the status of women; yet the matter is not quite that simple.

From its earliest official history in the 1720s, Freemasonry aroused criticism because of its conscious exclusion of women. Some of this tension was simply of a homophobic origin; opponents of the Hanoverian court attacked the lodges and hinted maliciously and darkly of their allegiance to the court, of sodomy and sadism.[68] No evidence exists to support such charges, but they did register and were countered by pro-Masonic literature and at least one Masonic play stressing the sentimental ideal of marriage where the women's right to choose her partner is stressed over prearranged marriages.[69] Throughout the eighteenth century, European Masonic literature echoes the point: Masons subscribe to the ideal of marriage freely entered into for love and, in turn, it is claimed that Masons make particularly virtuous and honourable husbands.[70] Indeed, their literature grew increasingly respectable on the subjects of sex and marriage and in the eighteenth-century Masonic song books the libertine songs almost uniformly date from the earliest part of the century.[71] Yet by the same token much of that same literature stressed the inferior sensibility of women, their inability to keep secrets, their essentially emotional nature.[72] In 1723, Anderson's *Constitutions* explicitly excluded from membership, not only 'stupid Atheists and Irreligious Libertines' but also 'no Bondmen, no Women, no immoral or scandalous Men'. For reasons unclear, the 1738 constitution sharpened the distinction to 'no Woman, no Eunuch', but that offensive passage was dropped from all subsequent editions.[73] Yet part of Masonic ritual entailed the presentation of two sets of gloves to the initiate, one for himself, the other for his wife or 'for the Lady whom he esteems most, if he has the good fortune to be still a bachelor' (149, 64–9). Wives were regularly toasted at Masonic banquets, while in one account of what must have been an originally artisan ceremony passed on to speculative Freemasonry, the apprentice must 'uncover his breast, to see that it is not a woman who has presented herself' (149, 69). All of this ritual and merry-making was accompanied by limericks or songs, of which one example is more than sufficient:

> No Mortal can more
> The Ladies adore
> Than a free and an accepted Mason.[74]

Masonic literature on the subject of women reveals an underlying tension, one that may prove to have been endemic to the new culture of Enlightenment. The advocacy of freedom of choice for women, and of course for men, as well as of companionship within marriage reflected a new, egalitarian ethic in family life that came into its own in the course of the eighteenth century.[75] Yet modernity is juxtaposed to sentiments that advocate women's natural inferiority or that are downright misogynist. If we assume that the significant growth of separate male fraternities and clubs in the eighteenth century constituted, from the perspective of social history, an alternative and a reaction to the new ideal of domesticity (even and perhaps most especially on the part of its practitioners) then Masonic literature would indeed tend to add further evidence for the growth of that ideal as well as for revealing one reaction to it. Freemasonry clearly advocated equality for men (other than bondsmen) within the lodges, glorified domesticity and sexual fidelity, yet at the same time betrayed resentment and discomfort on the question of women and their rights and abilities.

Although this pattern holds true in general for eighteenth-century Masonic literature and practice, does it hold specifically in the case of Masons who were philosophical and political radicals or who were in close proximity to them? One of the most extraordinary documents contained in the official manuscripts of Dutch Freemasonry is the constitution and membership list of an organised lodge of women and men that existed in The Hague from at least 1751 and which had a woman as 'grande maitresse', with the Baron de Wassenaer, a prominent Orangist and grand master for the Netherlands, as the 'protector' of the lodge. This lodge was never given public recognition by the Grand Lodge, yet it had official status, treated 'les soeurs' as absolutely full and equal members and certainly subscribed to 'the geometrical law' of human conduct, in effect to order and equality. It also gave its allegiance to 'the grand architect of the universe'.[76] Many members were married couples; others appear to have had an independent membership. Unwittingly perhaps, the egalitarian ideal of Masonry had led to one clandestine example of its inevitable logic. Elsewhere and later in Europe other lodges 'of adoption', that is, for both women and men, were established and openly justified by their adherents; but these lodges were always condemned by the official Masonic movement. To this author's knowledge, the women's lodge at The Hague is the earliest one of its kind that possessed rituals for both women and men. It constitutes an extraordinary example of a new culture, occasionally aristocratic but largely bourgeois, which cannot be explained without some attention to its intellectual milieu. Just as political ideas bear relation to political action, so too ideas about God and nature can influence social behaviour. Within the Masonic lodges of The Hague and Amsterdam could be found brothers in positions of leadership whose philosophical convictions were vastly out of step with Christian orthodoxy. It remains for us to explore those convictions and to examine the human implications for both men and women of a pantheistic creed that rendered the material world, and therefore civil society, the sole object of devotion and inquiry.

Notes: Chapter 6

1   Bernhard Fabian, 'English Books and Their Eighteenth-Century German Readers', in Paul Korshin (ed.), *The Widening Circle: Essays on the Circulation of*

Literature in Eighteenth Century Europe (Philadelphia, Penn.: University of Pennsylvania Press, 1976), pp. 155, 167. For the coffee house, see G. D. Schotel, *Het Maatschappelijk leven onzer vaderen in de zeventiende eeuw* (Haarlem, 1869), p. 62.

2   Marchand MSS 2, 16 September 1713; cf. his letters in Marchand MSS 1, which contains the surviving correspondence of the literary society; cf. Rapin to Marchand (or Levier), n.d. Marchand MSS 2; on 14 December 1713 le Bachellé voted 'yes' on Messrs Burnet, Mathurin and d'Artis; 'no' on a M. Brinkman. M. d'Artis was chaplain to the wife of the Duke of Portland. The new society of 1728 included s'Gravesande, de Joncourt, Sacrelaire and Marchand.

3   UL Leiden, Marchand, MSS 2, Fritsch to Marchand, Paris, 18 November 1712: 'Je passerai sous silence mes amusemens à Bruxelles, mais je suis obligé en conscience de ne pas laisser ignorer aux chevaliers de l'ordre l'acceuil honeste de M. Douxfils Coadjuteur et Vicaire de l'ordre . . .'. And from Brussels, 25 October 1712, Fritsch wrote, 'Nous arrivâmes donc hier au matin . . . à Bruxelles òu nous avons été parfaitement bien receu de tout le monde . . . Nous avons bue largement et copieusement à la santé de tous les Chevaliers, Amys et Amics . . .'. For Gilbert, see letters beginning 28 March 1714 in Marchand MSS 1.

4   On Gacon see Henry H. Grubbs, *Jean-Baptiste Rousseau – His Life and Works* (Princeton, NJ: Princeton University Press, 1941), pp. 21–2, 102n, 117. For Gacon's affiliation with the society see Marchand MSS 2, 17 December 1711: 'votre lettre . . . qu'elle est une marque certaine de la paix conclue entre tres hauts, tres puissants . . . tres poétiques seigneurs et princes Jaques Boyd, Charles Levier & François Gacon, d'une part, et très bas . . . frères Prosper Marchand et Gaspard Fritsch d'autre part.'

5   Marchand MSS 2, Dalber to Marchand, 9 January 1711; 31 April 1712.

6   J. N. S. Allamand (ed.), *Oeuvres philosophiques et mathématiques de Mr. W. J. s'Gravesandes* (Amsterdam: chez Marc-Michel Rey, 1774), p. lviii.

7   Marchand MSS 24c, 24a; letters from the 1730s.

8   Marchand MSS 2, 15 July 1716, Fritsch to Marchand, 'Dans une heure les s'Gravesande, les Alexandres, les Sacrelaires et plusiers autres les f[word cut out of letter] viendront boire le Theé chez moy. Nous boirons à Vostre Santé.' This sort of purposeful expurgation of words, coupled with the fact that the first letter of the excised word, 'f', and the size of the hole in the original renders the word 'frères' very likely, frustrates as much as it suggests. Cf. E. and E. Haag, *La France Protestante ou vies de Protestants français* (Paris, 1854–9), vol. 9, p. 74. Cf. Marchand MSS 1, F. le Bachellé to the Society: 'J'appris par ma propre expérience que les lettres s'y perdent fautement, je ne jugeai pas à propos d'hazarder témérairement le secret de la Société.' Marchand MSS 1, Alexandre to Marchand, 8 December 1713: He is proposing new members of the society, and ends the letter promising that he 'gardera religieusement le Secret.'

9   S'Gravesande, *Oeuvres*, vol. 2, pp. 316–17.

10   Roland Mortier (ed.), *Difficultés sur la religion proposées au Père Malbranche . . . texte intégral du 'Militaire Philosophe'* (Brussels: Presses Universitaires de Bruxelles, 1970), pp. 9–39, and text. Cf. Ira O. Wade, *The Clandestine Organization and Diffusion of Philosophic Ideas in France from 1700 to 1750* (Princeton, NJ: Princeton University Press, 1938), pp. 48–52; cf. E. Carayol, 'Themiseul de Saint-Hyacinthe'. Thèse, 3e cycle, Lettres', University of Paris, IV, 1971, vol. 2, p. 300, typewritten.

11   Frédérick Gerson, *L'Amitié au XVIIIe siècle* (Paris: La Pensée Universelle, 1974), pp. 79–80.

12   These anonymous signatories are identified in the copy of *Le Chef d'œuvre* at the BN, Res. Z. 2071, possibly the author's. Information about Johnson is contained in BL, MSS ADD. 4284, ff. 177–91; UL, Edinburgh, Johnson letters to Charles

Macky, Professor of Literature, Edinburgh. The use of the term *le chef d'œuvre* for this production may signal an identification with secret societies of artisans; French *compagnonnage* required *un chef d'œuvre* from its new members. I want to thank Joan Scott and William Sewell, Jr for drawing attention to these societies.

13   See Quentin Skinner, 'The principles and practice of opposition: the case of Bolingbroke versus Walpole', in Neil McKendrick (ed.), *Historical Perspectives. Studies in English Thought and Society in Honour of J. H. Plumb* (London: Europa Publications, 1974), pp. 113–27.

14   Marchand MSS 55b, no foliation, 'Les Grand Jours de l'Ignorance. Conte Hollandois' in the hand of Douxfils.

15   S.D.L.R.G. [Saint-Hyacinthe], *Mémoires littéraires* (The Hague: chez Charles Levier, 1716), preface. Saint-Hyacinthe may also have been suspected of dealing in subversive literature when in England. See his letter to Lord Carteret, n.d., PRO, S.P. Dom. George II, 146, f. 226.

16   F. Weil, 'Ramsay et la Franc-Maçonnerie', *Revue d'histoire littéraire de la France*, no. 63 (1963), pp. 272–8.

17   *Mémoires*, pp. 28–33.

18   Saint-Hyacinthe, *Letters Giving an Account of Several Conversations upon Important and Entertaining Subjects* (London, 1731), p. 124.

19   *Letters*, pp. 128, 164–5.

20   *Lettres critiques sur la Henriade de M. de Voltaire* (London, 1728), pp. 37, 46–7.

21   *Letters*, p. 14.

22   Marchand MSS 2, Saint-Hyacinthe to Levier, 30 April, n.a.

23   Spencer Research Library, University of Kansas, MS. B. 64, 'Travel Diary of John Mitchell', f. 60 on the burning in Ghent of one Kemnay, an artist, for sodomy.

24   Marchand MSS 2, Fritsch to Marchand, 17 November 1711, 'Mais Mr Gacon qu'a – il a démêler avec M. Le Clerc. Nostre ami nous fera un plaisir très sensible d'en agir modestement avec Luy, car cet homme est parmi les libraires ce que le diable est chez les Indiens, & il faut luy brusler une chandelle à fin qu'il ne fasse pas de mal . . .' See also 29 April 1716, Fritsch to Marchand: 'Je lui répondes que son dessein ne me convenoit pas, que M. Le Clerc ne m'ayant fait ni bien ni mal; je ne trouvois pas apropos d'imprimer contre lui de controverses qui pourroient aller trop loin et tourner en invectives . . .' One M. Masson had approached Fritsch to publish an attack on Le Clerc.

25   [Lambert Ignace Douxfils (ed.)], *Dissertation critique et analytique sur les Chrono-grammes, publiée en 1718. Nouvelle Édition revue et corrigée par l'Auteur* (Brussels: chez F. Foppens, 1741); Bibliothèque Royal, V.B. 7073^d: 'Je veux parler de l'affaire de la constitution . . .'

26   On Sallengre and the society see Marchand MSS 1; *L'Éloge de L'Yvresse* (The Hague, 1714), p. 107.

27   E. Benoist, *Mélange de remarques critiques . . . sur les deux dissertations de M. Toland . . .* (Delft, 1712); and *Bibliothèque angloise*, vol. 8, pt 2 (Amsterdam, 1720), pp. 318–21. Benoist died in Delft in 1728.

28   BL, MSS ADD. 4282, ff. 224–6, and ADD, 4287, de Sallengre to Desmaizeaux. Cf. J. H. Broome, 'An Agent in Anglo-French Relationship: Pierre des Maizeaux, 1673–1745', D. Phil. dissertation, University of London, 1949, pp. 222–35, 320–2.

29   *A Collection of Tracts Written by John Asgill, Esq.* (London, 1715), p. 80; M. Jacob, *The Newtonians* (p. 226); Caroline Robbins, *The Eighteenth Century Com-monwealthman* (Cambridge, Mass.: Harvard University Press, 1959), pp. 96–7.

30   Samber's MSS are in the Bodleian, Rawlinson collection. For Asgill and Samber, Rawl. 134b, f. 87. Boniface Oinophilus, *Ebrietatis Encomium: or the Praise of Drunkenness . . . confirmed by the Example of Heathens, Turks, Infidels, Primitive Christians . . . Philosophers, Peers, Free Masons . . .* (London, 1723), see ch. 5, 'Of Free Masons', pp. 83–91, not in the original.

31　Bodleian, Rawl. 134a, f. 196, 'Sir Isaac Newton. A Poem, 1729'.
32　Rawl. 134b, f. 119 *et seq.*, 'A new dissertation on the venereal disease'; cf. Edward Armitage, 'Robert Samber', *AQC*, vol. 11 (1948), pp. 103–17, esp. 115.
33　*Voyages et aventures de Jacques Massé* (Bordeaux, 1710 but probably The Hague, 1714).
34　H. Dethier, 'Vanini', *Tijdschrift voor de studie van de Verlichting*, vol. 2 (1974).
35　*Theatrum Fati, sive notitia scriptorum de providentia, fortuno et fato* (Rotterdam, 1712), pp. 1–2.
36　Marchand MSS 2, P.Fr. Arpe to Prosper Marchand, undated but mentions a meeting in Belgium (where Marchand may have been *en route* to The Hague in 1710) and Arpe's search for good publishers. The letter probably dates from 1710–12.
37　For Weyerman see G. M. Geerars, 'De Vrijdenkerij in de Journalistieke werken van Jakob Campo Weyerman', *Tijdschrift voor de studie van de Verlichting*, vol. 2 (1974). The MSS list of membership for this period at the Grand Lodge in The Hague does not include Weyerman, but the lists are not regarded as complete.
38　Marchand MSS 2, Rousset to Marchand, f.16, 18 August 1749.
39　Marchand MSS 1, M. Alexandre to Marchand, 8 December 1713; cf. G. d'Artis, *Projet pour l'instruction des jeunes gens* (The Hague, 1710).
40　Marchand MSS 2, Fritsch to Marchand, 3 November 1715 in Italian; Jean Frédéric Bernard, *Nouvelles Littéraires* (The Hague: Chez Henri du Sauzet, 1715); engraving of Minerva and Mercury on frontispiece; pp. 52–3, English freethinkers praised and then a retraction (pp. 71–2) based on Steele in the *Spectator*, Du Sauzet mentioned in Marchand MSS 2, Saint-Hyacinthe to Levier, n.d., f.6: 'M. du Sauzet doit vous donner les exemplaires des poésies de Villiers?'; and in Fritsch to Marchand, 3 November 1715 in Italian.
41　Bernard Picart, *Cérémonies*, Vol. 6, p. 252. Title-page engraving employs sun symbolism. In 1731–7 English edn, Vol. 6, pp. 202–3, the Freemasonry section has been pulled out by the English editors, explaining, 'The Free-Masons . . . are so well known in England . . . Besides, as it is not a religious Society, it is out of the Sphere of this Work.' Pious alternatives to Picart's anthology were quickly produced; see Thomas Broughton, *Bibliotheca historico-sacra* (London, 1738), first edition of *Historical Dictionary of All Religions* (1742).
42　*Praise of Hell*, pp. 44–5; *Réflexions morales, satiriques et comiques sur les mœurs de notre siècle* (Cologne: Chez Pierre Marteau, le Jeune, 1711), pp. 212–22.
43　For du Sauzet's membership in official Masonry, the Grand Lodge of the Netherlands, The Hague, 'Kronick Annales', 25 May 1748, 'La Loge d'Orange de Rotterdam soumisée à La Grande Maitrise des Provinces Unies . . . Louis Dagran, Grand Maitre; A. Huisken, J. Vermaat, Henry du Sauzet [the other officers]'. Du Sauzet's son (also Henry, d. 1785) admitted in 1755.
44　In Pierre Conlon, *Répertoire chronologique* (1715), no. 18047, a Catholic work is incorrectly attributed to Rousset: *Le Parti le plus sur . . .* (Brussels: les frères Serstevens, 1715). The Beinecke Library, Yale, incorrectly attributes it to Scheurleer.
45　Marchand MSS 2, Fritsch to Marchand, 15 July 1716, 'Mr Scheurleer croit faire merveilles à Paris, je le lui souhaitte; je lui ay donné ma bénédiction et quelques instructions qui ne me feront ny bien ny mal'.
46　Marchand MSS 2, Rousset to Marchand, f.36, n.d. but after 1749, '. . . je vous prie de saluer pour moi par le nombre fraternel'.
47　Marchand MSS 2, Rousset to Marchand, f.36, item no. 8, 'Votre anecdote de la Cassette de Franc-Maçon m'a fort diverti; si ma pré & post-face vous a plû . . .'
48　Marchand MSS 2, Rousset to Marchand, 8 April 1750, Brussels, f. 19; f. 35, Maersen, 18 October (n.a.), for 'maître Charles'; f.36, item no. 12, 'Je vous envoye avec celle-ci une Lettre du maçon de Nimegue [a work by Rousset] pour le frère

Charles, les Ministres Haverkamp & Broen & les deputés du Consistoire . . .'; f. 38, 'frère Charles'; f. 40, 'salut, Honor et argentium atque bonum appetitum à vous & au fr. Charles'; f. 41, 13 December 1752, 'Bon soir et bonne nuit pour vous & pour Charles, il ira sans doute chez Mr Doringer quand il sera parti . . .'; f.44, mention of 'frère Soyer'; f.46, 'Charles et Prosper pourraient ajouter à mon bonheur . . .'; f.47, 'Bon soir, portez-vous bien, répondez-moy, donnez-moi vos ordres . . .'; f.60, 'frère Charles'; f.61, 6 January 1753, 'frère Charles'; f.68, 10 April 1753, 'Je ne sai òu vous et Charles (dont j'ai reçu la Réponse que vous me prometez pour la semaine prochaine) avez trouvez dans mes lettres que j'aye intention *de renoncer à l'état tranquilé dont je jouis pour me replonger dans la tumulte des affairs publiques & Politiques & refréquenter la Cour et les grands.* Non mes chers amis, ce n'est point là mon intention . . .'; f.70, 10 May (n.a.), 'À propos du Prisonnier [that is, himself in exile], parlons de Mlle Roi & du fr. Charles; je l'ai importuné, c'est à dire le frère, parcequ'il me l'a permis pour le prier de faire passer à la première, le 1re quartier d'une petite pension que je lui ai accordée, . . . s'il voit Mlle le Roi, puisqu'elle est à Voorburg . . .'; f.74, 25 April (n.a.), 'J'espère envoyer de l'argent à Charles le 3 ou 4 mai pour Voorburg . . .' and 'Nos complimens [including Douxfils] au fr. Charles . . .'; f. 76, 'Vous prie de me renvoyer avec l'exemplaire que je vous demande & qui vous sera paié, si vous m'en marquez le prix le l. de Juillet m'envoyant au fr. Charles l'argent pour Mlle le Roi.'; f. 77, 29 June (n.a.), 'Je vous envoyeray 22f par le frère Charles quand je lui envoyerai le quart d'an de Mlle le Roi'; f. 81, 2 August 1753, 'J'envoyerai avant la fin de la semaine 48 fl à Charles pour envoyer à Mlle le Roy'; see also ff. 84, 89; f.96; f. 101, 1 February 1755 Maersen, 'J'ai reçu la lettre du frère Charles, qui m'afflige véritablement par raport à votre situation corporelle, je sens toute la peine . . .'

49 Marchand MSS 2, Allamand to Marchand, Leiden, 13 January 1755, 'J'ai parlé avec M^r De Bentinck sur ce qui a fait le sujet de notre dernière conversation: il mettra promtement la main à l'œuvre, pour vous procurer de la société une pension annuelle de 200 florins: pour cela il faut que votre Testament soit fait . . .'; Leiden 8 February 1755, 'J'éspérais de me rendre aujourdhui à la Haye avec M^r De Bentinck pour avoir le plaisir de passer la matinée de demain avec vous.'

50 Marchand MSS 2, Allamand to Marchand, 26 September 1754. Allamand also often makes mention of a mutual friend, M. de Beyer, and de Beyer's letters to Marchand, Marchand MSS 2, 1740s and 1750s, make constant reference to Freemasonry, e.g., 23 March 1743; de Beyer also knew Trembley; cf. Marchand 3, Jean de Bey, 29 April 1753, to Marchand, mention of M. van Laak, who was official Masonic publisher.

51 The Grand Lodge of the Netherlands, 'Persoonsnamen Correspondentie – *La Bien Aimée'*, 'Comte de Bentinck'; and 'Archief la Bien Aimée', no. 23, 1, letter dated 1 February 1757 by R. Schreuder.

52 Abraham Trembley, *Mémoires pour servir à l'histoire d'un genre de polypes* . . . (Leiden, 1744); cf. Marchand MSS 2, A. Trembley to Marchand, 2 May 1743; 16–27 November 1748 from London, 'J'ai reçu . . . par Mad. de Bentinck votre Lettre du 5 Nov. N.S.'

53 Koninklijk Huisarchief (The Hague), the correspondence of J. N. S. Allamand to Marc-Michel Rey, esp. ff. 30, 33, 43, 46, 64, 98, 99; Allamand refers to William Bentinck as 'M. De Roon'.

54 For the earliest description of official Dutch Masonry and its difficulties with the States of Holland, see Abbé Perau, *Le Secret des Francs-Maçons*, Nouvelle Edition (n.p., 1744), pp. 120–5, 'Extrait d'une lettre de Hollande du 17 Mars 1737'. On those events see *Daily Advertiser*, 5 November 1737, and in December 1735, on crowd disturbances against the Masons and accusations of homosexuality.

55 Marchand MSS 2, 18 November 1712; same to same, 3 November 1715. He is sometimes playfully called 'Dolce figlio' or just 'M. Doux'; Marchand 1, Paris, 23

March 1716, 'L'un des messieurs de la poste à pris sur lui à ma prière, de faire tenir le pacquet à Mr Doux à Bruxelles . . .' And from same to same, Paris, 6 April 1716, 'j'ai profité de la bonne volonté de Mr Pajot pour le faire tenir à Bruxelles sans frais, persuadé que M. Doux votre ami trouveroit pareille occasion pour vous le faire tenir de là á la Haye.'

56 ULC, Chol. 1102, Jaupain to Walpole, 16 February 1724, 'je ferai tout ce qui dépendra de moi, pour maintenir dans le Bureau, quelques personnes affidées, qui puissent rendre les même services . . .'; Thomas Tompson and Robert Jacomb were his contact men in England; cf. Paul Fritz, 'Anti-Jacobite intelligence, 1715–1745', *Historical Journal,* vol. 16 (1973), pp. 273–4.

57 Brussels, Archives Générales. Conseil Privé. Postes et Messageries, 1715–1750, no. 1217. I am grateful to the librarian, Ms Denise Van Derveeghde, for her assistance.

58 Österreichisches Staatsarchiv, Vienna, Protokolle v.32, for letters from Eugène to Hohendorf and Douxfils; v.33, f. 131, Douxfils described in 1718 as 'offr. des Postes à Brusselles'; f.125 on status of officers of the post with Emanuel Felbier singled out; f.360 to Hohendorf on the new edition of Palladio engraved by Picart; v.34, f.281 Eugène to Hohendorf's widow, that the continuation of a pension will be difficult 'as there are many widows'. For a guide to the archives, L. Bittner *et al.,* *Inventare des Wiener Haus-Hof- und Staatsarchivs* (Vienna, 1938).

59 About all we know of Douxfils, aside from his letters, comes from Arnelle [Mme de Clauzade], *Les Filles de Madame du Noyer, 1663–1720. Voltaire et Pimpette du Noyer, les fourberies de Cavalier, chef des Camisards* (Paris: Fontemoing et Cie, 1921), pp. 181–201.

60 Marchand MSS 2, Douxfils to Marchand, 6 February 1747, 'qu'une philosophie si relevée m'enchantoit . . . qu'un pareil ouvrage soit mis à côté des Voltaires et des Spinosa'.

61 [Lambert Ignace Douxfils], *L'Original multiplié ou Portraits de Jean Bruslé* (Liège, 1712). For Bruslé 'de Montpleinchamp, see *Biographie nationale . . . de Belgique,* Vol. 3, pp. 114–15. Cf. André Puttemans, *La Censure dans les Pays-Bas autrichiens* (Brussels: Palais des Académies, 1935), pp. 25 *et seq.*; M. J. Küntziger, 'Essai historique sur la propagande des encyclopédistes française en Belgique dans la seconde moitié du XVIIIème siècle', in *Mémoires couronnés et autres mémoires publiés par l'Académie Royale des Sciences, des Lettres et des Beaux-Arts de Belgique,* vol. 30 (Brussels, 1880).

62 See R. Darnton, 'Trade in the taboo: the life of a clandestine book dealer in prerevolutionary France', in Paul Korshin (ed.), *The Widening Circle. Essays on the Circulation of Literature in Eighteenth-Century Europe* (Philadelphia, Penn.: University of Pennsylvania Press, 1976).

63 This fascinating network is revealed in Marchand MSS 2, Douxfils to Marchand, 9 July 1747; 4 June 1747. There is just the possibility that M. Pajot may have been a Freemason. One Claude Pajot, probably a relative of the next generation, was inspector of mines in Flanders in the 1780s and he was a Mason; Louis Trenard, 'Les Lumières dans les Pays-Bas français', *Dix-huitième siècle,* vol. 10 (1978), p. 132. Masonry began in Lille in 1744. For Pajot's early involvement, Marchand MSS 1, de Sallengre to the society (Paris, April [?] 1716), and note 55.

64 Marchand MSS 2, Douxfils to Marchand, 3 February 1749.

65 Marchand 2, March 2 [?] 1735, Rousset to Marchand, actually a discussion of Voltaire's manuscript; d'Harnonville to Marchand, 9 July (n.a.), 'le Tholand Latin [8°]' which must be the *Pantheisticon*; Sebastian Hogguer to Marchand, St Gall, 23 April 1733, thanking him for *L'Histoire de Servet;* Crusius to Marchand, 27 July 1748, thanking him for *Les Bijoux indiscrets;* 7 August 1711, Fritsch to Marchand ordering 100 copies of the *Cymbalum* for the book fair in Basle.

66 Marchand MSS 2, Rousset to Marchand, f.57,

67   Marchand MSS 1, *varia*, unfoliated.

68   *The Free-Masons; an Hudibrastick Poem* (London, 1723), p. 5, 'And I take it Court Politicians and Free Masons are oftentimes ally'd . . .'; and p. 20. Curll is also mentioned as a bookseller to the society; he was rumoured to be a homosexual.

69   *The Perjur'd Free Mason Detected, and yet the Honour and Antiquity of the Society of Free Masons Preserv'd and Defended* (London, 1730). BL lists 'Defoe?' as possible author; *The Generous Free-Mason: or the Constant Lady with the Humours of Squire Noodle, and His Man Doodle. A Tragi-comi-farcical ballad Opera. By the Author of the Lover's Opera* (London, 1731). BL lists this as being by W. R. Chetwood.

70   *La Lire Maçonne, ou Recueil de Chansons des Francs-Maçons par les Frères de Vignoles et du Bois* (The Hague, 1766), published by R. van Laak, official publisher for the Grand Lodge of the Netherlands, pp. 244–5, 360–3; and *Chansons notées de la très vénérable confrérie des Maçons libres. Par Frère Naudot* (Paris, 1737).

71   ibid., pp. 16–18, 147–9, 471–3 on Minerva; pp. 142–4 on respectability; pp. 452–5 mention of d'Holbach.

72   *The Free-Masons Accusation and Defence. In Six Genuine Letters* (London, 1726), pp. 7–18.

73   M. Paillard (ed.), *The English and French Masonic Constitutions* (London: Watts, 1940), pp. 38, 56.

74   H. Poole, 'Masonic song and verse of the eighteenth century', *AQC*, vol. 40 (1928), p. 11.

75   Randolph Trumbach, *The Rise of the Egalitarian Family. Aristocratic Kinship and Domestic Relations in Eighteenth-Century England* (New York: Academic Press, 1978).

76   The Grand Lodge of the Netherlands, The Hague, 'Livre de Constitution . . . Constitution de notre grand loge d'adoption depuis Numero Un . . . De Saint Estienne, Député Maitre; Le Baron de Wassenaer, Grand Maitre'. Mariane, Baronne D'Honstein was "grande maitresse" and there were seventeen 'soeurs'. The Constitution begins: 'La Maconnerie, ayant pris naissances dans les vertus qui doivent gouverner sous une loy géometrique les moeurs des humains [,] a donné l'Etre dans ce siècle heureux [,] à un essain de coeurs soumis à cette loy, de l'un et de l'autre Sexe, qui dans ces climats cherche a estre favorisé d'un protecteur, qui étant reconnu pour grand maitre dans les provinces unies: l'autorise à professor sous l'auguste titre D'adoption les Devoirs que la morale de l'ordre Luy Impose.' Dated 1 May 1751. I am grateful to Margaret Hunt for assistance with this text and to the librarians of the Gemeente Archief, The Hague, for guidance in local history.

CHAPTER 7

Pantheistic Religion, Revolution and the New Science

Do you realize that if the theses [of the Abbé de Prades] had been passed at the same time as the 10 enormous volumes of the *Encyclopédie*, it would have led rapidly to Pantheism; the wits, the blue stockings, the light ladies, the dandies, all those Italian, English and French deists and atheists would have been rid of the yoke of religion   necessary in society if we are not to be slaughtered [by one another], and useful for nothing else but that is enough; but I must stop, I sound like 'le petit Encyclopédiste'.[1] (Rousset to Marchand, 1752)

A social world as rich and complex, not to mention as secretive, as that of Rousset, Marchand and their friends must only have been sustained by strong common interests as well as by strongly held common beliefs. We cannot know exactly how many 'frères' subscribed to the pantheism of Toland, Rousset and their friends but there is rich evidence that as young publishers and propagandists the Knights invented one of the most dangerously pantheistic manuscripts of the Enlightenment, the famous *Traité des trois imposteurs*. At every turn access to the printing press, and the clandestine channels of circulation gave importance to such projects far in excess of the relatively small social nexus that sustained them. But pantheism lay not simply in the propagating, but equally in the living of this curiously metaphysical, yet immensely secular, if not political, creed.

The attempt to disseminate pantheism, coupled with a commitment to the propagation of new scientific ideas, and in the case of Rousset, an ability to engage in scientific experiments, entwined with a religiously held, and we can also say, practised creed. The rituals and ceremonies of the Masonic lodge, with its emphasis on a common 'priesthood' and fraternity, could doubtless express a variety of creeds, Christian but just as likely, heretical. Likewise, the Masonic lodges must have provided immensely useful outlets, as well as subscribers,

for the various intellectual and literary projects, especially the journals, with which the Knights were involved, and also possibly for the
sale of Diderot's *Encyclopédie* – a project to which Rousset, if not his
other 'frères', gave a wholehearted endorsement. Much of our evidence for the meaning of this creed, as well as for the variety of political
and intellectual interests taken up by these radicals, comes from Rousset's private letters to Marchand (as well as from other correspondence
in Marchand's papers). Like the excerpt used to open this chapter,
which reveals· Rousset's concern that the French authorities, goaded
by the Jesuits, will succeed in suppressing the *Encyclopédie*, these
letters are explicit and frank because, as has been indicated, in this
period of exile after 1749 Rousset was able to send them to Marchand
through their Masonic friends in the Belgian post office.

To describe these pantheists simply as atheists, as indeed they were
in the eyes of the godly, might be to miss the constant insistence found
in this literature for order, harmony, and meaning in the natural and
human order. In 1734, Count Radicati, that itinerant Italian pantheist,
put it succinctly:

> But to say that Deists are Atheists is false; for they are so called by
> the Vulgar, and by those whose interest it is to decry them; [they]
> admit a first cause under the names of God, Nature, Eternal Being,
> Matter, universal Motion or Soul. Such were Democritus, Epicurus,
> Diagoras, Lucian, Socrates, Anaxagoras, Seneca, Hobbes, Blount,
> Spinoza, Vanini, St. Evremond, Bayle, Collins.[2]

In enlisting so many and disparate ancient and modern philosophers,
Radicati was trying to establish the intellectual lineage of this new
naturalism. Bayle would doubtless have been horrified to see himself
listed along with Spinoza, and various other worthies on the list would
have spurned the association. Yet the radicals were trying to give a
pantheistic interpretation to the freethinking tradition, and on a
polemical level they succeeded by 1750 in shifting the debate into their
quarter and in creating the most virulent form of philosophical heresy
in a century plagued by the disease.

Two texts served to propound the pantheism of the radicals:
Toland's *Letters to Serena*, published in English, but quickly translated
into French (a manuscript translation went to Vienna in Eugène of
Savoy's library); and more important, because of its much wider
circulation, the *Traité des trois imposteurs* (143). Toland's treatise
although openly published, was also the more overtly philosophical
and turgid of the two; its practical applications, except for advocating
an end to 'prejudices', remain largely implicit. Yet the materialistic
definitions it contained were clear and as such useful, 'all the matter in

Nature, every Part and Parcel of it, has bin ever in motion, and can never be otherwise' (Toland, p. 169). Locke was enlisted for verification of a metaphysic to which he did not subscribe, and so too was Newton, 'all the particular or local Motions of Matter are but the several Determinations of its general Action' (pp. 176–7). But Toland's definition of matter, in direct opposition to Newton's, stressed not only its inherent motion but also its infinity and its eternity, 'the World, with all the Parts and Kinds thereof, continuing at all times in the same condition' (pp. 190–1). Using his knowledge of the new science from biology through physics, and combining both with a revival of the mid-century sectarian heresy of mortalism, Toland articulated the metaphysics of eighteenth-century pantheism.

Toland's attack on the notion of the soul's immortality – 'it flattered Men with the Hopes of what they wish above all things whatsoever, namely, to continue their existence beyond the Grave; there being but few that can bear the very Thoughts of ever ceasing to live somewhere, and most People commonly choosing to be miserable, rather than not to be at all' (p. 153) – contained a social message that the Traité and other pantheistic and materialistic tracts would spell out. The worship of nature entails in effect the worship of the here and now, of civil society; there is no after-life, no spiritual society beyond our own. In an anonymous 1743 publication of earlier clandestine manuscripts, a collection dedicated to the memory of Anthony Collins, the point is made explicitly: the *philosophe*, and it is from this early eighteenth-century tract that we get the word used as a particular description of the man of enlightenment, knows that 'the existence of God is the most widespread and deeply engrained of all the prejudices'. In its place the *philosophe* puts civil society, 'it is the only divinity that he will recognize on earth'.[3] This new divinity, proclaimed in a collection of tracts whose metaphysical ambiance is explicitly pantheistic and materialistic, must be extolled and honoured by hard work and probity. Although there is no direct mention of Toland in this collection he would undoubtedly have agreed with the secular posture of *le philosophe*.

Yet by far the most famous – or infamous – and widely read clandestine tract of the Radical Enlightenment was the so-called *Traité des trois imposteurs*. Shrouded in mystery for centuries, the subject of endless monographs and essays, the manuscript's origins in the early eighteenth century were purposely obliterated (6). We now know who masterminded this obfuscation and the tract itself.

Late in their lives, Gaspar Fritsch, the former grand master, and Marchand, the original secretary of the Knights of Jubilation, resumed their correspondence. These are fairly cautious letters; much time has passed. Fritsch still clearly holds Marchand, although not all their 'brothers', in high regard. In February 1737, he thanks Marchand for having enlightened him about *La Vie et L'Esprit de Spinoza*, as the *Traité* was often called.[4] In fact on this subject, theirs was a mutually enlightening correspondence, but unfortunately only Fritsch's portion has survived. In October of that same year Fritsch revealed, in the letter printed in the appendix, that Levier got the *Traité* from Rousset de Missy and that Levier combined it with *La Vie de Spinoza*, a manuscript he copied in the library of Benjamin Furly. Then in 1740 when Marchand was compiling notes for his own *Dictionnaire* on the *Traité*, Fritsch writes:

> I will send you the rough draft for your essay on *The Three Impostors* [probably the one eventually published in Marchand's *Dictionnaire* (1758)]. It is quite true that one could do nothing without you. But this essay is perhaps such that you should disavow any hand in it when you make it public; while not forgetting the sad spectacle of the banning of *La Vie et L'Esprit de Spinoza* [by the Walloon churches].

Fritsch then reminds Marchand of his youthful transgression: Fritsch had arranged for his brother to carry *La Vie,* the manuscript from Furly's library, to Levier's house where he copied it 'very quickly. I kept the copy myself . . .'[5] Subsequently he has repented the fact that he showed that manuscript to a variety of people, and was doing so as late as 1736: 'I allowed them to copy as much as they wanted, entirely free of charge. It was total rubbish. Since then, I have come to think more seriously than I did.' As the letter later indicates Fritsch, now older and stricken with gout, has clearly come around to believing in God.

From these letters certain conclusions about the origins of the *Traité* present themselves: *La Vie* was clearly a separate manuscript from *L'Esprit*. Indeed there is no evidence that *L'Esprit* ever existed as a text prior to the *Traité*, and in the copy of *La Vie et L'Esprit* from Hohendorf's library and hence quite possibly from the Knights, *L'Esprit* appears to be identical with the *Traité*. And Levier got it from Rousset de Missy.[6] Fritsch stongly implies that Rousset was its author, although this is not to deny that the treatise may have been borrowed and concocted from a whole host of clandestine manuscripts (possibly from one called 'L'Esprit de Spinoza'), but also and not least of all from 'Le Theophrastus redivivus' (1659) which was French in origin and which Hohendorf had in his library where Marchand saw it. Some years ago, without this new evidence, Don Cameron Allen suggested Rousset de Missy as a likely candidate for this exercise in impiety, and that was a very good surmise (145). What is now also clear is that the

Knights were deeply involved in creating the *Traité*, in copying and disseminating it. Levier, apparently with the assistance of Toland's publisher, Thomas Johnson, did an extremely rare 1719 edition of it; Böhm did a shortened, perhaps somewhat different 1721 edition – both appear not to have survived. It is now possible to recreate the story of how this manuscript came to exist.

Accompanying many copies of the *Traité* is a brief exposition of its contents, commonly called the *Réponse*, which we now know to be written by Rousset and which was published separately and anonymously in 1716 by Henri Scheurleer. For decades prior to 1711 (the year Rousset gave the *Traité* to Levier) the rumour had circulated that someone had written a work in which it was claimed that Moses, Jesus and Mohammed were impostors. Various candidates for this final impiety were always being proposed: Aretino, Giordano Bruno, William Postel, Servetus, Bonaventure Des Périers, Campanella, Hobbes and Spinoza. The list was fairly distinguished and endless. As might be expected, philosophers indebted to the Hermetic tradition often found a place on it, as did thinkers whose ideas could be interpreted as tending to naturalism. Amid all these accusations and gossip a journalist named de la Monnoye published in 1694 an essay in which he concluded confidently that no such treatise on the three impostors had ever been written.

That essay was widely circulated and commented upon in the first decade of the eighteenth century, and perhaps the challenge was more than Rousset and his friends, with access to the superb library of heretical works in Benjamin Furly's home, could resist. It is just possible that the idea that the founder of Christianity had been an impostor had been hatched out with Toland; there is a manuscript among his private papers, only its table of contents survives, which claims to show that Jesus was a magician.[7] What better, in light of all the publicity, than to write, or to doctor significantly a pantheistic tract and to focus its attack against Christianity around the charge of imposture? What better polemical device by which to herald the birth of this new creed and to sound the death knell for its older, more established, rivals? In 1716 Rousset proclaimed to the world in his anonymous *Réponse* to de la Monnoye, which Fritsch knows Rousset to have written, that he had seen with his own eyes and possessed in his cabinet this famous little treatise.

Of course, we now know that Rousset was indeed telling the truth. He proceeded to give an exact description of the manuscript, by chapter and paragraph, one that conforms precisely with most extant copies. He further invented the fiction that he got the original Latin manuscript in Frankfurt-am-Main and that a German officer, Trawsendorf, and a student in theology, Frecht, had been involved in the transaction. As Fritsch notes to Marchand that was a complete fabrication.

But Rousset did not stop there. In effect his *Réponse* is a brief explication of the *Traité* that links it directly to Bruno's *Spaccio* – the same book of 'which Toland had published a translation in English a few years ago'.[8] Of course, Toland had carried the *Spaccio* all over Europe during his various forays, and the English translation had appeared in 1713. Furthermore, Rousset links the *Traité* very precisely with his own beliefs: it gives an idea of God that 'rather conforms to the system of the *Pantheists*, saying that the word *God* represents to us an infinite being of whom one of the attributes is to be an extended substance, and by consequence eternal and infinite' (Rousset's italics).[9] Rousset, in turn, then summarises the various chapters of the *Traité*, indicates in general the contents and offers no indication of disapproval. His *Réponse* was, in turn, answered by de la Monnoye in *Mémoires de Littérature* (1716) edited by de Sallengre and published by Henry du Sauzet. All of this added publicity in the pages of the *Mémoires* undoubtedly increased curiosity and indeed the 'frères' and their friends were, after all, businessmen. Years later, Marchand's posthumously published *Dictionnaire historique* (1758) contained a long essay on the *Traité* which repeated many of the fabrications, yet which is to this day one of the major sources of information about that tract.[10]

No one ever thought to ask how or why Marchand had got to know so much about that particular manuscript. The circulation of clandestine manuscripts was a dangerous business and identities had to be obscured. All the copies I have seen, from various libraries including Vienna and the Hohendorf collection, are neatly written by various hands. Never has a familiar piece of handwriting appeared; in almost every case, with the exception of that initial transmission described by Fritsch, the text must have been copied by hired scribes.

Imagine holding such a manuscript in your hands. In France you would have been imprisoned if caught doing so, and in no country were its contents legal. On its very first page the reader is informed that most men believe in the vain and the ridiculous, that is, Divinity, the Soul, Spirits, in short 'all the other objects which make up Religion'. They have been cajoled into this lamentable ignorance by religious impostors, Jesus, Moses and Mohammed. This confidence trick was perpetrated first by Moses, even though many of the prophets knew perfectly well that 'God is a purely corporeal being',[11] and then Moses used his army to make the lie stick. Why are people so gullible? Well, as Hobbes said, it is fear – 'those who are ignorant of physical causes have a natural fear . . . and this chimeric fear of invisible powers is the source of all these Religions'. Indeed, some men are so paralysed by fear that they have come to believe that 'the judgements of God are incomprehensible'. That error has happily been destroyed by 'mathematics, physics and some of the other sciences'.[12]

The new science provides the escape route from ignorance; it teaches that 'all final causes are only human fictions' and that natural causes can be found for all natural phenomena. Men seek to establish order in nature, but that order is nothing else than 'a pure effect of the human imagination'. It is absurd to think that God puts it there. With extraordinary sophistication about the meaning and uses of scientific knowledge, the manuscript tells us that the order in nature discerned by the new science is a necessary and valuable imposition of the human mind; science does not support the design arguments and the providentialism extracted from it by the Newtonians (and indeed by Newton himself). What then is this God of the theologians and the impostors? Adopting a personal style the author says, 'I respond that this word represents to us a universal being in which, to speak as Saint Paul, we have life, movement and being.' This God is nature, 'all is in God'.[13] Such a notion fulfils the Cartesian criterion of truth – it is clear and simple.

But there are plenty of men around who have a vested interest in retaining the god of the impostors. 'The vulgar' (*le peuple grossier*) want a god who resembles the kings of the earth, complete with pomp and 'celestial courtesans'. The laws of this vulgar god are 'human fictions' invented not by demons or evil genies but 'by the politics of Princes and Priests'. The survival of monarchies and churches depends vitally on the survival of religion, for through its laws princes have wanted 'to give greater weight to their authority' while priests 'have wanted to enrich themselves by the sale of an infinity of chimeras which they sell dearly to the ignorant'.[14]

The author of this manuscript would have us join in the work of destroying the old religion, founded on fear, repugnant 'to good sense and to reason', yet so appealing 'to the ignorant, that is to say the greater part of mankind'. Clearly this is a dangerous enterprise; political power is at stake here. Does Rousset advocate a revolution? In fact, he remarks, 'the seed of religion (I want to say hope and fear) fed by the diverse passions and opinions of men, has produced a great number of bizarre beliefs which are the causes of the ills (*maux*) and all the revolutions that occur in States'. So priests are the true revolutionaries, and the ministers of gods, 'these cunning men', have a great stake in preserving 'the lie'; they hate the truth.[15] The clear implication here, although one the tract stops short of advocating, is that a new kind of revolution (perhaps first in men's minds) will be necessary before the power accruing to priests, and by implication princes, will be eradicated.

This will be no easy task. Legislators since pagan times have been using the laws, cults and ceremonies of the gods to nurture whatever fanaticism they wanted to establish, and Moses, Jesus and Mohammed merely followed in this tradition. The author dwells at particular length on the duplicity of Moses. He was the son of a magician who was admitted into the priesthood of the Egyptians, men of great learning comparable in their social roles to the Druids in Gaul. As a result Moses became in his time 'a very great politician, a very learned Naturalist and a very famous Magician'. He used 'his pretended Magic' to rally the discontented peoples of the kingdom, including the Hebrews who were by far the 'most credulous', but who had also been treated most unjustly by the Egyptian kings. Through his knowledge of natural forces Moses contrived miracles and hoodwinked his followers into revering him 'like a god' – he had learned well the lessons taught by the Pharoah and his priests.[16]

Jesus followed in the footsteps of Moses – 'he was not ignorant of the precepts nor science of the Egyptians'. 'As the number of fools is infinite, Jesus Christ found his subjects among them.' In perhaps the most impious portion of the treatise, the author labels Jesus as the most cunning impostor of them all. He promised not to disrupt, to render to Caesar the things that were Caesar's; in other words, he acted like those princes who promise their subjects all sorts of privileges until their power is well established and then they renege on their promises.[17] In short, Jesus is portrayed as a kind of Machiavellian who saw 'the extreme corruption of the Jewish Republic' and who contrived, with the assistance of his ambitious followers, to 'cause those revolts that continued until the entire destruction of the ancient Republic of the Hebrews'. To seal his labours, Jesus and his followers, whose beliefs are just as absurd as those 'of women and idiots' taught that this new set of laws possessed eternal validity.[18] If Rousset is the author of this particular passage, rather than its copier, then as the opening quotation for this chapter would suggest, age and experience taught him to modify considerably his misogyny. Significantly, from the perspective of Rousset's later political involvements, he assails Jesus here as a corruptor of republics. Yet the author must admit that there is some merit in the morality of Jesus. Of course, his precepts can all be found in the writings of the ancient pagans; one does not find anything 'more useful or more sublime in the politics and morals of Christ than in the writings of the ancient Philosophers'.[19]

Mahametanism continues this pattern of subversion and upheaval, although the author is slightly less harsh on Mohammed than he is on Moses and Jesus. Mohammed is pushed into a role of leadership, but nevertheless the pattern of deceit and imposture holds true for he was one of 'the three celebrated legislators whose religions have subjugated a great part of the universe'.[20]

If all the major religions are built upon a tissue of lies, what are the alternatives? Clearly men must have a new god, and that must be 'nature, or, if one wants, the gathering of all beings, of all the properties and all the energies . . . a cause imminent and not distinct from its effects'. There can be 'no Gods, no hell, no spirits, no devils' – all that exists is the world around us – 'heaven is nothing else but the continuation of the air in which we live, a fluid in which the planets move'.[21]

In the *Traité* Rousset, possibly in conjunction with some previous author, leaves his readers with the foundation of a new religion of nature. Like some modern commentators and Biblical scholars, these early eighteenth-century pantheists have concluded that Jesus was an 'impostor', 'a magician', but unlike them they have gone further and offered in place of the traditional Western religions a new creed, based upon science, but also upon a naturalism first proclaimed by the ancient pagans.[22] The author attacks Descartes for not admitting that the soul is material, although he uses his arguments about motion in animals to conclude that what Descartes observed was their actual participation in 'the universal soul of the world'.[23]

Suddenly it is as if we have come full circle. Having abandoned 'the spirits' of traditional Christianity we once again encounter a form of spirit – 'it is certain that there is in the Universe a very subtle fluid or a very thin matter [une matière très-déliée], always in motion, whose source is in the sun'. Life and movement come from this semi-material soul of the world; 'what the poets and Theologians told us about another world is chimera'.[24] A few strong minds and sincere men have perceived this new truth and 'in spite of persecution they are crying out against the absurdities of their time' – and so they have given us this small treatise.[25]

The reference to the ether as well as to the sun conjures up the literature of magic, of astrology and alchemy. It is also one possible idication of the influence of the French spinozist and *parlementaire* mentioned in Chapter 5, the Comte de Boulainviller. He is almost certainly not involved in the *Traité* directly; his spinozism was far less extreme than that put forward by this radical cadre, and of course Boulainvillier was not a republican.[26] Yet his spinozist commentaries, replete with his references to astrology, were certainly all over the clandestine circuit. And there is something else to be learned from these references: pantheism, although so profoundly secular in its orientation, could slip, long before the Romantics got hold of it, into the language and metaphor of mysticism. The discovery of new gods, or even of a new God, the Grand Architect, and of new objects of social worship entailed, for both Newtonians and pantheists alike, not only rituals but also a profoundly emotional reverence which lent itself, perhaps inevitably, to mystical expression.

In the twentieth century, the anti-Mason and historian Bernard Fäy saw in Boulainvillier and his circle one of the main springs of European Freemasonry. Fäy's paranoid reading of that history, based upon little concrete evidence, contains a few half-truths worth noting in relation to the evidence we now possess. Fäy saw spinozism, of one variety or another, as close to the heart of Masonry, ignored entirely the Christian apologetics of the Newtonians, and thought that he could find an indigenous aristocratic French Masonry. If Fäy had stopped his polemics long enough to do some hard research in the Netherlands he might have seen that within at least one Masonic circle the subversive ideas he discerned in some late eighteenth-century French Masons had antecedents in these Huguenot and English republican circles.[27]

The *Traité* summarised a living creed; it was not simply an extrapolation from Bruno or Spinoza. It proclaimed a unique attempt to arrive at a new religion of nature based upon the old naturalism and also upon the new natural philosophies inherited from the Scientific Revolution. It had mystical elements; but it was not anti-scientific – although shortly we must focus our attention on the Radical Enlightenment's exact debt to the Scientific Revolution. Pantheism was, moreover, directly linked, as I have indicated, to republicanism. This spirit-in-matter philosophy must be seen, within those circles at least, as the philosophical foundation for republican and even democratic philosophies of government. If the world of ordinary people and daily events is rendered, in effect, sacred then systems of government justified by recourse to supernatural authority, even if reinforced by human contracts, lose all validity. In this 'secularism' – understood as another form of religiosity – to which pantheism inevitably leads we have also taken a step closer to evolutionary theories of development, not only of plants and animals but also of men and institutions. By implication, people can impose or dispose of established authorities; by the logic of circumstances they can much more easily (than by recourse to providential design) justify revolutionary action.

By linking the *Traité* directly with this coterie of French refugees new channels into the early Enlightenment are opened. Religion, natural philosophy, or in a more generic sense science, and politics are fused in the programme initiated by an international social world that was small but cohesive, with access to the printing press and hence to the whole of French-reading Europe. Its members plied their trade on a variety of literary projects, but wherever possible, these pantheists and republicans sought access to political power. They circulated around the court of Eugène of Savoy in The Hague, and years later Rousset told the Austrian minister, the Comte de Cobenzl, in whose service he was then employed, that he had on many occasions during the War of Spanish Succession given advice to that prince.[28] After his departure, some of these refugees appear to have served as agents for the British government; by the 1740s, as we shall see, Rousset and some of his Masonic friends have become avid Orangists as well as advocates of democratic reform.

And finally there is the connection between the Knights, their literary society and Freemasonry. Aristocratic, Newtonian, sycophantic of courts and kings in the main, yet Freemasonry was a potentially dangerous institution capable of housing republicans and pantheists and of nurturing their fantasies for social equality and political reform. Perhaps now we can see why, in the late eighteenth century and well beyond, at a time of revolutionary upheaval, proponents of the *ancien régime* fastened their paranoid theories of conspiracy around that very institution. There was no Masonic conspiracy to subvert the established order; but there certainly were Freemasons who from the early eighteenth century onwards brought their discontent with the post-revolutionary order in England on to the Continent and exported into northern Europe an institution that could provide a social nexus for displaced idealists, political agents and subversive thinkers. During the Dutch Revolution of 1747, Rousset de Missy, although a loyal Orangist, ultimately sided with its radical and reforming artisan contingent (see pp. 233 *et seq.*). After his exile from Paris, the Abbé Yvon, who wrote many of the articles that covertly explicated materialism for Diderot's *Encyclopédie*, turned up in Amsterdam and became an officer in one of its Masonic lodges. Indeed, for mid-century radicals, whether intellectual or political, pantheistic materialism, of the sort found in the *Traité*, remained a dominant creed and Masonic lodges offered an obvious place for its expression.

We shall never know what all the Knights of Jubilation thought about the literary masterpiece perpetrated by Rousset and Levier. Yet there is one clue that may help to relate it to their particular circumstances as French refugees with decided political interests and traditions. Marchand kept a copy of Rousset's *Réponse*, which usually accompanied the *Traité*, in his very private library. His larger library, donated to the University of Leiden was (and still is) grand indeed; his much smaller private one notably contained a heavy dose of pantheistic and naturalistic works, by Arpe and about Spinoza, by Toland and Collins, as well as translations of Algernon Sidney, and Newtonian works by s'Gravesande.[29] Marchand was a brilliant bibliographer whose unique system of classification, co-founded with his Parisian associate, Gabriel Martin, contributed decisively to the encyclopaedic method of cataloguing knowledge later refined by Diderot and d'Alembert (131, 15–16). His own library was meticulously catalogued according to subject matter and volume size. As his preserved catalogues indicate, when he classified a book he did so intentionally and with knowledge of its contents. What then was his logic in singling out Rousset's *Réponse* for special classification in his private library where it was accompanied by only one other book, and both under the heading 'books of politics'?

The companion volume, the *Vindiciae contra Tyrannos* (Basle, 1579), was one of the most radical political treatises of the sixteenth century, and it openly advocated rebellion against tyrannical authority (123, 305). This startling link, between the *Traité* and the *Vindiciae*, as perceived by Marchand, provides valuable historical background for the political thought of the Radical Enlightenment, and also explicates the political meaning of the *Traité*. These French Protestant refugees in The Hague, exiled and bitterly hostile towards Louis XIV and his absolutist regime, probably did not arrive there as politically naïve as the traditional accounts of their plight might imply. In one sense they did not need the English Commonwealthmen to teach them to theorise about the nature of tyranny and its political corrective, rebellion. The *Vindiciae* had been written by a French Protestant leader during the religious wars of the late sixteenth century. It spoke to a growing realisation within Huguenot circles at the time (1574–5) that in the wake of the St Bartholomew's Day Massacre (1572) the preservation of Protestantism in France would require open rebellion and that political compromise with monarchy itself appeared increasingly impossible.

Quite probably written by Phillippe du Plessis-Mornay (1549–1623) but aimed at a circle that included his young and devoted friend, Hubert Languet, as well as other revolutionaries such as François Hotman (125, 227, 274), the *Vindicae* announces that there is no justification 'for that preposterous servility that the sycophants of princes urge upon the simple-minded' (124, 145). Kings receive their power to rule from 'the people' with whom they have a covenant to rule justly and to protect true religion, that is the laws of God. If a king becomes a tyrant and persecutor, the people, through their magistrates, have a right to rise up against him. Central to the argument of the *Vindiciae* is the role of the magistrate, those public men to whom the people have transferred their power and who could be found in a variety of institutions, as leaders of the towns and cities, as judges in the *parlements*, as members of the Estates. Those magistrates alone have the right and authority to lead a rebellion, although the *Vindiciae* does grant that at certain times God may inspire private persons to 'initiate resistance if they are specially summoned for that purpose'. Utmost care must be enlisted, however, to guard against falsely inspired leaders; 'we should at least look for these internal signs . . . absence of all ambition, genuine and earnest zeal, conscientiousness and finally learning . . .' (124, 156).

Indeed the *Vindiciae* not only asserts the right of rebellion, it may also be interpreted as a 'republican' tract in that it asserts that 'the king is like a president among [the people he] possesses only primacy of place. For as the entire people is above the king, so these officers, although below the king as individuals, are above him when taken as a body' (p. 162). Seen from the perspective of the English Commonwealth tradition (the *Vindiciae* was first translated into English in 1648), early eighteenth-century readers could have interpreted the tract as asserting the primacy of representative institutions and lesser magistrates over the authority of monarchs or even ruling oligarchies for 'tyranny resembles oligarchy' (p. 186). As a document that proclaims contract theory as the basis of government and which asserts the primacy of citizen leaders, the *Vindiciae* offered a powerful critique of absolutism and one that was compatible with the beliefs held by Whig radicals. It is hard to believe that these French refugees were unfamiliar with its doctrines or hostile to its advocacy of rebellion before their arrival in The Hague.

Why, however, did Marchand place the *Traité*, as explicated by Rousset's *Réponse*, next to the *Vindiciae*? The author or authors of the *Vindiciae* were deeply Christian men committed to the Calvinist doctrine of predestination and to a literal faith in the sacred meaning of Scripture. Had not Calvin, in turn, burned freethinkers like Servetus whose anti-Trinitarianism and naturalism made him a hero to Toland, Collins, Rousset de Missy and their friends? The late sixteenth-century Calvinists worshipped the God of traditional Christianity; the early eighteenth-century pantheists worshipped nature. Yet both believed that the rules of political obligation could be derived from the laws of nature; their philosophical definitions of that concept simply differed profoundly. And both are linked in history by their violent opposition to absolutism and by their enforced exile in the Netherlands where on both occasions, as we shall see in our discussion of the Dutch Revolution of 1747, these Protestant refugees embraced the cause of the House of Orange. In the late sixteenth century, Huguenot revolutionaries belonged to an internationally linked Protestant network that practised secrecy for survival and that waged bitter war against the Spanish crown in the Netherlands, and after the Massacre of St Bartholomew's Day, against the French church and its king.[30] The Freemasonry to which Rousset and his friends were drawn fulfilled many of the same social needs as did the Calvinist churches, and like those churches in their time of persecution, but for very different reasons, it too was secret and international in scope.

Marchand's association of these anonymous tracts makes a good deal of historical sense. Both emanated from circles of French Huguenots bitterly alienated from monarchy and prepared to wage war against it. Did not Marchand, Rousset and their friends give their allegiance to Eugène of Savoy as that magistrate who would lead Protestant Europe against Louis XIV? Or did both groups, in their practice of secrecy, embrace the notion that in some sense they were the needed magistrates, or at least their educated mandarins? Furthermore, both tracts bitterly assail tyranny, only the *Traité* conflates political and religious tyranny and lays blame squarely on the major religions and their founders. Both imply that a few enlightened men must be found who can initiate the rebellion, the overthrow of tyranny. And both tracts, while asserting the fundamental role of 'the people', display a deep fear of their supposed ignorance. Both have democratic tendencies, the first because it asserts the people's contract with God and the king, the second because it would have all men be part of nature and hence inevitably equal.

The *Traité* and its authors parted company from the intellectual and social tradition of Huguenot radicalism from which they emerged on the crucial question of religion. Theirs would be of and from nature, devoid of priests but not of enlightened mandarins. They believed in the total authority of temporal rulers and human laws over the religious community, yet they also, like du Plessis-Mornay and his friends, believed in religious toleration. Political authority came from contracts and not from divine sanction. The radicals of the Enlightenment would champion Hobbes and Locke (for disparate reasons to be sure) in the first instance because they offered *de facto* theories of government and excluded any notion of divine right or providentially sanctioned authority. The Radical Enlightenment was a profoundly political movement, and the pantheism it brought to the Enlightenment served as one foundation for republicanism that would survive until well into the later part of the century.

Knowing now something about Marchand's understanding of the genre of literature to which the *Traité* belonged, can we, before turning our attention to the concrete political involvements as well as the other intellectual activities of the Knights and their associates, attempt to gauge the impact of the manuscript among its eighteenth-century readers? For instance, what relevance might it have had for the Masonic circles introduced in the previous chapter, for those men and women who had chosen to worship in the new temple of reason? That is the most difficult (probably impossible) question to answer, but there is one piece of evidence from The Hague that is so fascinating as to beg for our attention. The Royal Library possesses a unique manuscript version of the *Traité*, one of the many to be found all over Europe, but in this case it is bound with a copy of Arpe's essay on Vanini and his scurrilous *De tribus impostoribus*.[31] It is undated, but almost certainly comes from no later than 1750, and indeed given its location and this particular combination of manuscripts it could have come from someone in the Marchand–Rousset circle. The manuscript is also unique, however, in providing a final section where the anonymous reader of these clandestine manuscripts offers a short meditation on their meaning. 'A Moral Treatise, following the Principles of Nature'. This is amateur philosophising, and as a result all the more fascinating.

The idea of 'nature' presents this seeker of enlightenment with some problems, 'it is a composite of the works of the Creator, a general definition, that conforms to the idea of an All', but most important for this writer, within 'nature' there are individuals with an essence of their own.[32] The Creator can be nature, or if you like vice versa. What is important is the meaning derived from this philosophy of nature for the individual. This armchair philosopher had obviously been raised to believe in the traditional God and when he, or possibly she, moves away from that concept and embraces the idea of nature, words do not always mean what they should. But the author makes it clear that what is really interesting about these treatises are the practical, moral implications of this idea of nature for individuals. Why did nature make us? 'I have boldly decided that it was to make us happy'.[33] Man is the king of nature, sovereign of his reason, and he has available to himself the means of making himself more happy; our riches are in effect within us. This meditation on the practical morality implicit in the laws of nature, according to this author, will not be to the taste of the theologians but their orthodoxies have a practical effect contrary to the laws of nature.[34]

Real happiness consists in an intimate union of the body and the soul; the soul allows us to perceive clearly but it is also the seat of the passions. Nature put passions in individuals for a purpose: 'Nature does nothing in vain, she wants the body to be animated by the soul.'[35] In short, pantheism justifies sexual freedom. The major portion of this philosophical meditation concerns 'happiness for the two sexes'. The author states 'that men and women are equally sensible of their happiness, their nature is just about the same and the difference that one finds in their conduct is the effect of education'.

This practical philosopher has moved logically from the heady metaphysics of pantheistic materialism to trying to figure out how both men and women can better enjoy themselves and one another. Education benefits men in that they develop an independence of thought; they are not as bound by rules, 'they are able more easily to choose their pleasures'. But women in matters of pleasure 'are restrained by the rules that men have foolishly demanded of them'.[36] Hedonism runs aground on the obstacle of a woman's public image, 'reputation, in my opinion, is the poison of voluptuousness, it corrupts nature and debases our clearest pleasures'.[37]

This short treatise ends with a stirring denunciation of the tendency to choose reputation over nature, 'of all the passions there is none more tolerable than love, it purifies the spirit . . . love is the God of the fine arts, poetry and music are its faithful companions'.[38] Our hedonist ('I speak from experience') has found in the *Traité* and in the naturalistic tradition out of which it came, a philosophic justification for human sexual freedom. A variety of Enlightenment *philosophes* were to extract a similar message from that same materialist tradition.[39] Pantheism not only tended to level princes, it could also provide justification for the equality of the sexes as well as for a variety of pleasurable human freedoms. The advocacy of sexual freedom in itself, especially without the means of effective birth control, could not provide, any more than could private Masonic lodges for women, the foundation of social and sexual egalitarianism. Yet both might serve to suggest the failings of the prevailing social and sexual order. It was terribly important for individuals seeking to justify new varieties of human freedom to have available a coherent philosophical tradition and a call to action, such as was found in manuscripts like the *Traité*, from which they might find solace as well as inspiration.

If Marchand perceived the *Traité* as a political treatise, which among other things it was, then we might rightfully be led to expect a significant volume of political tracts attributable to the Knights and their friends. The republican statements of Saint-Hyacinthe and Jean Frédéric Bernard have already been noted as has been Rapin de Thoyras's association with this coterie. Jacques Boyd, one of the members of the literary society, was also a translator or possibly an editor of Algernon Sidney.[40] Shaftesbury, the great friend of Benjamin Furly, thought of his associates in the Netherlands as the 'Holland Whig Party' and endeavoured to distribute copies of Toland's edition of Harrington's *Works* among them (28, 44). The effect of this contact with the heady idealism of the radical Whigs was to render the Knights into Anglophiles of a sort. Years after those encounters, Rousset de Missy saw even Voltaire as an imitator of these famous 'freethinkers of London'. Inevitably some of these French converts became Whig propagandists. Yet dedicated to the abstractions of Whiggery, in the context of the Dutch Republic, produced a unique body of political literature that cannot be explained solely by reference to the English Revolution.

Rousset, in particular, put out an enormous volume of political propaganda, most of it in support of Whig foreign policy and the northern alliance of the Maritime Powers and Austria. If he was not paid for his services he should have been. His career as a propagandist began with the translation of Collins' *Discourse of Freethinking* (1713) which had been intended by Collins, as the preface to the French translation explains, as a piece of well-timed political propaganda and which Rousset, in turn, put out with his friend and life-long associate, the publisher Henri Scheurleer. Rousset also wrote, or translated, other works of a more orthodox character, intended to justify the Whig interpretation of 1688–9 as well as to defeat the Jacobite challenge (155). Furthermore, he contributed to the literature that apotheosised Eugène of Savoy, as did Bernard Picart who produced an elaborate engraving on the same theme.[41]

Likewise, the earliest journalistic publications of the Knights or their associates indicate a high degree of awareness of English political and cultural life and even a conscious desire to imitate and disseminate its achievements. Rousset published a journal modelled on the *Spectator*, while the journalism and translating into Dutch undertaken by Justus Van Effen is well known for its transmission of English, and in particular, Whig culture. An early journal done by Henri du Sauzet and Jean Frédéric Bernard (one dedicated to Minerva and Mercury) gave publicity to books published by the Knights, and to the *Traité*, but it also reported in detail on events in England. One issue recounted the Newtonian Richard Bentley's attack on Collins, Toland, et al. and praised the position adopted by the freethinkers. Then in a later issue, following Steele's attack on the extreme Whigs in the *Spectator*, the journal nervously withdrew its approbation.[42] Since we know that members of the Knights had contact with Whig agents in the Netherlands, one wonders if an effort was not made to enforce 'the party line'.

Certainly Whig interests and the northern alliance against France, even when it was out of fashion with Walpole and his ministers, were uniformly promoted by publications done by this coterie. Yet Rousset de Missy also carried on a one-man propaganda campaign against Cardinal Alberoni, the Spanish minister perceived as the archenemy in 1718 by a temporary alliance of France, England and Austria. This polemical treatment of Alberoni, whose evil Rousset perceives even in Alberoni's portrait, must have owed much to his reading of that vast literature, mostly published in the Netherlands and sometimes of Huguenot origin, that lashed out at the practitioners of absolutism (158). Rousset also, predictably, draws his examples from the classical tradition. The Italians, he notes, were enslaved 'under the Pagan Emperors, and those barbarous Nations, who most unworthily trampled under Foot the Senate and the Liberty of Italy'. He also lays blame for the menace of absolutism on the English Tories whose search for peace in 1712 thereby left 'Europe in those Difficulties from whence she might have then been extricated' (156, 252–60). Yet some monarchs because they now give their support to the northern alliance were worthy of praise, and Rousset wrote a long history of the reign of Catherine the Great precisely because she was perceived as an ally of the Maritime Powers.[43]

The political propaganda of this coterie, often buried in their literary journals, did seize the opportunity to praise signs of enlightened government where ever they might occur. Yet never before 1747 do they take up the arguments against Walpolean and Whig oligarchy with which they were doubtless familiar. Indeed, Rousset's knowledge of English affairs was quite substantial and his manuscripts include copies of the *Craftsman*, the opposition, Tory and 'country' paper of Walpole's era.[44] How much he and his friends may have approved of its critique of the government they saw as a necessary support for Dutch survival, we shall probably never know. Their republican analyses were confined to Continental affairs, to their reading of Dutch interests which, as we shall see, led them to support the Orangist cause, or to those occasions where they saw the possibility of spreading concepts of enlightened government to other parts of Europe.

Allegiance to the cause and person of Eugène of Savoy led to an identification with the Austrian empire and its interests, especially with its hostility to France. In the case of Rousset de Missy that allegiance was life-long; it is revealed in recently discovered letters to Austrian ministers, now housed in Vienna and Brussels, and it is displayed in one of his earliest printed tracts (1714) on the fate of Sardinia.[45] Freemasonry must have played a vital role in making possible this loyalty to a Catholic power. As Rousset states in one of his letters to the Austrian minister, he is a 'master mason' and hence he is 'from your royal order' and can be trusted.[46]

As indicated earlier, the Knights of Jubilation had firm connections in the Austrian Netherlands largely through the services of Lambert Ignace Douxfils and his friends. At first glance this dedication of pantheists and spinozists to the imperial Catholic monarchy may seem incongruous. Yet Austrian control over the southern Netherlands was perceived as crucial to the containment of France and the security of the Netherlands. Likewise, Hapsburg influence in the Mediterranean was regarded as equally vital to the maintenance of a European balance of power. If the universalist ideology of Freemasonry with its emphasis on state over church ever served to anchor political allegiances, it was in these disparate Austrian territories. In this respect, it is no accident that vast numbers of imperial civil servants, from Douxfils through Cobenzl to, in all probability, Gerard van Swieten, under Joseph II, were Freemasons.[47] Their Erastian and civil religion served as the antidote to the Gallicanising tendencies of the native clergy and the Jesuits.[48]

Rousset's tract on Sardinia gives insight into how the republican adherents of the northern alliance held their political ideas in some sort of balance with their, as they would have seen it, necessary political allegiances. In a piece of anti-Spanish propaganda that did not go unnoticed by the Jesuits, Rousset rejoiced in the fact that Sardinia had been wrested from the clutches of Spain during the War of Spanish Succession.[49] As an apologist for Austrian rule, Rousset insists that the Sardinians rejoice in their new sovereigns and that 'the people re-appear again with the liberty to contract new privileges, or to improve the old . . . the liberty of the people consists then in the power to accept or refuse a new sovereign . . . the people are not made to be bought and sold among kings as cattle are bargained among shepherds . . .'[50] While Rousset acknowledges that there are times when the people carry their search for privileges beyond reason, he sees in the recent changes in Sardinia the possibility of creating out of that barren land one of the 'most pleasant kingdoms in the universe'.

Rousset's gloss over the fact of conquest leaves the impression that the Sardinians had just experienced a self-made revolution and it ends with a plea for enlightened monarchy. In our discussion of the Dutch Revolution we shall encounter another, more historically important, example of radical idealism leading to a certain political myopia. Yet Rousset's early tract also reveals his commitment to the doctrine of popular sovereignity; one that he may have got either from his reading of Locke or from tracts like the *Vindiciae*. It also shows the mind of a radical propagandist at work, and reveals some of the contradictions that will become visible in the course of the Dutch Revolution of 1747, when Rousset de Missy attempts to combine his dedication to the House of Orange, as the reformer of a decadent and oligarchic republic, and his radicalism. Perhaps only in the intellectual lives of these radicals can we find a comfortable fit between their literary careers and their private beliefs. There they managed to unite their pantheistic faith with Freemasonry, and to combine both with an attempt to promulgate and apply the discoveries of the new science. But those intellectual lives were dramatically interrupted late in their maturity by the returning spectre of French invasion and by a con-commitant revolution in the Netherlands which was, significantly for our story, the only revolution to occur in a nation-state of Western Europe between the English Revolution of 1688–9 and the French Revolution of 1789.

The Dutch Revolution of 1747

The political history of the Dutch Republic after the death of William of Orange (William III, 1702), King of England and Stadholder of the Netherlands, was characterised by two interwoven and pressing con-cerns: during the War of Spanish Succession and long after, the fear of French encroachments on the hegemony, if not the territory, of the Netherlands, both north and south, and an increasingly obvious but slow commercial decline that was juxtaposed to the growing political power of Holland's rich urban 'notable' or regent elite (160, 50). In the absence of a direct heir to William's official and semi-monarchical authority, Dutch government became increasingly dominated by an oligarchy of about 200 extended families, centred in Amsterdam but well entrenched elsewhere. They had managed to lay claim to most essential offices in the various towns and cities of certain key provinces, most notably in Holland. They controlled taxation and its collection, and they had managed to place their own appointees as officers in the local citizen militias, the Dutch republican version of local police, as well as in the post offices, sensitive and vital links in communication and in the shipment and taxation of commercial goods. The States General, meeting at The Hague, reflected these particular commercial interests while being incapable, given its very limited constitutional powers, of becoming a significant agent of centralisation or reform. By the 1730s, it appeared to many observers that public squalor was complemented only by the growth of private wealth and the advancement of self-serving interests.

In foreign policy this oligarchic or 'true patriot' party, as it was called by its supporters, gave its critics greatest cause for alarm. Although committed in some sense to the alliance with England and the Austrian empire – the mainstay of Dutch foreign policy in the first half of the eighteenth century and beyond – the notables believed it possible to maintain neutral and commercially close relations with France. In consequence, they played down the dangers of French aggression in the southern Netherlands. As part of the territory ceded to Austria as a result of the War of Spanish Succession, Belgium (as it is now called) and its 'barrier fortresses' were perceived by the allies, and especially by the anti-French and increasingly Orangist party, as the first and essential line of defence against a possible French attack (162, 50).

In the course of the War of Austrian Succession (1740–8) the French army overran much of Belgium and the 'pro-French' foreign policy of the Dutch oligarchs was rendered bankrupt. The imminence of a French invasion into the Republic itself triggered off a popular uprising in Zeeland in April 1747 and in Holland in May. The crowds called for the restoration of the stadholder in the person of one William-Charles Friso, Prince of Orange-Nassau (163). One key element in the political base of this Orangist revival, and one directly relevant to Rousset de Missy's role in the Dutch Revolution of 1747, was the enormous popular support accorded any representative of the House of Orange. The antagonism of the artisan and petit-bourgeois town dwellers, as well as of rural tenants, toward the interests and policies of the great commercial oligarchs had, at moments, all the elements of class hatred.

In the 1730s, discontent with oligarchic rule coupled with the emergence of William-Charles Friso (1711–51), a cousin of William III, as a viable and legitimate claimant to the traditionally Orangist post of stadholder, gave new life to the Orangist Party. At its head were William and Charles Bentinck (164, 223–4) the sons of William III's most intimate adviser, and as indicated previously (pp. 198–200), enlightened aristocrats involved in Dutch Freemasonry. In consequence of their English schooling both regarded themselves as Whigs, although their conception of Whiggery, that is court-centred and ministerial, with a popular but powerless base, differed markedly from that of the radicals. Yet, first and foremost, the Bentincks were dedicated to the interests of the Dutch Republic and to the revitalisation, along Orangist lincs, of 'our bad constitution of government' (166, 37, 56, 77, 145).

Although the English government at first had the gravest misgivings about this new Orangist contender for the stadholderate, by the 1740s it was in active conspiracy with the Bentincks to effect an Orangist restoration.[51] While William-Charles Friso's foreign backing came from England and Austria, his support within the republic came from certain northern provinces as well as from a variety of ideological perspectives and interest groups. The traditional aristocratic and strict Calvinist elements who, in effect, favoured the institution of a monarchy and who were probably closest to William's own conception of his role as well as that shared by his wife, Anna of Hanover, daughter of George II (165), were joined by exasperated republicans as well as by radicals like Rousset and his followers who possessed strongly democratic tendencies. The restoration of the stadholder, even of one so relatively untested as William IV, seemed not only preferable but the only alternative to the 'corrupt and self-serving' rule of oligarchy (167). Elements within the Orangist Party saw the necessity of instituting massive reforms, while its specifically republican wing imagined that with these would come a reaffirmation of the traditional rights and privileges of the citizenry. Of course, William IV proved singularly incapable, as well as unwilling, to initiate such reforms, but none of that was clear until at least two years after the Revolution of 1747.

In 1734 William-Charles Friso and his wife set up 'court' in The Hague and, important from our perspective of the growing involvement of the radicals in the Orangist cause, their *chef de cuisine*, Vincent La Chapelle, opened the first official Masonic lodge there in that year (see pp. 110–11). The States of Holland promptly interrogated its leaders and forbade the spread of that movement precisely because of its Orangist associations. A look at the early Masonic membership list explains the grounds for those suspicions. Jean Corneille Radermacher is prominent on the list and he was rent master to William IV, while Dirk Wolters was received as an apprentice in January 1735 and he later acted as an agent for William Bentinck in the crucial months following the restoration of the stadholder.[52] Rousset's deep immersion in the allied and anti-French cause dates from at least 1710 and by the early 1740s the diplomatic correspondence of the Austrian government reveals him as one of its agents and spies. Of course this fits precisely with one of William Bentinck's almost obsessive concerns, that the alliance with Austria be seen as vital to Dutch interests. During the War of Succession the Duc d'Arenberg commanded the Belgian forces on the Austrian side, and he became a central figure in the Belgian government as well as a devoted follower of Maria Theresa. Lambert Ignace Douxfils, that early member of the Knights in Brussels and a devoted Freemason, was Arenberg's private secretary.[53] Years later, William Bentinck advised the young son of the then deceased William IV, that Bernard Picart had guided him into thinking about philosophy, and Bentinck offered the future William V a copy of Picart's works annotated by his friend, Marchand (171, IV, 471–2).

These Belgian, Dutch, and French refugee Masons should be seen as united in the first instance by their mutual dedication to this international military and diplomatic alliance against France, not necessarily by Orangism as such. For example, another Masons, Baron de Boetzelaar, was entrusted by Bentinck to bring the most secret instructions to England, and he was not, according to Bentinck, a dedicated Orangist (166, 96–102). Yet two of the most important Orangists of this period, Onno Zwier van Haren and his brother, William van Haren, were Freemasons. William wrote brilliant propaganda, both fictional and non-fictional, on behalf of the Orangist cause (166, 92–3). He embraced the concept of enlightened despotism found in Voltaire's *La Henriade* and became a minor figure of the Dutch Enlightenment.[54] Orangist propaganda, after the revolution, openly used Masonic symbolism, but long before (and after) 1747 the private correspondence of Rousset to Marchand crackled with the latest news of diplomatic intrigue and the fate of the Orangist cause.[55]

All of this Masonic involvement in the Orangist Party in turn rendered its Masonic membership prominent in the events of 1747–8 and also later, as the Bentincks attempted to consolidate William IV's power over that of the entrenched oligarchy. In May 1747, the States proclaimed William IV, stadholder, and he appointed Rousset de Missy as official historian of that revolution (169). Acting as an agent for Bentinck, Rousset also arranged to have published pertinent theoretical justifications for revolutionary change and, almost predictably, he sought the reprinting of the French edition of Locke's *Two Treatises*.[56] This use of Locke in a revolutionary situation, of course, presages his role in the American Revolution and reinforces an earlier point. As the Newtonians and moderate Whigs quickly realised, political theories based upon *de facto* definitions of political authority were inherently dangerous and in England after 1688–9 theorists intent upon justifying stability and strong ministerial government consistently shied away from Locke. But the Bentincks were Whigs who had conspired to make a revolution and Locke seemed to offer one obvious justification. They, however, unlike Rousset de Missy, did not take to its logical conclusion Locke's call for the popular foundation of political authority.

Rousset had long been an opponent of oligarchic rule; his *Mercure historique* begun in 1724, was notorious for its widely read critique of the existing order. In 1747, the restoration of the stadholder, an event so deeply indebted to the popular demonstrations witnessed throughout the republic, appeared to offer the possibility of sweeping reforms. As a prominent Orangist and reformer, Rousset suddenly emerged as one of the leaders of an Amsterdam-based coalition that attempted to push the revolution in a democratic direction. For a brief time he was imprisoned in Amsterdam and then The Hague, but William IV, unwisely as events were to show, ordered his release. By early 1748 Rousset had become an Orangist agent over whom his superiors had lost control. In collaboration with a wig-maker of French origin, Elie Chatin, who assisted him in his Dutch writings, Rousset rallied the largely artisan and small merchant classes around a series of demands for reform which became the platform of the radical wing of a movement known as the Doelistenbeweging (168, 83–6, 101–15, 144–5, 219).

At first that movement was led by Daniel Raap, an Amsterdam porcelain merchant, who under the influence of Rousset, presented a petition demanding that the stadholderate be made hereditary in the male and female lines, that all offices be sold 'for the profit of the country', that citizen leaders be chosen by the citizenry, and finally that the power of the guilds be restored. In brief, these reforms were intended to break the power of the oligarchy, not to destroy completely the place of wealthy men as elected officials, but rather to insure their responsibility to the citizenry. They also rested upon the vision of a supposed partnership between artisans and merchants which, it was claimed, had prevailed in the Dutch cities during mediaeval times. This vision of an ancient order of truly balanced government reinforced a decidedly modern sounding call for democratic reform. Among reformers more extreme than Raap and with whom Rousset eventually collaborated, these demands were set forth in a petition that called for, among other things, the placing of the post offices under the control of the stadholder and the appointment of tax collectors by the new government, to replace the tax-gathering role previously exercised by landlords whose abuses had been tolerated by the regents. By June 1748 riots had erupted in Amsterdam, Leiden, The Hague and Haarlem, and in this radical phase of the Doelisten-beweging Rousset along with Henry van Gimmig, a patternmaker from Haarlem, emerged as leaders.

What had begun as an Orangist revolution now threatened to become a lower-class movement for democratic reform. The response of the Prince of Orange and Bentinck was cautiously but resolutely hostile. Agents were sent to Amsterdam to confer with Rousset and his associates, and they were instructed to spend whatever money was necessary to try to win over other, more moderate followers, in effect to stem a tide that Bentinck, in his desire to whip up popular fervour for the prince, had been partially responsible for creating. A dangerous situation existed in Amsterdam where Doelisten pamphlets and wall posters had been seen in the poorest slums, and where pictures of the radical leaders, including Rousset, were openly displayed in the shop windows. It was only the eventual failure of the moderate faction, led by Raap, and the radicals, led by van Gimmig and Rousset, to agree on a common platform which created a wedge through which the government's authority could once again creep. At issue was the radicals' claim, articulated by Rousset to a representative of the court, that they had the right to overthrow the city government of Amsterdam (and by implication all governments) and to demand the right of all citizens, that is guild members, to elect their officers in the militia, and to control their shooting ranges, and to vote for various city officials.

In June 1749, Rousset was arrested, fined 1,000 guilders and banished by the States General from the country. His writings were also banned, (170, 78) and so ended the public career of a pantheist and journalist turned revolutionary. From his exile, Rousset often wrote to Marchand begging him to intercede on his behalf with Charles Bentinck, and bemoaned his absence from The Hague, from the world 'of the living'.[57] Yet he was also bitter in his repudiation of 'the tumult of public and political affairs' and he vowed never to return to the world of courts and grandees.[58] He claimed that his only desire was to obtain permission from the princess to be allowed to return to The Hague, solely for the purpose of seeing his 'dear friends'.

Rousset's disillusionment with the revolution was shared by other, far less radical, leaders like the Bentincks. William IV had proved manifestly incapable and unwilling to challenge the power of the great oligarchs, while in the face of the republic's financial and military weakness the English had despaired of their ally. Finally and not least, William's (d. 1751) widow had turned her back on the counsel provided by the Bentincks and they gradually drifted from power (171, II,

253–6, 275). Austria grew bitter and disillusioned with what it perceived as English double-dealing and Dutch weakness. Under the leadership of Kaunitz, Maria Theresa's brilliant administrator and advocate of centralisation, Austria broke with centuries of diplomatic tradition and effected the so-called 'diplomatic revolution' of 1756; it signed a treaty of mutual assistance with its traditional enemy, France.

Amid exile, disillusionment and ill-health, Rousset never stopped being profoundly concerned with European politics. Active in the 1740s as an agent for the Austrian government and probably as a spy, after 1749 Rousset continued to express his devotion to imperial authority[59] in opposition to the particularist interests of the electors of the empire and over the authority of the clergy. It was a common position to be found in enlightened circles, but Rousset combined it with imagining that somehow 'La République germanique' could be maintained in spite of, or in his opinion because of, these centralising tendencies. And in his correspondence with his Austrian paymasters (Rousset and later his family were rewarded for his services), he heaped special scorn on the Jesuits, whose power was seen to interfere with these efforts to achieve progressive and centralised government. His intelligence-gathering services to the empire also did not cease after his public disgrace, and in the face of Austria's increasing disinterest with the old alliance, Rousset frantically warned of the dangers posed to the empire by French bellicosity. Through his own secret correspondence with unnamed individuals in France, Rousset passed along evidence of France's hostile intentions. Yet he never forgot the business and necessities of patronage. He especially pleaded the case of Douxfils – 'un de mes anciens amis' – who, although a man of 'honesty' and 'talent', had fallen on hard times.

Before turning to a concluding discussion of the various intellectual projects that occupied and undoubtedly consoled these radical advocates of political reform, we must try to assess their political thought in relation to their political action, and to do so in the light of what we know about the English republican tradition with which they had once been in contact. We have moved many decades away from the 'neo-Harringtonian' republicanism of Toland and his associates and, of course, this new generation of radicals and republicans were at work in the Netherlands. In their violent opposition to French absolutism and in their desire to secure the independent survival of the Dutch Republic, they had also given their allegiance and service to that vast and complex international administration that held together the Austrian version of the *ancien régime*. Clearly dedication to her imperial majesty and to republicanism required some reconciling. Equally in need of explanation is the fact that Rousset, although a committed Orangist, became in those critical months after the restoration of the stadholder a central figure in the agitation for democratic reform and a major theoretician for cadres of artisans and shopkeepers.

Perhaps we can see in his proposal for universal suffrage for male citizens registered in the guilds (which would nevertheless permit only wealthy burghers to stand for office), with approval of elections as well as disinterested guidance coming from the stadholder, the influence of that originally English version of republicanism. These proposals seem to conjure up a vision of a balance of power among the people, a disinterested aristocracy and a carefully checked ruler that may owe something to Rousset's, and also to Marchand's, contact with Toland and Collins during those early years in The Hague. It may also be indebted to their having read or heard about the ideas of Sidney or Harrington. These French refugees, although involved at the highest levels of Dutch political life, appear to have had only a slight familiarity with Dutch political theory. Certainly their adoration of an idealised version of the British constitution remained with them throughout their lives. And finally pantheism, as revealed in the *Traité*, and the debt of its political message to Huguenot resistance theory must not be forgotten. This heady mixture of a purely naturalistic understanding of the world and man's place in it, coupled with English republicanism and with a distinctly Calvinist version of revolutionary ideology rendered Rousset, and probably quite a few of his friends, into truly dangerous men. Their *de facto* understanding of political authority meant that they could serve a variety of masters, and do so in good conscience. But given half the chance, as Rousset was in 1747, they were capable of acting out their historical roles as revolutionaries.

Decades before the French Revolution, some of the ideas we can now associate with the Radical Enlightenment, could possess and what is most important did actually possess, an ideological meaning that was in the context of the *ancien régime* truly revolutionary. The point needs stressing in the light of the continuing debate over the exact relationship between the ideals of the Enlightenment and the causes of the French Revolution. Perhaps one way of approaching that question might be to acknowledge that in the case of the eighteenth-century revolution in the Netherlands – one largely ignored until now in the historical literature – it is possible to show the existence of a radical underside deeply indebted, not to the moderate version of Enlightenment as represented by Voltaire, but to philosophical and political heresies nurtured in England but enriched by varieties of Continental materialism and possibly by Huguenot resistance theory. The history of this Masonic coterie, in effect, provides one link between the English Revolution of the seventeenth century and, in an attenuated sense, the democratic revolutions of the late eighteenth. We can now dispense with conspiracy theories and still show the survival throughout the first half of the eighteenth century of a social world that was often, but not necessarily, Masonic wherein some very dangerous ideas were in fact discussed and disseminated. It seems not unreasonable to suggest that this social circuit was international in scope while at the same time acknowledging that we still have a very imperfect account of the extent to which some Masonic lodges, under certain circumstances, would encourage a radical critique of the existing order.

Likewise, we have an inevitably unclear account, given the absence of documentary evidence, about the exact theoretical underpinning that made Rousset de Missy into a democrat at what was a most inauspicious moment in European politics to assume such a posture. Certainly there were some extremely forward-looking elements in his political programme; he would have a highly centralised republic that permitted a distinct element of democratic practice. Yet in Rousset's willingness to serve a variety of princes and rulers, Eugène of Savoy, Maria Theresa, William IV, undoubtedly without giving a moment's credibility to the mystique of monarchy, was there not also a certain myopia as regards their capabilities and intentions? Two decades later, after a dose of Orangism in practice, many Dutch republicans and reformers of the 1770s and beyond simply gave up any hope of making the House of Orange into a servant of the republic. Yet for Rousset and his associates, pressed as they were by the spectre of French invasion, the stadholderate seemed the only viable alternative. One other factor may have played a part in shaping their political understanding and that came out of their intensely personal and private experience of Freemasonry. It was, as Rousset reminded the Comte de Cobenzl, the 'royal art'. Did it simultaneously instruct its practitioners in the habits of democratic society while encouraging a camaraderie with the grandees that blurred the reality of their interests and power? It seems necessary to take a final look at that institution and its meaning in the intellectual lives of these radicals.

Freemasonry possessed great personal meaning for both Rousset and Marchand. Rousset's private letters attest to its importance and to the intensity of their private commitment, one so difficult to document from any other comparable eighteenth-century collection of published or unpublished letters or diaries. Through his later career, Rousset gave expression to this Masonic ardour by writing a variety of anonymous tracts in defence of the brotherhood. As his letters reveal he discussed the contents of these tracts with Marchand, Douxfils and 'frère Charles', in some cases before their publication. The universalist meaning and appeal of Freemasonry deeply concerned him: 'We are friends to all the world', he boasted to Marchand, but then quickly added 'except to the Jesuits, whom not one master of a lodge would receive in our order.' Rousset expressed particular indignation at the attacks levelled against Masonry by the Jesuits.[60] To these Huguenot opponents of the Jesuits, Freemasonry seemed to offer a fraternal and universalist alternative that could be pitted against an international clerical order. Rousset's correspondence constantly names a variety of 'frères', some of whom appear on the official membership lists now deposited in The Hague. Other times he simply refers to 'intimes frères', in Paris for instance, who supplied him with books and information.[61] Masonic fraternity filled his daily life; it provided Rousset with an outlet for his profound anti-clericalism and for his considerable talents as a propagandist and journalist.

At every opportunity this prominent Amsterdam grand master re-iterated and elaborated upon the ideals of Freemasonry. For example, all Masons 'on the earth' are brothers, 'and among them you will find all the charity, friendship and assistance that you may ever desire'.[62] It should not be forgotten that secrecy and mysteries are clearly 'the soul of Masonry'; without them a Mason would not 'ipso facto be a Mason'. Yet Masons have never refused to reveal those secrets to whomever presents himself for membership, to at least 'fifty thousand men in England and in France without counting Germany, Italy and Turkey' whom Rousset claims are members. They are the embodiment of respectability, 'there is nothing among us that is against religion, the state, or good morals'. Possibly because of that desire for acceptability, Marchand may have urged a strategic relaxation of secrecy; but Rousset was adamantly opposed. He simply asserted that the charges of 'libertinage, debauchery, deism, atheism and impiety, non-conformity and various other even greater abominations' are totally false; 'the pope himself knows that it is so'. 'The Emperor [Francis of Lorraine, husband of Maria Theresa], the king of England, the king of Prussia, all the princes of his house, the Elector of Cologne, almost all the English lords and many of the bishops in the same kingdom'[63] would not be members if these charges possessed any substance. The membership list presented by Rousset was impressive and extensive, and it was almost certainly accurate enough, although the figure of 50,000 he then asserted may be somewhat inflated. Notice that Rousset is careful to exclude pantheism from this list of impieties.

By the 1740s, European Freemasonry had come under attack as an institution subversive of state and church. One of the most widely read and repeated of these attacks, or 'exposures' as they are called, was an anonymous work emanating from Amsterdam and entitled *Les Francs-Maçons écrasés* (1747). It asserted the specifically English and republican origins of Freemasonry, accused its practitioners of wanting to destroy 'false religion' so that 'the Light of Nature in man's breast can once again shine forth' (149, 291). In short, it claimed that the Freemasons were seeking 'to introduce a new form of Religion and

Republic' and that both will be guided by the dangerous principles of liberty and equality (149, 282). This particularly paranoid account.[64] by someone who knew a great deal about the order, its rituals and ceremonies, deeply troubled Rousset. He remarked that 'as a master of the lodge of Amsterdam I have never known the author', a Florentine monk, one Botarelli, who Rousset asserts, keeps a house of prostitution in that city.[65] The anonymous author's accuracy on matters of ritual combined with a series of highly emotive half-truths struck Rousset as particularly threatening to the well-being of the order, and he appears to have written a number of anonymous works in contradiction of it.

Clearly that widely read 'exposure' had struck close to one aspect of European Freemasony, at least as it could be found in the Netherlands. That institution did bring radicals into touch with an international society which bridged the most extreme social differences, and Rousset often proudly pointed to that fact. The Masonic lodge could be a potentially dangerous place, as was clearly perceived by some contemporaries who attacked its democratic tendencies. Yet it could also enforce a profound social conservatism; even Rousset manifests pride at its princely membership. As a centre for religious worship – and that seems the only word by which to describe its ceremonies – Freemasonry was also linked in Rousset's mind with the most extreme forms of intellectual heresy, with pantheism and materialism. Most commonly his philosophical discussions occur in those letters with a significant Masonic content. For example, La Mettrie's *L'Homme machine* (1748), one of the most important materialistic works of the century, receives praise in a letter largely devoted to Masonic anecdotes and discussions.[66] Perhaps curiously from our perspective, yet understandable historically, in mid-eighteenth-century Europe heresy and the search for social equality, as well as adulation of aristocratic and princely masters, existed side by side; it was a balance that as the events of 1747–8 in the Netherlands revealed, could be undone.

In old age, as in youth, the Masonic originator of the *Traité des trois imposteurs* maintained his pantheistic faith intact. From that philosophy came consolation and in the face of the loss of a close friend, Rousset chided Marchand:

If you refuse the consolations of Philosophy, that is to say, of Nature's gift of reason I would turn for aid to the [?]; and I promise you that your endless grief, your overwhelming, mortal sorrow, are none other than reproaches levelled at Providence – behaviour which you condemn. At length, I would return to the order of *Nature*, which places us willy-nilly on this earth, not for ever but for a limited time, whose extent and final end are alike hidden from us;

this is the universal order, to which everyone, but especially men of reason, do well to submit themselves. In a word, I would urge you to let your sensibility bow to *Reason* and indeed to *Friendship*; you are not singular in your weakness . . . I urge you to make these efforts, on my own behalf and on behalf of all your other friends.[67]

Rousset's pantheism remained unshakeable, and he was unmoved by the arguments to the contrary put forward by 'the philosophers, the Mechanists and the Metaphysicians [who] by their measuring of the action, weight and elasticity of bodies', think that they can get 'inside' nature.[68] In keeping with the polemics of Toland and his associates, these pantheists remained unimpressed by the old metaphysics, even where supported by the new mechanical philosophy. Nevertheless, all the findings of the new science were to be savoured, only to be interpreted in pantheistic terms: eclipses, as Rousset explained, are, for one example, simply 'in the order of Nature'.[69]

During the early eighteenth century, the providentialist doctrine had been proclaimed most notably by the moderate, Newtonian phase of the Enlightenment, and it was intended to explain the operations of the ordered universe as explicated by the new science. In response, the radicals reserved special scorn for that intellectual construction. Douxfils regarded it as 'a perpetual contradiction', but then as he remarked he had great difficulty even entering a church although there was one only a few steps away from where he lived.[70] In a particularly revealing letter, Rousset dwelt upon the doctrine of providence calling it 'the divinity of the idlers' and implied that the lazy rely upon it.[71] For businessmen and refugees, such as were the Knights, life must have contained more than its usual quota of struggle and the element of supernaturally imposed order must have appeared sorely lacking. For Rousset, at least, if not his 'frères', 'the divinity of the Metaphysician' was, as he said, so much 'jargon'.

Yet life as prescribed by nature was far from random or meaningless for these 'frères'. In sickness and in death these now aged pantheists counselled for faith in nature: 'heaven or mother Nature will give us grace' and death is in effect a falling asleep.[72] In the end we return to nature and our understanding of this world while we are in it must be based upon 'reason' and 'true friendship'. Indeed, the theme of friendship and mutual aid runs through these letters, and that commitment was part of a larger ethic: 'You would admit that we are not in this world for ourselves alone, otherwise how would we serve society?' Perhaps because of the competitive world in which these publishers lived, and about which they complained endlessly in their letters, this ethic of mutual assistance and 'true friendship' could only find complete expression, or so it seemed, within the confines of the Masonic lodge.[73] In that closed world, these men of enlightenment embraced the central paradox of this new creed: in secrecy and with exquisitely restrained ceremonies and rituals they worshipped civil society at the altar of reason and order. They proclaimed universalism while carefully excluding all but the select company of 'frères'; they repudiated the old religions with their cults and rituals while discreetly participating in the formation of a new, if somewhat cerebral, version of that very impulse.[74] Their object of worship differed profoundly, however, from the God of 'the impostors'. The Freemasons and pantheists worshipped an entity that had been reinterpreted by the discoveries of the new science, by the Scientific Revolution that culminated in Newton's achievement (Chapter 1).

The New Science

As originally constituted under the careful leadership of the Newtonian, Desaguliers, official Freemasonry provided one agency for the inculcation of the new science. Although the exact educational role of individual Masonic lodges awaits historical investigation, it seems a safe assertion that in general Freemasons appear to have been particularly receptive to the new scientific learning and to have been generally comfortable with it. Certainly this holds true for the intellectual interests of the Knights of Jubilation, their literary society that published the *Journal littéraire*, as well as for the life-long scientific interests of Marchand and Rousset. In fact, Marchand and his associates turn out to have played important roles in the transmission and dissemination of the two major scientific achievements of the first half of the eighteenth century: the acceptance of the Newtonian synthesis on the Continent and the publication of Trembley's research on the self-generation of polyps. The literary society in The Hague, with s'Gravesande playing a particularly crucial role, took up Newton's science in the pages of the *Journal*, and in a systematic way and with Newton's personal encouragement, gave a wider exposition of his discoveries than had been available in any other French-language journal prior to 1713. This is not to denigrate the essential role played by Bolingbroke, Brook Taylor and Voltaire, as well as countless other Newtonians, in the destruction of Cartesianism. But it must be recognised that literary journals, such as the one produced by s'Gravesande, Marchand and company, reached a far larger literate audience, far earlier in the century, than did those individual propagandists.

Even before their arrival in the Netherlands during the War of Spanish Succession, Marchand and Picart, leading figures in the Knights of Jubilation, had been attracted to the new scientific learning. Marchand's Baconianism, his penchant for the systematic classification of knowledge, has already been noted, as has Picart's dedication to a freethinking interpretation of the Cartesian legacy and his practical interest in the microscope as a means of improving his technique as an engraver. Once they arrived in the Netherlands, s'Gravesande probably became their scientific tutor. The literary society formed by Marchand and his friends thereby ranks as one of the first circles on the Continent to be reasonably versed in Newton's science. The pages of the *Journal* attest to the sophisticated level of scientific understanding enjoyed by at least some of its editors, and even to their willingness to do polemical service against the critics of Newton's explanation of planetary motions.[75] As noted in Chapter 1, wherever we find the first stirrings of the new enlightened culture we find an intense interest in the new science.

But interest should not be equated with wholesale conversion to both the meaning and the content of the mechanical philosophy as articulated by Boyle and Newton. Newtonianism's fundamental interconnection with Christian metaphysics rendered it, if accepted complete with its understanding of inert matter and God's vital role in the universe, into an essentially moderate version of Enlightenment. This moderation must be seen as relative to the materialistic explanation of nature which had been extracted, with considerable effort, from Descartes, as well as relative to the pantheistic vision of the natural world extracted with little difficulty from a careful reading of Spinoza or a casual reading of Bruno. At precisely the time when the Knights established their literary society (1710–13) and began a journal committed to disseminating the new science, among other aspects of the new learning, their intense interest in Spinoza as well as in the naturalistic writers of the late Renaissance, Des Périers, Bruno and Vanini, has been established. It is no longer possible to assume, as did the German philosopher and historian Ernst Cassirer, a simple equation between the acceptance of Newtonianism and the origins of the Enlightenment. Within the Radical Enlightenment we find evidence instead that the mathematical and physical discoveries of the new science were grafted on to a natural philosophy that was essentially pre-scientific in its origins. In these circles nature was simultaneously deified and subjected to mathematical and experimental explication.

What precisely did the new science, that rich legacy of the seventeenth century, mean in the daily lives of these radical journalists and propagandists? Essentially it provoked two responses. The first entailed a personal interest in, and ability to follow with considerable sophistication, new scientific publications, and even to attempt one's own scientific experimentation. The second impulse was a more general desire to translate the scientific spirit into universal practice, into a systematic study of every aspect of human endeavour to be undertaken at every turn for the purpose of reforming or, if need be, of destroying certain established social institutions. For enlightened men with journalistic interests that scientific impulse took an encyclopaedic direction; it entailed the cataloguing and digesting, as well as the disseminating, of the new learning, the creation of literary projects often infused with subversive and polemical overtones.

In this spirit, Marchand and his associates edited and published the 1720 edition of Bayle's *Dictionnaire,* while Picart and Jean Frédéric Bernard began a massive and well-researched survey of all the world's religions. *Cérémonies et coutumes religieuses de tous les peuples du monde,* begun in 1722 and in turn translated into English and Dutch, was explicitly cynical about the evils of religious practice and graphically illustrated barbarous religious practices, with much emphasis on human sacrifice. Picart's engravings of these ceremonies forcefully impress the modern viewer and leave no doubt as to his own opinions about the absurdity of most religious practice. The Freemasons were among the few religious groups to get a decent press, while the preface to the English edition of this multivolumed and expensive encyclopaedia echoed sentiments about the world's religions not far from those found in the *Traité des trois imposteurs:* 'When we behold their depositions so destructive to the peace of the world . . . [we ask] whose mercy is over all [the Deity's] works?'.[76] Some decades after Marchand and Picart completed these various encyclopaedic projects, Rousset, in the letter to Marchand quoted at the beginning of this chapter, praised Diderot's *Encyclopédie* in language indicating that he rightly saw it as a continuation of that same scientific and subversive spirit.

By the early eighteenth century in Continental Europe scientific academies had been established in various cities and predictably at least one of these radical journalists, Rousset, enjoyed a fashionable membership in the Royal Academy of Arts and Sciences in Berlin as well as in the Academy of Science in St Petersburg. Their records leave no indication of what might have been Rousset's yearly contribution to the proceedings, but he was inordinately proud of his membership in both bodies. From St Petersburg he received scientific treatises, among them works by the important mathematician, Euler.[77] As his correspondence reveals, interest and skill in mathematics was combined by Rousset with microscopic investigations which on one occasion produced a scientific treatise on sea worms considered to be valuable in its day.[78] In the 1730s the wooden dikes around the Dutch coast were jeopardised by a plague of sea worms that threatened to weaken their foundations. Rousset turned his attention to these creatures and published a treatise, based upon his dissections, which outlined their structure and revealed his rather significant ability as a microscopic investigator. Throughout his life the microscope in his cabinet was among his most cherished possessions. More than biology and even medicine, about which he knew little but in which he entertained an interest, mathematics interested him most profoundly; he believed that mathematics 'rectifioient le jugement' and he seems to have been reasonably skilled in its practice.[79]

The editors of the *Journal littéraire*, and their collaborators in the Knights of Jubilation, laid down roots for the new scientific culture in the Netherlands that were to yield an unexpectedly rich legacy in the history of European materialism. One of the original 'frères' and a collaborator on the *Journal* was the French refugee, Isaac Sacrelaire (b. 1680). As a student of medicine and as an active participant in the intellectual life engendered by this secret literary society and its scientific leader, s'Gravesande, Sacrelaire acquired early in his career a familiarity with the most advanced scientific discoveries, as well as with the delicate questions posed by the new natural philosophies.

Those questions must have remained in his mind, when Sacrelaire became a collaborator and close friend to Abraham Trembley, the tutor to William Bentinck's children. While living at Bentinck's home in The Hague, and in daily contact with both William and Charles Bentinck, Trembley conducted extensive experiments on the reproductive behaviour of fresh-water polyps and came to the conclusion that they were capable of self-generation (52). That discovery, once wrested from his hands by materialists like La Mettrie, gave new life, some argued victory, to the materialist interpretation of natural phenomena. Trembley described Sacrelaire 'as the person who after me' knew most about that discovery and was best able to follow and assist him in his experiments.[80] Was Sacrelaire, like so many of his early 'frères', a materialist? We shall probably never know (certainly Trembley was not) but it is hardly coincidental that members of this scientific circle, given what we now know about its earliest history, would have been later drawn to questions and experiments that went to the heart of the Newtonian-materialist dialogue – we should really say polemic – which began with Toland and which was continued for decades on the Continent. In that war against Christian orthodoxy, the Dutch-based publishing firms and journalists played crucial roles as propagandists and disseminators of clandestine manuscripts as well as printed books. If Sacrelaire escaped a personal commitment to materialism, or pantheism as Toland and Rousset preferred to call it, Marchand did not. And at Trembley's request, Marchand brought his scientific discoveries about the polyp to publication, and thereby swung the debate in the direction of the materialists.

If it could be proven that living matter seemed capable of simply generating itself – and that was how the actions of this miniscule creature appeared to the most trained observers – then, the materialists argued, life, or motion, could indeed be inherent in nature, in matter itself. After decades of hard labour on the part of Newtonians, Cartesians and the followers of Leibniz – and on this one subject they were united – to prove that order, design and harmony in the universe rested on God's will and that animate matter was inherently incapable of forming and generating itself, suddenly it seemed that the new science revealed disturbing evidence that could play directly into the hands of philosophical and political radicals.

In the period after 1750, the materialism of the Radical Enlightenment was increasingly adopted by the French philosophes and its diffusion, often through the various editions of Diderot's *Encyclopédie*[81] with the coyly materialistic articles placed there by the Abbé Yvon, was alarmingly rapid. In the process, the republicanism and Freemasonry so vital to that early phase of the Enlightenment largely fell by the wayside. That is not, of course, to imply that the sources of French materialism can be explained largely by the impact of the projects, books and manuscripts now attributable to the radical coterie we have described here. Such an implication would amount to an egregious simplification of the history of a subversive doctrine as important as materialism became in eighteenth-century Europe and well beyond. Yet it has been already noted in passing that the Radical Enlightenment bears more than an ideological resemblance to doctrines later vital to the High Enlightenment in France. There were also social and personal links between this earlier generation of European materialists and the generation of philosophes and publishers who came into their own in the period after 1750. The unravelling of these links will be a treacherous business, in large measure because it involves a secret society as controversial as Freemasonry has become in French historiography. It would be safer to stop our historical knowledge of the Radical Enlightenment here, to be content to have traced some of its philosophical origins and its revolutionary heritage, to have examined its transmission to the Continent and its social world, and finally in this chapter to have outlined its institutions and political involvements. But inevitably the past bears some relation to what came after it. It remains for us to attempt a brief assessment of the relationship between the Radical Enlightenment and the mature years of Enlightenment culture in France. Perhaps it can be said that some new paths to the High Enlightenment have now been revealed.

Notes: Chapter 7

1 UL, Leiden, Rousset de Missy to Prosper Marchand, Marchand MSS 2, f. 47, 28 February (n.a., but from the context almost certainly 1752). The original reads: 'Savez vous que cela auroit été grand train vers le Panthéisme si ces Thèses eussent

passé et en même temps les 10 énormes vol. de L'Encyclopédie; on débarassoit les beaux Esprits, les femmes savantes & galantes, les petits-maîtres, tant de déistes et d'athées Italiens & Anglois et françois du joug de la Religion si nécessaire dans la société pour n'y être pas égorgé, et pas pour autre chose, et c'en est bien assez; mais [h]alte, je fais le petit Enciclopédiste.'

2 Albert, Count de Passeran, *Twelve Discourses concerning Religion and Government, Inscribed to All Lovers of Truth and Liberty* (London, 1734), p. 11.

3 *Nouvelles libertés de Penser* (Amsterdam, 1743), 'Le Philosophe', pp. 165, 188: 'La société civile est pour ainsi dire, la seule divinité qu'il reconnoisse sur la terre; il l'encense, il l'honore par la probité, par une attention exacte à ses devoirs . . .' Cf. J. O'Higgins, SJ, *Anthony Collins* (The Hague: Nijhoff, 1970), pp. 216–17.

4 UL, Leiden, Marchand MSS 2, 26 February 1737, 'Vous m'avez fait plaisir de m'instruire sur la Vie et l'Esprit de Spinosa; je suis bien aise d'être au fait de cette anecdote. Après ce que je vous en ay dit, il est aisé de s'apercevoir d'où elle vient'.

5 Marchand 2, 17 January 1740: 'Vous vous souvenés peut-être que c'étoit mon Frère qui nous en apporta le Msp. à la maison, appartenant à M. Furly. Levier le copia fort précipitamment: Je la garde encore cette Copie . . .'

6 See appendix, pp. 277–9. The original reads: 'Quant à ce que vous croyez que la Traduction imaginaire dont il s'agit dans Réponse en questions, ait quelque chose de Commun avec l'Esprit de Spinosa, j'en conviens avec vous. Levier la copia en 1711. Cette sorte de Livres etait sa marotte. Si, depuis ce temps, il a eu du commerce avec Rousset, tous les doutes la dessus se tournent en évidence. Il en est du Livre des trois Imposteurs comme des Clavicules de Salomon – dont j'ay veu plusiers Msp tous différens les uns des autres.'

7 BL, MSS ADD. 4295, ff. 69–70, 'Christopaedia, An Account of the Pueril Studies of Jesus Christ'.

8 *Réponse à la Dissertation de M. de la Monnoye sur Le Traité des trois imposteurs* (The Hague, 1716). In the 1768 edition of the *Traité*, the *Réponse* occurs on pp. 116–35; for Toland, p. 119. The Royal Library, The Hague, has Rousset's tract as a separate publication. (Italicising of 'Pantheists' my own.) Hassan El Nouty, 'Le panthéisme dans les lettres françaises au XVIIIᵉ siècle: aperçus sur la fortune du mot et de la notion', *Revue des sciences humaines,* vol. 27 (1960), pp. 435–57.

9 ibid., pp. 127–8. The *Traité* and the *Spaccio* were often circulated by the same people, e.g. S. Engel in Berne; cf. BL MSS. ADD. 12062 letter from Engel to Robinet prefixed to the *Spaccio*; Heinrich Dübi, *Das Buch von den drei Betrügern und das Berner Manuskript* (Berne: A. Francke, 1936), p. 14; BL, MSS ADD. 12064 for a copy of the *Traité*.

10 *Dictionnaire historique, ou mémoires critiques et littéraires, concernant . . . personnages distingués particulièrement dans la république des lettres* (The Hague: Pierre de Hondt, 1758), vol. I, pp. 312–29; cf. J. S. Spink, 'La diffusion des idées matérialistes et anti-religieuses au début du XVIIIᵉ siècle: le Theophrastus redivivus', *Revue d'histoire littéraire de la France?* (1937), pp. 44, 248–55. Cf. *Bibliotheca hohendorfiana* (1722), vol. 3, p. 234; see also Paul Vernière, *Spinoza et la pensée française avant la révolution* (17, II, 362). I doubt that there ever was a German doctor named Ferber involved in the 1721 edition. In the mythology of all this he ranks with Frecht and Aymon.

11 *Traité des trois imposteurs* (Amsterdam, 1768), ch. I, paras. 5–6. Rousset de Missy's system of describing the manuscript by chapter and 'paragraph' will be used to assist readers possessing different editions.

12 ibid., ch. 2, paras 1, 5.

13 ibid., ch. 2, paras 7, 10, 11.

14 ibid., ch. 2, para. 11.

15 ibid., ch. 3, paras 2, 3. Hobbes is specifically cited in the text; and para. 5.

16 ibid., ch. 3, paras 9, 10.
17 ibid., ch. 3, paras 12, 13.
18 ibid., ch. 3, paras 14, 15, 16. The term 'machiavellian' is not used.
19 ibid., ch. 3, paras 17, 19.
20 ibid., ch. 3, paras 22, 23. Here the text cites the Comte de Boulainvillier's life of Mahomet.
21 ibid., ch. 4, paras 2, 5.
22 For one such modern account see Morton Smith, *Jesus the Magician* (New York: Harper & Row, 1977). *Traité*, ch. 5, paras 5, 6.
23 *Traité*, ch. 5, paras 3, 6.
24 ibid., ch. 5, para. 7; cf. J. S. Spink, 'Libertinage et "Spinozisme": la théorie de l'âme ignée', *French Studies*, vol. 1 (1947), pp. 225–7.
25 *Traité*, ch. 6, para. 7.
26 R. Simon, *Henry de Boulainvillier, historien, politique, philosophe, astrologue, 1658–1722* (Paris: Boivin, 1941), pp. 450–5; ch. 3.
27 Bernard Fay, *Revolution and Freemasonry, 1680–1800* (Boston: Little, Brown, 1935); cf. Claire-Eliane Engel, *Mémoires du Chevalier de Gramont*, ed. Antoine Hamilton (Monaco, 1958).
28 Archives du Royaume de Belgique, Brussels, 'Correspondance du Comte de Cobenzl, ministre plénipotentaire aux pays-bas', 158ᵉ. V, no. 30, f. 26, 16 January 1755, 'Pendant la dernière guerre le Prince Eugène s'est fort bien trouvé de ses avis, & moi aussi en plusieurs occasions, où je l'ai trouvé bien informé . . .'
29 Marchand MSS 22, 'Catalogue des manuscrits et des imprimés de sa bibliothèque personelle'.
30 H. G. Koenigsberger, 'The organization of revolutionary parties in France and the Netherlands during the sixteenth century', *Journal of Modern History*, vol. 27 (1955), pp. 335–51.
31 The Royal Library, The Hague, MS. 132.D.30. In this manuscript the *Traité* is subtitled *L'Esprit de Spinoza*. My notion of dating comes from a general knowledge of writing styles, tone of argumentation, etc. The meditation on these tracts, 'Morale traitée, suivant les principes de la nature' occupies ff. 104–7.
32 ibid., f. 104: 'Ce que l'on appelle comunement nature est ce composé parfait des ouvrages du Créateur, définition générale, qui comporte l'ideé d'un tout, et qui renferme aussi sous Elle la nature particulière de chaque estre séparé du tout, c'est à dire ce qui fait l'essence propre et distincte de chaque individu; c'est à cette dernière ideé que je m'attache, come estant quelque chose de plus particulier, que nous appercevons plus distinctement . . .'
33 ibid.: 'Il est question d'examiner, quel a été le but de celui qui nous forma, et je decideraÿ hardiment, que ce fut pour nous rendre heureux . . .'
34 ibid., 'Nous voÿons clairement que nous avons tout ce qu'il nous faut pour estre heureux, Riches par nous mêmes, il ne nous manque que de faire de nos Thrésors un usage meilleur et c'est sur cela que je vais proposer mes idées, qui ne seront sans doute pas du gout des Théologiens, mais qui sont, ce me semble, plus dans celui du vraÿ, que leur Ortodoxie mal construé est d'une pratique si contraire aux loix de la nature.'
35 ibid., f. 106.
36 ibid.
37 ibid., f. 105v, 'La Réputation à mon avis est le poison de la volupte, c'est elle qui corompt la nature et avilit nos plus brillants privilèges . . .'
38 ibid., f. 106.
39 Aram Vartanian, 'La Mettrie, Diderot and sexology in the Enlightenment', in Jean Macary (ed.), *Essays on the Age of Enlightenment in Honor of Ira O. Wade* (Geneva: Droz, 1977), pp. 347–67; Stephen Werner, 'Diderot's Supplement and late Enlightenment thought', *Studies on Voltaire and the Eighteenth Century*, vol.

86 (1971), pp. 254–66; in Diderot's *Encyclopédie* see article on 'Jouissance'.

40   Marchand MSS 22; in this list of his private library, Marchand lists a rare translation of Sidney's *Discours sur le gouvernement* 'par Jacques Boyd' (Rotterdam, 1711). The more common translation of 1702 was by P. A. Samson. Marchand also had that edition; I have not seen a copy of the 1711 text.

41   Rousset de Missy, *Histoire militaire du Prince Eugène de Savoye, du Prince et Duc de Marlborough, et du Prince de Nassau-Frise. Par Mr. Dumont . . . augmentée d'un Supplément, par M. Rousset* (The Hague: chez Isaac van der Kloot, 1729); Bernard Picart, 'Explication du sujet simbolique . . . pour servir d'accompagnement aux Armes du Prince Eugène de Savoye', in Teylers Museum, Haarlem, Portfolio 188.

42   *Nouvelles littéraires* (The Hague: chez Henri du Sauzet, 1715), pp. 7, 52–3, 71–2.

43   See John J. Murray, *George I, The Baltic and the Whig Split of 1717. A Study in Diplomacy and Propaganda* (London: Routledge & Kegan Paul, 1969); M. M. Kleerkooper and W. P. van Stockum, *De Boekhandel te Amsterdam voornamelijk in de 17ᵉ eeuw* (159, II, 940) on Böhm publishing de Larrey's *Histoire de France sous de règne de Louis XIV* (Rotterdam, 1721).

44   The Royal Library, The Hague, MS. 131.B.15.

45   *La Sardaigne paranymphe de la paix aux souverains de l'Europe* (Boulogne, 1714); the identification of this tract with Rousset seems in this case to be correct. See Pierre Conlon, *Prélude au siècle des lumières en France. Répertoire chronologique de 1680 à 1715,* 6 vols (Geneva: Droz, 1970–5); and BL 1139.e.2.

46   Archives du Royaume de Belgique, Brussels, 'Correspondance du Comte de Cobenzl', f. 18, 'Votre Excell. connoit mon Ecriture qui ne paraitroit pas sur l'adresse et je signerais en frère maitre ◇ce que votre Excellence connoit sans doute puis que je sai qu'elle est de notre ordre Royal', from Rousset de Missy, 6 December 1754.

47   For a general account of the period see Ernst Wangermann, *Aufklärung und staatsbürgerliche Erziehung. Gottfried van Swieten als Reformator des österreichischen Unterrichtswesens 1781–1791* (Vienna: Verlag für Geschichte und Politik, 1978).

48   A. Renaudet, *Les Pays-Bas espagnols et les Provinces-Unies de 1598 à 1714* (Paris: Centre de Documentation Universitaire, 1960), pp. 262–9 for British support of anti-Jesuits.

49   Penfield Roberts, *The Quest for Security, 1715–1740* (New York: Harper & Row, 1947), pp. 13–16; on attention paid by the French Jesuits, *Mémoires pour l'histoire des sciences et des beaux arts. De L'Imprimerie à Trevoux* (September 1717), pp. 1,426–45.

50   *La Sardaigne,* pp. 113–16.

51   Richard Lodge, *Studies in Eighteenth Century Diplomacy 1740–48* (London: John Murray, 1930), p. 251; P. Geyl, 'Holland and England during the War of the Austrian Succession', *History,* vol. 10 (1925), pp. 47–51.

52   Nico Johannes Jacques de Voogd, *Die Doelistenbeweging te Amsterdam in 1748* (p. 109); C. Gerretson and P. Geyl (eds), *Briefwisseling . . .* (p. 261); the Grand Lodge of the Netherlands, The Hague, 'Kronick Annales', for Radermacher as one of the founders of the lodge, 'Le Veritable Zele', 24 October 1735.

53   Ghislaine de Boom, 'Les Ministres plénipotentiaires dans les Pays-Bas autrichiens principalement Cobenzl' (see bibliographical essay 89, 36–8, 43, 47, 55); Joseph Laenen, *Le Ministère de Botta Adorno dans les Pays-Bas autrichiens pendant le règne de Marie-Thérèse (1749–53)* (Antwerp: La Librairie Neérlandaise, 1901), pp. 61–2. Cf. C. Gerretson and P. Geyl (eds), *Briefwisseling . . .* (p. 144), for Bentinck's devotion to Arenberg; and for Douxfils see Marchand MSS 2, f. 29, 24 May (n.a.), Rousset to Marchand on how to address letters to him, i.e. to 'M. Lambert Douxfils, conseiller de S.A. le Duc d'Arenberg, rue de la Bergére à Bruxelles'; MSS Marchand 55b, song in the hand of Douxfils: 'Le grand Masson, &

ses deux Camarades,/En cette Cour tinrent les plus hauts grades.'

54 Huibert J. Minderhoud, 'La Henriade dans la littérature hollandaise', *Bibliothèque de la revue de littérature comparée*, vol. 33 (1927), pp. 4–6, 87, 102.

55 Gerrit van der Haar, *'t Leven van Willem Den IV. Princ van Oranje en Nassau . . .* (Amsterdam, 1752), Masonic symbolism employed in opening poem. My thanks to B. Croisset van Uchelen for bringing this poem to my attention; Marchand MSS 2, f. 8, Rousset to Marchand on 'Roy Theodore', an alias for the Baron de Neuhoff; f. 11, 21 January (prob. 1747) on the French ambassador; f. 35, 18 October (1750) on M. de Boissy and C. d'Athlone; f. 62, 6 January 1753 on Frederick the Great and Maupertius; f. 89, 20 November 1753, on spies in France. In Marchand MSS 2, Douxfils to Marchand, 16 October 1749 on conditions in the southern Netherlands; 15 November 1749, on same; 2 April 1753 on George II when Prince of Wales.

56 BL, Egerton, 1745, f. 486, Amsterdam, 26 June 1748, Rousset to Bentinck, 'Votre Excellence se souviendra sans doute de l'impressement avec lequel elle me fit venir à la Haye pour me donner ses ordres pour une publication ou reimpression du *Traité du Gouvernement de Lock . . .*'. Antonio Porta, *Joan en Gerrit Corver. De politieke macht van Amsterdam (1702–1748). Academisch Proefschrift . . . Universiteit van Amsterdam . . . 1975* (Assen: Van Gorcum, n.d.), p. 260; this work, only now (1980) seen, generally supports this account but does not make any reference to Rousset's letters or to the Masonic Archives.

57 Marchand MSS 2, Rousset to Marchand, f. 48, 14 October (n.a.); ff. 66–7, 27 March (n.a.), on attempts to have his sentence commuted so that he can visit his friends in The Hague.

58 ibid., f 68, 10 April 1753, 'Je ne sai où vous et Charles (dont j'ai reçu le Réponse que vous me prometez pour la semaine prochaine) avez trouvé dans mes lettres que j'aye intention *de renoncer à L'état tranquile et heureux dont je jouis pour me replonger dans la tumulte des affaires publiques et Politiques et refréquenter la Cour & les grands? Non mes chers amis, ce n'est point la mon intention . . .'*. He has written for permission to visit Holland, a request he has made through Kaunitz and Neny, i.e. the Austrian authorities. 'La Princesse me l'a promis et j'attends qu'elle exécute sa promesse; j'ira voir mes amis . . .'

59 Haus-Hof und Staatsarchiv, Vienna, in 'Alphabetischer Index zur Grossen Korrespondenz', GC.277, 328, 395 (some letters incorrectly listed under 'Roussel'). A letter from Frederick the Great to Prince of Wales included in this file; Rousset listed as 'agent de S.A. le Duc de Brunswick Wölfenbüttel'. On 29 March 1748, Rousset wrote to Kaunitz, 'Si je commencois à entrer dans le monde je ne désespérerois pas de voir tous les Electeurs Rois. V. E. n'ignore pas que les maximes d'un prince souverain et indépendant ne peuvent guerre être d'accord avec celle d'un vassal d'un fondataire, comme ces Rois Electeurs, l'étoient de L'Empire . . . Les Rois regardent un Empereur comme *primus inter pares*, ce que ne pouvoient faire les Electeurs . . .'

60 Marchand MSS 2, Rousset to Marchand, n.d., f. 36, item 8, 'Votre anecdote de la Cassete du Franc-Maçon m'a fort diverti, si ma pré & post-face vous a plû; mais révérence parlant, j'en apelle au pape même de l'injuste imputation de *Jesuitisme*, et vous ne nous connoissez pas. Nous sommes amis de tous le monde, excepté des Jesuites, dont aucun maître de loge ne voudroit recevoir un seul dans notre ordre'. Cf. f.75, 29 July (n.a.), '. . . c'est à dire un exemplaire pour vous & un pour mon frère Charles. Je ne sai ce que c'est que l'extrait de la *fraternité* Maçonique etc; pourez vous me faire voir cela en françois & en Hollandois.'

61 In 1737 Chevalier Ramsay estimated that there were 3,000 Masons; cf. B. Fäy, *Revolution and Freemasonry*, pp. 190–1.

62 Marchand MSS 2, Rousset to Marchand, 18 February (n.a.), f.46: 'Voici joint en françois, tout ce qui concerne la Maçonnerie en Gueldres avec une pré & post-face

de votre tr. H. S. qui ont eu le bonheur de plaire à l'archicritique de Bruxelles [Douxfils]. Votre Principe, *n'entreprenez rien etc.* est admis parmi nous en plein; on répond à toutes les questions qui y ont raport, & ensuite vous devenez postulant si vous voulez. Après vous avoir démontré (comme vous le verrez dans la lettre à Dr. Havercamp) qu'il n'y a rien chez nous contre la Relig., l'État & les bonnes mœurs, et vous avoir fait connaître qu'on ne vous cache que le secret, en vertu duquel vous vous trouvez frères de tout ce qu'il y a de Maçon sur la terre, et parmi lesquels vous trouverez toute la charité, l'amitié, les secours que vous pouvez souhaiter.' One of the tracts under discussion here is *Lettre d'un Franc-Maçon de la loge de S. Louis de Nimegue au venerable, pieux et savant Everhard Haverkamp, Ministre du St. Evangile dans la même Ville. Sur une partie de l'Application du Sermon, qu'il a pronouncé le 22 de Mars. 1752, Traduite du Hollandois. Dans le Monde Franc-Maçon. Aux dépens de l'ordre & des Lecteurs curieux,* 1752. The original is by Rousset de Missy and it concerns the controversy in Nimegue over a Dutch reformed church that denied admission to L. A. Merkes and F. C. Merkes, both Freemasons.

63 Marchand MSS, 15 December (n.a.), f. 64, 'Je m'étonne de l'aprobation que vous donnez à l'objection tirée de notre obstination à reveler nos Mistères, après avoir lû la lettre du Maçon de Nimegue, et les Etrennes au Pape du chev. de Lussy òu cette objection est pleinement refutée; j'ajouterai que c'est ce secret qui est l'âme de la Maçonnerie & que dès qu'il seroit révélé, il n'y auroit plus de Maçons, et quoique j'aie soutenu dans le préface de la traduction de la lettre de Nimègue que le caractère de fr. Maçon est indélibile; je dois reconnoitre que dès que la secret seroit révélé tous les *francs-maçons,* cesseroient *ipso facto* d'être Maçons. Ne comprendrez vous donc pas qu'on ne peut nous accuser de cacher des secrets des mistères que nous n'avons jamais refusé de révéler à qui s'est présenté pour les aprendre? peut-on dire qu'une chose est secrète quand elle est revélée à tous venans et est scu de 50 mille hommes au moins en Angleterre et en France, sans compter l'Allemagne, l'Italie & la Turquie. Quant aux accusation de libertinage, débauche, déisme, athéisme, impietéz, non-conformisme & autres encore plus abominables; les noms de ceux qui sont maçons, leur rang, leur vertu nous sauvent assez abominations . . . L'Empereur, le Roi d'Angleterre, le Roi de Prusse, tous les Princes de sa maison, l'Electeur de Cologne, presque tous les lords anglois, plusieurs des Evêques du même Royaume; le Pape même savent ce qui en est . . .' There are manuscript songs in the Marchand collection mocking Frederick the Great, despite his being a Freemason.

64 On the earliest mention of conspiracy in relation to Freemasonry in 1745 (in a book published in The Hague), see Robert Shackleton, 'When Did the French "Philosophes" Become a Party?', *Bulletin of the John Rylands University Library of Manchester,* vol. 60 (1977), p. 192.

65 Marchand MSS 2, Rousset to Marchand, f. 64, 15 December (n.a.), 'si ce n'est en ce qu'etant Maître de la loge d'Amsterdam je n'ai pas voulu reconnoître l'auteur (Botarelli, moine de Florence qui t'ent a présent bordel à Amsterdam) pour franc-maçon – il déclare lui même dans *les Francs-Maçons trahis* qu'il n'a jamais été reçu en loge . . .'

66 Marchand MSS, Rousset to Marchand, f. 36.

67 ibid., f. 86, 9 September (n.a.); italics in original.

68 ibid., f. 41, 13 December 1752.

69 ibid., f. 83, n.d., 'L'Eclipse dont vous me parlez et ses effets sont dans l'ordre de la Nature et du théâtre'.

70 Marchand MSS 2, 15 November 1749, Douxfils to Marchand; and also 9 July 1747.

71 Marchand MSS 2, 24 May (n.a.), Rousset to Marchand, f. 29: 'Je voudrois que ces grands Providenciers donnassent une définition courte, simple, & bien distincte de ce qu'ils entendent par providence. Je crois que c'est la divinité des Paresseux,

comme étoit cet ami, mais il a trouvé a la fin qu'elle l'a fort mal servi parcequ'il n'a pas suivi un conseil que des Théologiens prôuent fort haut comme etant parole divine (aide toy dieu t'aidera) qu'un fameux rabin m'a dit n'être pas dans toute la bible. Mais que le Talmud y est formel trouvant cette ordonnance dans la lettre II.'

72 Marchand MSS 2, f. 35, 18 October (n.a.).

73 Marchand MSS 2, f. 102, 'Le Ciel ou la mére Nature nous en fasse la grace. Je crois que ce seroit un charme de s'endormir & de ne se pas réveiller.' In f. 101 Rousset indicates that he has had a letter from 'fr. Charles' on Marchand's failing condition. Since paralysis seems to have occurred suddenly we may presume that he had suffered a stroke. And from f. 87, 20 October, 1753, 'Vous conviendrez que nous ne sommes pas dans ce monde pour nous seuls, autrement à quoi serviroit la société.'

74 See Harry Payne, 'Elite versus popular mentality in the eighteenth century', in Roseann Runte (ed.), *Studies in Eighteenth-Century Culture*, Vol. 8 (Madison, Wis.: University of Wisconsin Press, 1979), p. 15.

75 C. Berkvens-Stevelinck, 'Nicolas Harsoeker contre Isaac Newton ou pour quoi les planètes se meuvent-elles?', *Lias*, vol. 2 (1975), pp. 313–28.

76 Bernard Picart, *The Ceremonies and Religious Customs of the Various Nations of the Known World*, (London, 1737), Vol. 1, preface, p. v; cf. Margaret Hodgen, *Early Anthropology in the Sixteenth and Seventeenth Centuries* (Philadelphia, Penn.: University of Pennsylvania, 1964), pp. 203, 344, 353.

77 Marchand MSS 2, f. 54, Rousset to Marchand.

78 *Observations sur l'origine, la structure, et la nature des vers de mer, qui percent les vaisseaux et les pilliers, les Jetées, et des estrades* (The Hague, 1733). A Dutch translation was published in the same year; cf. Margaret Jacob, 'Newtonian science and the Radical Enlightenment', *Vistas in Astronomy*, vol. 22 (1978), pp. 545–5. For Rousset's interest in science and medicine his letters to Dr Bernard, an Amsterdam physician, are useful: UL, Leiden, 242; and Marchand MSS 2, f. 68, 10 April 1753, on his still possessing a microscope.

79 Marchand MSS 2, f. 78, in the 1750s.

80 Maurice Trembley, *Correspondance inédite entre Reaumur et Abraham Trembley* (Geneva: Georg & Cie, 1943), pp. 74, also 77, 84. Cf. John R. Baker, *Abraham Trembley of Geneva, Scientist and Philosopher 1710–1784* (London: Edward Arnold, 1952).

81 See Robert Darnton, *The Business of Enlightenment. A Publishing History of the Encyclopédie 1775–1800* (Cambridge, Mass.: Harvard University Press, 1979).

Epilogue: New Paths to the High Enlightenment

One literary project, perhaps more than any other, has come to symbolise the mature years of the European Enlightenment and its by then predominantly French character. Diderot's *Encyclopédie*, conceived in 1745 as a revision of Chambers's *Cyclopædia* (1728, see pp. 125–6), quickly became a new enterprise in itself; it became encyclopaedism on a grand scale. The project enlisted the talents of major philosophers like Voltaire and d'Holbach and its list of contributors, nearly 200 strong, included virtually every minor and major thinker of the day, as well as various scientists, artisans and innumerable hack writers. At the core of the project were its Parisian publishers, Le Breton, Durand, the elder David and Briasson, as well as Diderot, the editor whom they chose, and his small circle of confidants and associates among them the Abbé Claude Yvon (1714–91), who has been described as the metaphysician of the *Encyclopédie* (173, *passim*). With skill and not a little cunning he injected the predominant materialism of Diderot and the influential members of his circle into certain key articles on immaterialism, the soul, polytheism and moral liberty.

Yvon's compatriot in heresy and fellow cleric, the Abbé Jean Martin de Prades (1720–82), also belonged to this circle although he appears to have produced only one article for the *Encyclopédie*. In November 1751, de Prades presented a thesis to the Sorbonne that was blatantly materialistic and implied among other things that Moses had been a liar (174). To that austere institution's embarrassment the thesis was carelessly passed, but when this gross negligence was discovered a storm broke over the heads of de Prades and his associates. On 11 February 1752 the Parlement of Paris ordered his arrest, and in a panic de Prades and Yvon fled to Holland. The *Encyclopédie* itself appeared in jeopardy and its radical sympathisers in the Netherlands watched this spectacle of censorship and persecution with concerned interest.

Given the camaraderie and heretical proclivities of this encyclopaedic circle, and the still disputed role of Freemasonry during the French Revolution, some late eighteenth-century opponents of that event, notably the Abbé Barruel, levelled the charge that Diderot's *Encyclopédie* (1751) had been a Masonic project (176). Subsequently it has been argued on the basis of no concrete evidence that Diderot was a Freemason, or that his publishers, either Le Breton or Laurent

Durand, were Freemasons of sorts, or that various contributors to the *Encyclopédie* possessed Masonic sympathies (179). Various scholars have elaborated upon this idea (178), and not a few have dismissed it as unproveable. Most recently Robert Shackleton has presented convincing evidence that very few of its contributors were Masons and that, therefore, Diderot's project had nothing to do with that institution. In pressing his conclusion Shackleton did not have available the evidence we now possess. As a result he could not give attention to the historical links, evinced in the 1720 edition of Bayle's *Dictionnaire* done by some of the Knights of Jubilation and in the publication of Chambers's *Cyclopædia*, between encyclopaedism as a mentality and an approach to learning, and early Freemasonry. While there is no proof that any of the *Encyclopédie*'s publishers were Masons – although Briasson had dealings with Marchand and Henri Scheurleer, Rousset's publisher – we now know that the Abbé Yvon was a Freemason in the Netherlands and that he and his close friend, the Abbé de Prades, knew and conferred with Rousset de Missy.[1]

It is necessary to take another look at Diderot's *Encyclopédie* and the question of Freemasonry, in order to reformulate our understanding of that relationship. If the frankness of the Rousset-Marchand correspondence serves to settle any historical dispute, it ought to be to prove that the *Encyclopédie* was not a Masonic project. Never is it mentioned in those terms – but it is mentioned, and so are various people associated with it. These Freemasons in the Netherlands were avidly interested in Diderot's great project and they knew well at least two of its key contributors – Yvon and another important encyclopaedist and Huguenot refugee, Louis Chevalier de Jaucourt (1704–80). Jaucourt wrote nearly a quarter of the articles in the *Encyclopédie*, and he had worked as a contributor and journalist for s'Gravesande who, among others, edited the *Bibliothèque rasonnée* (Morris, Lough, Schwab and Fletcher, 181). Rousset was also a regular contributor to that journal and part of the inner circle that produced it.

Perhaps it was associations like these, coupled with the desire to sell copies to lodges or their members, that prompted Diderot in the 1760s to commission a frontispiece for the *Encyclopédie* which was engraved by the Freemason, Charles-Nicolas Cochin, and which employed discernibly Masonic symbolism.[2] The first volumes issued in 1751 also pictorially appealed to Minerva and Apollo, and as we have seen, she had special meaning in the early history of European Freemasonry, having been the patron deity of the Knights of Jubilation. This link between encyclopaedism and Freemasonry was perceived by Masons themselves as early as the 1730s. Indeed, the Chevalier Ramsay, the prime architect of French Freemasonry of a Christian variety (95, 157–8) and a bitter enemy of spinozism, addressed himself to that rapport when he publicly urged 'all the grand masters in Germany, in England, in Italy and in all of Europe, to exhort the learned and all the artists in the fraternity, to unite for the purpose of furnishing material for a universal dictionary of all the liberal arts and useful sciences, with the exception of Theology and Politics'. Referring almost certainly to Chambers's text, he noted that such a project was already under way in England. In the same speech he also acknowledged that Minerva has special meaning for 'our solemnities' but then cautioned that the pagan deities had sunk into impiety.[3]

Ramsay's now famous address to a Masonic meeting has been used to argue that he was pointing towards Diderot's project. But if the speech is read carefully it is clear that Ramsay is desperately concerned that Freemasonry should become a force to augment Christian piety, to rid the world of 'irreligion and libertinism'.[4] Rather than trying to encourage projects (whether by Masons or non-Masons) such as was produced by Diderot and Yvon, it is more likely that Ramsay was concerned to prevent just such a project, possibly one that could emanate from the journalistic and Masonic circles at work in Amsterdam and The Hague. He wanted to see encyclopaedism harnessed to the service of Christian piety and appealed to the international Masonic community to effect that linkage. In the process, of course, Ramsay's appeal for a Masonic encyclopaedism would certainly, if unwittingly, have enhanced the sales of Diderot's *Encyclopédie* among lodges and their members.

By 1751, contemporary Freemasons, like Rousset de Missy, had also seen the compatibility between Masonry as they understood it, and the just-published *Encyclopédie*. In general, Rousset regarded Diderot as the 'second La Mettrie', and even before publication of the *Encyclopédie* Douxfils passed along information about Diderot's 1749 imprisonment, a punishment meted out, in Douxfils's opinion, for the author's philosophical as well as his pornographic works.[5] There was, of course, the ideological consistency between Diderot's materialism, for which he owed some debt to Toland's writings (Crocker and Flam, 180), and the pantheism of Rousset and his associates. Rousset was, as we have seen, quick to perceive that the *Encyclopédie* would promote the spread of his beliefs. But the relationship between Freemasonry and the *Encyclopédie* did not rest solely on ideology. Although there is no evidence that de Jaucourt was a Freemason, it can be argued that he got his training as a journalist when he lived in Leiden in the 1730s, journeyed frequently to Amsterdam, and contributed to s'Gravesande's journal. S'Gravesande was, of course, one of the original 'frères' in that literary society whose membership was so deeply entwined with the Knights of Jubilation.

In one of Rousset's more complex and secretive letters to Marchand, describing the mysterious comings and goings of Theodore Etienne, Baron de Neuhoff, for a time King of Corsica, Rousset indicates that Jaucourt and his close friend, Theodore Tronchin, had assisted this beleaguered adventurer financially.[6] King Theodore, as he was called, was a freethinker and international conspirator who joined up with the Corsicans in their revolt against Genoa. He then persuaded the Corsicans to make him their king (1736), and set out on an international mission to raise money and arms for their cause.[7] His freethinking undid him with the clergy, while the complexity of his financial dealings led to the confiscation of his throne by creditors. What is important about this bizarre episode, aside from it providing evidence for a commonality of interests between Rousset and the encyclopaedist, Jaucourt, is that almost predictably, wherever we find revolutionaries on the European scene, so too we find our Freemasons. What labyrinths of political intrigue lie yet to be uncovered can only be conjectured.

Happily we need only pursue here the links between Jaucourt, the radicals and the *Encyclopédie*. After Jaucourt became the workhorse of the *Encyclopédie*, he infused certain of his articles with attacks on Bourbon absolutism and with the old Whig and country ideology of Bolingbroke (Morris, Lough, Schwab and Fletcher, 181). In both intellectual and practical ways Jaucourt put to good use the training he received from our first generation of Enlightenment encyclopaedists among whom Freemasonry figured so prominently.

Could Jaucourt have been the bridge between Rousset de Missy and the Abbés Yvon and de Prades? The origins of that connection, prior to Yvon's flight from Paris, are wholly obscure, but Rousset's familiarity with these two heretical abbés raises some unsettling questions.[8] When Yvon's name turns up in April 1755, on the records of the lodge Concordia Vincit Animos he is already an officer in it. Positions of leadership within lodges were not awarded quickly or haphazardly. The real possibility exists that Yvon had become a Freemason before his flight from Paris, in other words at a time more or less coincidental with his writing for the *Encyclopédie*. It could also be the case that Yvon sought shelter and solace in his exile and that either through Jaucourt or Durand, one of the *Encyclopédie*'s publishers who knew Rousset, Yvon was introduced to Rousset or Marchand and hence to the Masonic movement. That explanation for his membership would also, however, have to include the postulate that this French abbé became such a devoted Freemason that his rapid elevation in the lodge largely bypassed the normal time limits. Yvon's Masonic membership, whatever the date of his initiation, strongly suggests a commonality of interests and outlook between the intellectual leadership of Dutch Freemasonry and the originators of the great *Encyclopédie*. Certainly,

Rousset followed the progress of these itinerant abbés, and he sent a witty and sardonic aphorism to Marchand about de Prades accusing his friend Yvon of re-embracing theism, probably for strategic reasons.[9] In fact such a transformation did eventually overtake the exiled abbé who then made his way back to France and to a clerical position of relative security.

Through a variety of channels, some of them doubtless Masonic, Rousset avidly gleaned news from Paris about the trials and tribulations of the encyclopaedists. Some of that information he could have obtained, even though he was in exile in Maersen, from the Abbé de Prades himself, who promised to visit him there.[10] Rousset regarded Diderot's great project as a continuation of Bayle's *Dictionnaire*,[11] and in a methodological sense he was basically correct. The evidence linking the first generation of Enlightenment radicals with the French encyclopaedists of mid-century argues not for a Masonic conspiracy, but rather for an ideological continuity between the radicalism of these Hugenot exiles, with their adoration for English culture and institutions, and the beliefs and values at the heart of a project that became central to the High Enlightenment. Encyclopaedism had many roots to be sure, but the journalists and Freemasons often at work in the Netherlands in the period prior to 1750 deserve more credit than has heretofore been accorded them.

Likewise, the role of publishers and publishing must be seen as central to the Enlightenment. A more detailed account of the journalistic and publishing enterprises undertaken by the Knights of Jubilation and their attendant literary society should now be written. Here it has been possible only to highlight some of their most important achievements, in particular the *Traité des trois imposteurs*. This research adds further weight to the contention that the early spread of Enlightenment culture cannot be understood separately from the study of the clandestine manuscript and book trade; and I would add, from the study of secret societies and their networks. After 1750, however, more and more of those originally clandestine manuscripts received publication and indeed by the 1760s one publisher seemed to hold a virtual monopoly on the irreligious and heretical.

Marc-Michel Rey (1720–80) migrated from Lausanne to Amsterdam where he became a member of the Walloon community and where he was admitted to the publisher's guild.[12] Little is known about his early years as a publisher; but here I should like to emphasise his contacts with the radical circles we have been describing. Entrée was undoubtedly provided by his wife, the daughter of Jean Frédéric Bernard, Picart's long-time collaborator. She, unlike her father, appears to have been devout and thus while his family followed conventional religious practices, Rey published some of the most outrageous works of the High Enlightenment. He appears not to have had a religious burial.

Rey was also a man of some learning and the lengthy correspondence of J. N. S. Allamand, s'Gravesande's successor in Leiden, to Rey (unfortunately Rey's replies have not been preserved) attests to Allamand's respect for Rey's knowledge of what he was publishing (although not for 'all the heterodox pieces that have come out of your shop').[13] These letters make clear that Rey was servicing the book needs of the Bentincks and this evidence coupled with remarks made by Rousset and Douxfils indicate that early in his career Rey moved into the business world of these radicals and Freemasons. There is absolutely no indication that he ever became a Mason; indeed Rousset did not even much like Rey, calling him in one letter 'a fop'. But Rey published books that appealed to the old friends of his father-in-law, and that habit began with an edition of the works of Jean-Baptiste Rousseau. Douxfils took an immediate interest in this edition; he, Rousset and Rousseau had all been very good friends. He wrote off to Marchand about it, as did Rousset, and considerable correspondence among these three concerned Rey's project.[14] Frequently Rousset refers to Rousseau as 'ce grand Maître', and in the context and given his youthful and deep involvement with Eugène of Savoy, it seems probable that Rousseau had also been initiated into Masonry. The young Rey may have been 'a fop' in the eyes of Rousset, but he was no fool. He pursued his business contacts with this internationally linked circle whose activities in the clandestine book trade must have made them very useful people to know. By the late 1760s, Rey was the most important publisher of the major philosophes of that era, Jean-Jacques Rousseau and the Baron d'Holbach, and he also published Rousset's (d. 1762) old text, the *Traité*. It was suggested to him by d'Holbach's coterie in Paris.

Scholars have long believed that Rey helped to finance the first and Parisian edition of Diderot's *Encyclopédie*. But his involvement may also have extended to the publication and/or circulation of certain of its volumes. In a letter to Marchand, Rey comments on Diderot's total preoccupation with the *Encyclopédie,* and then offers to send Marchand a copy of its fifth volume, 'if the reading of this work would give you pleasure.'[15] That offer was made in December 1754, but of course the fifth volume was only published in November 1755. It would seem that the text was being 'read' or proofed in Amsterdam, although more evidence would have to be forthcoming before we could proclaim with certainty Rey's firm as one of the real or contemplated manufacturing centres of Diderot's great work. One wonders, also, if Marchand ever took up Rey's offer and saw that volume in advance of its publication, and what contribution, if any, he may have made to its contents. In assessing Rey's career, so central as it is to the later years of the Enlightenment, we must acknowledge that he, like the radical publishers of the first generation, knew the 'business of Enlightenment' well, and we can only speculate about how much he learned from his family and business associates in the Netherlands. This radical coterie stood at the heart of the early Enlightenment in the Netherlands, and it was not without its assistance that Rey became the foremost publisher of the European Enlightenment.

His industry specialised in the literature of materialism. By the 1760s one coterie had monopolised the genre and it was led by the Baron d'Holbach in Paris. His writings and his circle have been the subject of a vast and growing literature, which has been partly inspired by the desire to know more about the roots of European materialism because that philosophy of nature stands as central to the socialist tradition. Until recently d'Holbach and his coterie have been often portrayed as avid radicals, revolutionaries in fact, who defied convention at every turn. Of late we have seen their intense involvement in the financial and social life of the *ancien régime* and focused upon their inevitable commitment to its survival in some form (183). Certainly d'Holbach's political writings, although hostile to courts and the abuse of monarchical authority, should not be described as republican.

In drawing forth some of the paths from the Radical Enlightenment to the High Enlightenment the continuity between the pantheism of Toland and Rousset and the materialism of d'Holbach should be emphasised. Various scholars have acknowledged that whole sections of d'Holbach's *Système de la Nature* (1770) come from Toland's *Letters to Serena,* which d'Holbach had translated into French and which Rey had published. Certainly none of d'Holbach's materialistic predecessors would have quarrelled with his metaphysics: 'A great variety of matter, combined in an infinity of forms, receives and communicates incessantly, a variety of motions. The different properties of this matter . . . constitute for us, the essence of beings . . . of which the sum total makes what we call, Nature.'[16] From this conception of nature, based in part on his own and Toland's rendering of the Newtonian concept of force,[17] this French materialist attempted to construct a new religion of nature and to argue for the ethical foundations of government based upon consent and law.[18] In the process the characteristic republicanism of the earlier pantheism appears muted, almost irrelevant. Materialism embraced the secular order whatever it might be. In the context of post-revolutionary England, Toland and his associates agitated for reforms through Parliament; in revolutionary Amsterdam Rousset sided with the artisan reformers; in the late *ancien régime* d'Holbach fantasised about benevolent and ethical governments led by infinitely wise, carefully checked monarchs. In general, where we find pantheistic materialsim in pre-industrial Europe we shall find it linked to a republican vision. But that linkage, although strong, was soluble. By far the most essential political element in European materialism, prior to the French Revolution, was its realism. Materialists possessed no illusions about monarchy and they could work for any strong leader, if his goals were compatible with theirs. And in every instance, from Toland through Rousset, La Mettrie and d'Holbach, the materialist was primarily concerned with religion, with destroying the old and creating the new. Inevitably the construction of a new religious institution, based in this instance on artisan socialising now rendered speculative and symbolic, became an integral part of the history of materialism in both England and the Continent.

D'Holbach's materialism obviously had other roots, some of them in the life sciences, besides what he read in Toland. Yet that English legacy appears to have been vital and to have been learned from young English radicals when they and d'Holbach were students in Leiden. There he was on intimate terms with the later Whig radical, John Wilkes – they belonged to the same 'club' – and d'Holbach knew the young English poet, Mark Akenside, whose verse betrays the influence of pantheistic speculation.[19] From them he also received books and we can easily imagine that Wilkes supplied a heavy dose of republican literature. Although Wilkes was a Freemason, a member of Asgill's old lodge at the Three Tuns, and received some Masonic support during the 1760s and his confrontation with the government, no evidence exists to link d'Holbach with the Masonic movement. Yet in this period Masonic songs hailed him and his philosophy.[20]

Freemasonry, as transmitted in the first instance to Protestant and largely French circles in the Netherlands must now be reckoned as central to the history of European radicalism and as supplying one of the links between English republicanism, that revolutionary legacy, and republican thought and schemes on the Continent. Likewise, the scientific culture of the seventeenth century, as mediated by conflicting political ideologies, produced two versions of Enlightenment, one that was moderate, deistic, Newtonian, and supportive of court-centred government, the other that was pantheistic, politically radical, and often republican. Only late in the century did the Radical Enlightenment find its grand *philosophes*, men like d'Holbach and his atheistic friend, Naigeon. Prior to 1750, it survived and flourished among highly educated men of trade and commerce about whom it has at last been possible to construct the outlines of a history. They bring a new dimension to the Enlightenment and draw our vision away from the Parisian salons and the great *philosophies*. For the Radical

Enlightenment prior to the 1750s we must look to the bookshops of The Hague. There we have found a social world of journalists, refugees, a scientist or two, foreign agents and spies, and in their midst we have discovered profoundly secular men who worshipped in a new temple and who sometimes gave reverence only to the deity within themselves.

Notes: Epilogue

1 The Grand Lodge of the Netherlands, The Hague, 'Annales de Dagran', Yvon is listed on the roles of 'Concordia Vincit Animos' lodge; and on 'Persoonsnamen Ordearchief', listed alphabetically. For Briasson's four letters to Marchand, see Marchand MSS 2, UL, Leiden. Briasson conveys Marchand's greetings to 'M. Falconnet', possibly Etienne Falconet, who contributed an article and knew Diderot. See John Lough, *The Contributors to the 'Encyclopédie'* (London: Grant & Cutler, 1973), p. 81.

2 There has been controversy over the specifically Masonic nature of this symbolism; I am of the opinion that it is. See also Georges May, 'Observations on an allegory: the frontispiece of the *Encyclopédie*', *Diderot Studies*, vol. 16 (1973), pp. 171–3. On Cochin as a Freemason see Robert Shackleton (176); also useful is S. Rocheblave, *Charles-Nicolas Cochin, Graveur et Dessinateur* (Paris: G. Vanoest, 1927), pp. 81–2.

3 [Chevalier Ramsay], 'Discours prononcé à la Recéption des Franc-Maçons', in *Lettres de M. de V****, avec plusiers pièces de differens auteurs (The Hague: P. Paupie, 1738), pp. 58–61.

4 ibid., p. 53. On Ramsay's politics and piety, see G. H. Luguet, *La Franc-maçonnerie et l'Etat en France au XVIIIme siècle* (Paris: Editions Vitiano, 1963), pp. 157–8.

5 Marchand MSS 2, 18 August 1749, Douxfils to Marchand. Aram Vartanian has arrived at a similar conclusion; see item 179 cited in the 'Bibliographical Essay'.

6 Marchand MSS 2, Rousset to Marchand, f.8, n.d., 'Mrs Tronchin and Neuville se donnerent beaucoup de mouvement, & plusieurs personnes signerent pour 1000, pour 600, pour 500 . . . flor. dont je connois Mrs Listernon, ter Smelt, Smith libr., Voordag, Beecks, van Collen etc. . . .' This description begins: 'Th[eodore] partit de l'isle de Corse pour aller chercher les secours qu'il avoit promis aux Corses . . . parcequ'on lui avoit promis à lui même, & qu'on lui manquoit de Parole. Il s'est rendu directement & *secrètement* à la Cour d'Espagne, où il a obtenu des remises sur cette ville [Madrid] pour y acheter l'artillerie & les munitions dont il avoit besoin. Il a passé par la France . . .' Bernard Tronchin belonged to Yvon's lodge.

7 See Thadd E. Hall, *France and the Eighteenth Century Corsican Question* (New York: New York University Press, 1971), p. 32 on King Theodore, seen by the French as working for English and Dutch interests in the Mediterranean.

8 Marchand MSS 2, Rousset to Marchand, f. 36, item no. 4, 'L'Abbé Yvon confrère de Prades est à Amsterdam, ainsi qu'un abbé de Loncourt Lorain, le premier travaille à l'apologie de Prades & à la sienne qui est sous presse; il est douteux qu'il aille joindre son confrère.

9 ibid., f. 38, 'J'ai vu des Lettres, qui disent, que le R. de Pr. a chassé de Prade de ses Etats, . . . ce qui empêche Yvon de le suivre: réponse de l'Abbé de Prade à l'Abbé Yvon, qui se proposoit d'aller s'établir à Berlin . . . car, vous croyez encore en Dieu'; f. 39, 'S'il a été chassé pour avoir tenu un langage contradictoire à sa fameuse Thèse, cette circonstance pourrait être ajouteé à son apologie . . .'; cf. also f. 52 on Rey and Yvon.

10 ibid., f. 45, February (n.a.), 'Je n'ai pas le tems de répondre à votre lettre mais je

vous dirai que les dévotes viennent de jouer un diable de tour aux encyclopédistes; ils ont engagé la Reine à renvoyer l'exemplaire qui étoit dans son cabinet avec défense d'y remettre un livre aussi impie et rempli de sentimens pires que ceux de Spinosa...'; f. 46, 21 August (n.a.), 'Prades avoit promis de me venir voir; mais le R. de Prus. l'a invité ainsi que son compagnon Yvon à se rendre à Berlin, óu ils sont allés d'abord...'; f. 47 on de Prades; f. 89 for Rousset's somewhat suspicious attitude to Yvon as a Frenchman. In Berlin de Prades was suspected of spying.

11 ibid., f. 49.

12 The best place to start with Rey is Max Fajn, 'Marc-Michel Rey: Boekhandelaar op de Bloemmark (Amsterdam)', *Proceedings of the American Philosophical Society*, vol. 118, no. 3 (1974), pp. 260–8. Rey MSS are in the Koninklijk Huisarchief, The Hague, and in the Bibliotheek van de vereeniging ter bevordering van de belangen des boekhandels, Amsterdam.

13 Koninklijk Huisarchief, The Hague, Autograph collection, KHA, f. 33, 6 November 1767.

14 Jean-Baptiste Rousseau, *Portefeuille* (Amsterdam: Marc-Michel Rey, 1751), with letter from M[r] R. D. M., January 1745, to L. D. that is Rousset to Douxfils; Vol. 2 adorned with a Picart engraving. Cf. Marchand MSS 2, Douxfils to Marchand, 25 May 1750; 9 April 1753, *et seq.*; Rousset to Marchand, Brussels, 8 April 1750, f. 19, supplying manuscript material for the edition; ff. 20, 22; f. 29 on Rousseau's religious beliefs; f. 35 on further business dealings with Rey; f. 41 on Rey's business dealings in Paris, 'Rey qui en a été averti par 3. Sauveur (son protecteur consul de France, dont Rey passa pour l'Espion) a redemandé son exempl[aire] à Noncourt...'; f. 44 on proposing to Rey that he publish *L'Ecole de l'homme*; f. 46, 21 August (n.a.), 'Rey est un petit fat'; f. 50, complaining about Rey; f. 69; f. 83, 'Votre petit Rey est digne du prénom de son beau Père J. F. Bernard, vous savez, comme on expliquoit le J. F.; sa femme a été ici 15 jours pour sa santé, j'étois où arrive la barque quand il est venu la chercher... ainsi tout ce que vous me dites de son ingratitude à votre égard après celle dont j'ai à me plaindre, ne m'étonne point.' Rey also employed Yvon.

15 Lough, *The Contributors to the 'Encyclopédie'*, pp. 19–20; Vol. 4 appeared in October 1754; UL, Leiden, Marchand 2, Rey to Marchand, 'Mr Diderot est toujours occupé à l'Encyclopédie dont je viens de recevoir le tom. 4, on travaille au 5me, tous les matériaux sont prets, si la lecture de cet ouvrage peut vous faire plaisir je vous l'expedierai; a vous le lirez à votre loisir...' Amsterdam, 12 December 1754.

16 Paul Heinrich Dietrich von d'Holbach, *Système de la Nature* (Paris, 1770); a convenient but not very good English translation, *The System of Nature* (London: G. Kearsley, 1797), p. 31 (here altered slightly).

17 ibid., pp. 49–50.

18 d'Holbach, *Ethocratie ou le gouvernement fondé sur la morale* (Amsterdam: Marc-Michel Rey, 1776), pp. 12–13.

19 BL, MSS ADD. 30867, f. 14, 9 August 1746, 'There I see my Dear Wilkes, What a Hurry of Passions! Joy, fear of a second parting! What charming tears? What sincere Kisses...'; ff. 20–1, 'Mr Dowdeswell being left alone of our Club at Leyden...', and on Wilkes sending books. W. H. Wickwar, *Baron d'Holbach. A Prelude to the French Revolution* (London: Allen & Unwin, 1935), pp. 18 *et seq.*; p. 74 on Toland and d'Holbach, p. 63 on Akenside.

20 Frères de Vignoles et du Bois, *La Lire Maçonne* (The Hague: van Laak, 1766), p. 454:

> Ce temple est notre retraite;
> Le Sage y doit commander;
> Notre attente est satisfaite
> D'H ... va présider.

For Wilkes, see John Brewer, *Party Ideology and Popular Politics at the Accession of George III* (Cambridge: Cambridge University Press, 1976), pp. 181, 194–6.

Appendix

The first document comes from the manuscripts of John Toland (1670–1722) deposited in the British Library (ADD. 4295, ff. 18–19). His editor and associate, Pierre Desmaizeaux, chose, for whatever reason, not to publish it. Obviously Toland thought this meeting record of a secret society important enough to preserve among his papers. It dates from the period, 1708–10, when Toland lived in The Hague, and the original, here translated, was written in French by Prosper Marchand. As has been indicated in Chapter 5, the manuscript qualifies as the earliest Masonic document from the Continent. 'The Knights of Jubilation' formed a private Masonic lodge, probably inaugurated by Toland, although it received no 'official' standing at the founding of the Grand Lodge of London in 1717. There is no evidence to suggest that this lodge ever sought formal affiliation with the Grand Lodge, and it is doubtful that its members would have been particularly welcome given the Grand Lodge's antipathy to 'atheists and libertines'.

This meeting record recounts one evening in the lives of its members who, as the manuscript reveals, were a jolly crew. The original document displays a distinct deterioration in the clarity of the handwriting, a fact perhaps best explained by the 'good wine' consumed on the occasion. The text is vitally important not only for its contents but also for the fact that it is signed. The meeting place, 'Gaillardin', may have been one of the many and fashionable coffee houses in The Hague (although it could also have been a private home), and the word itself rather than denoting the name of the actual place was intended to indicate any place of ribaldry and jest. From the playful tone of the text it appears that Brother Jean Gleditsch had decided to marry, to enter into 'the grave of all laughter and fun'. Note the use of the terms 'brothers', 'constitution' and 'grand master' – all essential attributes of eighteenth-century Masonry. The title 'grand master' was later adopted by official Freemasonry and was not used in the seventeenth century operative lodges. It may well owe something to aristocratic orders such as the Knights of the Bath or have been in imitation of usages supposedly found among the Knights Templar. The reference to the 'bourgeois gentilhomme' may refer to Molière's satiric play of that name, and since many of the Knights were members of the publishers' guild in The Hague they did also rightfully qualify as bourgeoisie, citizens of their town or city. Note also the references to the donation of Constantine and the Testament of Charles II. The latter refers to the falsity of French claims to the Spanish throne, an issue of vital concern as the War of Spanish Succession raged to the south. That last will and testament asserting those claims is compared to another great historic forgery, the Donation of Constantine first exposed during the Renaissance, and used by Protestants to show the duplicity of the papacy and the shaky foundations of its claim to control the papal territories. The signatories of this 1710 meeting record were all Protestants, and most were French refugees from religious persecution.[1]

Extract from Records of the Chapter-General of the Knights of Jubilation, held at Gaillardin, the Order's Meeting House, on 24 November 1710.

We, the Knights of Jubilation, to all those who will see these words: Greetings, Joy, Good Health! [and also] pigeons, chickens, and lots of fat pullets, and capons, and partridges; [together with] pheasants, and woodcocks, cooked tongues and hams; *Bonum vinum, atque semper bonum apetitum,* etc. [and good wine, and a continually healthy appetite.].

Let it be made known, then, that at the request of Chevalier *Böhm*, cupbearer of the Order, we were gathered happily in general convocation around a table, laden with a huge sirloin *together with fricassés and salads;* and, having eaten *with the utmost discernment,* and drunk *quite uncommonly well* [in the original, *cum summo judicio, et bu admodum egregie*]. We listened, with all attention the noise of our [revelry] allowed us to muster, to the complaints put forward by the aforesaid cupbearer against fr. ['frère' or brother] *Jean Frederick Gleditsch*, whom he has denounced for infraction against our most gallant and joyful *constitution*, and for being the first man to disturb the happiness and tranquillity which has always been a part of our Order from its foundation up until the present day. [And here are the words of the accusation]:

Whereas the aforesaid Knight Jean Frederick Gleditsch, being sworn under solemn oath to observe in perpetuity the *statutes* and *rules* of our order, which consist in the requirement to be always merry, high-spirited, happy, ready to eat and drink, to sing and to dance, to gamble and to joke and to frolic and play pranks, and moreover to abstain from all love, whether clandestine or matrimonial, since love is the complete opposite of all joy, and marriage the grave of all laughter and fun; and whereas he was admitted amongst us only after he had sworn to abjure love as he would the plague and the wine of [Roechiz?]; nevertheless he, in spite of his vows, and to the great scandal of our Order, has violated his word and his promises, and committed the crime of *lèse-jubilation* [high treason against rejoicing], which is most horrid, detestable and utterly deplorable apostasy, namely, to allow the drear poison of love to enter his heart: which is a heresy *ipso facto* punishable, and to be punished by excommunication, and the extinguishing of all the little beauties of love [?], to be carried out by all the chapters and constitutions of our order; and whereas he has incurred the penalty of excommunication *major, minor,* minima, minimula, minimulissima, and all the *issimas* in the world; that Brother Böhm has kindly and charitably required us to proceed without mercy against him, as against a rebel of the joy-inspiring statutes of our Order.

And whereas we, always mindful of the frailties of our brothers in living up to the continual gaity to which we are dedicated, have heard with sadness this astonishing news; nevertheless at the advice of our honourable, scientifically-minded, and [?] member, M. Gaspar Fritsch, our good-humoured and charming Grand Master, we have come to the conclusion that we ought to put the judgement once more before the new Order, since it is our custom never to condemn someone without first consulting the pints and pots.

And, this being the case, Brother Gottlieb Gleditsch, also chevalier of this Order and younger brother of the accused, has generously put himself forward to defend his case, and has given him a strong defence, after first, be it noted, lengthily and copiously saluting the health of the Grand Master, on the following grounds (and there is no doubt that the outcome will have been greatly aided thereby): First, he has denied that the Chevalier J. Frederick Gleditsch ever made any vows; Second, he has represented to us most elegantly and wittily that even if these vows were not as imaginary as the Donation of Constantine, or the Testament of Charles II,[2] even so one ought not to treat the accused without either indulgence or mercy, since no woman is proof against the graces and charms of a handsome face; and furthermore that if there is any crime pardonable in the eyes of the world, this, without doubt, is the one, and this he proved to us quite conclusively using the irrefutable authority of one of the Ancients and one of the Moderns, by repeating in an indescribably comic imitation of the 'Bourgeois Gentilhomme', *Amor omnia vincit, omnia vincit amor, vincit Amor omnia* [Love conquers all, everything conquers love, may he conquer all love].

Therefore, impressed as we are with the affectionate zeal he has shown in defence of a brother, and mindful of his inveterate attachment to happiness, and frivolity, and merry-making; but wishing at the same time to make something of an example of him, *ad perpetuam rei memoriam* [to fix the matter forever in his mind], and furthermore to keep the Knights up to the mark:

We, in the fullness of our power, certain knowledge and 'jubilational' authority, have at the present time declared and ordained, one and all, that the said J. Frederick Gleditsch will be exempt from excommunication by him [the Grand Master], on the one condition that he remits and reimburses into the safekeeping of our Treasurer, G. Gleditsch, the sum of 200 [the currency is unclear but probably *livres tournois*], a modest sum whose modesty has been urged upon us by our charming Grand Master, whose moderation is always so striking. Signed and sealed at Gaillardin, in the eighteenth thousand and third year of our foundation, and in the presence of

Our Grand Master His Most Serene Highness Don Gaspar of 'de Cocodrillos y de la Cueva' –
   [G. Fritsch, Grand Master][3]
M. Böhm, Cupbearer of the Order,
G. Gleditsch, Treasurer of the Order,
Ch. LeVier, Harlequin and Buffoon of the Order,
Bernard Picart, Dauber and Engraver of the Order,
M. De Bey, Keeper of the Seals of the Order,
P. Marchand, Secretary of the Order,
and all the rest of our Devil-may-care-gentlemen.

2   The next few documents come from manuscripts bequeathed by Prosper Marchand (d. 1756) to the University Library in Leiden (Marchand MSS 1, *varia*). Some of the sheets are undated and since the collection is unbound the exact sequence of the folios that Marchand might have intended, cannot accurately be determined. All these excerpts date from the period 1711 to 1717 (although not every manuscript is dated) and they represent a small portion of over twelve folios that are in some cases folded and written on in a most haphazard fashion. These are notes, made by M. Alexandre, from the proceedings of the literary society that published the *Journal littéraire* and that contributed to Saint-Hyacinthe's *Le Chef d'œuvre d'un inconnu* (1714). S'Gravesande belonged to this group, as did de Sallengre, Marchand, and possibly Justus Van Effen, as well as the still obscure M. Alexandre. If this literary society was not in fact Masonic, its links to the Knights, established by the use of the terms 'brother' and 'order' and the obvious secrecy of its proceedings, render it difficult to find any other word to describe its character. Some of the folios may be copies of letters written to the society by an absent member, in one case by s'Gravesande himself, to be read to the assembled; others appear to be copies of speeches made at various meetings. During the eighteenth century it became commonplace for Masonic lodges to establish just such societies, where members, not all of whom were necessarily initiated brothers, read books of common interest or even attempted to compose their own literary masterpieces. The aim, at every turn, was self-improvement and the attainment of skills in the seven liberal arts.

The manuscripts open with the complaints of one member, clearly abroad, against a journalist or publisher in Holland who has made financial claims against him. The journalist is identified only by the initials 'M. La F.' This complaint may very well be from s'Gravesande, commonly listed as one of the authors of *L'Chef d'œuvre,* because he is troubled by this enemy's claim that he 'had had the manuscript [of *L'Chef d'œuvre*] in his possession, although I was positive that the manuscript had not been out of my hands except when it left for the printer's' (f.2).

The next folio (f. 3–3a, 3b, here printed) is a speech given to the membership, possibly by the grand master, in which the link with the pagan deities is made explicit. Various of the brothers mentioned have not been identified.

This society, as the title-pages of books published by them indicates, did adopt Minerva and Mercury as their standard bearers. The speech is a superb example of the Enlightenment at work among educated practical men intent upon getting on in business and yet improving their wit and learning. The speaker is practising the art of rhetoric, replete with classical allusions, while urging his brothers on to achieve new skills, in the sciences as well as in business.

My very dear brothers:

I would be unworthy of addressing you in this way if during the time that all the members of our worthy secret society were working with their advancement in mind and to shed some glory on themselves, I alone remained with my arms shackled. While some distinguish themselves by polished and eloquent speeches, as for instance Brother André, and others make a name by starting to edit in writing our happenings and difficulties [à rediger par écrit vos faits & gênes] as does Brother Antoine, or in giving learned and erudite lectures to our gatherings as Brother Jean is due to do today (as someone informs me). Myself, paltry abortion of our Order, not daring to fly so high, because I know that I would be the most anxious if I raised myself too high (since someone told me this in seeing that I was falling from Parnassus),[4] I limit all my studies to looking for a subject which can meet with your approval. I would be happy only if you do not say that I have done nothing worthwhile, although I have scratched my ears and rubbed my head; but I would be a thousand times happier to find that I have succeeded, and that I have not laboured in vain.

My advice would be therefore, my very dear brothers, if you approve, that we take for the body of our motto [notre devise] a sapling, which Minerva plants, and Mercury waters, to make it grow . . . [a sapling may soon grow into a tree]. It is that which has made me choose this device – it is the connection it has not only with all the Order in general, but also with each member in particular. Our worthy reverend, who we had regarded as so far only a tender sapling planted at the foot of Parnassus, if I may dare to speak in this fashion, has become in a short time one of its noblest ornaments, owing to his learning and eloquence. Our Vicar, Brother Laurent, after being tied for a long time to one of the galleys of trade, vulgarly called a shop-counter, has at last taken the steering into his own hands, and is happily taking charge of his own ship; it could be said that he has become Mercury's Bishop. Brother Jean and Brother Thomas, who when our Order began dared not abandon their writings to public view without having made their wise adviser first correct their style, are presently in the position of giving lessons to others; there is no one with a grain of taste who would not take great pleasure in reading their works, and we see that they are in demand throughout Europe, and in other parts of the world. The weather is too cold for me to amuse myself in deducing for you from the bill of fare the progress that our Brothers Nicholas, Antoine, André and Simon have made. You are better informed on them than I am, and that will be sufficient. There is only Brother Jacques who up to this point has not yet become a Grand-Clerc, but he hopes to arrive at this point with time, if not in ability, at least with seniority. In the meantime he is going to try to show that the device that he has had the honour of proposing to you is more or less agreeable at the very least to the Order in general rather than to each member in particular. Let us compare them. You are well aware, I know, that our Order, although illustrious, is not at present the largest nor the most powerful in the world, but it could become so. This is why I compare it to a small shoot, which with time will grow into a large tree. It is planted by Minerva, goddess of wisdom and the Protectress of those who cultivate the sciences, to show that we have had exactly the same aim in mind: [the cultivation of] our society, from which we are instructed and we become sages, if it is possible. Thus Mercury waters a little shoot to make it grow: this is my thought.

Riches help a lot in making states, commonwealths and private persons important: thus our Order will both appear to be and will be great indeed when our treasury is full. But how is it to be filled? Father Laurent has told us several times that it is by Trade [*le Negoce*], that we can make our organisation rich by Trade, over which Mercury presides as God. I believe one couldn't do better than to introduce this into my device.

This is what I have proposed to you and it is for you to decide whether I have done well or badly. Cut it, pare it, add to it, amplify it – I am in agreement with all that you will do to it, and I will be indebted to you, for you have more brains than I have, but you have no qualms about being less reserved.

The following excerpt also occurs on a single folio in Marchand MSS 1, *varia*, and appears to be minutes jotted down at one meeting. The tone is playful here and the emphasis is clearly on clubbing as such than on mutual self-improvement. Anyone who has ever tried to organise a new club or society will recognise certain historical constants.

Meeting convened by Brother Nicolas.
Held at Brother Laurent's house, 30 September 1711
(1)   The Minutes [*le Journal*] of the previous meeting were not read.
(2)   Brother Nicolas did not bore us by reading a long discourse since he had prepared neither a long nor a short one.
(3)   Some of the brothers paid what they owed to the Treasurer
(4)   Some others didn't pay anything.
(5)   There was no work done on the business affairs of the Order.
I proposed that we ought to compose a more extended record [*Journal*] of a meeting as fruitless as the one of which we speak. It seems that it [the meeting] resembled that at 'La Mondanité' [possibly a coffee house] in which the Convener was in effect dead while he was absent. Also was it not the first he had come to since his return? It must be hoped that he will be recompensed for the time lost on the first occasion.[5] However, since he was abroad it was impossible to discharge this. The evening passed in conversation on several subjects, after which each one left.
(6)   Brother Thomas didn't come because he was ill.
(7)   Brothers Jean and André came too late.

The next set of minutes, dated 16 March 1712, are fuller, and amply illustrate the closed, exclusive quality of these meetings. Although outsiders were allowed to attend, they were judged harshly when observed to be lacking in rhetorical skills or to be obsessed with material interests. That this was the thirty-fifth meeting in the period of 1711–12 indicates a considerable frequency, and note the insistence upon regular dues payment. Both became common characteristics of organised European Freemasonry.

(1)   **Brother Laurent, who convened the meeting, made these opening remarks:** he should have begun with a talk, but he hadn't had the time to compose one, so he would offer one off the cuff. All the brothers having arrived he made good his promise in these words:

My brothers [Mes F: = frères] the discourse that I have devised for you consists in two points: here they are – and so saying he deposited an escalin [a coin] with each hand on the table – (these were certainly quite tangible points) and then he continued, Brother André will make the explication and Brother Jean the application.

I spoke as follows:

In saying this, one might assume that Brother Laurent has paid all he owes for making no discourse according to all the rules. But this would be a wrong assumption. For Brother André declares in taking from him the two escalins that he has paid all that he owes. But Brother Jean, who hates equivocation, has decided rightly to take exception to this, since there can be no real excuse except ignorance.

(2)   We began the reading of the records, but only a part of the minutes of the sixth meeting were covered because of the arrival of a . . . I do not know what name to give to the animal who then came in. Judged from the outside one would consider him human, but when he opened is mouth he was no better than an animal.

From Paris to Peru, from Japan to Rome
No animal there is more bestial than Man.
[first line also crossed out to read,
'From here to Japan, from Japan to Rome',
etc. etc.]

He looked for all the world like a traveller newly disembarked from Moscow. And his personality corresponded exactly with his appearance. He hadn't got the faintest notion of proper reasoning, but he talked and talked. Well, a woodpecker talks, a starling talks, a parakeet can talk – these creatures can all say something prettily if you teach them; but as for him, whatever you said or remarked to him, he had the knack of hanging on to its least significant part. He was well-travelled, and had spent his money freely, but it was all money wasted. The proverb 'Men who travel beyond the sea change the climate but not their characters' couldn't apply more exactly to him. He wore the most wonderful clothes, but this is all that was attractive about him. His wig was made in Paris, and cost him 80f. I know this only too well, for he said so, five or six times in the space of an hour. This character, whom I have just described quite without exaggeration, uttered five or six words as soon as he came in to the assembled company: in other words, he made five or six silly remarks. And the rest of his conversation was just like the beginning: it was simply a concoction of nonsense, relieved from time to time by some good opinions, laden with superlatives and bombastic expressions. All that we learned from him was the price of his perriwig, and that he had dined and drunk well. May the skies above, which shine on us as much as on him, show him disfavour; and if this were to happen, we wouldn't be found together, for fire would rain down on us, which we're certainly not looking for! But so be it.

The last manuscript from the society's records that is of interest to us, records the secretary's last meeting and the departure of a brother, possibly the secretary himself. Note that amid all the nonsense and good humour of the preceding minutes we find here an expression of life-long friendship and the assertion that membership in the society will continue for life, 'in whatever part of the world' this departing brother may find himself. The clear implication is that the society will continue, and indeed a few years later s'Gravesande and Marchand did put out another version of the *Journal littéraire* (1713–22; 1729–36).

Here follows, so far as I can judge, the last meeting at which I assisted before my removal.

Do not expect me, my dear brothers, to make you a lengthy speech, persuading you that I am desolate. I think that you can be in no doubt about it, and so it would be pointless to attempt to persuade you with many fine phrases. If I had the gift of expressing myself feelingly and dolefully, I would give myself the pleasure of charming the tears out of you by an affecting and tender farewell: for tears like that would flatter my ego! But since, unfortunately for me, all my talent, if I have any at all, is a talent for saying things amusingly, and I would rather make you laugh than cry, I will just have to put up with a lowering of my self-esteem. So be content, then, if I say to you with all the seriousness I can muster, that I will regret nothing so much after my departure from here as being without my friends. I will never forget the many marks of friendship I have received from you as a whole as well as individually. It is quite impossible for me to give you sufficient assurance of my appreciation of this. I flatter myself that for your part, you will wish to remember poor Brother Jaquez occasionally. You can certainly rest assured that in him you have, in whatever part of the world he may be, a zealous and faithful member, and that he will glory in this for as long as he lives.

In one of his anonymous publications Toland claimed to have established a secret society. The exact relationship between Toland's Socratic society and ritual, revealed in his infamous *Pantheisticon* (1720), and the Knights of Jubilation may never be known. Yet in a letter to Baron Hohendorf dated 1711 Toland indicated that his philosophical liturgy was nearing completion, and Hohendorf knew the Knights and they in turn cherished the exploits of Eugène of Savoy. Three curious items that survive in Marchand's papers make explicit mention of the *Pantheisticon*, a text which he obviously knew well. They are printed below.

The first is a loose and impious fragment, a prayer to Bacchus, written in Latin but here translated. It is signed 'W. Feilding' – clearly an English name and not one easily identified. Among Walpole's friends in Norfolk there was a William Feilding; but not enough is known about him to suggest anything about his religious persuasions. There was a Robert Feilding (d. 1712) who had a libertine reputation as well as a brother – but, alas, his name is not known. The existence as well as the tone of this manuscript adds further evidence for the English and freethinking affiliations of the Knights. The next fragment (Marchand MSS 62) is a poem about Toland – also in Latin – that labels him as more dangerous than Spinoza and Vanini.

The last and longer manuscript (also Marchand MSS 62) is a letter about Toland that Marchand sent to Thomas Johnson, who was a publishing associate but not a member of the literary society. He was the first publisher of the *Journal* and he specialised in English literature. He did a brisk business selling in England because he was able to sell works cheaper than his English competitors. His letters in the University Library, Edinburgh, also reveal that he slipped a few clandestine books into his shipments and that he was a man of polished literary tastes. Johnson had obviously asked Marchand about the *Pantheisticon* and Marchand's letter claims no knowledge of Freemasonry; the letters of Rousset de Missy to Marchand reveal, however, that Marchand was a Freemason. Of course, he had no reason to be frank with Johnson on that score. Unfortunately the letter is undated; it concerns notes made on the *Pantheisticon* by the French refugee in England, Michel Maittaire.

(1) **Formula to be inserted in the Pantheisticon**
All-powerful, external Bacchus, who hast established human society especially in drinking, grant, being propitious, that the heads of these men, who are heavy from yesterday's drinking, be lightened by today's, and that this be done, through cups of cups. Amen.

W. Feilding

(2) **Land of Britain**, more pestilential than Africa, why rearst thou monsters, scarce known to distant ages, and hostile to that Christian name which is they boast? The author of this book [the *Pantheisticon*] has produced a sort of unmentionable sect. The creeping poison, scarce to be washed off with the sea, drips on more men. Whatever impiety has hitherto emerged, will seem piety compared with this hydra. Vaninus and Servetus will then be harmless. Thine opinions, Spinoza, will be less condemned: our times know of one Spinosier.

(3) **These for Mr Johnson, Bookseller at The Hague:**
All the mss which accompany this ed. of the Pantheisticon are in the hand of the late Michel Maittaire and were probably written by him; certainly he compiled them. He gathered them from copies belonging to doctors Richard Mead and Hans Sloane, faous as medics and for their collections of natural curiosities and for their Libraries which will probably go to the Royal Society. After Maittaire's death a mutual friend passed them on to me, knowing my fondness for literary and bibliographical 'curiosities'.
    He [Maittaire] noticed that there were two eds. of the *Pantheisticon* so similar that one might not see the difference very easily; in one of the vignettes, the grey letters and the lamp-ends are engraved in copper and in the other in wood. The number of pages, the rubrics [the Red letters] and the date are also the same. Maittaire added that the word aratra appears on p. 73 in both. That may be so in the two eds. he saw, but it is not so in this one, where the word is aratro. Still it would be wrong to imagine that there was a 3rd ed. This was only so in the case of the wood-engraved ed., where a leaf was inserted to rectify the error and put the word aratro.

Not worth the trouble for Maittaire to deal with all the different readings, curiosities and etymologies, agreement of sentences etc. in the Mss Notes, just to illustrate (explain) this libertine and irreligious bantering, against which both he and the wisest English [?] have raised the alarm. The work is said to be Toland's and indeed it seems to 'fit' him, although he frequently disclaimed it. It would not be the first time that such a bacchanalian liturgy has appeared; it was to be found in 16th c. England, e.g. the Missa de Potia[?], id est Missa bacchanalis Formula ludicra, prophana, ac blasphema; ex vetusto codice, in quodam Angliae monasterio, inter Londin et Norwicien. anno 1535 invento, cf. Bibl. Uffenbachiana, 3, p. 536. In 18th c. we saw the Bacchanalian matins, composed after the manner of canonical 'Hours' full of libertine, irreligious and impious verses . . . Not knowing the Lodges of the Freemasons I would take care not to judge indiscreetly, but from what one can deduce of their unique and bizarre ceremonies, their gestures and what is said, they seem to so resemble the *Pantheisticon* and other bacchanalian liturgies as to be the same thing under a different name.

Chapelle was blamed for letting his bantering and mocking vein run away with him rather than allow him to let the public see the enormity of Toland's writings; what was worse he translated the stuff into French. Maty took him to task for this in his Doctrine of the Trinity explained and defended from Scripture (in the preface).

I think that Chapelle, reformed minister in London and then at The Hague, refuted Toland best in his Extract of the *Pantheisticon,* where under pretext of not being able to believe that the author is also *Nazarenus* he ridicules both works. It's a good refutation of Spinozism, esp. in the long passage from Bayle contained in it.

The various popular festivals . . . which one finds in all countries associated with saints or with times of the year, which are processions, rogations or banquets etc., are all survivals of pagan antiquity. The Protestant Churches have accused the Roman Catholic of retaining such idolatry. [One final paragraph not included here.]

Marchand's extant correspondence is vast and spans over forty years. One of his intermittent correspondents was the Grand Master of the Knights, Gaspard Fritsch. He returned to Frankfurt in 1715, and continued the family's publishing business which was extensive. He wrote occasionally to Marchand, a respected *savant* and publisher, for information about Enlightenment books and also to convey what he knew. This next letter is a good example of the correspondence between two thoroughly professional publishers; it also reveals the origin of the *Traité des trois imposteurs.* In a letter that could easily have been opened (unlike Rousset de Missy, Fritsch appears to have had no Masonic friends in the post office) the tone is cautious – condemnatory of impiety but, nevertheless, anticlerical. *La Vie de Spinoza* could not refer to Colerus's life (1706) which was available in book form and in no sense impious. *L'Esprit* and *La Vie* were usually bound together and indeed the *Traité* was first called *La Vie et l'Esprit de Spinosa* (1719 edn in 8vo, 208 pp., very rare).[6] Only the most relevant portions of the letter are published here. Note also that Fritsch has stopped signing himself 'le Grand Maître' and the letters make no specific allusions to any common fraternity except for references to 'the royal family' which was a term of reference used by the Knights and their friends in the period 1710–17. The letter also reveals that Fritsch, an original member of the Knights, socialised with Van Effen, one of the early editors of the *Journal* and a member of its literary society.

Leipzig, 7 September 1737

Honoured sir and dear friend,

I have had the honour and pleasure of receiving your letters of 5th July, 5th October, and a note via M. Neaulme. I am very much obliged to you for all the trouble you are taking over my affairs. Since you have been relying on the news about the discontinuation of printing that edition of *Etienne's Treasury* at Basle, I have been curious to find out more about it: and I would be especially interested to know what those fellows there have done with the first 60 or 80 pages of the print-run. I do know that the Wetstein and Smith partnership have their eye on the London edition and that they would be the only people in Holland who would be able to combine and promote it with the Basle edition. They must have refused to do it in order to help out the Basle people with their edition. It would be very kind of you if you could do me the favour of telling me everything you know for certain about all this, together with any details which you can commit to paper in your spare time.

You were quite right to include the *Memoirs of Berwyk* among the other trashy pieces. If I were you, I would add the *Sequel to Bonneval,* the *Memoirs of the Duc d'Ormond*, the *Gallant Saxon*, and a whole lot of others to the pile. I had 20 copies of *Berwyk* off M. Neaulme; it wasn't Paupie[7] who printed them, it was someone in Paris or Rouen. How come people in Holland are prepared to get bogged down in such a load of rubbish?

Do you know anything about the *History of Louis XIV* by de la Hode, with plates, 6 vols, quarto, which Van Duren has just announced, to be brought out by public subscription? The author's reputation is a complete unknown factor and the publishing house isn't very well established yet. Would you be able to give me some idea of the author's general standing and his ability? Also, have we got anything coming shortly from the next piece of work undertaken by the author of the *Mémoirs de Torbin*? I must thank you very much for all your comments on the character and present circumstances of the Marquis d'Argens: he certainly deserves to be properly known. I could certainly wish we didn't owe his best pieces of work to his youthful frolics, for a man who thinks and writes so well certainly deserves a better fate: but this is all George Dandin's fault – that was the way he wanted it.

The consignment of the *History of the Revolution in Corsica* has arrived, together with your gifts, which I will treasure very dearly and for which I give you my most heartfelt thanks. *La Vie de Spinosa* was copied word for word from the copy made by Levier from Furly's manuscript: there is nothing added but some notes, the advertisement, and the catalogue of his

other works. But *l'Esprit de Spinosa* has been touched up and added to –
one can venture to ask who was responsible? It would satisfy my curiosity to
know whether it was Rousset who was the author of the *Réponse* etc. This
book, together with the *Letter from M. de la Monoye to President Bouhier,*
vol. 4 of *Menagiana* and *La Vie de Spinosa* have to be taken all together.
With regard to the purported *Narration* by Frecht and Tausendorf, it is all a
complete fabrication: I made inquiries about it once in Frankfurt: the
History has only been in existence since 1704. Everyone was in complete
ignorance of it. It was said to be a commission from a Prince of Saxony, who
could quite possibly have had some contact with the former Prince of Lower
[?] Saxony, the one who had the library which included a selection of
irreligious books. However, anything of that nature would have been
undertaken personally by his agent Weidmann, who certainly wouldn't
have let the light of such a *Literary News* get hidden beneath a bushel.
There is nothing more to be said about that whole tirade – 'Oh, the terrible
daring! the outrageous insolence!' etc., etc. . . . As to what you believe
about the imaginary translation which is mentioned in the aforesaid
Réponse, I quite agree with you that it has something in common with the
L'Espirit de Spinoza. Levier copied it in 1711. This sort of book was his
particular hobby-horse. If he has had some contact since then with Rousset,
then I should think that all the uncertainties surrounding it are answered.
The book of the *Three Impostors* is not unlike the *Collar-bones of Solomon,*
of which I have seen several manuscripts, all differing from one another;
just the kind of thing the rabble manipulate according to their whims, to
trap the unwary. It's sad to think this sort of thing goes on in a civilised and
Christian nation: it would be more excusable among Hottentots,
Caribbeans or Iroquois Indians. But you have to look to the behaviour of
priests for the source of all the trouble: men full of religion comprising
fables and self-interested dogmas which are both absurd and useless, who
fasten on to purity and innocence. It is intellectually abhorrent, but it gives
credence to impostors to hold sway, for the gift of good judgement is shared
out only among the few.

I have never heard any mention of the *Tragic Odes of d'Aubigné,* so my
debts to you only increase; they are affording me much pleasure – so far I
have looked only at those you have marked. I shall look after them as I
would a treasure-trove.

Your edition of Marot has come in good time to go alongside the two
little editions of 16° size, the one from Lyon dated 1546, and the other,
Paris, 1547.[8] They are very different from each other; I don't care much
myself for the Abbé Langlet's edition. He is the only classic French poet I
collect; [Jean-Baptiste] Rousseau together with his pupil.

You [ought?] to have been able to tell me about Baron Van Effen's[9]
death. I do not know by what misadventure it took place – it was about six
weeks ago, according to the obituary in our German-language *Literary
News;* – a place, indeed, worthy of the aforesaid gentleman. He certainly
used to be my *bête noire* in company but I can pardon him all that now that
we are saved from his other faults – his fussy manner, his conceit and so on.
Have you any idea why he went to live in Bois-le-Duc? And also is it true

there was a certain beautiful but boring princess who went there who was formerly attached to him?

Your *Histoire des Revolutions de Corse* is very instructive. But you may have been pipped at the post by a German writer in Nuremburg. His book has an edge over yours in that it gives a *Geographical Sketch* of the island, which is very useful in getting to understand the movements of the insurgents. What he gives in the way of historical material is new and not so badly done as the usual hack productions from Nuremburg. He ends with the departure of King Theodore. I think you ought to add a second volume to yours, especially as the scenes are changing there, if it is true that the French court is getting involved in the politics of this island. M. Paupie's samples arrived at a good moment. Some foreign booksellers who were around when the packets were opened relieved me of almost all of them . . .

Any news on *The History of Printing*?

As for the rest, please don't have any reservations regarding the reception of your letters: however long they are, I prefer them far and beyond any number of Literary Memoirs etc. At present I don't have enough time to make this present letter any longer. At the moment I am preoccupied with hearing the latest about an important sale in the city. A fop called Sellius, who used to live in Utrecht, spent his wife's fortune on Pictures, Shells, nicknacks and books, and has now run out of money. After useless efforts at Göttingen, and at Halle most recently, now sadly under the thumb of the King of Prussia, he has been forced to come here to borrow, and now, his credit exhausted, to sell all his possessions. His library has been brought here. It is very fine, containing a number of old editions and some other very rare books. They are selling so well that I feel I am assisting at the proceedings of the great hall of The Hague.

I greet you with all my heart, and rest assured, sir and very dear friend, that I am

your very humble and obedient servant,

Gaspar Fritsch.

P.S. News of the royal family is always welcome.

Since modern, easily accessible editions of Anderson's Masonic *Constitutions* of 1723 are rare, it is included here. In addition to the explication given in Chapter 4, the contents of the constitutions, undoubtedly comprised by a variety of hands, reveal the rich complexity of traditions, ethics, political ideology and customs which lay at the heart of European Freemasonry. It repays a careful reading, and it is particularly useful in showing the merger of 'operative', that is, old craft practices, with 'speculative' elements, the latter by 1717 largely predominant. Such was the nature of much of eighteenth-century Freemasonry.

The Charges of a Free-Mason,
Extracted From
The Ancient Records of Lodges beyond the Sea, and of those in England,

Scotland, and Ireland, for the Use of the Lodges in London:
To Be Read
At the making of New Brethren, or when the Master shall order it.

The General Heads, viz.
(I)   Of God and Religion.
(II)   Of the Civil Magistrate supreme and subordinate.
(III)   Of Lodges
(IV)   Of Masters, Wardens, Fellows, and Apprentices.
(V)   Of the Management of the Craft in working.
(VI)   Of Behaviour, viz.
    (1)   In the Lodge while constituted.
    (2)   After the Lodge is over and the Brethren not gone.
    (3)   When Brethren meet without Strangers, but not in a Lodge.
    (4)   In Presence of Strangers not Masons.
    (5)   At Home, and in the Neighbourhood.
    (6)   Towards a strange Brother.

(I) Concerning God and Religion.

A mason is oblig'd, by his Tenure, to obey the moral Law; and if he rightly understands the Art, he will never be a stupid Atheist, nor an irreligious Libertine. But though in ancient Times Masons were charg'd in every Country to be of the Religion of that Country or Nation, whatever it was, yet 'tis now thought more expedient only to oblige them to that Religion in which all men agree, leaving their particular opinions to themselves; that is, to be good Men and true, or men of honour and honesty, by whatever denominations or persuasions they may be distinguish'd; whereby Masonry becomes the centre of union, and the means of conciliating true friendship among persons that must have remain'd at a perpetual distance.

(II) Of the Civil Magistrate Supreme and Subordinate.

A Mason is a peaceable subject to the Civil Powers, wherever he resides or works, and is never to be concern'd in plots and conspiracies against the peace and welfare of the nation, nor to behave himself undutifully to inferior magistrates; for as Masonry hath been always injured by war, bloodshed, and confusion, so ancient kings and princes have been much dispos'd to encourage the craftsmen, because of their peaceableness and loyalty, whereby they practically answer'd the cavils of their adversaries, and promoted the honour of the fraternity, who ever flourish'd in times of peace. So that if a Brother should be a rebel against the State, he is not to be countenanc'd in his rebellion, however he may be pitied as an unhappy man; and, if convicted of no other crime, though the loyal Brotherhood must and ought to disown his rebellion, and give no umbrage or ground of political jealousy to the government for the time being; they cannot expel him from the Lodge, and his relation to it remains indefeasible.

(III) Of Lodges.

A Lodge is a place where Masons assemble and work: hence that assembly, or duly organis'd Society of Masons, is call'd a Lodge, and every Brother ought to belong to one, and to be subject to its By-Laws and the General Regulations. It is either particular or general, and will be best understood by attending it, and by the regulations of the General or Grand Lodge hereunto annex'd. In ancient times, no master or fellow could be absent from it, especially when warn'd to appear at it, without incurring a severe censure, until it appear'd to the master and wardens, that pure necessity hinder'd him.

The persons admitted members of a Lodge must be good and true men, free-born, and of mature and discreet age, no bondmen, no women, no immoral or scandalous men, but of good report.

(IV) Of Masters, Wardens, Fellows, and Apprentices.

All preferment among Masons is grounded upon real worth and personal merit only; that so the Lords may be well served; the brethren not put to shame, nor the Royal Craft despis'd: therefore no Master or Warden is chosen by seniority, but for his merit. It is impossible to describe these things in writing, and every brother must attend in his place, and learn them in a way peculiar to this Fraternity: only Candidates may know, that no Master should take an Apprentice, unless he has sufficient Imployment for him, and unless he be a perfect youth, having no maim or defect in his body, that may render him uncapable of learning the Art, of serving his Master's Lord, and of being made a Brother, and then a Fellow-Craft in due time, even after he has served such a term of years as the custom of the country directs; and that he should be descended of honest parents; that so, when otherwise qualify'd, he may arrive to the honour of being the Warden, and then the Master of the Lodge, the Grand Warden, and at length the Grand-Master of all the Lodges, according to his merit.

No Brother can be a Warden until he has pass'd the part of a Fellow-Craft; nor a Master until he has acted as a Warden, nor Grand-Warden until he has been Master of a Lodge, nor Grand Master unless he has been a Fellow-Craft before his election, who is also to be nobly born, or a Gentleman of the best fashion, or some eminent Scholar, or some curious Architect, or other Artist, descended of honest parents, and who is of singular great merit in the opinion of the Lodges. And for the better, and easier, and more honourable discharge of his office, the Grand-Master has a power to chose his own Deputy Grand-Master, who must be then, or must have been formerly, the Master of a particular Lodge, and has the privilege of acting whatever the Grand-Master, his Principal, should act, unless the said principal be present, or interpose his authority by a letter.

These Rulers and Governors, supreme and subordinate, of the ancient Lodge, are to be obey'd in their respective stations by all the Brethren, according to the old Charges and Regulations, with all humility, reverence, love, and alacrity.

(V) Of the Management of the Craft in working.

All Masons shall work honestly on working days, that they may live creditably on holy Days; and the time appointed by the Law of the Land, or confirm'd by Custom, shall be observ'd.

The most expert of the Fellow-Craftsmen shall be chosen or appointed the Master, or Overseer of the Lord's work; who is to be call'd Master by those that work under him. The Craftsmen are to avoid all ill language, and to call each other by no disobliging name, but Brother or Fellow; and to behave themselves courteously within and without the Lodge.

The Master, knowing himself to be able of cunning, shall undertake the Lord's work as reasonably as possible, and truly dispend his goods as if they were his own; nor to give more wages to any Brother or Apprentice than he really may deserve.

Both the Master and the Masons receiving their wages justly, shall be faithful to the Lord, and honestly finish their work, whether task or journey; nor put the work to task that hath been accustom'd to journey.

None shall discover envy at the prosperity of a Brother, nor supplant him, or put him out of his work, if he be capable to finish the same; for no man can finish another's work so much to the Lord's profit, unless he be thoroughly acquainted with the designs and draughts of him that began it.

When a Fellow-Craftsman is chosen Warden of the work under the Master, he shall be true both to Master and Fellows, shall carefully oversee the work in the Master's absence to the Lord's profit; and his Brethren shall obey him.

All Masons employ'd, shall meekly receive their wages without murmuring or mutiny, and not desert the Master till the work is finish'd.

A younger Brother shall be instructed in working, to prevent spoiling the materials for want of judgment, and for increasing and continuing of Brotherly Love.

All the tools used in working shall be approved by the Grand Lodge.

No Labourer shall be employ'd in the proper work of Masonry; nor shall Free Masons work with those that are not free, without an urgent necessity; nor shall they teach Labourers and unaccepted masons, as they should teach a Brother or Fellow.

(VI) Of Behaviour, viz.

(1) In the Lodge while constituted.

You are not to hold private Committees, or separate Conversation, without Leave from the Master, nor to talk of any thing impertinent or unseemly, nor interrupt the Master or Wardens, or any Brother speaking to the Master: Nor behave yourself ludicrously or jestingly while the Lodge is engaged in what is serious and solemn; nor use any unbecoming Language upon any Pretence whatsoever; but to pay due Reverence to your Master, Wardens, and Fellows, and put them to worship.

If any Complaint be brought, the Brother found guilty shall stand to the Award and Determination of the Lodge, who are the proper and competent Judges of all such Controversies, (unless you carry it by Appeal to the Grand Lodge) and to whom they ought to be referr'd, unless a Lord's Work be hinder'd the mean while, in which Case a particular Reference may be made; but you must never go to Law about what concerneth Masonry, without an absolute Necessity apparent to the Lodge.

(2) Behaviour after the Lodge is over and the Brethren not gone.

You may enjoy yourselves with innocent Mirth, treating one another according to Ability, but avoiding all Excess, or forcing any Brother to eat or drink beyond his Inclination, or hindering him from going when his Occasions call him, or doing or saying any thing offensive, or that may forbid an easy and free Conversation; for that would blast our Harmony, and defeat our laudable Purposes. Therefore no private Piques or Quarrels must be brought within the Door of the Lodge, far less any Quarrels about Religion or Nations, or State Policy, we being only, as Masons, of the Catholick Religion above-mention'd; we are also of all Nations, Tongues, Kindreds, and Languages, and are resolv'd against all Politicks, as what never yet conduc'd to the Welfare of the Lodge, nor ever will. This Charge has been always strictly enjoin'd and observ'd; but especially ever since the Reformation in Britain, or the Dissent and Secession of these Nations from the Communion of Rome.

(3) Behaviour when Brethren meet without Strangers, but not in a Lodge form'd.

You are to salute one another in a courteous manner, as you will be instructed, calling each other Brother, freely giving mutual Instruction as shall be thought expedient, without being overseen or overheard, and without encroaching upon each other, or derogating from that Respect which is due to any Brother, were he not a Mason: For though all Masons are as Brethren upon the same Level, yet Masonry takes no Honour from a Man that he had before; nay rather it adds to his honour, especially if he has deserv'd well of the Brotherhood, who must give Honour to whom it is due, and avoid ill Manners.

(4) Behaviour in Presence of Strangers not Masons.

You shall be cautious in your Words and Carriage, that the most penetrating Stranger shall not be able to discover or find out what is not proper to be intimated; and sometimes you shall divert a Discourse, and manage it prudently for the Honour of the worshipful Fraternity.

(5) Behaviour at Home, and in your Neighbourhood.

You are to act as becomes a moral and wise Man; particularly, not to let your Family, Friends, and Neighbours know the Concerns of the Lodge, &c., but wisely to consult your own Honour, and that of the ancient Brotherhood, for Reasons not to be mentioned here. You must also consult your Health, by not continuing together too late, or too long from home, after Lodge Hours are past; and by avoiding of Gluttony or Drunkenness, that your Families be not neglected or injured, nor you disabled from working.

(6) Behaviour towards a strange Brother.

You are cautiously to examine him, in such a Method as Prudence shall direct you, that you may not be impos'd upon by an ignorant false Pretender, whom you are to reject with Contempt and Derision, and beware of giving him any Hints of Knowledge.

But if you discover him to be a true and genuine Brother, you are to respect him accordingly; and if he is in want, you must relieve him if you can, or else direct him how he may be reliev'd: You must employ him some Days, or else recommend him to be employ'd. But you are not charged to do beyond your Ability, only to prefer a poor Brother, that is a good Man and true, before any other poor People in the same Circumstances.

Finally, All these Charges you are to observe, and also those that shall be communicated to you in another way; cultivating Brotherly-Love, the Foundation and Cape-stone, the Cement and Glory of this ancient Fraternity, avoiding all Wrangling and Quarrelling, all Slander and Backbiting, nor permitting others to slander any honest Brother, but defending his Character, and doing him all good Offices, as far as is consistent with your Honour and Safety, and no farther. And if any of them do you Injury, you must apply to your own or his Lodge: and from thence you may appeal to the Grand Lodge at the Quarterly Communication, and from thence to the annual Grand Lodge, as has been the ancient laudable Conduct of our Forefathers in every Nation; never taking a legal Course but when the Case cannot be otherwise decided, and patiently listening to the honest and friendly Advice of Master and Fellows, when they would prevent your going to Law with Strangers, or would excite you to put a speedy Period to all Law-Suits, that so you may mind the Affair of Masonry with the more Alacrity and success; but with respect to Brothers and Fellows at Law, the Master and Brethren should kindly offer their Mediation, which ought to be thankfully submitted to by the contending Brethren; and if that Submission is impracticable, they must however carry on their Process, or Law-Suit, without Wrath and Rancour (not in the common way) saying or doing nothing which may hinder Brotherly Love, and good Offices to be renew'd and continu'd; that all may see the benign Influence of Masonry, as all true Masons have done from the Beginning of the World, and will do to the End of Time.

Amen so may it be said.

Postscript

A Worthy Brother, learned in the Law, has communicated to the Author (while this Sheet was printing) the Opinion of the Great Judge Coke upon the Act against Masons, 3 Hen. VI. Cap. I. which is Printed in this Book, Page 35, and which Quotation the Author has compar'd with the Original, viz.

Coke's Institutes, third Part, Fol. 99.

The Cause wherefore this Offence was made Felony, is for that the good Course and Effect of the Statutes of Labourers were thereby violated and broken. Now (said my Lord Coke) all the Statutes concerning Labourers, before this Act, and whereunto this Act doth refer, are repeal'd by the Statue of 5 Eliz. Cap. 4. whereby the Cause and End of the making of this Act is taken away; and consequently this Act is become of no Force or Effect; for, cessante ratione Legis, cessat ipsa Lex: And the Indictment of Felony upon this Statute must contain, that those Chapters and Congregations were to the violating and breaking of the good Course and Effect of the Statutes of Labourers; which now cannot be so alleg'd, because these Statutes be repealed. Therefore this would be put out of the Charge of Justices of Peace, written by Master Lambert, page 227.

This Quotation confirms the Tradition of old Masons, that this most learned Judge really belong'd to the ancient Lodge, and was a faithful Brother.

General Regulations,

Compiled first by Mr. George Payne, Anno 1720, when he was Grand-Master, and approv'd by the Grand Lodge on St. John Baptist's Day, Anno 1721, at Stationer's-Hall, London; when the most noble Prince John Duke of Montagu was unanimously chosen our Grand-Master for the Year ensuing; whose chose John Beal, M.D. his Deputy Grand-Master; and Mr. Josiah Villeneau, and Mr. Thomas Morris, jun., were chosen by the Lodge Grand-Wardens. And now, by the Command of our said Right Worshipful Grand-Master Montagu, the Author of this Book has compar'd them with, and reduc'd them to the ancient Records and immemorial Usages of the Fraternity, and digested them into this new Method, with several proper Explications, for the Use of the Lodges in and about London and Westminster.

(I) The Grand-Master, or his Deputy, hath Authority and Right, not only to be present in any true Lodge, but also to preside wherever he is, with the Master of the Lodge on his left hand, and to order his Grand-Wardens to attend him, who are not to act in particular Lodges as Wardens, but in his Presence, and at his Command; because there the Grand-Master may command the Wardens of that Lodge, or any other Brethren he pleaseth, to attend and act at his Wardens pro tempore.

(II) The Master of a particular Lodge has the Right and Authority of congregating the Members of his Lodge into a Chapter at pleasure, upon any Emergency or Occurrence, as well as to appoint the time and place of their usual forming: And in case of Sickness, Death, or necessary Absence of the Master, the senior Warden shall act as Master pro tempore, if no Brother is present who has been Master of that Lodge before; for in that Case the absent Master's Authority reverts to the last Master then present; though he cannot act until the said senior Warden has once congregated the Lodge, or in his Absence the junior Warden.

(III) The Master of each particular Lodge, or one of the Wardens, or some other Brothers by his Order, shall keep a Book containing their By-Laws, the Names of their Members, with a List of all the Lodges in Town, and the usual Times and Places of their forming, and all their Transactions that are proper to be written.

(IV) No Lodge shall make more than Five new Brethren at one Time, nor any Man under the Age of Twenty-five, who must be also his own Master; unless by a Dispensation from the Grand-Master or his Deputy.

(V) No man can be made or admitted a Member of a particular Lodge, without previous notice one Month before given to the said Lodge, in order to make due Enquiry into the Reputation and Capacity of the Candidate; unless by the Dispensation aforesaid.

(VI)   But no Man can be enter'd a Brother in any particular Lodge, or admitted to be a Member thereof, without the unanimous Consent of all the Members of that Lodge then present when the Candidate is propos'd and their Consent is formally ask'd by the Master; and they are to signify their Consent or Dissent in their own prudent way, either virtually or in form, but with Unanimity: Nor is this inherent Privilege subject to a Dispensation; because the Members of a particular Lodge are the best Judges of it; and if a fractious Member should be impos'd on them, it might spoil their Harmony, or hinder their Freedom; or even break and disperse the Lodge; which ought to be avoided by all good and true Brethren.

(VII)   Every new Brother at his making is decently to cloath the Lodge, that is, all the Brethren present, and to deposite something for the Relief of indigent and decay'd Brethren, as the Candidate shall think fit to bestow, over and above the small Allowance stated by the By-Laws of that particular Lodge; which Charity shall be lodg'd with the Master or Wardens, or the Cashier, if the Members think fit to chose one.

And the Candidate shall also solemnly promise to submit to the Constitutions, the Charges, and Regulations, and to such other good Usages as shall be intimated to them in Time and Place convenient.

(VIII)   No Set or Number of Brethren shall withdraw or separate themselves from the Lodge in which they were made Brethren, or were afterwards admitted Members, unless the Lodge becomes too numerous; nor even then, without a Dispensation from the Grand-Master or his Deputy: And when they are thus separated, they must either immediately join themselves to such other Lodges as they shall like best, with the unanimous Consent of that other Lodge to which they go (as above regulated) or else they must obtain the Grand-Master's Warrant to join in forming a new Lodge.

[These detailed Masonic rules continue in this fashion, ending with rule no. 39, which as you will note, is dated and indicates the approximate number of initiated members, at least in the London area:]

(XXXVIII)   The Grand-Master or his Deputy, or some Brother appointed by him, shall harangue all the Brethren, and give them good Advice: And lastly, after some other Transactions, that cannot be written in any Language, the Brethren may go away or stay longer, as they please.

(XXXIX)   Every annual Grand-Lodge has an inherent Power and Authority to make new Regulations, or to alter these, for the real Benefit of this ancient Fraternity: Provided always that the old Land-Marks be carefully preserv'd, and that such Alterations and new Regulations be proposed and agreed to at the third Quarterly Communication preceding the Annual Grand Feast: and that they be offered also to the Perusal of all the Brethren before Dinner, in writing, even of the youngest Apprentice; the Approbation and Consent of the Majority of all the Brethren present being absolutely necessary to make the same binding and obligatory; which must, after Dinner, and after the new Grand-Master is install'd, be solemnly desired; as it was desir'd and obtain'd for these Regulations, when propos'd by the Grand-Lodge, to about 150 Brethren, on St. John Baptist's Day, 1721.

In contrast to the sober quality of official Masonic publications stand the fanciful musings of an early Masonic writer, Robert Samber, whose private papers at the Bodleian reveal him to have been both a true eccentric and a devout Mason (see p. 194). The following long excerpt from his dedicatory address to the Freemasons prefixed to a French work that he translated stands as one of the first printed texts to discuss the meaning of the newly organised and speculative Freemasonry. Samber was no 'official' spokesman and hence his perspective is all the more interesting. Clearly he sees Freemasonry as a form of religious worship; he also appears to have dabbled in the Hermetic and magical literature. Indeed this dedicatory address was prefaced to his translation of a work on longevity, a subject the author had coupled with ideas on the elixir of life – a combination well suited to the magical sensibility. Samber's understanding of religion, so curiously pious and yet heterodix ('God is Nature'), complements his fanciful account of ancient history and the role of Masonry as the preserver of true religion. Just that sort of historical myth-making, particularly with emphasis on the Egyptians, flourished in eighteenth-century Masonic literature. In short, Samber's tract illustrates, far better than Anderson's *Constitutions* the variety of meanings to be extracted from speculative Freemasonry by 'ordinary' zealots whose numbers grew significantly in the course of the century.

[Rober Samber],
Long Livers: A curious History of Such Persons of both Sexes who have liv'd several Ages, and grown Young again: . . . By Eugenius Philalethes, F.R.S. Author of the Treatise of the Plague . . . London . . . 1722.

[Dedication]

To the Grand Master, Masters, Wardens and Brethren, of the Most Ancient and most Honourable Fraternity of the Free Masons of Great Britain and Ireland, Brother Eugenius Philalethes Sendeth Greeting.

Men, Brethren,

I Address my self to you after this Manner, because it is true Language of the Brotherhood, and which the primitive Christian Brethren, as well as those who were from the Beginning, made use of, as we learn from the holy Scriptures, and an uninterrupted Tradition.

I present you with the following Sheets, as belonging more properly to you than any else. By what I here say, those of you who are not far illuminated, who stand in the outward Place, and are not worthy to look behind the Veil, may find no disagreeable or unprofitable Entertainment: and those who are so happy as to have greater Light, will discover under these Shadows somewhat truly great and noble, and worthy the serious Attention of a Genius the most elevated and sublime: The Spiritual Celestial Cube, the only true, solid and immoveable Basis and Foundation of all Knowledge, Peace, and Happiness.

I therefore, my dearest Brethren, greet you most heartily, and am glad of this Opportunity to rejoice with you, inasmuch as it hath pleased the

Almighty, One, Eternal, Unalterable God, to send out his Light, and his Truth, and his vivifying Spirit, whereby the Brotherhood begins to revive again in this our Isle, and Princes seek to be of this sacred Society, which hath been from the Beginning, and always shall be; the Gates of Hell shall never prevail against it, but it shall continue while the Sun and Moon endures, and till the general Consummation of all Things; for since God, my dearest Brethren, is for us, who can be against us?

This being so, I shall speak to you a few Words on this important Subject; and perhaps I am the first that ever spoke to you after this Manner. I shall as briefly as I can, present you with a true and faithful Mirrour, and Mirrour which will not, which cannot flatter (Flattery be eternally banish'd from the Brotherhood) wherein you may see, or rather be remembered, what you are: and then you need not be told very much how you ought to act. And in this I shall use that Liberty and Freedom, which is our essential Difference, richly distinguishes us from all others, and is indeed the very Soul and Spirit of the Brotherhood.

The Style I shall make use of is most catholick, primitive and Christian; it is what is extracted from the sacred Scriptures. Remember that you are the Salt of the Earth, the Light of the World, and the Fire of the Universe. Ye are living Stones, built up a spiritual House, who believe and rely on the chief *Lapis Angularis,* which the refractory and disobedient Builders disallowed, you are called from Darkness to Light, you are a chosen Generation, a royal Priesthood.

This makes you, my dearest Brethren, fit Companions for the greatest Kings; and no wonder, since the King of Kings hath condescended to make you so to himself, compared to whom the mightiest and most haughty Princes of the Earth are but as Worms, and that not so much as we are all Sons of the same one Eternal Father, by whom all things were made; but inasmuch as we do the Will of his and our Father which is in Heaven.

You see now your high Dignity; you see what you are; act accordingly, and shew yourselves (what you are) MEN, and walk worthy the high Profession to which you are called. But while I say this, do not imagine I set up for a Rabbi, Master, or Instructor, who am one of the least of you, a meer Novice, a Cathechumen, and know nothing. However, do not despise my Mite, which I throw into your Treasury, since 'tis all I have; others may do more in Quantity, but not in Proportion.

Remember then what the great end we all aim at is; Is it not to be happy here and hereafter? For they both depend on each other: The Seeds of that eternal Peace and Tranquillity and everlasting Repose must be sown in this Life; and he that would glorify and enjoy the Sovereign Good then, must learn to do it now, and from contemplating the Creature gradually ascend to adore the Creator.

You know, no one is worthy to be of you that does not know, or at least love, one or more of the seven Liberal Arts, which in some sort depend on each other; Musick, Harmony, and Proportion run thro' all; but the grandest and most sublime of all is Astronomy, by which it has been given to Men from above to do such Wonders, and has so amply displayed the Glories of the most High. The Heavens speak forth the Glory of God, and the Firmament announceth the Works of his Hands.

This Earth which we inhabit is indeed a wonderful Piece of Structure, replenished with infinite Variety of rich Productions of Vegetables and Minerals, which all discover a Divine Origin, as much as the Animal Kingdom; where a little Fly is as much the Wonder of the most penetrating Philosopher, as proud haughty Man, who plumes himself up with being Rational, and yet makes so bad use of his being so; stiles himself the Lord of the Creation, and like a true Tyrant devours one third (and that the most innocent part) of it, to keep up his Royalty. This little despicable Animal has all its proper Organs as regularly posited as the other; its Members as justly proportioned and adapted; its littly Eye has its Uvea, Retina, and crystalline Humour; and its Body its proper Vessels, its Blood and Lymphae. O Lord our God, how wonderful is thy Name in all the Earth!

But alas! my Brethren, what are we and our little Globe below, to that stupendous Celestial Masonry above! where the Almighty Architect has stretch'd out the Heavens as a Curtain, which he has richly embroidered with Stars, and with his immortal Compasses, as from a Punctum, circumscribed the mighty ALL; is himself the Centre of all Things, yet knows no Circumference? who lets down his golden Balance, and weighs all Things according to eternal incorruptible Justice, and where the Actions of the best of Men are frequently found too light; who has created infinite Worlds, for what we know, above us; and those vast Luminaries within our Ken, to which he has given Laws, and allotted them their peculiar Influences, Intelligences and Dæmons.

In these Contemplations the Royal Psalmist was lost in Wonder and Amazement; these humble the proudest Spirits, and make the most haughty Philosopher own, that all he knows is, that he knows nothing. Can any then, who thinks after this manner, be an Atheist? No, my dearest Brethren, there never was such an hideous Monster in the World. Be not therefore carried away with every Blast of Doctrine, or fondly imagine anyone, who is so unhappy as to be branded with this odious Appellation, to be what the detestable Term imports. The best and most learned Men have not escaped the opprobrious Names of Atheists and Hereticks; it has ever been the Practice of poor narrow-soul'd Animals, when they meet with an elevated Genius, who, Eagle like, soars to the Sun, and contemplates that bright Luminary in all his Glories, which dazle and confound their weak Sight, when they are at a Loss in Argument, vainly to persuade their Audience (as wise as themselves) by Noise and senseless Clamour, and the everlasting Din of Heresy and Atheism. This I hint to you as a Caution not to run on with the unthinking Herd, or give into rash Judgment, whereby good Men have been too often injured; and the Slanderer, if ever he is so happy as to reflect and look upwards, finds nothing but a troubled Conscience, and a perpetual Incapacity of making Restitution for his Crime.

I hope none of the Brethren will ever lie under these Aspersions; but no one can answer for the Effects of the Folly and Malice of ignorant and designing Men. However, be not uneasy at Sounds which have no Meaning in them; for thus to affirm any one who believes in the Almighty, Eternal Father, and adores his divine and most glorious Attributes, to be an Atheist, is the most impudent, most abominable, and most unpardonable piece of Villany and Ignorance in the world, a flagrant Contradiction; for those two are as repugnant as Light to Darkness, and Heaven to Hell.

Those indeed who hold, or would persuade the Vulgar that they hold, (what they themselves know they do not believe) a Plurality of Gods, deserve infinitely more that charitable predicate; for a Multitude of Gods is utterly inconsistent with the Idea of the Divinity; it is the same as a Multitude of First Beings, Nonsense the most blasphemous and enormous; for he that believes there are many Gods, believes in no God at all. And who could ever have imagined, (had not History so informed us) that the whole World, except the Brotherhood, should have been guilty of so much Folly and Madness as to adore a wretched Company of Ribbalds, lewd Harlots, and their consecrated Bastards, with which holy Fry the Heathens peopled their Heavens, with a notorious Whoremaster at their Head, and of whose hopeful Issue the whole Band of *puisne* Gods (*Magnum Jovis incrementum*) were composed.

But if to cashier for ever out of our Creed this infinite ribble-rabble of spurious Divinities both he and she; if to own one cannot believe the eternal Magazine of holy Trumpery, and bend (like Isacher's Ass) beneath the insupportable Luggage of Infidel and Pagan Legendary Superstition, the Reveries of pamper'd dreaming Enthusiasts, whose Brains, ever pester'd with a thousand fluttering inconsistent Ideas, and incoherent Phantoms, the Effects of the Fumes of Wine and indigested Luxury, who retail out their spiritual Haberdashery of small Wares and holy Baubles, to the childish unthinking Idiot Multitude: If to do all this, and believe only in one God the Father Almighty, Maker of Heaven and Earth, and of all Things visible and invisible, the most grand, essential, the prime, eternal, everlasting, Fundamental Article of the most holy, catholick, universal, and Christian Faith (of which we are) makes one an Atheist; such, my dearest Brethren, are we all, and we glory in it. Let the Infidel and Pagan World say what they will, we shall have the Suffrages of all Christians, under whatever other Denomination distinguished, who cannot be so inconsistent with themselves, as to take Umbrage at those who believe the prime Article of their (that is, our) holy Faith.

After this manner, thank our great God, have we learned Christ, and after the Way such call Atheism and Heresy (I speak in Brother St Paul's Style) So worship we the God of our Fathers, who (we know) is but One as is our Faith. There is one God, one Faith, one Baptism, one Lord and Saviour of us all.

O thou Eternal One! thou Immortal Unite! though Incomprehensible Monas! Never let us swerve from these everlasting Truths. Send out thy Light and thy Truth, that they may lead and bring us to thy holy Hill and thy Tabernacle. We are imprisoned, who shall deliver us from the Body of this Death? We are exiled Children from our Country, when shall we return? Here thou has placed us as Novices and Probationers, when shall we be professed amongst those blessed Fraternities above, and be made free Denizons of the celestial Jerusalem, not built with Hands, and be reinstated in our Innocence? Here we wander in the dark gloomy Vale of Tears and the Shadow of Death, where we remember nothing, and know nothing, and who dares say What dost thou? Here hast thou placed us for

Reasons best known to thy Almighty Justice, and thy inscrutable Counsels, into which the curious Pryer is struck blind by the radiant Majesty of thy Glories, thou inaccessible Light! thou eternal Power! Wisdom! Love!

Pardon me, my dearest Brethren, this Digression, which probably however may not be without its Profits, and into which my Meditation on this divine Science generally leads me, of which tho' I know nothing, yet perhaps I have said too much. However, to acquire this, as well as any of the other Sciences, whereby you will come to know, love and honour God, a diligent Application is absolutely necessary, and that cannot be without inward Peace; to obtain which, you must avoid all Tumult, much Company, and the Hurry of all Publick Employment; for which Reasons avoid as much as possible the Court, where a Man must indispensably be obliged to wear the Mask, and where the Language and Customs very ill agree with the Simplicity of the Brotherhood; where the Baits to do Ill are so many and enticing, and the Encouragements to Virtue so few and cold, that a good Man has much ado to hinder himself from being carried away with the Torrent; and ten to one but all his honest Endeavours to serve his Prince and Country, are represented in a wrong Light, and his faithful Service repaid with Disgrace; there being ever about great Men some fawning Sycophants whose Interest it is to keep honest Persons from them, lest they come to know the Truth of Things. This is the State of all Princes; for let them be never so good themselves, they must see through other People's Eyes, and hear through other People's Ears.

But if any of you should happen to be in any Employment which obliges your constant Attendance here; if your Prince, who knows how to distinguish Merit, should cast his Honours on you unsought, unlookt for; exert your selves like Men. Be affable and courteous to all Men, and that not in Words only, but in Reality; and especially to the Brethren; it is your Duty particularly to be kind to them; they will ask nothing unreasonable, they cannot do it; (*Natura paucis contenta*) and they least of all will envy your high Station. Alas! they are sensible the Heights of Honour are not only very slippery, but shew you to all the World, where every one will see your Spots, but few sound your Virtues. The Crowd indeed is pleased with Show and Pageantry; all see your Pomp, but few know your Sorrows. A true Brother (Heaven defend us, as from the bluest Plagues, from false ones) envies no one who is mounted on the high Battlements of State; he had infinitely rather live in Security than Grandeur; the Pleasure in such lofty Stations he knows (even of the few Good) can be but little, but the Ruine long, if they chance to fall. He would chose to hide himself in the Clefts of the Rock, or securely pass his Days in some sweet quiet Shade, happy in Leisure and profoundest Obscurity. His Happiness is, not to be taken notice of; and whilst others place all their imaginary Joy and Satisfaction in Noise and being popular, he desires (to use the Style of a great, but obscure Philosopher) that his soft Minutes may glide away in Obscurity (like subterraneous Streams) unheard, unknown. And thus, when his Days are past away in Silence, would die a good, plain, honest Man; knowing that Death cannot chose but be to him a mighty Terror, who is popularly known to all the World, and dies only to himself a Stranger. Be wise therefore, ye great ones of this World, be learned, ye that are Judges of the Earth. Kiss the Son, lest he be angry, and so ye perish from the right way; lest he bruise you with his Rod of Iron, and crush you into Pieces like a Potter's Vessel: Remember you must die, and with her meanest Sons pay that Debt of Nature, and be reduced to your primitive Earth, which then will be no ways different from that of the poorest Cottager. Here the Weary rest from Labour, here the Prisoner sleeps in Peace, the Rich and the Poor, the haughty Monarch and the abject Slave lie promiscuous, undisturbed, and have no Distinction in the cold silent Grave. This is the End of all human Glory. Do therefore Justice, yet be merciful; discharge faithfully your respective Duties, and then if you fall from your eminent Heights, you will carry Peace of Mind along with you, and a good Conscience; if you do not die rich, you will die honest Men, and that is much better; for a good Name is better than Riches.

The next Thing that I shall remember you of is, to avoid Politicks and Religion: Have nothing to do with these, as you tender your own Welfare; they will be destructive to your beloved Peace and Quiet, and have undone Millions; and therefore in these latter Days, happy are they who do not trouble themselves about either. You know what I mean. But lest the rash censorious World, or such into whose Hands this Book may fall, from hence fancy we have neither Religion nor Politicks, let such know their Error: Ours is the best Policy, it is Honesty; it is the Policy of the holy Jesus, who never disturbed Governments, but left them as he found them, and rendered to Cæsar the Things that were Cæsar's. Thus shall Princes love and cherish you, as their most faithful and obedient Children and Servants, and take delight to commune with you, inasmuch as amongst you are found Men excellent in all kinds of Sciences, and who thereby may make their Name, who love and cherish you, immortal.

It is the same thing in relation to the Religion we profess, which is the best that ever was, or will, or can be; and whoever lives up to it can never perish eternally, for it is the Law of Nature, which is the Law of God, for God is Nature. It is to love God above all things, and our Neighbour as our self; this is the true, primitive, catholick, and universal Religion, agreed to be so in all Times and Ages, and confirmed by our Lord and Master Jesus Christ, who tells us, that on these hang all the Law and the Prophets. And now I have a convenient Opportunity, hearken to me a little in this Point. You know when the Almighty Architect, after framing this goodly Universe, had built up Man, he gave him a Law to walk by; this Law was absolutely perfect in itself, for it was God's Law, and consequently wanted nothing to make it better than it was; this Law indeed Man transgressed, and thence flowed all our Misery. However, after he was put out of Paradise, we do not read he had any other to square his Actions by, no more than his first Sons, the two first Brothers in the World. And now the Infant World, consisting but of a very few People, lived in common according to this Divine Law, till the eldest of the two (the first false Brother) growing sick of Virtue, and swoln with Pride and Cruelty according to the Flesh, (as is after his Example usual in such Cases) persecuting him who was humble according to the Spirit, inhumanly murder'd his and our Brother. O dire Effects of the Lust of Rule and Empire!

However, God repaired this Loss to our common Father, by his third Son Seth; while Cain, who by the Parricide of his Brother founded (as almost all ambitious Thirsters after Empire have since done) his Dominion in Blood, and despising the holy Law of Nature, and confiding in his own Strength, first usurped sovereign Sway; was the first who constituted arbitrary Government, and began to oppress with Force, Rapine, Servitude, and wicked Laws, Men created by God Free, and the Sons of a Generation, till these, God's Judgments being now also by them contemned, and all Flesh corrupted, begot those Giants in Iniquity who oppressed the Poor, raised themselves to high Stations by Plunderings and Robberies: and, priding themselves in their Wealth, made their Names famous, imposing them on Regions, Cities, Mountains, Rivers, Waters, and the Sea; whose first Parent (Cain) was malicious, envious, incorrigible by God's Correction, a dissembling Traytor, a Spiller of fraternal Blood, an accursed Wanderer and Vagabond, and who added Blasphemy to his Malediction; in short, a FALSE BROTHER.

This wicked and impious Race (for the whole Creation groaned under their Impieties) the Almighty washed off from the Face of the Earth by the Deluge, excepting Noah, a just Man in the Generations of Seth, with his Family. This good holy Man endeavoured, after the Flood, to restore the Law of Nature which had been so long obscured by the Pride and Impiety of those that perished. But his Sons and their Issue following the Example of the Giants, began to domineer in like manner over their Inferiors, to build mighty Cities and form Kingdoms, so that from Noah till Abraham there is no mention made of any just Man; for till his Time these haughty Rulers continued most flagrant and enormous Examples of hardy and robust Improbity, Impiety, Confusion, tyrannick Power, Violence, Oppression, Hunting, Luxury, Pomp, and Vanity, and the like Wickedness and Folly, which the Sons of Noah had introduced; amongst whom was Cham or Ham, who, as he was the most wicked of them, so he obtained by Violence the largest share of Dominion. From him descended Nimbroth, whom the Scripture describes to be powerful in the Earth, and a mighty Hunter; he built Babylon, and was the Beginning of the Confusion of Tongues. This mighty Hunter of Men, as well as Beasts, made severe and rigorous Laws, instituted Degrees of Honour, and Offices, introduced Slavery, and laid heavy Taxes on the People, raised vast Armies, waged cruel Wars, and set up Images and pompous Rites and Ceremonies in Worship, and was, as is believed, the Founder and Father of Idolatry.

In his Time too, it is highly probable, that bloody Sacrifices were invented. It was easy to persuade a Criminal against the Gods, that he might expiate what he deserved to die for, by the Death of a poor Beast; and if the Gods did not eat the reserved Part of the Sacrifice, which was always the best, their Ministers or Viceregents (the Sacrificators) who in all likelihood had hunted with their Grand Monarch, and loved his Roast-Meat, would eat it for them, and that was as well.

From this same Cham proceeded Cush, Mizraim, and Canaan, whence descended the Ethiopians, Egyptians, and Canaanites, all great and most noble Nations indeed, but withal most wicked and abominable, and cursed by God, inasmuch as they condemned his Law, which he gave from the Beginning, and turned aside from his true Worship, and transferred the Glory of the one immortal God to a thousand of his Creatures, to the Sun, and Moon, and Planets, and all the Host of Heaven.

In this condition was the World, when the Almighty chose another just Man, Abraham the Father of the Faithful, who by unerring Tradition had received the Divine Truths; for our Great God has always a Number of those who believe in him aright, and worship him in Spirit and in Truth, and write his Law, not in Tables of Stone, but in their Hearts, and who live in Quiet and Peace, private and unknown; as he told the Prophet afterwards, that he had 7000 who had not bent the Knee to Baal.

The holy Patriarch and his Posterity persevered in their Justice till they were in Danger in Egypt to lose it by the Cruelty of a wicked Prince, (who knew not Joseph) and their Conversation with the Professors of a pompous luxurious Idolatry: Then God raised up Moses, a great Astronomer, and a learned Man in Men and Things, who wonderfully freed them from their Servitude after having eased and despoiled their Enemies of their superfluous Gold.

These People he delivered from Servitude after a wonderful Manner from the Fury of an impious King. In the Desert they continued forty Years, tho' their Deliverer might have brought them into the Land of Promise in forty Days: But as this was a most excellent piece of Policy, and worthy the Foresight of Moses, so it cannot be sufficiently commended; he knew that a Company of raw undisciplined People, trained up for the most part in keeping of Sheep, would not be a Match for those warlike People, whose Cities and Kingdoms they were to take from them; besides that they might be in Danger of falling into Idolatry, to which by their Long Residence in Egypt, and their being acquainted with their Flesh-pots, Ragous, or made Dishes (probably deriving their Origin from luxurious Sacrifices) he had observed they were too much addicted.

Every body knows that the Egyptians (to whom we owe the Invention of the Zodiac) adored the Sun under those Symbols; so because that glorious Luminary enters Aries in the Month of March, they worshipped him under the Symbol of a Lamb, or a human Figure with that Animal's Head, as they did in the following Month under the Symbol of a Calf, or young Bull. Moses, whose grand Design was to bring them back to their original divine and most perfect Law, given Man by God Almighty in the Beginning, was resolved to bend all his Thoughts to efface those Tinctures of Idolatry that they had received in their Servitude, by constituting a Religion wonderfully adapted to the present Occasion, with pompous Sacrifices, Rites and Ceremonies, magnificent Sacerdotal and Levitical Vestments, and a vast Number of mystical Hieroglyphics, as the Egyptians had; but with this essential Difference, that these mystic Shadows all tended to set forth the Glory of one God the Creator; whereas those were entirely subservient to the Worship of a Multitude of Creatures, an Opposition greater than which could never be.

The first publick Act then of Religion after their Deliverance was the Passover, or the Ceremony of eating the Paschal Lamb, which was in the Month of March; so that, in that very Month that the Egyptians adored the Ram, the Israelites were roasting and eating up this their God, and that too after such a manner, being shod, girded, and with their Staves in their Hands, in a Hurry, and with bitter Herbs, as evidently shewed the highest Contempt and Disdain of this imaginary Deity.

However, as a Specimen of their Propensity to Idolatry, one cannot give a more notorious Instance than the setting up the Golden Calf, which was made of those Earrings and Ornaments they a little before had borrowed of the Egyptians. It is true, this piece of Pageantry lasted not long; the well-grounded Zeal of Moses, who had the Honour to discourse a long while very familiarly with God, put a Stop to their religious Mirth and Gallantry; the Idol was broken in pieces, burnt, and ground to Powder, and the Crime was no otherwise expiated, than with the Blood of 3000 Souls. It was now high time for Moses to look about him; the Law then was form'd with all convenient Diligence and Expedition, and the Decalogue written over again, and that too (to speak in the Hebrew Style) by the Finger of God. And certainly, well may it be said to be divinely penn'd, inasmuch as it comprehends whatever Man is to act in relation to his God and Neighbour. Whoever will give himself the trouble to read over Leviticus, will find what Rites and Ceremonies were superadded in order to keep up this external Pomp and Magnificence, so necessary at that time for the People, who could not at once be brought back to the pure worshipping of the most High in Spirit and in Truth . . .

[Here the text continues describing in detail the failings of the Jews.]

But, during this general Corruption, it must not be imagined but there were some few who were not carried away with the Stream; The Brotherhood continued unshaken, and kept their Integrity; amongst whom some of the holy Prophets were inspired to denounce the heavy Judgments of God against these notorious Monsters of Impiety; but they were soon silenc'd for their unseasonable Babbling, by some little harmless Corrections, as having their Brains knocked out, or being sawed asunder, and the like wholsome Severities.

But as the Laity continued in their Wickedness, the Princes were not one jot the better, but rather much worse; so that the High Priest's Office was bought and sold, and fought for, and at last two Persons executed that high Charge by turns.

Thus stood the Affairs of the Jewish Nation in the Time of Augustus Cæsar, when there was a profound Peace all over the World, which was never more polite, and perhaps never more vicious.

The Sceptre having now departed from Judah, the Messiah, the Prince of Peace, came into the World, and came (as he himself says) not to destroy but to fulfil: But how, my dearest Brethren, must that be [un]derstood? it is certain he came to destroy the Shadows, Types, Hieroglyphicks, the bloody Sacrifices, and the whole Ceremonial Law, or else his Disciples and Followers have led us in the dark. He came not then to destroy, but to fulfil, what was couched under all these, and all what was delivered by the Prophets, in relation to his Kingdom; to be the Restorer of corrupted Nature, and to bring back Man again to his primæval State of Integrity, which the Mosaick

Law could never do; to deliver us from Bondage, and make us Free, to bring us from Darkness into Light, and to be our Lord, Master, Saviour, and Redeemer from utter Perdition and Ruine for ever . . .

Thus suffered our Great, our Immortal Master, who came into the World to do the Will of his Father which is in Heaven, and whose Brethren we are (as he says himself) if we do so too. If you ask me what this Will of his Father is, I answer, it is Christ's Will, who is of one and the same Will and Substance with his Father; and this I need not to repeat to you, it is as plain as the Noon-day Sun, to be found in what he himself says, and whom alone if we hear, it is sufficient; his Precepts are clear and expressive, obvious to the meanest Capacity. And it would have been better for the Christian World, had they kept up to this Divine Rule, and not obscured his sacred Religion with so many senseless impertinent Speculations, Aristotelian and Heathenish Distinctions, and the unintelligible Jargon of the Schools, by which they have almost distinguished all Religion out of the World; so that too often we see many a Venerable Professor pass many Years to acquire the Faculty of rattling out a company of barbarous Terms, that had no manner of Meaning in them, and by which, after so long a Study, they are not one jot the honester, and omit the easy and amiable Practice of the common Duties of Love and Charity.

You see now what is our Profession; it is the Law of Nature, which being almost lost, was endeavoured to be retrieved, or, at least some how kept up by the Shadows of Moses, but entirely restored by the Law of Grace, by Jesus Christ the Son of God.

You have been remembered, that under the Law of Nature Mankind had no Propriety, but lived in common, and as there was no Superfluity, so there was nothing wanting; no anxious Cares then of heaping up Riches, or Solicitude for future Provisions distracted their Repose, or interrupted their sweet Contemplations. This way of Life continued in the Generations of Seth, who were called the Sons of God, till some of them, allured by the Daughters of Men, the Children of Cain, corrupted themselves, and fell into those extravagant Impieties that drew down the Deluge.

This same way of living was revived by Noah after the Flood, till the Pride of his Posterity, who ran into those tyrannic Proprieties which have undone the World, and almost destroyed it. It came however down by Tradition to Abraham and his Descendants, who were Keepers of Sheep in the Land of Egypt for 430 Years. After their Delivery they lived in the same manner, and tho' afterwards the Generality, when they began to live in Cities, abandoned it, yet this Spirit remained amongst their greatest Men for Wisdom, and in the Colleges of the Prophets and their Sons, and which was brought in a more particular manner to its primitive Lustre by Jesus Christ, who called and composed a Fraternity first of the Apostles, who afterwards admitted others, whom they thought worthy, into the Society, where the Contempt of the World, and Money (no otherwise than it subserved to the Necessities of Life, and charitable Uses) was always kept up as a distinguishing Mark of the Faithful, that is, the Brethren, for they were first called Christians at Antioch, so that they were of one Heart and one Soul, neither said any of them that aught of the Things which he possessed was his own, but they had all Things in common, neither was any among them that lacked; for as many of them as were Possessors of Lands or Houses sold them, and brought the Prices of the Things that were sold, and laid them down at the Apostles' Feet, and Distribution was made unto every Man according as he had need. Avarice (the Bane of humane Society) was detested, loathed, abhorred, as the Root and Foundation of all Evil; it was what, my dearest Brethren, ruined Judas Iscariot, and made him the first False Brother under the Law of Grace, who for a little sordid Pelf proved the most wicked Traitor in the World, the Horrors of whose Perfidy lay so terrible on his Conscience, that he could not survive them, but growing desperate, put an end to his Sorrows by an ignominious Death; he hanged himself, and burst asunder, and all his Bowels gushed out, and his Bishop-rick another took.

You may remember, that the next terrible Punishment of a False Brother was on Ananias, who had indeed a Desire to come into the Brotherhood and Apostolical way of Life; and accordingly (for this was a Prerequisite thereto) sold a Possession and kept back Part of the Price, and brought a certain Part, and laid it at the Apostles Feet, for which fraudulent Act he was struck dead by holy Brother St. Peter.

This living in common was looked upon as an essential Point among the Brethren (who, as I observed before, were at Antioch first called Christians) that the primitive Brethren kept it up for 300 Years successively after the Death of their Lord and Master, the Holy Jesus; and the Bishops of Rome, who were almost all of them martyr'd for the Religion of the Brotherhood or Christianity (which is the same thing) religiously maintained it.

These Bishops, or Overseers (as the Name imports) had the Care and Oversight of the common Treasury, then worthily called the Treasure of the Church, and dispensed to every one according to their several Necessities. And Brother Lawrence, a Deacon to Bishop (or Overseer) Xystus, or Sixtus, was put to a most cruel Death, broiled on a Grid-iron, because, as the Tyrant thought, he mocked him, when he told him that there (pointing to some poor Brethren) he had disposed of the Church's Treasure.

Nor was this State interrupted till Constantine the Great turned Christian, who rebuilt or repaired Byzantium to rival Rome, and called it, (as Romulus did Rome) after his Name, Constantinople; to which he transferred the Empire, and (in this too like the Founder of Rome) laid its Foundation in Parricide, in the Blood of his Sister's Husband and Son, and that of his own Wife and Child.

The Courtiers and great Men, who always conform to the Example of the Prince, turned Christians too, and the Draught of Fishes was so very great, that the Net broke, and there were found infinitely more bad than good. The Truth of it was, the Church then grew at ease, and had certain Stipends settled on her Priests and Pastors, who now (so true it is that the Blood of Martyrs is the Seed of the Church) living at Ease and Plenty, forgot by Degrees their original Institution, and conversing with the Court, learned its Modes and Fashions, and took on themselves high Titles; the poor Pastors or Bishops swelled into Lords, and the humble Successor of St.

Peter, the Servant of the Servants of God, from an Overseer grew into a Sovereign Pontiff, or PONTIFEX MAXIMUS, which meant no more amongst the antient Romans than Bridge-Master General. A great Number too of Pagan Rites and Ceremonies were introduced to make it a glorious Church, fit for Emperors and Kings, and People of Quality; but as these Titles were of little moment, and these Ceremonies innocent enough in themselves, and might conduce to outward Decency, they could not in the main be any Hindrance to Devotion, and consequently no Cause of Separation.

But this was not all; the Philosophy of Aristotle, and dark obscure Terms and Sophisms were introduced into Christian Schools, with ridiculous Subtilities, vocal and nominal Controversies, chimerical Notions, Entia Rationis, Genereitas in Concreto, Ubications, Quandations, with all the confused barbarous Ribaldry, and venerable Gibberish of noise, empty, positive, conceited, dogmatical ignorant Pædagogues and scientifical Blockheads.

After these Reverend Fooleries, the whole World ran a whoring, as the Israelites did after Gideon's Ephod; and these learned Doctors and Magistri nostri, being thus employed in these sublime Speculations; things of greater Moment, forgot to inculcate the Practice of good Works, the Mechanical Part of Religion; so that all Immorality flowed in like an irresistible Deluge, and there was more Wickedness and Impiety practised amongst Christians, than ever amongst the Jews and Infidels; and nothing left but the very Names of Christ and Christianity, which were often abused to carry on the Designs of wicked, ambitious, and turbulent Men; so that the Religion of the Prince of Peace was made to patronise and countenance all sorts of Violence, Rapine, Murders, Sacrileges, Tyrannies, and Rebellions; and the holy Scriptures, as the Casuists knew how, were made a Nose of Wax, and contending Parties, tho' never so diametrically opposite to each other, had God on their side, with whose most adorable Name all their several Parricides, Burnings, Massacres and Plunderings were sanctified.

Neither did things rest here; People were to be dragooned into Religion; Whips, Wracks, Tortures, Burnings, Inquisitions, Star-Chambers, Spiritual Courts, Ecclesiastical Censures, Excommunications (I aim at no Sect or Communion in particular, they were all alike) were set up as wholsome, Soul-saving Engines to screw People into Peace of Conscience, while perhaps the poor Culprit, tho' he could not express himself in the uncouth Language of the Schools was as Orthodox as the spiritual inquisitive Bloodhound, who could notwithstanding be so charitable as to change all Penalties into a pecuniary Mulct, if the Party could but provide a sufficient Quantity of that Catholicon which cures all things, tho' never so inveterate, and is every where orthodoxly current . . .

Good Men lamented these Calamities, and the Brethren sighed to Heaven, and wished a Reformation. The several religious Orders in the Churches of Rome and Greece aimed at it, and had very good Notions and Designs for that Work; and tho' amongst these Recluses, Sciences have been in a great Measure encouraged, and to these Bodies we owe several invaluable Treasures, yet because their Fraternitys consist only of single

Persons, and lie under particular Restrictions they do not altogether answer the Ends of the Brotherhood, who cannot subsist without being Free.

However, it is earnestly to be wished, that some Prince or Great Men would (and they would if they knew us) cast on us a favourable Eye, by this means would they encourage Arts and Sciences, which have been always worthy the Care of the wisest and best of Men; this would open a glorious way to celebrate the wonderful Works of the Almighty, and to do good to Men (which is all our End and Aim) and of consequence should we most cordially pray for our Noble and Illustrious Benefactors, and transmit their Name with Honour to remotest Posterity.

Drawing now towards a Conclusion, I shall beg your Attention to two or three Things more, before I take my Leave of you.

Avoid all Companies where ridiculing of Religion is thought witty, and more especially when the wretched Discourse is turned upon the adorable Mystery of the most Holy Trinity, which is an eternal Doctrine, believed by Wise Men in all Ages. The antient Philosophers, who had no revealed Religion, no other Light but the Light of Nature, taught and believed this most sacred Truth, as I could shew in a proper place as clear as the Sun. The Platonics, for Example, to instance no more, acknowledge in the Godhead three Persons, the first they called the Father of the Universe, or of all things; the second the Son and first Mind; that is, according to Plotinus and Philo, the Divine Intellect, flowing from God the Father, as Light from Light, or the Word that is spoken from the Speaker: Hence he was called the VERBUM, or WORD, Light of Light, and the Splendour of God the Father; and the third they called the Spirit or Anima Mundi, which Dove-like sate brooding on the Face of the Waters, and with its celestial, amatorial, genial Heat, hatcht the Universe.

All this, and much more, could I shew, if required, from a Cloud of Witnesses, abstracting from the commonly-received Doctrines of Christianity, which these witty Gentlemen (pretend what they will) seem to have very little regard to.

It is also well-becoming the Brotherhood to be very respectful to all Clergymen, especially those of the Established Church. In the next place, never on any account connive at what the Wits of the Age call roasting of a Parson; which besides that it does no ways suit with a Gentleman or honest Man (which is the same thing) is barbarous and cruel; it brings him that is thus baited into Contempt with the People, who are easily carried away with flashy Wit and Ridicule (for nothing is so easy as to ridicule Religion) so that by degrees, when People despise his Instructions, no body will go to hear him, which is a sacrilegious Robbery of his good Name, according to all Divines, a Hindrance to his Preferment, and consequently to the better providing for his Family. There is no Tradesman but would think this Usage very cruel.

Take care also not to be concerned in your Dealings with litigious Persons, who on every Trifle are for going to Law; rather make up your Difference, though you lose by it. Remember the Words of your Divine Master; If any Man will sue thee at the Law, and take away thy Coat, let him have thy Cloak also. The Reason is obvious, viz. lest the Lawyer come with his *Fieri facias*, and strip thee to the Skin. I speak not of the good, for there are a great many very worthy Members of this Profession, Men of true Honour and Integrity, our Bulwarks against Oppression and Injustice; but I speak of those poor, wretched, ignorant, pitiful Sollicitors, Cause-Pedlars, Sowers of Discord, Pettifoggers, and Setters, those scandalous Vermin of the Law; those rapacious Harpies, insatiate Cormorants, Canibals and Devourers of Mankind, who tear out and gnaw our Bowels, and suck our Blood and Vitals, and for a trivial, scandalous, little, sordid Lucre, bring frequently irreparable Ruine on such as are so unhappy as to come in their way; regardless, like the deaf Adder, to the Tears of the helpless Orphan and Widow.

These are the very Dregs of Mankind, miserable abandoned Wretches, who as they live, so, without a miraculous Act of the Divine Goodness, die without Remorse; or, if they reflect before they go hence, how racking, how torturing must those dire and dreadful Reflections be, when they find themselves not able to make Restitution for their dishonest Gains, and without which it is impossible according to the best Divines to have any Hopes of future Happiness? These Makebates, Incendiaries, and common Barreters, of all Men are most miserable, for they take such Care by their Rapacity (like some wretched Botchers) never to be employed twice, and are therefore ever poor, and the Scorn and Contempt (being indeed the Outcast and Offal) of Mankind.

But these Monsters can no more affect the Honour of the sage Administrators of the Law, than a prating, noisy, nonsensical Mountebank the skilful Physician, or a false Brother our sacred Fraternity; that sacred Fraternity, whose very Soul and Life is Charity, which is to love and honour all Men, to comfort the feeble minded, to support the weak and infirm, to heal the Sick, to help the Fatherless and Widow, and cover the Frailties of our Neighbour; for Charity (I speak in the Words of Brother Saint Paul) is kind, not easily provoked, thinketh no Evil.

Let us therefore, my dearest Brethren, never be easily persuaded to think Evil of any one, much less of a Brother, if we hear any evil Report of him; let us, according to the Divine Rules of Love and Charity, believe it not, but stifle the Viper in its Birth, and admonish our Brother; who, if we do it with a Spirit of Sincerity and brotherly Love, will thank us (nothing making Instruction so unacceptable as a haughty, dogmatical Utterance) so shall we be a Stay and Comfort to him from malicious and envious Tongues, from whose poisonous Effects the best of Men are not sure to be free.

O my dearest Brethren, let us love one another. This is the sacred Advice of Saint John the Divine, that beloved Disciple of the Holy Jesus, our blessed Master; for (says he) Love is of God, and every one that loveth is born of God, and knoweth God: He that loveth not, knoweth not God, for God is Love. If a Man say he loveth God, and hateth his Brother, he is a Liar; for he that loveth not his Brother whom he hath seen, how can he love God whom he hath not seen?

[The tract continues to exhort the Freemasons to behave morally, and it does so in language that becomes increasingly mystical.]

Notes: Appendix

1   The translation of these French documents for publication was undertaken by Dr Clarissa Campbell Orr. Latin translations were supplied by Wilfrid Lockwood, University Library, Cambridge.

2   Robert Darnton first brought this allusion to my attention, and helped to identify the currency mentioned in the text.

3   In the document a line has been put through his name. The year of foundation is a jest; but in the eighteenth century Freemasons commonly claimed an ancient foundation, often dating it from pre-Christian times.

4   Written as an aside, 'qu'on me dit en me voyant tomber patatrai (?) du M. Parnasse'.

5   On the side of the manuscript appears an explanatory note: 'A man of the world I met by chance at Brother Laurent's, and who did not leave until the Brothers' meeting broke up on whose account our hands were tied.' This comment about, 'un Mondain', an uninitiated man about town whose presence frustrated the meeting's proceedings, further illustrates the habit of secrecy.

6   S. Spink, 'La diffusion des idées matérialistes et anti-religieuses au début du XVIIIᵉ siècle: le theophrastus redivivus', *Revue d'histoire littéraire de la France*, vol. 44 (1937), pp. 248–55.

7   Fritsch probably refers to M. Paupie (the original adds a 'd' to his name) who was in fact a prominent publisher at The Hague.

8   This refers to the sixteenth-century French court poet, Clement Marot, whose works were enjoyed in libertine circles.

9   This is, of course, Justus Van Effen, an early associate of the Knights who became a homophobic attacker of libertine culture.

Index